W9-AOU-782

SOURCES

Notable Selections in *Psychology*

SECOND EDITION

About the Editor

TERRY F. PETTIJOHN is a professor of psychology at the Ohio State University at Marion, where he has been teaching introductory psychology for two decades. As an undergraduate, he attended Alma College and Michigan State University, where he earned his B.S. in 1970. He obtained his M.A. in 1972 and his Ph.D. in experimental psychology in 1974 from Bowling Green State University. He is the author of a number of teaching publications for the introductory psychology course, including *Psychology: A Concise Introduction,* 3rd ed. (Dushkin Publishing Group/ Brown & Benchmark Publishers, 1992), as well as the accompanying teaching and testing materials. He has served as editor of the *MicroPsych Computer Network Newsletter,* and he currently serves on the Advisory Board for *Annual Editions: Psychology* (Dushkin Publishing Group/ Brown & Benchmark Publishers). In addition to introductory psychology, he teaches social and experimental psychology, learning and memory, motivation, adjustment, psychobiology, and research methods. Dr. Pettijohn has been recognized for his teaching efforts, including being a recipient of the Ohio State University Distinguished Teaching Award three times. His current research interests include the study of human emotion, memory, and animal social behavior. He is a member of the American Psychological Society, the Psychonomic Society, the Animal Behavior Society, the Society for Computers in Psychology, and the American Psychological Association, where he is affiliated with the Division of the Teaching of Psychology.

SOURCES

Notable Selections in *Psychology*

SECOND EDITION

Edited by
TERRY F. PETTIJOHN
Ohio State University

Dushkin Publishing Group/Brown & Benchmark Publishers
A TIMES MIRROR HIGHER EDUCATION GROUP COMPANY

Manufactured in the United States of America

Second Edition

10 9 8 7 6 5 4 3 2 1

Library of Congress Cataloging-in-Publication Data
   Main entry under title:
      Sources: notable selections in psychology/edited by Terry F. Pettijohn.—2nd ed.
      Includes bibliographical references and index.
      1. Psychology. I. Pettijohn, Terry F., *comp.*

                                                                                                        150
      0–697–34331–6   96–85797

 Printed on Recycled Paper

ACKNOWLEDGMENTS

1.1   From *The Principles of Psychology* (Vol. 1, pp. 1, 4–8) by W. James, 1950. New York: Dover Publications. (Original work published 1890.) Notes omitted.

1.2   From "Psychology as the Behaviorist Views It" by J. B. Watson, 1913, *Psychological Review, 20,* pp. 158–177.

1.3   From "Teachers' Expectancies: Determinants of Pupils' IQ Gains" by R. Rosenthal and L. Jacobson, 1966, *Psychological Reports, 19,* pp. 115–118. Copyright © 1966 by Southern Universities Press. Reprinted by permission.

1.4   From "The Fragmentation of Psychology?" by G. H. Bower, 1993, *American Psychologist, 48,* pp. 905–907. Copyright © 1993 by The American Psychological Association. Reprinted by permission.

2.1   From "Hemisphere Deconnection and Unity in Conscious Awareness" by R. W. Sperry, 1968, *American Psychologist, 23,* pp. 723–733. Copyright © 1968 by The American Psychological Association. Reprinted by permission.

Acknowledgments and copyrights are continued at the back of the book on pages 359–361, which constitute an extension of the copyright page.

Preface

Although barely a century old as a formal discipline, the study of psychology has revolutionized how we look at ourselves and others. Psychology is the science of behavior and cognition; it is a rigorous brain science and, at the same time, it seeks to help people. Psychologists study behaviors, such as eating, talking, writing, running, or fighting, precisely because they can be directly observed and recorded. But psychologists also study mental processes, such as dreaming, thinking, remembering, and problem solving, which are not directly observable and are often studied through reports provided by human research subjects.

Psychologists are also interested in the physiological processes that often accompany both overt behavior and cognition. Finally, some psychologists are concerned with applying psychological principles to help people.

As a discipline, psychology has evolved its own history of ideas and thinkers, research methods, and theories. In this volume I have put directly into your hands those researchers and writers whose works are essential to the study of psychology.

Sources: Notable Selections in Psychology, 2d ed., brings together 50 selections of enduring intellectual value—classic articles, book excerpts, and research studies—that have shaped the study of psychology and our contemporary understanding of it. The book includes carefully edited selections from the works of the most distinguished psychological researchers and practitioners, past and present, from Sigmund Freud and Jean Piaget to Robert Rosenthal and Mary D. Salter Ainsworth. These selections allow you to obtain a behind-the-scenes look, so to speak, at psychology in the making.

Sources represents over 100 years of psychological thought and application. The actual dates of publication range from 1890 to 1995. I have made every effort to portray psychology as a dynamic and changing discipline. Obviously, new research has modified our understanding of some of the ideas covered in some of the selections; nonetheless, using these original sources will enrich your understanding of psychology and its elemental concepts.

Revision procedure The challenge of revising this book was carefully considered. In the first edition, I paid great attention to finding those classic works that could best communicate the excitement of psychology. Readability was the top priority, and each selection was carefully edited so that the essence of the original work could be readily understood. These goals also guided the development of the second edition.

I wanted to ensure that the second edition continued to be truly representative of the breadth of psychology, both in terms of the distinguished people and of the important issues. I began by reviewing the hundreds of sources that were not included in the first edition, as well as the most historical and contemporary influential articles. Computer searches allowed me to identify writings by some of the most well respected names in psychology. The first edition was reviewed by current users, and their evaluations of each selection were extremely valuable in making decisions about which ones to replace. I also asked my students to provide feedback on the most effective selections as well as the ones that were not quite as informative. Unfortunately, much of the feedback I received was extremely positive on almost all of the selections, so the process of replacing selections was a very difficult one. Although not everyone will agree with the final decisions on individual selections, I believe that with the advice of many people I was able to significantly strengthen the book by including some of the best work of the past century.

New to the second edition are 21 selections from some of the most distinguished researchers, theorists, writers, and practitioners in psychology. Care was taken to include gender and cultural diversity issues as they relate to the discipline of psychology. I am confident that the final compilation of writings will challenge students to think about and discuss the core issues that make up psychology today. Some of the selections provide theories that have shaped our discipline; some discuss crucial issues that have confronted psychologists during the past century; and many present the results of original research studies. Together the selections compose a snapshot of psychology as it currently exists, including important landmarks in its development.

Organization of the book The selections are organized topically around the major areas of study within psychology: Part 1 includes selections on the Foundations of Psychology; Part 2, Perceptual Processes; Part 3, Learning and Cognitive Processes; Part 4, Motivation and Emotion; Part 5, Personality and Adjustment; Part 6, Psychological Disorders; and Part 7, Social Processes. The selections are organized so as to parallel most introduction to psychology textbooks. This means that these original sources, these classic works that underlie the key psychological concepts covered in the textbooks, can be easily read along with any textbook. But each selection is independent and can be read in any order and used in any way an instructor deems appropriate.

Suggestions for reading each selection As you read these original writings, it is important to keep in mind that ideas and standards have changed over the last century. In particular, changes in ethical concerns and in how language is used need to be mentioned here. Currently, there are very strict ethical guidelines for conducting human and animal research. Today researchers must submit proposals to committees that ensure that ethical standards are met. Some of the studies carried out in the past would not be approved now. As you read these selections, consider how the research contributed to psychology and whether or not the benefits outweighed the potential harm to the subjects.

Each selection is representative of the time in which it was written. Just as psychologists have become more sensitive to ethical considerations over the years, so too have they become more aware of the issue of gender, particularly as regards language. Many of the older articles use the masculine pronoun *he* when referring to both men and women, and many of the early studies had only male subjects. I recommend that you view each selection in the context of when it was written and focus on the psychological issues it reveals. These classic studies have had a major impact on the development of psychology as a discipline and should be read from that perspective.

Each selection is preceded by an introductory headnote that establishes the relevance of the selection, provides biographical information about the author, and includes a brief background discussion of the topic. I have also provided suggestions for understanding statistical tests and thought questions designed to guide critical thinking. It is important to read the headnote before beginning the selection itself.

Try to take an active approach when reading each selection. For example, when reading an experiment, determine what the research hypothesis is, identify the independent and dependent variables, and analyze the research methodology. Does the experiment raise ethical considerations? Do the conclusions follow from the results? Are there any extraneous variables or alternative explanations for the results? When reading a theoretical or summary article, organize the main themes, identify the conclusions, evaluate the relevance of the theory, and question the applications to everyday situations.

Let me make a couple of suggestions to help you get the most out of each selection. First, be sure to read the headnote to gain background information on the topic and the author. Recognize that some of these selections are easy to read and understand, whereas others may have more challenging language, theories, or statistical concepts. Try to focus on the main ideas and important concepts in each selection. Remember that journal research articles include an introduction to the problem, a description of the research methods, a presentation of the results, and a discussion of the significance of the results. When you finish reading a selection, reread the headnote to make sure that you focused on the important concepts. Finally, take notes on the selection and reflect upon the importance of the writing to your understanding of psychology.

Psychology resources on the Internet Each part in *Sources: Notable Selections in Psychology,* 2d ed., is preceded by an "On the Internet" page. On these pages, I have provided several Internet links that should be of interest to you as you investigate the topics presented in the book. I have tried to include links that were focused and relevant to the specific selections in each part.

There are many resources available on the Internet to help you learn about psychology. In addition to the ones included for each part, here are some general sites that contain information and additional links to other resources:

American Psychological Association—This APA site provides numerous resources in all areas of psychology.

http://www.apa.org

American Psychological Society—This APS site provides resources for teaching and research in scientific psychology.

http://psych.hanover.edu/APS

PsychWeb—This Georgia Southern University site provides numerous psychology resource links in all areas

http://www.gasou.edu/psychweb/psychweb.htm

Psyc Site—This Nipissing University psychology site provides extensive resource links.

http://www.unipissing.ca/psyc/info.htm

Yahoo Psychology Search—This is a general psychology search site.

http://www.yahoo.com/Science/Psychology/

A word to the instructor An *Instructor's Manual With Test Questions* (including multiple-choice and essay questions) is available for instructors using *Sources: Notable Selections in Psychology,* 2d ed., in the classroom.

Acknowledgments I was extremely excited when Rick Connelly, former president and publisher of the Dushkin Publishing Group, Inc., first approached me with the idea for *Sources: Notable Selections in Psychology.* For a long time I had wanted to be able to introduce my students to original writings in psychology. I was thrilled to be able to share with students the excitement of learning directly from some of the most influential figures in psychology.

This project is very much a joint effort. Although my name as editor is the only one on the cover, I had lots of help from many people. Whenever I had a question about the readability or relevance of an article, my psychology students provided comments and suggestions. I thank the many students who used the first edition of the book and took the time to provide evaluative feedback. I especially appreciate the efforts of Tina Spurlock and Annette Nemeth, who provided outstanding library assistance. I also want to thank Mary Kuhn, who truly enjoyed the first edition. I sincerely want to thank the reviewers of the first edition:

Michael Gamble
Malaspina College

Thomas Rabon
Campbell University

Catherine Weir
Colorado College

Doug Wessel
Black Hills State University

Mary Wood
St. Mary's College

George Yatchism
University of California,
    Santa Barbara

They provided many suggestions on potential sources and specific direction for the second edition. David Dean, List Manager for the Sources series, kept everything functioning smoothly. Tammy Ward, Administrative Assistant, provided helpful information as I needed it. My wife, Bernie, typed the reference lists, headnotes, and test questions, and she provided much emotional support. And my family, Terry and his wife Shelley, Karen, and Tommy, were patient as I worked on this project and missed family activities.

Sources: Notable Selections in Psychology, 2d ed., is designed particularly to meet the needs of those instructors who want to convey to students the richness of the psychological perspective through original writings. I have worked hard to produce a valuable resource, and I would very much appreciate any comments or suggestions you might have on the book. Although I feel that these selections represent some of the most significant studies in psychology, not everyone will agree with all of the particular selections. I promise to carefully consider all of your suggestions as the book goes through the revision process (my e-mail address is Pettijohn.1@osu.edu). I hope you find this collection useful in your teaching.

Terry F. Pettijohn
Ohio State University

Contents

interaction provides the baby with opportunity to build up expectations of the mother and, eventually, a working model of her as more or less accessible and responsive."

"Actually, as soon as we talk with children about morality, we find that they have many ways of making judgments which are not 'internalized' from the outside, and which do not come in any direct and obvious way from parents, teachers or even peers."

"Concern over sexism in language raises a number of interesting questions for which the psychologist can provide empirical answers. How do people process gender-neutral uses of 'he?' How do they interpret that pronoun when they hear it?"

"There are certain important ways in which gender is implicated in social behavior—ways that may be obscured or missed altogether when behavior is summed across all categories of social partners."

"[I]s experience really the teacher? Or is the ability to perceive and avoid a brink part of the child's original endowment? Answers to these questions will throw light on the genesis of space perception in general."

"The *Gestalt-Theorie* is more than a theory of perception: it is even more than a mere psychological theory. Yet it originated in a study of perception and the investigation of this topic has furnished the better part of the experimental work which has been done."

PART ONE

Foundations of Psychology

On the Internet . . .

Sites appropriate to Part One

Description of and information on the divisions of the American Psychological Association (APA).

> http://www.apa.org/division.html

The APA's historical database is a collection of dates and brief descriptions of over 3,100 events in the history of psychology.

> http://www.cwu.edu/~warren/today.html

A tutorial on brain structures by Dr. John H. Krantz, Hanover College.

> http://psych.hanover.edu/Krantz/neurotut.html

CHAPTER 1 Introducing Psychology

1.1 WILLIAM JAMES

The Scope of Psychology

The American psychologist William James's *Principles of Psychology*, published in 1890, marked a major milestone in the history of psychology. In it, James asserts that psychology should focus on the functions of consciousness, an idea that helped establish the school of functionalism and that continues to be important to the study of psychology today.

James (1842–1910) obtained his M.D. from Harvard University in 1869 and accepted a teaching position in psychology there three years later. During his lifetime, he wrote on a variety of topics, including consciousness, emotion, personality, learning, and religion.

This selection is taken from James's most famous work, the two-volume *Principles of Psychology.* In it, James argues that psychology is the "science of mental life." Although he includes feelings and cognitions in his definition of psychology, he emphasizes the role of the brain in behaviors that serve the function of survival. His book formed the cornerstone of many early psychology courses, and it encouraged psychologists to take a broad view of their discipline. This book is still very much read and studied today.

Key Concept: an early definition of psychology

*P*sychology is the Science of Mental Life, both of its phenomena and their conditions. The phenomena are such things as we call feelings, desires, cognitions, reasonings, decisions, and the like; and, superficially considered, their variety and complexity is such as to leave a chaotic impression on the observer. . . .

[R]eflection shows that phenomena [experience in the outer world] have absolutely no power to influence our ideas until they have first impressed our senses and our brain. The bare existence of a past fact is no ground for our remembering it. Unless we have seen it, or somehow *undergone* it, we shall never know of its having been. The experiences of the body are thus one of the conditions of the faculty of memory being what it is. And a very small amount of reflection on facts shows that one part of the body, namely, the brain, is the part whose experiences are directly concerned. If the nervous communication be cut off between the brain and other parts, the experiences of those other parts are non-existent for the mind. The eye is blind, the ear deaf, the hand insensible and motionless. And conversely, if the brain be injured, consciousness is abolished or altered, even although every other organ in the body be ready to play its normal part. A blow on the head, a sudden subtraction of blood, the pressure of an apoplectic hemorrhage, may have the first effect; whilst a very few ounces of alcohol or gains of opium or hasheesh, or a whiff of chloroform or nitrous oxide gas, are sure to have the second. The delirium of fever, the altered self of insanity, are all due to foreign matters circulating through the brain, or to pathological changes in that organ's substance. The fact that the brain is the one immediate bodily condition of the mental operations is indeed so universally admitted nowadays that I need spend no more time in illustrating it, but will simply postulate it and pass on. . . .

Bodily experiences, therefore, and more particularly brain-experiences, must take a place amongst those conditions of the mental life of which Psychology need take account. . . .

Our first conclusion, then, is that a certain amount of brain-physiology must be presupposed or included in Psychology.

In still another way the psychologist is forced to be something of a nerve-physiologist. Mental phenomena are not only conditioned . . . by bodily processes; but they lead to them. . . . That they lead to *acts* is of course the most familiar of truths, but I do not merely mean acts in the sense of voluntary and deliberate muscular performances. Mental states occasion also changes in the calibre of blood-vessels, or alteration in the heart-beats, or processes more subtle still, in glands and viscera. If these are taken into account, as well as acts which follow at some *remote period* because the mental state was once there, it will be safe to lay down the general law that *no mental modification ever occurs which is not accompanied or followed by a bodily change*. The ideas and feelings, *e.g.*, which these present printed characters excite in the reader's mind not only occasion movements of his eyes and nascent movements of articulation in him, but will some day make him speak, or take sides in a discussion, or give advice, or choose a book to read, differently from what would have been the case had they never impressed his retina. Our psychology must therefore take account not only of the conditions antecedent to mental states, but of their resultant consequences as well.

William James

But actions originally prompted by conscious intelligence may grow so automatic by dint of habit as to be apparently unconsciously performed. Standing, walking, buttoning and unbuttoning, piano-playing, talking, even saying one's prayers, may be done when the mind is absorbed in other things. The performances of animal *instinct* seem semi-automatic, and the *reflex acts* of self-preservation certainly are so. Yet they resemble intelligent acts in bringing about the *same ends* at which the animals' consciousness, on other occasions, deliberately aims. Shall the study of such machine-like yet purposive acts as these be included in Psychology?

The boundary line of the mental is certainly vague. It is better not to be pedantic, but to let the science be as vague as its subject, and include such phenomena as these if by so doing we can throw any light on the main business in hand. It will ere long be seen, I trust, that we can; and that we gain much more by a broad than by a narrow conception of our subject. At a certain stage in the development of every science a degree of vagueness is what best consists with fertility. On the whole, few recent formulas have done more real service of a rough sort in psychology than the ... one that the essence of mental life and of bodily life are one, namely, 'the adjustment of inner to outer relations.' Such a formula is vagueness incarnate; but because it takes into account the fact that minds inhabit environments which act on them and on which they in turn react; because, in short, it takes mind in the midst of all its concrete relations, it is immensely more fertile than the old-fashioned 'rational psychology,' which treated the soul as a detached existent, sufficient unto itself, and assumed to consider only its nature and properties. I shall therefore feel free to make any sallies into zoology or into pure nerve-physiology which may seem instructive for our purposes, but otherwise shall leave those sciences to the physiologists.

Can we state more distinctly still the manner in which the mental life seems to intervene between impressions made from without upon the body, and reactions of the body upon the outer world again? Let us look at a few facts.

If some iron filings be sprinkled on a table and a magnet brought near them, they will fly through the air for a certain distance and stick to its surface. A savage seeing the phenomenon explains it as the result of an attraction or love between the magnet and the filings. But let a card cover the poles of the magnet, and the filings will press forever against its surface without its ever occurring to them to pass around its sides and thus come into more direct contact with the object of their love. ...

If now we pass from such actions as these to those of living things, we notice a striking difference. Romeo wants Juliet as the filings want the magnet; and if no obstacles intervene he moves towards her by as straight a line as they. But Romeo and Juliet, if a wall be built between them, do not remain idiotically pressing their faces against its opposite sides like the magnet and the filings with the card. Romeo soon finds a circuitous way, be scaling the wall or otherwise, of touching Juliet's lips directly. With the filings the path is fixed; whether it reaches the end depends on accidents. With the lover it is the end which is fixed, the path may be modified indefinitely.

Such contrasts between living and inanimate performances end by leading men to deny that in the physical world final purposes exist at all. Loves and desires are today no longer imputed to particles of iron or of air. No one supposes now that the end of any activity which they may display is an ideal purpose presiding over the activity from its outset.... The end, on the contrary, is deemed a mere passive result, ... having had, so to speak, no voice in its own production. Alter the pre-existing conditions, and with inorganic materials you bring forth each time a different apparent end. But with intelligent agents, altering the conditions changes the activity displayed, but not the end reached; for here the idea of the yet unrealized end co-operates with the conditions to determine what the activities shall be.

The pursuance of future ends and the choice of means for their attainment are thus the mark and criterion of the presence of mentality in a phenomenon. We all use this test to discriminate between an intelligent and a mechanical performance. We impute no mentality to sticks and stones, because they never seem to move for *the sake of* anything, but always when pushed, and then indifferently and with no sign of choice. So we unhesitatingly call them senseless.

Just so we form our decision upon the deepest of all philosophic problems: Is the [C]osmos [the universe] an expression of intelligence rational in its inward nature, or a brute external fact pure and simple? If we find ourselves, in contemplating it, unable to banish the impression that it is a realm of final purposes, that it exists for the sake of something, we place intelligence at the heart of it and have a religion. If, on the contrary, in surveying its irremediable flux, we can think of the present only as so much mere mechanical sprouting from the past, occurring with no reference to the future, we are atheists and materialists.

Psychology as the Behaviorist Views It

From the 1920s through the 1960s the field of psychology was largely dominated by behaviorists, who focus on the objective measurement of behavior. The founder of the school of behaviorism was John B. Watson, whose view of psychology as a "purely objective experimental branch of natural science" had a major influence on early psychologists. Watson's belief that psychology should be the science of overt behavior, modeled after the natural sciences, is expressed in this selection.

Watson (1878–1958) earned his Ph.D. in experimental psychology from the University of Chicago in 1903. He began teaching at the Johns Hopkins University in 1908 and stayed there until he resigned in 1920. Although he left academic psychology after only 12 years of teaching, his influence is still felt in the discipline today.

This selection is from "Psychology as the Behaviorist Views It," published in *Psychological Review* in 1913. This article marked the introduction of the school of behaviorism. In it, Watson discards the subject of consciousness and the method of introspection from psychology and argues for an objective study of the behavior of both people and animals. His goal is to help psychology become more applicable in other areas (such as education, law, and business) as it develops into an experimental natural science.

Key Concept: school of behaviorism

*P*sychology as the behaviorist views it is a purely objective experimental branch of natural science. Its theoretical goal is the prediction and control of behavior. Introspection forms no essential part of its methods, nor is the scientific value of its data dependent upon the readiness with which they lend themselves to interpretation in terms of consciousness. The behaviorist, in his efforts to get a unitary scheme of animal response, recognizes no dividing line between man and brute. The behavior of man, with all of its refinement and complexity, forms only a part of the behaviorist's total scheme of investigation. . . .

The time seems to have come when psychology must discard all reference to consciousness; when it need no longer delude itself into thinking that it is making mental states the object of observation. We have become so enmeshed in speculative questions concerning the elements of mind, the nature of conscious content (for example, imageless thought, attitudes, . . . etc.) that I, as an experimental student, feel that something is wrong with our premises and the types of problems which develop from them. There is not longer any guarantee that we all mean the same thing when we use the terms now current in psychology. Take the case of sensation. A sensation is defined in terms of its attributes. One psychologist will state with readiness that the attributes of a visual sensation are *quality, extension, duration,* and *intensity.* Another will add *clearness.* Still another that of *order.* I doubt if any one psychologist can draw up a set of statements describing what he means by sensation which will be agreed to by three other psychologists of different training. Turn for a moment to the question of the number of isolable sensations. Is there an extremely large number of color sensations—or only four, red, green, yellow and blue? Again, yellow, while psychologically simple, can be obtained by superimposing red and green spectral rays upon the same diffusing surface! If, on the other hand, we say that every just noticeable difference in the spectrum is a simple sensation, and that every just noticeable increase in the white value of a given color gives simple sensations, we are forced to admit that the number is so large and the conditions for obtaining them so complex that the concept of sensation is unusable, either for the purpose of analysis or that of synthesis. Titchener, who has fought the most valiant fight in this country for a psychology based upon introspection, feels that these differences of opinion as to the number of sensations and their attributes; as to whether there are relations (in the sense of elements) and on the many others which seem to be fundamental in every attempt at analysis, are perfectly natural in the present undeveloped state of psychology. While it is admitted that every growing science is full of unanswered questions, surely only those who are wedded to the system as we now have it, who have fought and suffered for it, can confidently believe that there will ever be any greater uniformity than there is now in the answers we have to such questions. I firmly believe that two hundred years from now, unless the introspective method is discarded, psychology will still be divided on the question as to whether auditory sensations have the quality of 'extension,' whether intensity is an attribute which can be applied to color, whether there is a difference in 'texture' between image and sensation and upon many hundreds of others of like character. . . .

I was greatly surprised some time ago when I opened Pillsbury's book and say psychology defined as the 'science of behavior.' A still more recent text states that psychology is the 'science of mental behavior.' When I saw these promising statements I thought, now surely we will have texts based upon different lines. After a few pages the science of behavior is dropped and one finds the conventional treatment of sensation, perception, imagery, etc., along with certain shifts in emphasis and additional facts which serve to give the author's personal imprint. . . .

This leads me to the point where I should like to make the argument constructive. I believe we can write a psychology, define it as Pillsbury, and never go back upon our definition: never use the terms consciousness, mental states, mind, content, introspectively verifiable, imagery, and the like. . . . It can be done in terms of stimulus and response, in terms of habit formation, habit integrations and the like. Furthermore, I believe that it is really worth while to make this attempt now.

The psychology which I should attempt to build up would take as a starting point, first, the observable fact that organisms, man and animal alike, do adjust themselves to their environment by means of hereditary and habit equipments. These adjustments may be very adequate or they may be so inadequate that the organism barely maintains its existence; secondly, that certain stimuli lead the organisms to make the responses. In a system of psychology completely worked out, given the response the stimuli can be predicted; given the stimuli the response can be predicted. Such a set of statements is crass and raw in the extreme, as all such generalizations must be. Yet they are hardly more raw and less realizable than the ones which appear in the psychology texts of the day. I possibly might illustrate my point better by choosing an everyday problem which anyone is likely to meet in the course of his work. Some time ago I was called upon to make a study of certain species of birds. Until I went to Tortugas I had never seen these birds alive. When I reached there I found the animals doing certain things: some of the acts seemed to work peculiarly well in such an environment, while others seemed to be unsuited to their type of life. I first studied the responses of the group as a whole and later those of individuals. In order to understand more thoroughly the relation between what was habit and what was hereditary in these responses, I took the young birds and reared them. In this way I was able to study the order of appearance of hereditary adjustments and their complexity, and later the beginnings of habit formation. My efforts in determining the stimuli which called forth such adjustments were crude indeed. Consequently my attempts to control behavior and to produce responses at will did not meet with much success. Their food and water, sex and other social relations, light and temperature conditions were all beyond control in a field study. I did find it possible to control their reactions in a measure by using the nest and egg (or young) as stimuli. It is not necessary in this paper to develop further how such a study should be carried out and how work of this kind must be supplemented by carefully controlled laboratory experiments. . . . In the main, my desire in all such work is to gain an accurate knowledge of adjustments and the stimuli calling them forth. My final reason for this is to learn general and particular methods by which I may control behavior. . . . If psychology would follow the plan I suggest, the educator, the physician, the jurist and the business man could utilize our data in a practical way, as soon as we are able, experimentally, to obtain them. Those who have occasion to apply psychological principles practically would find no need to complain as they do at the present time. Ask any physician or jurist today whether scientific psychology plays a practical part in his daily routine and you will hear him deny that the psychology of the laboratories finds a place in his scheme of work. I think the criticism is extremely just. One of the earliest conditions which made me dissatisfied with psychology was the feeling that there was no realm of application for the principles which were being worked out in content terms.

What gives me hope that the behaviorist's position is a defensible one is the fact that those branches of psychology which have already partially withdrawn from the parent, experimental psychology, and which are consequently less dependent upon introspection are today in a most flourishing condition. Experimental pedagogy, the psychology of drugs, the psychology of advertising, legal psychology, the psychology of tests, and psychopathology are all vigorous growths. These are sometimes wrongly called "practical" or "applied" psychology. Surely there was never a worse misnomer. In the future there may grow up vocational bureaus which really apply psychology. At present these fields are truly scientific and are in search of broad generalizations which will lead to the control of human behavior. For example, we find out by experimentation whether a series of stanzas may be acquired more readily if the whole is learned at once, or whether it is more advantageous to learn each stanza separately and then pass to the succeeding. We do not attempt to apply our findings. The application of this principle is purely voluntary on the part of the teachers. In the psychology of drugs we may show the effect upon behavior of certain doses of caffeine. We may reach the conclusion that caffeine has a good effect upon the speed and accuracy of work. But these are general principles. We leave it to the individual as to whether the results of our tests shall be applied or not. Again, in legal testimony, we test the effects of recency upon the reliability of a witness's report. We test the accuracy of the report with respect to moving objects, stationary objects, color, etc. It depends upon the judicial machinery of the country to decide whether these facts are ever to be applied. For a 'pure' psychologist to say that he is not interested in the questions raised in these divisions of the science because they relate indirectly to the application of psychology shows, in the first place, that he fails to understand the scientific aim in such problems, and secondly, that he is not interested in a psychology which concerns itself with human life. The only fault I have to find with these disciplines is that much of their material is stated in terms of introspection, whereas a statement of terms of objective results would be far more valuable. . . .

In concluding, I suppose I must confess to a deep bias on these questions. I have devoted nearly twelve years to experimentation on animals. It is natural that such a one should drift into a theoretical position which is in harmony with his experimental work. Possibly I have put up a straw man and have been fighting that. . . . Certainly the position I advocate is weak enough at present and can be attacked from many standpoints. Yet when all this is admitted I still feel that the considerations which I have urged should have a wide influence upon the type of psychology which is to be developed in the future. What we need to do is to start work upon psychology, making *behavior*, not *consciousness*, the objective point of our attack. Certainly there are enough problems in the control of behavior to keep us all working many lifetimes without ever allowing us time to think of consciousness. . . . Once launched in the undertaking, we will find ourselves in a short time as far divorced from an introspective psychology as the psychology of the present time is divorced from faculty psychology.

1.3 ROBERT ROSENTHAL AND LENORE JACOBSON

Teachers' Expectancies: Determinants of Pupils' IQ Gains

Psychological research is sometimes difficult to interpret correctly, in part because people can unintentionally bring bias into the research setting. Without being aware of it, a person's expectations can alter his or her perceptions and behavior. The pioneering work of Robert Rosenthal and Lenore Jacobson has helped psychologists become more aware of the potential for bias in research studies.

Rosenthal earned his Ph.D. in psychology in 1956 from the University of California, Los Angeles. He is currently a professor of psychology at Harvard University. Jacobson was with the South San Francisco Unified School District when the research reported in this selection was performed. Rosenthal and Jacobson coauthored a book on expectancy effect entitled *Pygmalion in the Classroom: Teacher Expectations and Pupils' Intellectual Development* (Holt, Rinehart & Winston, 1968).

This selection is from "Teachers' Expectancies: Determinants of Pupils' IQ Gains," which was published in *Psychological Reports* in 1966. It demonstrates how teacher expectancy (in this study, expectancy that certain students would "intellectually bloom" during a school year) had a significant effect on student behavior (the randomly selected students increased their IQ scores). As you read this selection, think about your elementary school years. Did you do best in classes in which your teachers expected high performance? How does expectancy play a role in our everyday lives? How could research studies be designed to minimize the effects of expectancy?

Key Concept: bias in psychological research

*E*xperiments have shown that in behavioral research employing human or animal *S*s, *E*'s expectancy can be a significant determinant of *S*'s response (Rosenthal, 1964, in press). In studies employing animals, for example, *E*s led to believe that their rat *S*s has been bred for superior learning ability obtained performance superior to that obtained by *E*s led to believe that their rats had been bred for inferior learning ability (Rosenthal & Fode, 1963; Rosenthal & Lawson, 1964). The present study was designed to extend the generality of this finding from *E*s to teachers and from animal *S*s to school children.

Flanagan (1960) has developed a nonverbal intelligence test (*Tests of General Ability* or *TOGA*) which is not explicitly dependent on such school-learned skills as reading, writing, and arithmetic. The test is composed of two types of items, "verbal" and "reasoning." The "verbal" items measure the child's level of information, vocabulary, and concepts. The "reasoning" items measure the child's concept formation ability by employing abstract line drawings. Flanagan's purpose in developing the TOGA was "to provide a relatively fair measure of intelligence for all individuals, even those who have had atypical opportunities to learn" (1960, p. 6).

Flanagan's test was administered to all children in an elementary school, disguised as a test designed to predict academic "blooming" or intellectual gain. Within each of the six grades in the school were three classrooms, one each of children performing at above average, average, and below average levels of scholastic achievement. In each of the 18 classes an average of 20% of the children were assigned to the experimental condition. The names of these children were given to each teacher who was told that their scores on the "test for intellectual blooming" indicated that they would show unusual intellectual gains during the academic year. Actually, the children had been assigned to the experimental condition by means of a table of random numbers. The experimental treatment for these children, then, consisted of nothing more than being identified to their teachers as children who would show unusual intellectual gains.

Eight months after the experimental conditions were instituted all children were retested with the same IQ test and a change score was computed for each child. Table 1 shows the mean gain in IQ points among experimental and control *S*s in each of the six grades. For the school as a whole those children from whom the teachers had been led to expect greater intellectual gain showed a significantly greater gain in IQ score than did the control children ($p = .02$, one-tail). Inspection of Table 1 shows that the effects of teachers' expectancies were not uniform across the six grade levels. The lower the grade level, the greater was the effect ($rho = -.94$, $p = .02$, two-tail). It was in the first and second grades that the effects were most dramatic. The largest gain among the three first grade classrooms occurred for experimental *S*s who gained 24.8 IQ points *in excess* of the gain (+16.2) shown by the controls. The largest gain among the three second grade classrooms was obtained by experimental *S*s who gained 18.2 IQ points in excess of the gain (+4.3) shown by the controls. . . .

There are a number of possible explanations of the finding that teachers' expectancy effects operated primarily at the lower grade levels, including: (a) Younger children have less well-established reputations so that the creation of expectations about their performance would be more credible. (b) Younger

TABLE 1

13

Mean Gains in IQ

*Robert
Rosenthal and
Lenore Jacobson*

Grade	Controls		Experimentals		Diff.	t	p†
	M	σ	M	σ			
1	12.0	16.6	27.4	12.5	15.4	2.97	.002
2	7.0	10.0	16.5	18.6	9.5	2.28	.02
3	5.0	11.9	5.0	9.3	0.0		
4	2.2	13.4	5.6	11.0	3.4		
5	17.5	13.1	17.4	17.8	-0.1		
6	10.7	10.0	10.0	6.5	-0.7		
Weighted M	8.4*	13.5	12.2**	15.0	3.8	2.15	.02

*Mean number of children per grade = 42.5
**Mean number of children per grade = 10.8
† p one-tailed.

children may be more susceptible to the unintended social influence exerted by the expectation of their teacher. (c) Younger children may be more recent arrivals in the school's neighborhood and may differ from the older children in characteristics other than age. (d) Teachers of lower grades may differ from teachers of higher grades on a variety of dimensions which are correlated with the effectiveness of the unintentional communication of expectancies.

The most important question which remains is that which asks how a teacher's expectation becomes translated into behavior in such a way as to elicit the expected pupil behavior. Prior research on the unintentional communication of expectancies in experimentally more carefully controlled interactions suggests that this question will not be easily unanswered (Rosenthal, in press).

But, regardless of the mechanism involved, there are important substantive and methodological implications of these findings. . . . For now, one example, in question form, will do: How much of the improvement in intellectual performance attributed to the contemporary educational programs is due to the content and methods of the programs and how much is due to the favorable expectancies of the teachers and administrators involved? Experimental designs to answer such questions are available. (Rosenthal, in press) and in view of the psychological, social and economic importance of these programs the use of such designs seems strongly indicated.

REFERENCES

FLANAGAN, J. C. *Tests of general ability: technical report.* Chicago, Ill.: Science Research Associates, 1960.

ROSENTHAL, R. The effect of the experimenter on the results of psychological research. In B. A. Maher (Ed.), *Progress in experimental personality research.* Vol. I. New York: Academic Press, 1964. Pp. 79–114.

ROSENTHAL, R. *Experimenter effects in behavioral research.* New York: Appleton-Century-Crofts, in press.

ROSENTHAL, R. & FODE, K. L. The effect of experimenter bias on the performance of the albino rat. *Behavioral Science,* 1963, 8, 183–189.

ROSENTHAL, R. & LAWSON, R. A longitudinal study of the effects of experimenter bias on the operant learning of laboratory rats. *Journal of Psychiatric Research,* 1964, 2, 61–72.

The Fragmentation of Psychology?

How do we define the scope of the discipline of psychology? Since the emergence of psychology from philosophy and biology over 100 years ago, psychologists have been trying to answer this question. In recent years, there has been a trend toward increasing specialization. As president of the American Psychological Association (APA), Gordon H. Bower addressed this issue.

Bower (b. 1932) earned his Ph.D. in experimental psychology in 1959 at Yale University. He then joined the faculty at Stanford University, where he is currently a professor of psychology. He served as president of the APA in 1992.

This selection is from "The Fragmentation of Psychology?" which was published in *American Psychologist* in 1993. In it, Bower discusses the trend toward specialization in psychology. Psychologists study a range of topics, and each area requires specialized training. Bower points out, however, that there are common issues that involve all psychologists, and national organizations such as the American Psychological Association and the American Psychological Society provide opportunities for communication and common action. How do you define psychology? As you study the various subfields, try to focus on the core issues in psychology as a discipline.

Key Concept: the discipline of psychology

The topic of this article—the fragmentation of psychology—is one of those perennial chestnuts to which there is no agreed-upon answer at present, nor is one likely in the near future. Probably William James and Titchener argued about this at the first meeting of the American Psychological Association (APA) 100 years ago. The basic difficulty is that psychology itself is an ill-defined field; few of us could agree on what is the proper purview of the discipline of psychology. Similarly, the unity or fragmentation of any intellectual discipline can be assessed from many different perspectives, such as agreement among its devotees regarding the legitimate problems to be investigated or agreement in their philosophical orientation, fundamental concepts, or methods of investigation.

A simple resolution might be to define the field of psychology in operational terms, as simply the collection of professional activities that people who call themselves psychologists engage in. And if we discover that psychologists engage in many different types of activities, then we can conclude that there are many different types of psychologists or fragments of the field.

Now there is no question that people who call themselves psychologists are working in large numbers of vastly different settings doing vastly different things. Some of us are university teachers, laboratory researchers, survey researchers studying social problems or human-factors specialists interfacing people to machines. Some of us study or intervene in large organizations, such as commercial enterprises, communities, or prisons; others counsel school children, help the mentally or physically handicapped, help improve preschool programs, or provide psychotherapy to distressed individuals. Even the laboratory psychologists differ greatly in what they actually study and do.

So, if we classify psychologists by what we do, there is little doubt that the field has been fragmented for years, and its fragmentation is increasing as psychologists become involved in an ever-expanding range of activities. We may ask, what is causing this fragmentation, and does fragmentation portend bad things for the science and profession of psychology?

I think the fragmentation reflects two different trends. One trend has been the development of a diverse range of applications of psychology to many different sorts of problems. Each applied setting has its own breed of specialist, from industrial organizations to the school counselor's office, from mental health clinics to rehabilitation centers, and so on. Psychologists also tend to cluster into topical interest groups, such as those with interests in political or religious behavior, conflict resolution, women's issues, minorities, or cross-cultural studies. These applied and topical interests have spawned the many divisions of APA that attract their adherents to specialized meetings within and beyond the APA convention. So, that is one reason for the fragmentation of psychology.

A second reason is that fragmentation is a perfectly natural outgrowth of the maturing of a science. We are following in exactly the same path as older sciences, such as mathematics, chemistry, and biology. A science grows over time by covering more ground, addressing new but related problems, distinguishing between cases and differentiating among types of things or topics that it formerly lumped together, and obtaining new findings and elaborating new concepts and theories around them. A frequent metaphor for the growth of a science views it as an expanding tree that sends out branches, then more branches on those branches as more phenomena are discovered and as new concepts are developed to explain them. To carry this metaphor to an unflattering extreme, an individual scientist is like a small bug feeding on a succulent leaf at one end of a tiny branch and perhaps talking to the other bugs feeding on the same leaf.

Each branch is a topical specialty. In psychology as in other disciplines, we have many hierarchical levels of specialization. For example, in the study of human abilities, one high-level ability is sensory perception, which divides into different senses of vision, audition, and so forth. Each of these divides further (e.g., vision divides into the perception of color, brightness, motion, objects, depth, and scenes). Furthermore, each of these subspecialties can be examined from different perspectives, in neurophysiological or behavioral terms, or one can study its development from infancy. In this manner, it is only a bit of a stretch for us to understand why someone might become a specialist in comparative development of neurophysiological substrates of color vision in mammals and still be called a psychologist.

This last example also illustrates another division in psychology that we all live with, namely, that psychology really has three distinct subject matters. Roughly speaking, they are behavior and its neurobiological substrates and phenomenological experience. Although psychologists typically specialize in one of these subject matters, we occasionally try to tie together two or more of the areas. Some of the more interesting research attempts to correlate brain events with either behavioral or phenomenological events. For example, Mike Posner and his associates (Posner, Petersen, Fox, & Raichle, 1988) have correlated a higher metabolic rate in a frontal cortical area as measured by position emission tomography (PET scan) with a specific kind of cognitive operation in humans, or electrophysiologists have correlated the P300 bump in the evoked cortical response with the subjective experience of being surprised. In fact, human neuropsychology is a field dedicated to looking for correlations between brain events and psychological functions.

To return to the theme of the fragmentation of psychology, I have noted that it is a consequence of the natural maturation of the science and the expanding range of its applications. But rather than call this *fragmentation*, why not label the process one of *specialization*, which has fewer negative connotations? After all, most people do not think specialization is so bad, especially when they need a doctor who specializes in what ails them.

I do not deny that this increasing specialization creates serious tensions when we must decide what topics and specialties should be covered in training students at both undergraduate and graduate levels. We are all familiar with these vexing questions: "What is the core of psychology? What must be taught, and in what order? How do we certify sufficient expertise by the teachers or by the students who want to become credentialed psychologists?" Many of these are local decisions best left to the training faculty at a given school. Then I think we should permit free market forces to operate, letting students and the society as a whole decide, by voting with their feet, whether they want to pay for that kind of training or hire graduates of that kind of training program. But these issues are highly politicized at present, and it would be foolhardy to try to do justice to them in this brief essay. . . .

However, despite this specialization, I still firmly believe that there are several important functions to be performed by large national umbrella organizations such as APS [American Psychological Society], APA, and the Federation. Such organizations provide many professional services for their members, such as publications, international exchanges, job placement services, and interesting newsletters that maintain a sense of community. The societies also help to set uniform standards for professional ethics and for accreditation of training programs, and they hold national conventions at which members can exchange information and at least try to talk to one another.

National umbrella organizations also provide us with a forum and a platform in which we can come together to reaffirm our common interests and values. As a group, psychologists share a large number of personal and scientific values and beliefs. These include an interest in understanding the mind and behavior, a respect for empirical evidence to decide whatever issues it can, a preference for data over tradition and authorities, and a generally liberal political agenda that includes using our knowledge to reduce suffering and to promote mental health, social equality, personal freedom, and human welfare. We certainly should not be reticent to acknowledge or promote these common values.

But for me personally, one strong reason to support national professional organizations is that, unlike the smaller specialty groups, the umbrella organizations help us to aggregate and focus our advocacy of policy issues that are under consideration by Congress, the administration, regulatory agencies, and federal agencies. One need not be a rocket scientist to realize that the health of our profession, our educational system, and our mental-health delivery system is strongly impacted by the actions of Congress and the administration because they make funding and regulatory decisions that trickle down to affect nearly every one of us, whether we be academics or practitioners.

REFERENCE

Posner, M. I., Petersen, S. E., Fox, P. T., & Raichle, M. E. (1988). Localization of cognitive operations in the human brain. *Science, 240,* 1627–1631.

CHAPTER 2

Psychobiology

2.1 ROGER W. SPERRY

Hemisphere Deconnection and Unity in Conscious Awareness

The fact that the human brain is divided into two cerebral hemispheres has always intrigued scientists. In the 1950s, neurosurgeon Philip Vogel developed the technique of cutting the corpus callosum (the neural bundle connecting the two cerebral hemispheres) to reduce the severity of seizures in epileptic patients. This allowed researchers, particularly Roger W. Sperry, to study the conscious behavior of so-called split-brain patients.

Sperry (1913–1994) received his Ph.D. from the University of Chicago in 1941. He became a professor of psychobiology at the California Institute of Technology in 1954. Sperry initially studied cerebral hemisphere disconnection in cats, then he moved on to study humans who underwent split-brain surgery. In 1981, Sperry received a Nobel Prize in physiology and medicine for his research on the brain.

This selection from "Hemisphere Deconnection and Unity in Conscious Awareness," which was published in 1968 in *American Psychologist*, describes some of the research conducted by Sperry and his colleagues. Through his research, Sperry discovered that the two cerebral hemispheres have distinct functions—the left side is involved in reasoning, language, and writing, whereas the right side is involved in nonverbal processes, such as art, music, and creativity. This selection conveys the excitement of discovering how human consciousness functions and the intricacies of the human brain.

Key Concept: split-brain research

*T*he following article is a result of studies my colleagues and I have been conducting with some neurosurgical patients of Philip J. Vogel of Los Angeles. These patients were all advanced epileptics in whom an extensive midline section of the cerebral commissures had been carried out in an effort to contain severe epileptic convulsions not controlled by medication. In all these people the surgical sections included division of the corpus callosum in its entirety, plus division also of the smaller anterior and hippocampal commissures, plus in some instances the massa intermedia. So far as I know, this is the most radical disconnection of the cerebral hemispheres attempted thus far in human surgery. The full array of sections was carried out in a single operation.

No major collapse of mentality or personality was anticipated as a result of this extreme surgery: earlier clinical observations on surgical section of the corpus callosum in man, as well as the results from dozens of monkeys on which I had carried out this exact same surgery, suggested that the functional deficits might very likely be less damaging than some of the more common forms of cerebral surgery, such as frontal lobotomy, or even some of the unilateral lobotomies performed more routinely for epilepsy.

The first patient on whom this surgery was tried had been having seizures for more than 10 years with generalized convulsions that continued to worsen despite treatment that had included a sojourn in Bethesda at the National Institutes of Health. At the time of the surgery, he had been averaging two major attacks per week, each of which left him debilitated for another day or so. Episodes of *status epilepticus* (recurring seizures that fail to stop and represent a medical emergency with a fairly high mortality risk) had also begun to occur at 2- to 3-month intervals. Since leaving the hospital following his surgery over 5½ years ago, this man has not had, according to last reports, a single generalized convulsion. It has further been possible to reduce the level of medication and to obtain an overall improvement in his behavior and well being (see Bogen & Vogel, 1962).

The second patient, a housewife and mother in her 30s, also has been seizure-free since recovering from her surgery, which was more than 4 years ago (Bogen, Fisher, & Vogel, 1965). Bogen related that even the EEG has regained a normal pattern in this patient. The excellent outcome in the initial, apparently hopeless, last-resort cases led to further application of the surgery to some nine more individuals to date, the majority of whom are too recent for therapeutic evaluation. Although the alleviation of the epilepsy has not held up 100% throughout the series (two patients are still having seizures, although their convulsions are much reduced in severity and frequency and tend to be confined to one side), the results on the whole continue to be predominantly beneficial, and the overall outlook at this time remains promising for selected severe cases.

The therapeutic success, however, and all other medical aspects are matters for our medical colleagues, Philip J. Vogel and Joseph E. Bogen. Our own work has been confined entirely to an examination of the functional outcome, that is, the behavioral, neurological, and psychological effects of this surgical disruption of all direct cross-talk between the hemispheres. Initially we were concerned as to whether we would be able to find in these patients any of the numerous symptoms of hemisphere deconnection that had been demonstrated in the so-called "split-brain" animal studies of the 1950s (Myers, 1961; Sperry, 1967a, 1967b). The outcome in man remained an open question in view of the historic Akelaitis (1944) studies that had set the prevailing doctrine of the 1940s and 1950s. This doctrine maintained that no important functional symptoms are found in man following even complete surgical section of the corpus callosum and anterior commissure, provided that other brain damage is excluded.

These earlier observations on the absence of behavioral symptoms in man have been confirmed in a general way to the extent that it remains fair to say today that the most remarkable effect of sectioning the neocortical commissures is the apparent lack of effect so far as ordinary behavior is concerned. This has been true in our animal studies throughout, and it seems now to be true for man also, with certain qualifications that we will come to later. At the same time, however—and this is in contradiction to the earlier doctrine set by the Akelaitis studies—we know today that with appropriate tests one can indeed demonstrate a large number of behavioral symptoms that correlate directly with the loss of the neocortical commissures in man as well as in animals (Gazzaniga, 1967; Sperry, 1967a, 1967b; Sperry, Gazzaniga, & Bogen, 1968). Taken collectively, these symptoms may be referred to as the syndrome of the neocortical commissures or the syndrome of the forebrain commissures or, less specifically, as the syndrome of hemisphere deconnection.

One of the more general and also more interesting and striking features of this syndrome may be summarized as an apparent doubling in most of the realms of conscious awareness. Instead of the normally unified single stream of consciousness, these patients behave in many ways as if they have two independent streams of conscious awareness, one in each hemisphere, each of which is cut off from and out of contact with the mental experiences of the other. In other words, each hemisphere seems to have its own separate and private sensations; its own perceptions; its own concepts; and its own impulses to act, with related volitional, cognitive, and learning experiences. Following the surgery, each hemisphere also has thereafter its own separate chain of memories that are rendered inaccessible to the recall processes of the other.

This presence of two minds in one body, as it were, is manifested in a large number and variety of test responses which, for the present purposes, I will try to review very briefly and in a somewhat streamlined and simplified form. First, however, let me take time to emphasize that the work reported here has been very much a team project. The surgery was performed by Vogel at the White Memorial Medical Center in Los Angeles. He has been assisted in the surgery and in the medical treatment throughout by Joseph Bogen. Bogen has also been collaborating in our behavioral testing program, along with a num-

FIGURE 1 *Apparatus for Studying Lateralization of Visual, Tactual, Lingual, and Associated Functions in the Surgically Separated Hemispheres*

ber of graduate students and postdoctoral fellows, among whom M. S. Gazzaniga, in particular, worked closely with us during the first several years and managed much of the testing during that period. The patients and their families have been most cooperative, and the whole project gets its primary funding from the National Institute of Mental Health.

Most of the main symptoms seen after hemisphere deconnection can be described for convenience with reference to a single testing setup—shown in Figure 1. Principally, it allows for the lateralized testing of the right and left halves of the visual field, separately or together, and the right and left hands and legs with vision excluded. The tests can be arranged in different combinations and in association with visual, auditory, and other input, with provisions for eliminating unwanted stimuli. In testing vision, the subject with one eye covered centers his gaze on a designated fixation point on the upright translucent screen. The visual stimuli on 35-millimeter transparencies are arranged in a standard projector equipped with a shutter and are then back-projected at $\frac{1}{10}$ of a second or less—too fast for eye movements to get the material into the wrong half of the visual field. Figure 2 is merely a reminder that everything

FIGURE 2 *Things Seen to the Left of a Central Fixation Point With Either Eye Are Projected to the Right Hemisphere and Vice-versa*

23

Roger W. Sperry

seen to the left of the vertical meridian through either eye is projected to the right hemisphere and vice versa. The midline division along the vertical meridian is found to be quite precise without significant gap or overlap (Sperry, 1968).

When the visual perception of these patients is tested under these conditions the results indicate that these people have not one inner visual world any longer, but rather two separate visual inner worlds, one serving the right half of the field of vision and the other the left half—each, of course, in its respective hemisphere. This doubling in the visual sphere shows up in many ways: For example, after a projected picture of an object has been identified and responded to in one half field, we find that it is recognized again only if it reappears in the same half of the field of vision. If the given visual stimulus reappears in the opposite half of the visual field, the subject responds as if he had no recollection of the previous exposure. In other words, things seen through the right half of the visual field (i.e., through the left hemisphere) are registered in mental experience and remembered quite separately from things seen in the other half of the field. Each half of the field of vision in the commissurotomized patient has its own train of visual images and memories.

This separate existence of two visual inner worlds is further illustrated in reference to speech and writing, the cortical mechanisms for which are centered in the dominant hemisphere. Visual material projected to the right half of the field—left-hemisphere system of the typical right-handed patient—can be described in speech and writing in an essentially normal manner. However, when the same visual material is projected into the left half of the field, and hence to the right hemisphere, the subject consistently insists that he did not see anything or that there was only a flash of light on the left side. The subject acts as if he were blind or agnostic for the left half of the visual field. If, however, instead of asking the subject to tell you what he saw, you instruct him to use his left hand to point to a matching picture or object presented among a collection of other pictures or objects, the subject has no trouble as a rule in pointing out consistently the very item that he has just insisted he did not see.

We do not think the subjects are trying to be difficult or to dupe the examiner in such tests. Everything indicates that the hemisphere that is talking to the examiner did in fact not see the left-field stimulus and truly had no experience with, nor recollection of, the given stimulus. The other, the right or nonlingual hemisphere, however, did see the projected stimulus in this situation and is able to remember and recognize the object and can demonstrate this by pointing out selectively the corresponding or matching item. This other hemisphere, like a deaf mute or like some aphasics, cannot talk about the perceived object and, worse still, cannot write about it either.

If two different figures are flashed simultaneously to the right and left visual fields, as for example a "dollar sign" on the left and a "question mark" on the right and the subject is asked to draw what he saw using the left hand out of sight, he regularly reproduces the figure seen on the left half of the field, that is, the dollar sign. If we now ask him what he has just drawn, he tells us without hesitation that the figure he drew was the question mark, or whatever appeared in the right half of the field. In other words, the one hemisphere does not know what the other hemisphere has been doing. The left and the right halves of the visual field seem to be perceived quite separately in each hemisphere with little or no cross-influence.

When words are flashed partly in the left field and partly in the right, the letters on each side of the midline are perceived and responded to separately. In the "key case" example shown in Figure 2 the subject might first reach for and select with the left hand a key from among a collection of objects indicating perception through the minor hemisphere. With the right hand he might then spell out the word "case" or he might speak the word if verbal response is in order. When asked what kind of "case" he was thinking of here, the answer coming from the left hemisphere might be something like "in *case* of fire" or "the *case* of the missing corpse" or "a *case* of beer," etc., depending upon the particular mental set of the left hemisphere at the moment. Any reference to "key case" under these conditions would be purely fortuitous, assuming that visual, auditory, and other cues have been properly controlled.

A similar separation in mental awareness is evident in tests that deal with stereognostic [involving tactile recognition] or other somesthetic [related to bodily sensations] discriminations made by the right and left hands, which are projected separately to the left and right hemispheres, respectively. Objects put in the right hand for identification by touch are readily described or named in speech or writing, whereas, if the same objects are placed in the left hand, the subject can only make wild guesses and may often seem unaware that anything at all is present. As with vision in the left field, however, good perception, comprehension, and memory can be demonstrated for these objects in the left hand when the tests are so designed that the subject can express himself through nonverbal responses. For example, if one of these objects which the subject tells you he cannot feel or does not recognize is taken from the left hand and placed in a grab bag or scrambled among a dozen other test items, the subject is then able to search out and retrieve the initial object even after a delay of several minutes is deliberately interposed. Unlike the normal subject, however, these people are obliged to retrieve such an object with the same hand with which it was initially identified. They fail at cross-retrieval. That is, they cannot recognize with one hand something identified only moments before with the other hand. Again, the second hemisphere does not know what the first hemisphere has been doing.

When the subjects are first asked to use the left hand for these stereognostic tests they commonly complain that they cannot "work with that hand," that the hand "is numb," they they "just can't feel anything or can't do anything with it," or that they "don't get the message from that hand." If the subjects perform a series of successful trials and correctly retrieve a group of objects which they previously stated they could not feel, and if this contradiction is then pointed out to them, we get comments like "Well, I was just guessing," or "Well, I must have done it unconsciously." . . .

Much of the foregoing is summarized schematically in Figure 3. The left hemisphere in the right-handed patients is equipped with the expressive mechanisms for speech and writing and with the main centers for the comprehension and organization of language. This "major" hemisphere can communicate its experiences verbally and in an essentially normal manner. It can communicate, that is, about the visual experiences of the right half of the optic field and about the somesthetic and volitional experiences of the right hand and leg and right half of the body generally. In addition, and not indicated in the figure, the major hemisphere also communicates, of course, about all of the more general, less lateralized cerebral activity that is bilaterally represented and common to both hemispheres. On the other side we have the mute aphasic and agraphic right hemisphere, which cannot express itself verbally, but which through the use of nonverbal responses can show that it is not agnostic; that mental processes are indeed present centered around the left visual field, left hand, left leg, and left half of the body; along with the auditory, vestibular, axial somatic, and all other cerebral activities that are less lateralized and for which the mental experiences of the right and left hemispheres may be characterized as being similar but separate.

It may be noted that nearly all of the symptoms of cross-integrational impairment that I have been describing are easily hidden or compensated un-

FIGURE 3 *Schematic Outline of the Functional Lateralization Evident in Behavioral Tests of Patients With Forebrain Commissurotomy*

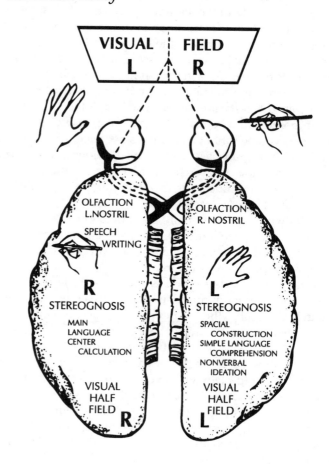

der the conditions of ordinary behavior. For example, the visual material has to be flashed at $1/10$ of a second or less to one half of the field in order to prevent compensation by eye movements. The defects in manual stereognosis are not apparent unless vision is excluded; nor is doubling in olfactory perception evident without sequential occlusion of right and left nostril and elimination of visual cues. In many tests the major hemisphere must be prevented from talking to the minor hemisphere and thus giving away the answer through auditory channels. And, similarly, the minor hemisphere must be prevented from giving nonverbal signals of various sorts to the major hemisphere. There is a great diversity of indirect strategies and response signals, implicit as well as overt, by which the informed hemisphere can be used to cue-in the uninformed hemisphere (Levy-Agresti, 1968).

Normal behavior under ordinary conditions is favored also by many other unifying factors. Some of these are very obvious, like the fact that these two separate mental spheres have only one body, so they always get dragged to the same places, meet the same people, and see and do the same things all the time and thus are bound to have a great overlap of common, almost identical, experience. Just the unity of the optic image—and even after chiasm section in animal experiments, the conjugate movements of the eyes—means that both hemispheres automatically center on, focus on, and hence probably attend to, the same items in the visual field all the time. Through sensory feedback a unifying body schema is imposed in each hemisphere with common components that similarly condition in parallel many processes of perception and motor action onto a common base. To get different activities going and different experiences and different memory chains built up in the separated hemispheres of the bisected mammalian brain, as we do in the animal work, requires a considerable amount of experimental planning and effort. . . .

Let me emphasize again in closing that the foregoing represents a somewhat abbreviated and streamlined account of the syndrome of hemisphere deconnection as we understand it at the present time. The more we see of these patients and the more of these patients we see, the more we become impressed with their individual differences, and with the consequent qualifications that must be taken into account. Although the general picture has continued to hold up in the main as described, it is important to note that, with respect to many of the deconnection symptoms mentioned, striking modifications and even outright exceptions can be found among the small group of patients examined to date. Where the accumulating evidence will settle out with respect to the extreme limits of such individual variations and with respect to a possible average "type" syndrome remains to be seen.

REFERENCES

Akelaitis, A. J. A study of gnosis, praxis, and language following section of the corpus callosum and anterior commissure. *Journal of Neurosurgery*, 1944, 1, 94–102.

Bogen, J. E., Fisher, E. D., & Vogel, P. J. Cerebral commissurotomy: A second case report. *Journal of the American Medical Association*, 1965, 194, 1328–1329.

Bogen, J. E., & Vogel, P. J. Cerebral commissurotomy: A case report. *Bulletin of the Los Angeles Neurological Society*, 1962, 27, 169.

Gazzaniga, M. S. The split brain in man. *Scientific American*, 1967, 217, 24–29.

Levy-Agresti, J. Ipsilateral projection systems and minor hemisphere function in man after neocommissurotomy. *Anatomical Record*, 1968, 160, 384.

Myers, R. E. Corpus callosum and visual gnosis. In J. F. Delafresnaye (Ed.), *Brain mechanisms and learning*. Oxford: Blackwell, 1961.

Sperry, R. W. Mental unity following surgical disconnection of the hemispheres. *The Harvey lectures*. Series 62. New York: Academic Press, 1967. (a)

Sperry, R. W. Split-brain approach to learning problems. In G. C. Quarton, T. Melnechuk, & F. O. Schmitt (Eds.), *The neurosciences: A study program*. New York: Rockefeller University Press, 1967. (b)

Sperry, R. W. Apposition of visual half-fields after section of neocortical commissures. *Anatomical Record*, 1968, 160, 498–499.

Sperry, R. W., Gazzaniga, M. S., & Bogen, J. E. Function of neocortical commissures: Syndrome of hemisphere deconnection. In P. J. Vinken & G. W. Bruyn (Eds.), *Handbook of neurology*. Amsterdam: North Holland, 1968, in press.

2.2 LARRY R. SQUIRE

Memory and the Hippocampus: A Synthesis from Findings With Rats, Monkeys, and Humans

For many years, psychologists have been trying to discover how memory is stored in the brain. After numerous false starts, much progress has recently been made on identifying the specific brain structures involved in memory storage and retrieval. Researchers are also finding that different kinds of memory involve different structures. One researcher at the forefront of memory research is Larry R. Squire.

Squire (b. 1941) earned his Ph.D. in cognitive psychology in 1968 from the Massachusetts Institute of Technology. He joined the faculty at the University of California, San Diego in 1970, where he is currently a professor of psychiatry. He also serves as a research career scientist at the San Diego Veterans Affairs Medical Center. Squire and his colleagues have studied memory using imaging techniques that allow them to view the activity of the brain while the subject is processing information. Among Squire's numerous publications is his book *Memory and the Brain* (Oxford University Press, 1987).

This selection is from "Memory and the Hippocampus: A Synthesis from Findings With Rats, Monkeys, and Humans," which was published in *Psychological Review* in 1992. In it, Squire reviews information indicating that the hippocampus is important for one type of memory called *declarative memory*, which includes semantic memory (for facts) and episodic memory (for events). Squire argues that the hippocampus is therefore important in forming new relationships. He further states that *nondeclarative memory* (skills and habits, simple conditioning) does not involve the hippocampus. As you read this selection, think about the value of understanding the structures involved in memory formation. How might this information be useful to us as we continue to learn and remember events in our lives?

Key Concept: the role of the hippocampus in memory

*I*n recent years a consensus has been developing about the role of the mammalian hippocampal formation in learning and memory. The idea that the hippocampus is important for memory is not in itself new. What is new is that this idea is now supported by direct and compelling evidence for each of the three species that has been important to this work: rats, monkeys, and humans. In addition, there have been major gains in understanding exactly how the hippocampal formation is involved in memory. . . .

MULTIPLE MEMORY SYSTEMS

Progress in identifying the structures and connections that make up the medial temporal lobe memory system has been paralleled by gains in understanding how this system participates in memory functions. An important step in this achievement was the insight that the hippocampal formation is important for only a particular kind of memory. The implication was that memory is not a single entity but consists of multiple processes or systems. Converging evidence about the selective role of the hippocampal formation in memory is now available from rats, monkeys, and humans.

It took time for the idea of multiple memory systems to become firmly established. In 1962, the severely impaired amnesic patient H. M. was reported to be capable of day-to-day improvement in a hand-eye coordination skill, despite having no memory for the practice sessions (Milner, 1962). Nevertheless, subsequent discussions of memory in general and amnesia in particular tended to set aside motor skill learning and to focus on the unitary nature of the rest of memory. Amnesia was considered to impair memory globally, with the recognition that an exception should be made for motor skills. . . .

Subsequently, it was discovered that motor skills are just one example of a broader category of skill learning that is intact in amnesic patients (Cohen, 1984; Cohen & Squire, 1980; Squire, 1982). At the same time, the success of partial information at the time of retrieval in eliciting recall in amnesic patients came to be better understood (e.g., word stems like inc____ or mot____ as cues for recently studied words). It turned out that only one kind of instruction yields normal performance (complete the stem to form the first word that comes to mind; Graf, Squire, & Mandler, 1984). With conventional memory instructions (use the stem as a cue to recall a recently presented word), normal subjects maintain their advantage over amnesic patients (Graf et al., 1984; Squire, Wetzel, & Slater, 1978). Intact performance by amnesic patients on such tasks, when indirect instructions are used, is now understood as an example of word priming, and a large body of work has accumulated with both normal subjects and amnesic patients in support of the idea that priming reflects a different kind of memory than the kind that is tapped in conventional memory experiments (Shimamura, 1986; Tulving & Schacter, 1990). . . .

Larry R. Squire

The tradition of work with amnesic patients explains why the idea of multiple memory systems led naturally to a consideration of what kind of memory depends on the integrity of the brain structures, including hippocampus, that are damaged in amnesia. In addition, the idea that the hippocampus might be involved in only one kind of memory appeared independently in the animal literature, on the basis of the selective effects of limbic lesions (Gaffan, 1974; Hirsch, 1974; O'Keefe & Nadel, 1978; Olton et al., 1979). The sections that follow suggest that the findings from humans and experimental animals, including rats and monkeys, are now in substantial agreement about the kind of memory that depends specifically on the hippocampus and related structures.

This kind of memory has been termed *declarative* (Cohen & Squire, 1980) in the sense that one can bring to mind or declare the content of this kind of memory (for its earlier use in psychology, see Anderson, 1976). The term *declarative* was derived from work with human subjects and has been difficult to apply usefully to experimental animals. The problem is not that declarative memory seems to imply an ability to declare one's knowledge verbally. Indeed, declarative memory includes memory for faces, spatial layouts, and other material that is declared by bringing a remembered image to mind rather than by verbalizing. The difficulty is that the term *declarative* is often linked to the notion of conscious memory. In the sections that follow, the idea of declarative memory is developed more fully in an attempt to make contact with similar ideas about memory systems derived from work with experimental animals. Declarative memory is also contrasted with a heterogeneous collection of nondeclarative (implicit) memory abilities, which are expressed only through performance and which are independent of the structures damaged in amnesia (Figure 1).

An additional point about the term *declarative* memory might be useful at this juncture. Many terms have been used to describe a particular kind of memory (e.g., *declarative, explicit, relational*, or *configural*), and many other terms have also been used to describe a kind (or kinds) that are dissociable from the first kind (e.g., *nondeclarative, implicit*, or *habit*). However, terms themselves are not the proper focus. If one considers the various biological and purely psychological concepts that have been used, it is striking that they sort themselves out in terms of ideas about what the hippocampus does and does not do in the service of memory. It should not be surprising that these terms place themselves on either side of a biologically meaningful boundary. The brain is the machinery that accomplishes memory, and history shows that other fundamental psychological distinctions have proved to be prominent in the organization of brain systems (e.g., short-term and long-term memory). Accordingly, the term *declarative* is used here to describe one kind of memory, but not with the idea that it is especially different from other terms. The more important point is that the terms *explicit* memory and *declarative* memory, when one considers the properties that have been associated with each, describe a biologically real component of memory that depends on particular structures and connections in the brain. Accordingly, it is to be expected that these terms have much in

FIGURE 1 *A Memory Taxonomy*

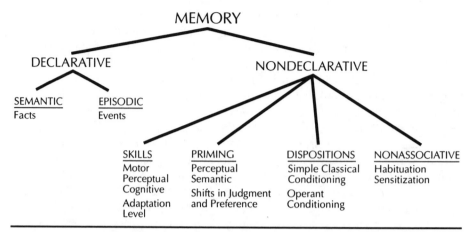

Declarative memory includes memory for facts and events and depends on the integrity of the hippocampus and related structures. Nondeclarative memory refers to a heterogeneous collection of distinct learning and memory abilities where performance changes but without affording access to the experience or experiences that caused the change. From "Neuropsychological Investigations of Memory and Amnesia: Findings From Humans and Nonhuman Primates," p. 437, by S. Zola-Morgan and L. R. Squire, 1990, in A. Diamond, *The Development and Neural Bases of Higher Cognitive Functions,* New York: New York Academy of Sciences. Copyright 1990 by the New York Academy of Sciences. Reprinted by permission.

common with each other and with the terms *relational* and *configural,* which come from work with rats.

Recall, Recognition, and the Feeling of Familiarity

What kind of information is acquired as declarative memory and how is it best assessed? The assessment of memory has relied traditionally on two methods: free recall and recognition. In normal subjects, both recall and recognition are typically accompanied by a sense of familiarity about the past. Amnesic patients perform poorly on tests of recall and recognition, and they have a diminished feeling of familiarity, as reflected in the low confidence ratings that they attach to their recognition choices. Recall and recognition have usually been taken as reflections of declarative memory (Tulving, 1983). . . .

THE ROLE OF THE HIPPOCAMPAL FORMATION: ESTABLISHING CONJUNCTIONS

A consideration of the anatomical and physiological organization of the hippocampus suggests that it functions as a device for forming conjunctions between ordinarily unrelated events (Squire, Shimamura, & Amaral, 1989). One possible associative device is long-term potentiation (LTP), a rapid-developing and long-lasting form of synaptic plasticity (Bliss & Lomo, 1973; Gustafsson & Wigstrom, 1988). LTP is cooperative: it depends on convergent inputs occurring nearly simultaneously, and it provides a mechanism by which conjunctions can be formed and stored. Similar proposals identify the hippocampus as the storage site for a simple memory, a summary sketch, a gross trace, an index, a device for constructing unique configurations among stimuli, or for collating widely stored pieces of experience (Halgren, 1984; Marr, 1971; McNaughton & Nadel, 1990; Moscovitch, 1989; Rolls, 1990; Sutherland & Rudy, 1989; Teyler & Discenna, 1986). In psychological terms, the hippocampus contributes to the forming of new relationships, such as those established when associating stimuli with their spatial and temporal context (thus representing a new episode) or those established when associating a fact with the semantic context to which it belongs (thus representing a new concept).

It is clear that the hippocampal formation must perform a critical function at the time of learning if declarative memory is to be established in an enduring and usable way. In the case of transient amnesic episodes, the events that occur during the period of anterograde amnesia do not subsequently reappear in memory after recovery from amnesia. New learning becomes possible, but events from the amnesic episode do not return.

Because memories do not return after transient amnesic episodes, it appears that, in the absence of the hippocampus, representations that had been established in short-term memory are literally lost, become disorganized, or achieve some abnormal fate. In this sense, it seems reasonable to suppose that the hippocampus is needed for memory storage to occur. Yet, one could also propose that its role is to permit retrieval by establishing relationships at the time of learning with distributed neocortical storage sites. However, because neural plasticity is prominent in the hippocampus, in the form of a mechanism that seems well suited for forming and storing conjunctions (LTP), it seems more reasonable to view the hippocampus as a site that, together with other sites, actually stores an experience. Also, a purely retrieval view of hippocampal function cannot be correct because chronic amnesic patients do not recover from their retrograde amnesia as time passes, even though normally stored memories do become gradually independent of the hippocampus.

Configural Associations

One view that is similar to what is being proposed here is that the hippocampus is essential for memory tasks that require the development of configural as opposed to simple associations (Sutherland & Rudy, 1989). Certain operations, such as the exclusive-OR operation, cannot be accomplished by strengthening or weakening simple associations between stimulus and response elements. It has been proposed that the hippocampus is required for those kinds of learning in which unique combinations of stimuli must be remembered. The clearest demonstration of this idea is the report that rats with hippocampal lesions could not solve a negative patterning discrimination problem. Specifically, they did not learn to discriminate correctly in a case where either a light (L) or a tone (T) was rewarded, but the light-tone compound stimulus (LT) was unrewarded (Rudy & Sutherland, 1989). . . .

Relational and Flexible Memory

One way in which the original notion of declarative memory is making useful contact with studies of experimental animals is found in the idea that the hippocampus is essential for establishing flexible representations on the basis of relationships among stimuli (Eichenbaum et al., 1988). Whereas configural associations do not imply either flexibility or inflexibility, declarative memory entails a specific view of this issue (Cohen, 1984; Squire, 1987). By this view, the hippocampus, and the system to which it belongs, is essential for acquiring information about relationships, combinations, and conjunctions among stimuli, such that the resulting representation is flexible and accessible to multiple response systems.

This idea is still insufficiently formal and quantitative. Moreover, it remains difficult to predict beforehand which memory system will be engaged. Humans are overwhelmingly declarative; that is, they are memorizers and will readily engage hippocampus-dependent memory. Rats will readily adopt a simple associational strategy. Thus, it is difficult to know when a rat, in the presence of a light and a tone, for example, will simply form a conditioned response to the compound cue and when the rat will form a relational, hippocampus-dependent memory. However, the key idea is that the two kinds of memory, once acquired, have different characteristics. . . .

Nondeclarative (Implicit) Memory

The term *procedural memory* was traditionally used to contrast with declarative memory (Winograd, 1975). *Procedural memory* aptly describes the knowledge acquired during skill learning, but it is not clear that this same term is useful for the many examples of learning and memory now known to be independent of the hippocampus. The more neutral term *nondeclarative* was subsequently introduced to describe this collection of memory abilities (Squire & Zola-Morgan, 1988). The term *implicit* memory (Reber, 1967; Schacter, 1987) has a similar meaning. Nondeclarative memory includes skillful behavior or habits (perceptuo-motor, perceptual, and cognitive skills), simple conditioning (including emotional learning), the phenomenon of priming, and other instances where experience changes the facility for operating in the world but without affording conscious access to past episodes. Whereas declarative memory concerns recollection, nondeclarative memory concerns behavioral change. In nondeclarative memory, information is acquired as changes within specific perceptual or response systems, independently of memory for the prior encounters that led to behavioral change.

2.3 BARRY L. JACOBS

Serotonin, Motor Activity and Depression-Related Disorders

Recently, a great deal of attention has been devoted to the study of how brain chemicals called neurotransmitters can affect people's behavior and moods. Of particular interest are drugs such as Prozac, which alter neuro-transmitters, because they appear to have great abilities to treat psychologi-cal disorders. How does the brain chemical serotonin affect behavior and mood? Psychologist Barry L. Jacobs and his colleagues are trying to find out.

Jacobs is currently a professor of psychology and director of the neurosci-ence program at Princeton University in Princeton, New Jersey. His research on serotonin makes him one of the leading authorities in this field.

This selection from "Serotonin, Motor Activity and Depression-Related Disorders," which was published in *American Scientist* in 1994, provides an exciting look into the chemical processes affecting depression. Especially intriguing is the finding that motor activity could be important in treating depression and obsessive-compulsive disorder. The technical details of this selection may be challenging, but is is more important to focus on the implications for better understanding everyday emotion. Does exercise im-prove your mood? How might an exercise program be developed to help people who feel depressed?

Key Concept: neurotransmitters and behavior

*P*rozac, Zoloft and Paxil are drugs that have been widely celebrated for their effectiveness in the treatment of depression and obsessive-compulsive disorders. The popular press has also made much of Prozac's ability to allevi-ate minor personality disorders such as shyness or lack of popularity. The glamorous success of these drugs has even inspired some writers to propose that we are at the threshold of a new era reminiscent of Aldous Huxley's *Brave*

New World, in which one's day-to-day emotions can be fine-tuned by simply taking a pill. Yet for all the public attention that has been focused on the apparent benefits of Prozac-like drugs, the fundamental players in this story—the cells and the chemicals in the brain modified by these drugs—have been largely ignored.

This is partly a consequence of the complexity of the nervous system and the fact that so little is known about *how* the activity of cells in the brain translates into mood or behavior. We do know that Prozac-like drugs work by altering the function of neurons that release the signaling chemical (neurotransmitter) serotonin. Serotonin has been implicated in a broad range of behavioral disorders involving the sleep cycle, eating, the sex drive and mood. Prozac-like drugs prevent a neuron from taking serotonin back into the cell. Hence Prozac and related drugs are collectively known as selective serotonin reuptake inhibitors, or SSRIs. In principle, blocking the reuptake of serotonin should result in a higher level of activity in any part of the nervous system that uses serotonin as a chemical signal between cells. The long-term effects of these drugs on the function of a serotonin-based network of neurons, however, are simply not known.

My colleagues and I have attempted to understand the role of serotonin in animal physiology and behavior by looking at the activity of the serotonin neurons themselves. For more than 10 years at Princeton University, Casimir Fornal and I have been studying the factors that control the activity of serotonin neurons in the brain. I believe these studies provide the linchpin for understanding depression and obsessive-compulsive disorders and their treatment with therapeutic drugs. Our work provides some unique and unexpected perspectives on these illnesses and will serve, we hope, to open new avenues of clinical research.

SEROTONIN, DRUGS AND DEPRESSION

Communication between neurons is mediated by the release of small packets of chemicals into the tiny gap, the synapse, that separates one neuron from another. The brain uses a surprisingly largely number of these chemical neurotransmitters, perhaps as many as 100. However, the preponderance of the work is done by four chemicals that act in a simple and rapid manner: glutamate and aspartate (both of which excite neurons) and gamma-aminobutyric acid (GABA) and glycine (both of which inhibit neurons). Other neurotransmitters, such as serotonin, norepinephrine and dopamine are somewhat different. They can produce excitation *or* inhibition, often act over a longer time scale, and tend to work in concert with one of the four chemical workhorses in the brain. Hence they are also referred to as neuromodulators.

Even though serotonin, norepinephrine and dopamine may be considered to be comparatively minor layers in the overall function of the brain, they appear to be major culprits in some of the most common brain disorders: schizophrenia, depression and Parkinson's disease. It is interesting to observe that glutamate, aspartate, GABA and glycine are generally not centrally involved in psychiatric or neurological illnesses. It may be the case that a primary dysfunction of these systems is incompatible with sustaining life.

Serotonin's chemical name is 5-hydroxytryptamine, which derives from the fact that it is synthesized from the amino acid *L*-tryptophan. After a meal, foods are broken down into their constituent amino acids, including tryptophan, and then transported throughout the body by the circulatory system. Once tryptophan is carried into the brain and into certain neurons, it is converted into serotonin by two enzymatic steps.

Serotonin's actions in the synapse are terminated primarily by its being taken back into the neuron that released it. From that point, it is either recycled for reuse as a neurotransmitter or broken down into its metabolic by-products and transported out of the brain. With this basic understanding of serotonin neurotransmission, we can begin to understand the mechanisms of action of antidepressant drugs.

One of the earliest antidepressant drugs, iproniazid, elevates the level of a number of brain chemicals by inhibiting the action of an enzyme, monoamine oxidase, involved in their catabolism. For example, monoamine oxidase inhibitors (MAOIs) block the catabolism of serotonin into its metabolite, 5-hydroxyindole acetic acid (5-HIAA), leading to a buildup of serotonin in the brain. Unfortunately, because monoamine oxidase catabolizes a number of brain chemicals (including norepinephrine and dopamine), there are a number of side-effects associated with these drugs. Some interactive toxicity of MAOIs is also a major drawback for their use in the treatment of depression.

Tricyclic antidepressants (so named because of their three-ringed chemical structure), do not share the interactive toxicity of MAOIs. Tricyclics such as imipramine act to block the reuptake of serotonin from the synapse back into the neuron that released it. In a sense, this floods the synapse with serotonin. These drugs are quite effective in treating depression, but they also induce some unpleasant side-effects, such as constipation, headache and dry mouth. This may be due to the fact that tricyclic antidepressants not only block the reuptake of serotonin, but also exert similar effects on norepinephrine and dopamine.

The obvious benefit of the selective serotonin reuptake inhibitors is that their action is effectively limited to the reuptake of serotonin. This probably accounts for the fewer side-effects experienced by people taking SSRIs. Like other antidepressant drugs, the SSRIs have a therapeutic lag. They typically require 4 to 6 weeks to exert their full effects. Claude DeMontigny and his colleagues at McGill University have suggested that one of the consequences of increasing the levels of serotonin in the brain is a compensatory feedback inhibition that decreases the discharge of brain serotonergic neurons. This results in a "zero sum game" in which there is no net increase in functional serotonin. However, with continuous exposure to serotonin, the receptors mediating this feedback inhibition (the 5-HT$_{1A}$ receptor) become desensitized. It is hypothesized that after several weeks this results in progressively less feedback, increased serotonergic neurotranmission and clinical improvement.

BEHAVIOR OF SEROTONIN NEURONS

Essentially all of the serotonin-based activity in the brain arises from neurons that are located within cell clusters known as the raphe nuclei. These clusters of serotonin neurons are located in the brainstem, the most primitive part of the brain. It is not surprising, then, that serotonin appears to be involved in some fundamental aspects of physiology and behavior, ranging from the control of body temperature, cardiovascular activity and respiration to involvement in such behaviors as aggression, eating and sleeping.

The broad range of physiology and behavior associated with serotonin's actions is at least partly attributable to the widespread distribution of serotonin-containing nerve-fiber terminals that arise from the raphe nuclei. Indeed, the branching of the serotonin network comprises the most expansive neurochemical system in the brain. Serotonin neurons project fibers to virtually all parts of the central nervous system, from the various layers of the cerebral cortex down to the tip of the spinal cord. . . .

Serotonin neurons have a characteristic discharge pattern that distinguishes them from most other cells in the brain. They are relatively regular, exhibiting a slow and steady generation of spikes. Serotonin neurons retain this rhythmic pattern even if they are removed from the brain and isolated in a dish, suggesting that their clocklike regularity is intrinsic to the individual neurons.

One of the first significant discoveries about the behavior of serotonin neurons in the brain was that the rate of these discharges was dramatically altered during different levels of behavioral arousal. When an animal is quiet but awake, the typical serotonin neuron discharges at about 3 spikes per second. As the animal becomes drowsy and enters a phase known as slow-wave sleep, the number of spikes gradually declines. During rapid-eye movement (REM) sleep, which is associated with dreaming in human beings, the serotonin neurons fall completely silent. In anticipation of waking, however, the neuronal activity returns to its basal level of 3 spikes per second. When an animal is aroused or in an active waking state, the discharge rate may increase to 4 or 5 spikes per second. . . .

Interestingly, some serotonin neurons tend to become active just *before* a movement begins. Their activity may also occasionally synchronize with a specific phase of the movement—discharging most, for example, during a particular aspect of the quadrupedal stepping cycle. Moreover, the rate of the spike discharge often increases linearly with increases in the rate or strength of a movement, such as an increase in running speed or the depth of respiration.

One final observation provides a noteworthy clue to the function of serotonin neurons. When an animal is presented with a strong or novel stimulus, such as a sudden loud noise, it often suppresses all ongoing behavior, such as walking or grooming, and turns toward the stimulus. This orienting is essentially a "what is it?" response. In such instances serotonin neurons fall completely silent for several seconds, and then resume their normal activity.

Anatomical evidence supports these observations about the activity of serotonin neurons. For one thing, serotonin neurons preferentially make contacts with neurons that are involved in tonic and gross motor functions, such as those that control the torso and limbs. Reciprocally, serotonin neurons tend not to make connections with neurons that carry out episodic behavior and fine movements, such as those neurons that control the eyes or the fingers.

Our observations of the activity of serotonin neurons during different aspects of an animal's behavior lead us to conclude that the primary function of the brain serotonin system is to prime and facilitate gross motor output in both tonic and repetitive modes. At the same time, the system acts to inhibit sensory-information processing while coordinating autonomic and neuroendocrine functions with the specific demands of the motor activity. When the serotonin system is not active (for example, during an orientation response), the relations are reversed: Motor output is disfacilitated, and sensory-information processing is disinhibited.

BRAIN CELLS AND MENTAL DISORDERS

Although we are far from understanding the precise neural mechanisms involved in the manifestation of any mental illness, a number of studies have linked serotonin to depression. One of the most notable findings is that the major metabolite of serotonin (5-HIAA) appears to be significantly reduced in the cerebrospinal fluid of suicidally depressed patients. Our own studies suggest that serotonin neurons may be centrally involved in the physiological abnormality that underlies depression-related disorders. Recall that serotonin neurons appear to play crucial roles in facilitating tonic motor actions and inhibiting sensory-information processing. If an animal's serotonin neurons are responding abnormally, such that the rate or pattern of their activity is modified, then one might expect that both motor functions and sensory-information processing would be impaired.

Depression is frequently associated with motor retardation and cognitive impairment. If serotonin neurons are not facilitating tonic motor activity, then it should not be surprising that depressed patients feel listless and often appear to require enormous effort merely to raise themselves out of bed. Inappropriate activity during sensory-information processing might also account for the lapses of memory and the general lack of interest in the environment experienced by depressed patients. It might also be worth noting here that the well-known efficacy of REM-sleep deprivation for treating depression is at least partly dependent on serotonin. Since serotonin neurons are usually silent during REM sleep, depriving an animal of REM sleep maintains a generally higher level of activity in the system. Preliminary research in my laboratory suggests that the deprivation of REM sleep also increases the activity of serotonin neurons when the animal is in the awake state.

The activity of serotonin neurons may also be central to the manifestation of obsessive-compulsive disorders. Since our results show that repetitive motor acts increase serotonin neuronal activity, patients with this disorder may be engaging in repetitive rituals such as hand washing or pacing as a means of self-medication. In other words, they have learned to activate their brain serotonin system in order to derive some benefit or rewarding effect, perhaps the reduction of anxiety. Since the compulsive acts tend to be repeated, often to the point of becoming continuous, such activity may provide an almost limitless supply of serotonin to the brain. (The same may also be true for repetitive obsessional thoughts, but this is obviously difficult to test in animals.) Treating obsessive-compulsive disorders with a selective serotonin reuptake inhibitor ultimately accomplishes the same neurochemical endpoint, thus allowing these people to disengage from time-consuming, socially unacceptable and often physically harmful behavior.

Our studies suggest that regular motor activity may be important in the treatment of affective disorders. For example, if there is a deficiency of serotonin in some forms of depression, then an increase in tonic motor activity or some form of repetitive motor task, such as riding a bicycle or jogging, may help to relieve the depression. Indeed, there are various reports that jogging and other forms of exercise have salutary effects for depressed patients. This does not mean that exercise is a panacea for depressive disorders. Since the long-term effects of exercise on brain serotonin levels are not known, the benefits may prove to be transient. On the other hand, exercise may be an important adjunct to drug treatments, and may permit a reduction in the required drug dosage. . . .

CONCLUSION

Our research raises the issue of why the manipulation of a system that is primarily a modulator of motor activity has profound effects on mood. Aside from recognizing that the raphe nuclei are connected to regions of the brain that are known to be involved in the emotions (such as the limbic system), it is worth noting that a common organizational plan underlies the distribution of serotonin cell bodies and fiber terminals in essentially all vertebrate brains. This implies that the system has been conserved through evolution, and suggests that there may be some adaptive significance to linking mood and motor activity.

Consider the following possibility. We know that emotions play a role in allowing an animal to withdraw from an ongoing sequence of activities to consider alternative paths. When something bad (perhaps even life-threatening) transpires, it seems reasonable to suppress motor activity and to contemplate the available options. To put it another way: If something negative has happened in one's world, it might be counterproductive, or even dangerous, to explore and engage the environment. The most adaptive response is to withdraw and ruminate. In this light, emotions act at a higher level of complexity in the service of effective motor behavior. When one's mood is bright and expansive, on the other hand, it may be profitable to explore new options. Wide mood swings may allow an exploration of a broader spectrum of perspectives and thus may be related to the well-documented relationship between mood disorders and creativity in artists, writers and composers.

Barry L. Jacobs

As a final note, the brain serotonin system may be involved in some nonclinical aspects of human behavior. Why do some people endlessly engage in rhythmic leg bouncing? What is rewarding about chewing gum? What underlies the therapeutic or reinforcing effects of breathing exercises, and the twirling or dancing movements employed by various cults and religious groups? The reader can probably think of other behaviors that increase serotonin release in his or her brain.

Environment and Genes: Determinants of Behavior

The importance of nature (genetics) and nurture (environment) on behavioral development has been debated for centuries. Only in the past few decades, however, have psychologists begun to discover the specific mechanisms by which heredity influences cognition and behavior. At the same time, psychologists have found that behavior is also influenced by one's environment and that, in fact, all behavior is the result of the interaction of heredity and the environment. Behavior geneticist Robert Plomin has been studying this interaction.

Plomin (b. 1948) earned his Ph.D. in biological psychology from the University of Texas at Austin in 1974. Currently working at Pennsylvania State University, he has been actively involved in behavioral genetic research, and he is coauthor of the textbook *Behavioral Genetics: A Primer*, 2d ed. (W. H. Freeman, 1989).

This selection is from "Environment and Genes: Determinants of Behavior," which was published in *American Psychologist* in 1989. In it, Plomin reviews some of the research findings in the field of behavior genetics that came to light during the 1980s. The field of behavior genetics is important because it helps us understand ourselves and those around us. Today, reports are being made regularly on how specific genes influence intelligence, personality, and psychopathology, as well as other bodily processes. As you read this selection, notice Plomin's emphasis on how both heredity and environment influence human behavior.

Key Concept: behavior genetics

*A*BSTRACT: *Recent behavioral genetic research has demonstrated that genetic influence on individual differences in behavioral development is usually significant and often substantial and, paradoxically, also supports the important role of the environment. This article reviews research on the heritability of intellectual factors, personality factors, and psychopathology It discusses the importance of investigating within-family*

Robert Plomin

Increasing acceptance of hereditary influence on individual differences in development represents one of the most remarkable changes in the field of psychology that has occurred during the decade since the 1979 special issue of the *American Psychologist* on children. Even for IQ scores, traditionally one of the most controversial areas, a recent survey of over 1,000 scientists and educators indicates that most now believe that individual differences in IQ scores are at least partially inherited (Snyderman & Rothman, 1987). Recent behavioral genetic research providing the empirical basis for this trend is reviewed in the first half of this article.

The wave of acceptance of genetic influence on behavior is growing into a tidal wave that threatens to engulf the second message of this research: These same data provide the best available evidence for the importance of environmental influence. Variability in complex behaviors of interest to psychologists and to society is due at least as much to environmental influences as it is to genetic influences. Because its methods recognize both environmental and genetic influences on behavior, behavioral genetic research has made some novel advances in understanding the environment. . . .

Although the brevity of this article precludes a discussion of the theory and methods of behavioral genetics, the two major methods are the twin design, in which identical twin resemblance is compared with fraternal twin resemblance, and the adoption design, in which genetically related individuals reared apart and genetically unrelated individuals reared together are studied. These methods are used to assess heritability, a statistic that describes the proportion of observed variance for a behavior that can be ascribed to genetic differences among individuals in a particular population. . . .

Two conceptual issues about the field of behavioral genetics need to be mentioned. First, behavioral genetic theory and methods address the genetic and environmental sources of differences among individuals. Behavioral genetics has little to say about universals of development (e.g., why the human species uses language) or about average differences between groups (e.g., why girls perform better than boys on verbal tests). This critical issue, the cause of much misunderstanding, is discussed at length elsewhere (Plomin, DeFries, & Fulker, 1988). Second, when genetic differences among children are found to relate to differences in their behavior, this is a probabilistic relationship in much the same way as finding associations between environmental factors and children's development. . . . [G]enetic influences on behavior are multifactorial—that is, they involve many genes, each with small effects—as well as environmental influences. In other words, genetic influences on the complex behaviors of interest to psychologists do not fit the deterministic model of a single-gene effect—like Mendel's pea-plant characteristics or like some genetic diseases such as sickle-cell anemia—which operates independently of other genes or of environmental influences. . . .

HIGHLIGHTS OF RECENT BEHAVIORAL GENETIC RESEARCH

This section provides a brief overview of recent human behavioral genetic research indicating that behavior can no longer be considered innocent of genetic influence until proven guilty. The litany includes intellectual factors, including IQ, specific cognitive abilities, academic achievement, reading disability . . . ; personality factors, including extraversion and neuroticism, temperament in childhood, and attitudes and beliefs; and psychopathology, including schizophrenia, affective disorders, delinquent and criminal behavior, and alcoholism.

Intellectual Factors

IQ. More behavioral genetic data have been obtained for IQ than for any other trait. A summary of dozens of studies prior to 1980 includes nearly 100,000 twins and biological and adoptive relatives and makes it difficult to escape the conclusion that heredity importantly influences individual differences in IQ scores (Bouchard & McGue, 1981). For example, genetically related individuals adopted apart show significant resemblance, and identical twins are substantially more similar than fraternal twins. An interesting twist is that, for reasons as yet unknown, studies in the 1970s yielded lower estimates of heritability (about 50%) than older studies (about 70%; Plomin & DeFries, 1980; cf. Loehlin, Willerman, & Horn, 1988).

Recent studies include two ongoing studies of twins reared apart that will triple the number of identical twins reared apart who have been studied for IQ and will also, for the first time, add hundreds of pairs of the equally important group of fraternal twins reared apart. Preliminary reports from these two studies indicate that their results are in line with the rest of the behavioral genetics literature in implicating substantial genetic influence on IQ scores (Bouchard, 1984; Pedersen, McClearn, Plomin, & Friberg, 1985). . . .

Specific cognitive abilities. Although there is some evidence that verbal and spatial abilities show greater genetic influence than do perceptual speed tests and memory tests, the general message is that diverse cognitive tests show significant and often substantial (almost as much as for IQ) genetic influence throughout the life span (Plomin, 1988). In 10 twin studies, tests of creativity show less genetic influence than any other dimension within the cognitive domain, especially when IQ is controlled (R. C. Nichols, 1978).

Research on specific cognitive abilities during the past decade includes a study of over 6,000 individuals in nearly 2,000 families, three twin studies in childhood and one in adulthood, and several parent–offspring adoption studies in addition to the two studies of twins reared apart mentioned in relation to IQ (Plomin, 1986).

Academic achievement. Although no new behavioral genetic research on school-relevant behavior has been reported during the past decade, genetic influence is pervasive here as well. Twin studies of academic-achievement test scores show substantial genetic influence, about the same as for specific cognitive abilities. Even report-card grades and years of schooling show substantial genetic influence. Vocational interests are also substantially influenced by genetic factors, as shown in twin and adoption studies. (For references, see Plomin, 1986.)

Reading disability.   Reading disability shows considerable familial resemblance (DeFries, Vogler, & LaBuda, 1985). One recent twin study found evidence for a genetic basis for this familial resemblance (DeFries, Fulker, & LaBuda, 1987); another twin study found genetic influence on spelling disability but not on other aspects of reading disability (Stevenson, Graham, Fredman, & McLoughlin, 1987). A single-gene effect has been proposed for spelling disability (Smith, Kimberling, Pennington, & Lubs, 1983), although subsequent analyses have not confirmed the linkage (Kimberling, Fain, Ing, Smith, & Pennington, 1985; McGuffin, 1987). . . .

Personality Factors

Extraversion and neuroticism.   One focus of recent research on personality involves two "super factors" of personality: extraversion and neuroticism. A review of research involving over 25,000 pairs of twins yielded heritability estimates of about 50% for these two traits (Henderson, 1982). This review also pointed out that extraversion and other personality traits often show evidence for nonadditive genetic variance. Nonadditive effects of genes involve unique combinations of genes that contribute to the similarity of identical twins but not to the resemblance of first-degree relatives. These conclusions are supported by a recent large-scale twin study in Australia (N. G. Martin & Jardine, 1986) and by two studies of twins reared apart (Pedersen, Plomin, McClearn, & Friberg, 1988; Tellegen et al., 1988). The presence of nonadditive genetic variance may be responsible for the lower estimates of heritability from adoption studies of first-degree relatives (Loehlin, Willerman, & Horn, 1982, 1985; Scarr, Webber, Weinberg, & Wittig, 1981).

Emotionality, activity, and sociability (EAS).   Extraversion and neuroticism are global traits that encompass many dimensions of personality. The core of extraversion, however, is sociability, and the key component of neuroticism is emotionality. From infancy to adulthood, these two traits and activity level have been proposed as the most heritable components of personality, a theory referred to with the acronym EAS (Buss & Plomin, 1984). A review of behavioral genetic data for these three traits in infancy, childhood, adolescence, and adulthood lends support to the EAS theory (Plomin, 1986). However, note that many personality traits display genetic influence, and it is difficult to prove that some traits are more heritable than others, perhaps because of the pervasive genetic influence of extraversion and neuroticism (Loehlin, 1982). . . .

Attitudes and beliefs. Surprisingly, some attitudes and beliefs show almost as much genetic influence as do other behavioral traits. One focus of recent interest is traditionalism, the tendency to follow rules and authority and to endorse high moral standards and strict discipline. For example, a large twin study estimated that half of the variance on this measure is due to genetic influence (N. G. Martin et al., 1986), and a report of twins reared apart has also found substantial genetic influence for traditionalism (Tellegen et al., 1988). Religiosity and certain political beliefs, however, show no genetic influence.

Psychopathology

Behavioral genetic research on psychopathology in children and adults is especially active (Loehlin et al., 1988; Vandenberg, Singer, & Pauls, 1986). This section provides a brief overview of recent research in schizophrenia, affective disorders, delinquent and criminal behavior, alcoholism, and other psychopathology.

Schizophrenia. In 14 older studies involving over 18,000 first-degree relatives of schizophrenics, the risk for first-degree relatives was about 8%, eight times greater than the risk for individuals chosen randomly from the population (Gottesman & Shields, 1982). Recent family studies continue to yield similar results.

Twin studies suggest that this familial resemblance is due to heredity. The most recent twin study involved all male twins who were veterans of World War II (Kendler & Robinette, 1983). Twin concordances were 30.9% for 164 pairs of identical twins and 6.5% for 268 pairs of fraternal twins. Adoption studies of schizophrenia support the twin findings of genetic influence on schizophrenia. . . .

Affective disorders. Although twin results for affective disorders suggest even greater genetic influence than for schizophrenia, adoption studies indicate less genetic influence (Loehlin et al., 1988). In one recent adoption study, affective disorders were diagnosed in only 5.2% of biological relatives of affectively-ill adoptees, although this risk is greater than the risk of 2.3% found in the biological relatives of control adoptees (Wender et al., 1986). The biological relatives of affected adoptees also showed greater rates of alcoholism (5.4% vs. 2.0%) and attempted or actual suicide (7.3% vs. 1.5%). . . .

Delinquent and criminal behavior. The spotlight on controversies concerning genetic influence on IQ has switched to criminal behavior with the publication of a recent book (Wilson & Herrnstein, 1985) claiming that biology affects such behaviors. Six twin studies of juvenile delinquency yielded 87% concordance for identical twins and 72% concordance for fraternal twins, suggesting slight genetic influence and substantial environmental sources of resemblance (Gottesman, Carey, & Hanson, 1983). A recent quantitative study of delinquent acts indicated greater genetic influence than did earlier studies that attempted to diagnose delinquency (Rowe, 1983b).

It has been suggested that juvenile delinquents who go on to become adult criminals may have a genetic liability (Wilson & Herrnstein, 1985). Eight older twin studies of adult criminality yielded identical and fraternal twin concordances of 69% and 33%, respectively. Adoption studies are consistent with the hypothesis of some genetic influence on adult criminality, although the evidence is not as striking as in the twin studies (Mednick, Gabrielli, & Hutchings, 1984).

Alcoholism. Alcoholism runs in families. Alcoholism in a first-degree relative is by far the single best predictor of alcoholism (Mednick, Moffitt, & Stack, 1987). About 25% of the male relatives of alcoholics are themselves alcoholics, as compared with fewer than 5% of the males in the general population. Although twin studies of normal drinkers show substantial genetic influence (for example, Pedersen, Friberg, Floderus-Myrhed, McClearn, & Plomin, 1984), no twin studies have focused on alcoholism per se. A Swedish adoption study provides the best evidence for genetic influence on alcoholism, at least in males (Bohman, Cloninger, Sigvardsson, & von Knorring, 1987; cf. Peele, 1986). Twenty-two percent of the adopted-away sons of biological fathers who abused alcohol were alcoholic, suggesting substantial genetic influence.

Other psychopathology. Although most research on psychopathology has focused on psychoses, criminality, and alcoholism, attention has begun to turn to other disorders. Areas of recent research include a family study of anxiety neurosis sometimes known as panic disorder, twin and family studies of anorexia nervosa, and family and adoption studies of somatization disorder that involves multiple and chronic physical complaints of unknown origin (Loehlin et al., 1988).

Summary

The first message of behavioral genetic research is that genetic influence on individual differences in behavioral development is usually significant and often substantial. Genetic influence is so ubiquitous and pervasive in behavior that a shift in emphasis is warranted: Ask not what is heritable, ask what is not heritable.

The second message is just as important: These same data provide the best available evidence of the importance of the environment. The data reviewed in this section suggest pandemic genetic influence, but they also indicate that nongenetic factors are responsible for more than half of the variance for most complex behaviors. For example, identical twins show concordance of less than 40% for schizophrenia. Because identical twins are genetically identical, most of the reason one person is diagnosed as schizophrenic and another is not has to do with environmental rather than genetic reasons. The phrase "behavioral genetics" is in a sense a misnomer because it is as much the study of nurture as nature. In addition to documenting the importance of environmental variation, it provides a novel perspective for viewing environmental influences, especially the family environment, in the context of heredity. . . .

The move away from a rigid adherence to environmental explanations of behavioral development to a more balanced perspective that recognizes genetic as well as environmental sources of individual differences must be viewed as healthy for the social and behavioral sciences. The danger now, however, is that the swing from environmentalism will go too far. During the 1970s, I found I had to speak gingerly about genetic influence, gently suggesting heredity might be important in behavior. Now, however, I more often have to say, "Yes, genetic influences are significant and substantial, but environmental influences are just as important." This seems to be happening most clearly in the field of psychopathology, where evidence of significant genetic influence has led to a search for single genes and simple neurochemical triggers at the expense of research on its psychosocial origins. It would be wonderful if some simple, and presumably inexpensive, biochemical cure could be found for schizophrenia. However, this happy outcome seems highly unlikely given that schizophrenia is as much influenced by environmental factors as it is by heredity.

Furthermore, as mentioned earlier, genetic effects on behavior are polygenic and probabilistic, not single gene and deterministic. The characteristics in the pea plant that Mendel studied and a few diseases such as Huntington's disease and sickle-cell anemia are due to single genes that have their effects regardless of the environment or the genetic background of the individual. The complexity of behaviors studied by psychologists makes it unlikely that such a deterministic model and the reductionistic approach that it suggests will pay off. There is as yet no firm evidence for a single-gene effect that accounts for a detectable amount of variation for any complex behavior. . . .

As the pendulum swings from environmentalism, it is important that the pendulum be caught midswing before its momentum carries it to biological determinism. Behavioral genetic research clearly demonstrates that both nature and nurture are important in human development.

REFERENCES

Bohman, M., Cloninger, R., Sigvardsson, S., & von Knorring, A. L. (1987). The genetics of alcoholisms and related disorders. *Journal of Psychiatric Research, 21*, 447–452.

Bouchard, T. J. (1984). Twins reared together and apart: What they tell us about human diversity. In S. W. Fox (Ed.), *Individuality and determinism* (pp. 147–178). New York: Plenum Press.

Bouchard, T. J., Jr., & McGue, M. (1981). Familial studies of intelligence: A review. *Science, 212*, 1055–1059.

Buss, A. H., & Plomin, R. (1984). *Temperament: Early developing personality traits.* Hillsdale, NJ: Erlbaum.

DeFries, J. C., Fulker, D. W., & LaBuda, M. C. (1987). Evidence for a genetic etiology in reading disability in twins. *Nature, 329*, 537–539.

DeFries, J. C., Vogler, G. P., & LaBuda, M. C. (1985). Colorado Family Reading Study: An overview. In J. L. Fuller & E. C. Simmel (Eds.), *Behavior genetics: Principles and applications II.* (pp.357–368). Hillsdale, NJ: Erlbaum.

Donis-Keller, H., Green, P., Helms, C., Cartinhour, S., & Weiffenbach, B. (1987). A human gene map. *Cell, 51*, 319–337.

Egeland, J. A., Gerhard, D. S., Pauls, D. L., Sussex, J. N., & Kidd, K. K. (1987). Bipolar affective disorders linked to DNA markers on chromosome 11. *Nature, 325,* 783–787.

Gottesman, I. I., Carey, G., & Hanson, D. R. (1983). Pearls and perils in epigenetic psychopathology. In S. B. Guze, E. J. Earls, & J. E. Barrett (Eds.), *Childhood psychopathology and development* (pp. 287–300). New York: Raven Press.

Gottesman, I. I., & Shield, J. (1982). *Schizophrenia: The epigenetic puzzle.* Cambridge, England: Cambridge University Press.

Gusella, J. F., Wexler, N. S., Conneally, P. M., Naylor, S. L., Anderson, M. A., Tanzi, R. E., Watkins, P. C., & Ottina, K. (1983). A polymorphic DNA marker genetically linked to Huntington's disease. *Nature, 306,* 234–238.

Henderson, N. D. (1982). Human behavior genetics. *Annual Review of Psychology, 33,* 403–440.

Kendler, K. S., & Robinette, C. D. (1983). Schizophrenia in the National Academy of Sciences–National Research Council twin registry: A 16-year update. *American Journal of Psychiatry, 140,* 1551–1563.

Kimberling, W. J., Fain, P. R., Ing, P. S., Smith, S. D., & Pennington, B. F. (1985). Linkage analysis of reading disability with chromosome 15. *Behavior Genetics, 15,* 597–598.

Loehlin, J. C. (1982). Are personality traits differentially heritable? *Behavior Genetics, 12,* 417–428.

Loehlin, J. C., Willerman, L., & Horn, J. M. (1982). Personality resemblances between unwed mothers and their adopted-away offspring. *Journal of Personality and Social Psychology, 42,* 1089–1099.

Loehlin, J. C., Willerman, L., & Horn, J. M. (1985). Personality resemblance in adoptive families when the children are late adolescents and adults. *Journal of Personality and Social Psychology, 48,* 376–392.

Loehlin, J. C., Willerman, L., & Horn, J. M. (1988). Human behavior genetics, *Annual Review of Psychology, 38,* 101–133.

Martin, J. B. (1987). Molecular genetics: Applications to the clinical neurosciences. *Science, 238,* 765–772.

Martin, N. G., Eaves, L. J., Heath, A. C., Jardine, R., Feingold, L. M., & Eysenck, H. J. (1986). Transmission of social attitudes. *Proceedings of the National Academy of Sciences, USA, 83,* 4364–4368.

Martin, N. G., & Jardine, R. (1986). Eysenck's contributions to behaviour genetics. In S. Modgil & C. Modgil (Eds.), *Hans Eysenck: Consensus and controversy* (pp. 13–27). Philadelphia: Falmer.

McGuffin, P. (1987). The new genetics and childhood psychiatric disorder. *Journal of Child Psychology and Psychiatry, 28,* 215–222.

Mednick, S. A., Gabrielli, W. F., Jr., & Hutchings, B. (1984). Genetic influences in criminal convictions: Evidence from an adoption cohort. *Science, 224,* 891–894.

Mednick, S. A., Moffitt, T. E., & Stack, S. (1987). *The causes of crime: New biological approaches.* New York: Cambridge University Press.

Nichols, R. C. (1978). Twin studies of ability, personality, and interests. *Homo, 29,* 158–173.

Pedersen, N. L., Friberg, L., Floderus-Myrhed, B., McClearn, G. E., & Plomin, R. (1984). Swedish early separated twins: Identification and characterization. *Acta Geneticae Medicae et Gemellologiae, 33,* 243–250.

Pedersen, N. L., McClearn, G. E., Plomin, R., & Friberg, L. (1985). Separated fraternal twins: Resemblance for cognitive abilities. *Behavior Genetics, 15,* 407–419.

Pedersen, N. L., Plomin, R., McClearn, G. E., & Friberg, L. (1988). Neuroticism, extraversion, and related traits in adult twins reared apart and reared together. *Journal of Personality and Social Psychology, 55,* 950–957.

Peele, S. (1986). The implications and limitations of genetic models of alcoholism and other addictions. *Journal of Studies on Alcohol, 47,* 63–73.

Plomin, R. (1986). *Development, genetics, and psychology.* Hillsdale, NJ: Erlbaum.

Plomin, R. (1988). The nature and nurture of cognitive abilities. In R. J. Sternberg (Ed.), *Advances in the psychology of human intelligence* (Vol. 4, pp. 1–33). Hillsdale, NJ: Erlbaum.

Plomin, R., & DeFries, J. C. (1980). Genetics and intelligence: Recent data. *Intelligence, 4,* 15–24.

Plomin, R., DeFries, J. C., & Fulker D. W. (1988). *Nature and nurture during infancy and early childhood.* New York: Cambridge University Press.

Roew, D. C. (1983b). Biometrical genetic models of self-reported delinquent behavior: Twin study. *Behavior Genetics, 13,* 473–489.

Scarr, S., Webber, P. I., Weinberg, R. A., & Wittig, M. A. (1981). Personality resemblance among adolescents and their parents in biologically related and adoptive families. *Journal of Personality and Social Psychology, 40,* 885–898.

Smith, S. D., Kimberling, W. J., Pennington, B. F., & Lubs, H. A. (1983). Specific reading disability: Identification of an inherited form through linkage analysis. *Science, 219,* 1345–1347.

Snyderman, M., & Rothman, S. (1987). Survey of expert opinion on intelligence and aptitude testing. *American Psychologist, 42,* 137–144.

Stevenson, J., Graham, P., Fredman, G., & McLoughlin, V. (1987). A twin study of genetic influences on reading and spelling ability and disability. *Journal of Child Psychology and Psychiatry, 28,* 229–247.

Tellegen, A., Lykken, D. T., Bouchard, T. J., Wilcox, K., Segal, N., & Rich, S. (1988). Personality similarity in twins reared apart and together. *Journal of Social and Personality Psychology, 54,* 1031–1039.

Vandenberg, S. G., Singer, S. M., & Pauls, D. L. (1986). *The heredity of behavior disorders in adults and children.* New York: Plenum.

Wender, P. H., Kety, S. S., Rosenthal, D., Schulsinger, F., Ortmann, J., & Lunde, I. (1986). Psychiatric disorders in the biological and adoptive families of adopted individuals with affective disorders. *Archives of General Psychiatry, 43,* 923–929.

Wilson, J. Q., & Herrnstein, R. J. (1985). *Crime and human nature.* New York: Simon & Schuster.

Wyman, A. R., & White, R. L. (1980). A highly polymorphic locus in human DNA. *Proceedings of the National Academy of Sciences, 77,* 6754–6758.

Preparation of this article was supported in part by grants from the National Science Foundation (BNS-8643938) and the National Institute of Aging (AG-04563).

CHAPTER 3

Development

3.1 JEAN PIAGET AND
BÄRBEL INHELDER

The Sensori-motor Level

Psychologists have traditionally had difficulty studying cognitive development in children because young children cannot effectively communicate their thoughts to others. Swiss psychologist Jean Piaget, however, became interested in cognitive development in infants and children, and he spent nearly 60 years investigating the differences between the thought processes of children and those of adults. Piaget was greatly assisted during 48 of those years by his student and chief collaborator, Bärbel Inhelder.

Piaget (1896–1980) earned his Ph.D. in zoology from the University of Neuchâtel in 1918. His training helped him in his studies on children's cognitive development because he learned how to make careful observations of noncommunicative organisms solving problems. He theorized that when children are unsuccessful at solving particular problems, they develop more complex mental structures to help them in the future. Piaget was the founder and director of the International Center of Genetic Epistemology in Geneva and a professor of psychology at the University of Geneva. Inhelder (b. 1913), coauthor with Piaget of *The Psychology of the Child* (Basic Books, 1969), was a professor of child and adolescent psychology and the chairperson of genetic and experimental psychology at the University of Geneva before she retired in 1983. She also pioneered the application of genetic epistemology to the study of mental deficiency, to cross-cultural research, and to learning.

This selection is from chapter 1, "The Sensori-motor Level," of *The Psychology of the Child*. The book summarizes Piaget's theory of cognitive development. Because cognition is central to psychology today, it is critical to understand how we develop our ability to think and reason. As you read this selection, try to understand development from the perspective of a child.

Key Concept: cognitive development

*I*f the child partly explains the adult, it can also be said that each period of his development partly explains the periods that follow. This is particularly clear in the case of the period where language is still absent. We call it the "sensori-motor" period because the infant lacks the symbolic function; that is, he does not have representations by which he can evoke persons or objects in their absence. In spite of this lack, mental development during the first eighteen months[1] of life is particularly important, for it is during this time that the child constructs all the cognitive substructures that will serve as a point of departure for his later perceptive and intellectual development, as well as a certain number of elementary affective reactions that will partly determine his subsequent affectivity.

SENSORI-MOTOR INTELLIGENCE

Whatever criteria for intelligence one adopts—purposeful groping (E. Claparède), sudden comprehension or insight (W. Köhler or K. Bühler), coordination of means and ends, etc.—everyone agrees in recognizing the existence of an intelligence before language. Essentially practical—that is, aimed at getting results rather than at stating truths—this intelligence nevertheless succeeds in eventually solving numerous problems of action (such as reaching distant or hidden objects) by constructing a complex system of action-schemes[2] and organizing reality in terms of spatio-temporal and causal structures. In the absence of language or symbolic function, however, these constructions are made with the sole support of perceptions and movements and thus by means of a sensori-motor coordination of actions, without the intervention of representation or thought.

Stimulus-Response and Assimilation

There certainly is such a thing as a sensori-motor intelligence, but it is very difficult to specify the exact moment when it appears. Actually, the question makes no sense, for the answer always depends upon an arbitrary choice of criterion. What one actually finds is a remarkably smooth succession of stages, each marking a new advance, until the moment when the acquired behavior presents characteristics that one or another psychologist recognizes as those of "intelligence." (All writers are in agreement in attributing this quality to at least the last of these stages, from twelve to eighteen months.) There is a continuous progression from spontaneous movements and reflexes to acquired habits and from the latter to intelligence. The real problem is not to locate the first appearance of intelligence but rather to understand the mechanism of this progression.

For many psychologists this mechanism is one of association, a cumulative process by which conditionings are added to reflexes and many other acquisitions to the conditionings themselves. According to this view, every acquisition, from the simplest to the most complex, is regarded as a response to external stimuli, a response whose associative character expresses a complete control of development by external connections. One of us,[3] on the other hand, has argued that this mechanism consists in *assimilation* (comparable to biological assimilation in the broad sense): meaning that reality data are treated or modified in such a way as to become incorporated into the structure of the subject. In other words, every newly established connection is integrated into an existing schematism. According to this view, the organizing activity of the subject must be considered just as important as the connections inherent in the external stimuli, for the subject becomes aware of these connections only to the degree that he can assimilate them by means of his existing structures. In other words, associationism conceives the relationship between stimulus and response in a unilateral manner: $S \rightarrow R$; whereas the point of view of assimilation presupposes a reciprocity $S \rightleftarrows R$; that is to say, the input, the stimulus, is filtered through a structure that consists of the action-schemes (or, at a higher level, the operations of thought), which in turn are modified and enriched when the subject's behavioral repertoire is accommodated to the demands of reality. The filtering or modification of the input is called *assimilation*; the modification of internal schemes to fit reality is called *accommodation.*

Stage 1

The point of departure of development should not be sought in the reflexes conceived as simple isolated responses, but in the spontaneous and total activities of the organism (studied by E. von Holst and others). There are relatively fixed and predictable reflexes embedded in this total activity, but they can be viewed as a differentiation of this global activity, as we shall see. Some of these reflexes are developed by exercise instead of remaining unchanged or atrophying and are the points of departure for the development of schemes of assimilation.

On the one hand, it has been shown by the study of animal behavior as well as by the study of the electrical activity of the nervous system that the organism is never passive, but presents spontaneous and global activities whose form is rhythmic. On the other hand, embryological analysis of the reflexes (G. E. Coghill and others) has enabled us to establish the fact that reflexes are formed by differentiation upon a groundwork of more global activities. In the case of the locomotive reflexes of the batrachians [frogs and toads], for example, it is an overall rhythm which culminates in a succession of differentiated and coordinated reflexes, and not the reflexes which lead to that rhythm.

As far as the reflexes of the newborn child are concerned, those among them that are of particular importance for the future (the sucking reflex and the palmar reflex, which will be integrated into later intentional grasping) give rise to what has been called a "reflex exercise"; that is, a consolidation by means of functional exercise. This explains why after a few days the newborn child nurses with more assurance and finds the nipple more easily when it has slipped out of his mouth than at the time of his first attempts.[4] The reproductive or functional assimilation that accounts for this exercise also gives rise to a generalizing assimilation (sucking on nothing between meals or sucking new objects) and a recognitive assimilation (distinguishing the nipple from other objects).

We cannot label these modifications of sucking acquisitions in a strict sense, since the assimilating exercise does not yet go beyond the preestablished boundaries of the hereditary apparatus. Nevertheless, the assimilation fulfills a fundamental role in developing this activity. This makes it impossible to regard the reflex as a pure automatism and also accounts for later extensions of the reflex scheme and for the formation of the first habits. In the case of sucking we observe, sometimes as early as the second month, the commonplace but nonetheless instructive phenomenon of a baby sucking his thumb. Fortuitous or accidental thumbsucking may occur as early as the first day. The more advanced sucking is systematic and dependent upon a coordination of the movements of arm, hand, and mouth. Associationists see here only an effect of repetition (but what is the source of this repetition, since it is not imposed by external connections?), and psychoanalysts already see a symbolic behavior by representative identification of the thumb and the breast (but what is the source of this symbolic or evocative power, well before the formation of the first mental images?). We suggest that this acquisition be interpreted as a simple extension of the sensori-motor assimilation at work as early as the reflex. It is quite clear that this is a genuine case of acquisition in a broad sense, since there exists no reflex or instinct for sucking one's thumb (indeed, the appearance of this activity and its frequency are subject to variation). But this acquisition is not a random affair: it is introduced into a reflex scheme that is already formed, extending it through the integration of sensori-motor elements hitherto independent of this scheme. Such integration already characterizes Stage 2. Although the child's actions seem to reflect a sort of magical belief in causality without any material contact, his use of the same means to try to achieve different ends indicates that he is on the threshold of intelligence.

Stage 2

Some such pattern characterizes the formation of the first habits, whether they depend directly upon an activity of the subject, as in the foregoing case, or seem to be imposed from the outside, as in the case of "conditionings." A conditioned reflex is never stabilized by the force of its associations alone, but only by the formation of a scheme of assimilation: that is, when the result attained satisfies the need inherent in the assimilation in question (as with Pavlov's dog, which salivates at the sound of the bell as long as this sound is identified with a signal for food, but which ceases to salivate if food no longer follows the signal).

But even if we use "habits"—for lack of a better word—to refer to acquired behavior while it is being formed as well as after it has become automatized, habit is still not the same as intelligence. An elementary "habit" is based on a general sensori-motor scheme within which there is not yet, from the subject's point of view, any differentiation between means and ends. The end in question is attained only by a necessary succession of movements which lead to it, without one's being able to distinguish either an end pursued from the start or means chosen from among various possible schemes. In an act of intelligence, on the other hand, the end is established from the outset and pursued after a search for the appropriate means. These means are furnished by the schemes known to the subject (or "habit" schemes), but they are used to achieve an aim that had its source in a different scheme.

Stage 3

The most interesting aspect of the development of sensori-motor actions during the first year of the child's life is that it not only leads to elementary learning experiences which are the source of simple habits on a level where intelligence, strictly speaking, is not yet observed, but it also provides a continuous series of intermediaries between habitual and intelligent reactions. Thus after the reflex stage (Stage 1) and the stage of the first habits (Stage 2), a third stage (Stage 3) introduces the next transitions after the beginning of coordination between vision and prehension—around four and a half months on the average. The baby starts grasping and manipulating everything he sees in his immediate vicinity. For example, a subject of this age catches hold of a cord hanging from the top of his cradle, which has the effect of shaking all the rattles suspended above him. He immediately repeats the gesture a number of times. Each time the interesting result motivates the repetition. This constitutes a "circular reaction" in the sense of J. M. Baldwin, or a new habit in the nascent state, where the result to be obtained is not differentiated from the means employed. Later you need only hang a new toy from the top of the cradle for the child to look for the cord, which constitutes the beginning of a differentiation between means and end. In the days that follow, when you swing an object from a pole two yards from the crib, and even when you produce unexpected and mechanical sounds behind a screen, after these sights or sounds have ceased the child will again look for and pull the magic cord. Although the child's actions seem to reflect a sort of magical belief in causality without any material connection, his use of the same means to try to achieve different ends indicates that he is on the threshold of intelligence.

Stages 4 and 5

In a fourth stage (Stage 4), we observe more complete acts of practical intelligence. The subject sets out to obtain a certain result, independent of the means he is going to employ: for example, obtaining an object that is out of reach or has just disappeared under a piece of cloth or a cushion. The instrumental acts appear only later and they are obviously seen from the outset as means: for example, seizing the hand of an adult and moving it in the direction of the unreachable object, or lifting the screen that masks the hidden object. In the course of this fourth stage, the coordination of means and ends is new and is invented differently in each unforeseen situation (otherwise we would not speak of intelligence), but the means employed are derived only from known schemes of assimilation. (In the case of the object that is hidden and found again, the combination is also new, as we shall see in the next section. But the fact of seizing and moving a cushion corresponds to a habitual scheme.)

In the course of a fifth stage (Stage 5), which makes its appearance around eleven or twelve months, a new ingredient is added to the foregoing behavior: the search for new means by differentiation from schemes already known. An example of this is what we call the "behavior pattern of the support." An object has been placed on a rug out of the child's reach. The child, after trying in vain to reach the object directly, may eventually grasp one corner of the rug (by chance or as a substitute), and then, observing a relationship between the movements of the rug and those of the object, gradually comes to pull the rug in order to reach the object. An analogous discovery characterizes the behavior pattern of the string, studied first by Bühler and then by many others: bringing the objective to oneself by pulling the string to which it is attached.

Stage 6

Finally, a sixth stage marks the end of the sensori-motor period and the transition to the following period. In this stage the child becomes capable of finding new means not only by external or physical groping but also by internalized combinations that culminate in sudden comprehension or *insight*. For example, a child confronted by a slightly open matchbox containing a thimble first tries to open the box by physical groping (reaction of the fifth stage), but upon failing, he presents an altogether new reaction: he stops the action and attentively examines the situation (in the course of this he slowly opens and closes his mouth, or, as another subject did, his hand, as if in imitation of the result to be attained, that is, the enlargement of the opening), after which he suddenly slips his finger into the crack and thus succeeds in opening the box.

It is at this same stage that one generally finds the well-known behavior pattern of the stick, first studied by Köhler in chimpanzees and later by others in the human infant. But Köhler, like Bühler, considers that there is an act of intelligence involved only in cases where there is sudden comprehension. He banishes groping from the domain of intelligence and classifies it with the behavior of substitution, etc. Claparède, on the other hand, saw groping as the criterion of intelligence, attributing the onset of hypotheses to an externalized groping. This criterion is surely too broad, since groping exists as early as the reflex and the formation of habits. But the criterion of *insight* is certainly too narrow, for it is by means of an uninterrupted succession of assimilations on various levels (Stages 1 through 5) that the sensori-motor schemes lead to those new combinations and internalizations that finally make immediate comprehension possible in certain situations. This last level (Stage 6) cannot therefore be separated from the others; it merely marks their completion.

Jean Piaget and Bärbel Inhelder

NOTES

1. Ages indicated in this book are always average and approximate.
2. A scheme is the structure or organization of actions as they are transferred or generalized by repetition in similar or analogous circumstances.
3. Jean Piaget, *The Origins of Intelligence in Children* (New York: International Universities Press, 1951; London: Routledge and Kegan Paul, 1953).
4. Similar reflex exercises are observed in animals too, as in the groping that characterizes the first efforts at copulation in Lymnaeae.

Infant–Mother Attachment

How babies form attachments to their parents is of interest to a variety of people, from parents to educators to psychologists. Especially intriguing is the notion that there are different patterns of attachment behavior shown by infants. A major contribution in this area has been provided by psychologist Mary D. Salter Ainsworth.

Ainsworth earned her Ph.D. in personality psychology in 1939 from the University of Toronto. She taught at Johns Hopkins University from 1956 to 1975, when she became a professor emeritus at the University of Virginia. Among her many publications in the area of development and attachment is her book *Infancy in Uganda: Infant Care and the Growth of Love* (Johns Hopkins University Press, 1967).

This selection is from "Infant–Mother Attachment," which was published in *American Psychologist* in 1979. In it, Ainsworth describes her classic research on the development of attachment. Her "strange situation" is used to test the behavior patterns of infants, and it has shown at least three distinguishable attachment patterns. Ainsworth argues that the infant's crying is a key to determining how the infant–mother interaction will develop. As you read this selection, speculate about the long-term development of attachment patterns. How will the secure, anxious, and avoidant babies relate to other people when they become adults?

Key Concept: infant attachment

*B*owlby's (1969) ethological–evolutionary attachment theory implies that it is an essential part of the ground plan of the human species—as well as that of many other species—for an infant to become attached to a mother figure. This figure need not be the natural mother but can be anyone who plays the role of principal caregiver. This ground plan is fulfilled, except under extraordinary circumstances when the baby experiences too little interaction with any one caregiver to support the formation of an attachment. The literature on maternal deprivation describes some of these circumstances, but it cannot be reviewed here, except to note that research has not yet specified an acceptable minimum amount of interaction required for attachment formation.

However, there have been substantial recent advances in the areas of individual differences in the way attachment behavior becomes organized, differential experiences associated with the various attachment patterns, and the value of such patterns in forecasting subsequent development. These advances have been much aided by a standardized laboratory situation that was devised to supplement a naturalistic, longitudinal investigation of the development of infant–mother attachment in the first year of life. This *strange situation*, as we entitled it, has proved to be an excellent basis for the assessment of such attachment in 1-year-olds (Ainsworth, Blehar, Waters, & Wall, 1978).

The assessment procedure consists of classification according to the pattern of behavior shown in the strange situation, particularly in the episodes of reunion after separation. Eight patterns were identified, but I shall deal here only with the three main groups into which they fell—Groups A, B, and C. To summarize, Group B babies use their mothers as a secure base from which to explore in the preseparation episodes; their attachment behavior is greatly intensified by the separation episodes so that exploration diminishes and distress is likely; and in the reunion episodes they seek contact with, proximity to, or at least interaction with their mothers. Group C babies tend to show some signs of anxiety even in the preseparation episodes; they are intensely distressed by separation; and in the reunion episodes they are ambivalent with the mother, seeking close contact with her and yet resisting contact or interaction. Group A babies, in sharp contrast, rarely cry in the separation episodes and, in the reunion episodes, avoid the mother, either mingling proximity-seeking and avoidant behaviors or ignoring her altogether.

COMPARISON OF STRANGE-SITUATION BEHAVIOR AND BEHAVIOR ELSEWHERE

Groups A, B, and C in our longitudinal sample were compared in regard to their behavior at home during the first year. Stayton and Ainsworth (1973) had identified a security–anxiety dimension in a factor analysis of fourth-quarter infant behavior. Group B infants were identified as securely attached because they significantly more often displayed behaviors characteristic of the secure pole of this dimension, whereas both of the other groups were identified as anxious because their behaviors were characteristic of the anxious pole. A second dimension was clearly related to close bodily contact, and this was important in distinguishing Group A babies from those in the other two groups, in that Group A babies behaved less positively to being held and yet more negatively to being put down. The groups were also distinguished by two behaviors not included in the factor analysis—cooperativeness and anger. Group B babies were more cooperative and less angry than either A or C babies; Group A babies were even more angry than those in Group C. Clearly, something went awry in the physical-contact interaction Group A babies had with their mothers, and as I explain below, I believe it is this that makes them especially prone to anger.

Ainsworth et al. (1978) reviewed findings of other investigators who had compared A–B–C groups of 1-year-olds in terms of their behavior elsewhere. Their findings regarding socioemotional behavior support the summary just cited, and in addition three investigations using cognitive measures found an advantage in favor of the securely attached.

COMPARISON OF INFANT STRANGE-SITUATION BEHAVIOR WITH MATERNAL HOME BEHAVIOR

Mothers of the securely attached (Group B) babies were, throughout the first year, more sensitively responsive to infant signals than were the mothers of the two anxiously attached groups, in terms of a variety of measures spanning all of the most common contexts for mother–infant interaction (Ainsworth et al., 1978). Such responsiveness, I suggest, enables an infant to form expectations, primitive at first, that moderate his or her responses to events, both internal and environmental. Gradually, such an infant constructs an inner representation—or "working model" (Bowlby, 1969)—of his or her mother as generally accessible and responsive to him or her. Therein lies his or her security. In contrast, babies whose mothers have disregarded their signals, or have responded to them belatedly or in a grossly inappropriate fashion, have no basis for believing the mother to be accessible and responsive; consequently they are anxious, not knowing what to expect of her.

In regard to interaction in close bodily contact, the most striking finding is that the mothers of avoidant (Group A) babies all evinced a deep-seated aversion to it, whereas none of the other mothers did. In addition they were more rejecting, more often angry, and yet more restricted in the expression of affect than were Group B or C mothers. Main (e.g., in press) and Ainsworth et al. (1978) have presented a theoretical account of the dynamics of interaction of avoidant babies and their rejecting mothers. This emphasizes the acute approach–avoidance conflict experienced by these infants when their attachment behavior is activated at high intensity—a conflict stemming from painful rebuff consequent upon seeking close bodily contact. Avoidance is viewed as a defensive maneuver, lessening the anxiety and anger experienced in the conflict situation and enabling the baby nevertheless to remain within a tolerable range of proximity to the mother.

Findings and interpretations such as these raise the issue of direction of effects. To what extent is the pattern of attachment of a baby attributable to the mother's behavior throughout the first year, and to what extent is it attributable to built-in differences in potential and temperament? I have considered this problem elsewhere (Ainsworth, 1979) and have concluded that in our sample of normal babies there is a strong case to be made for differences in attachment quality being attributable to maternal behavior. Two studies, however (Connell, 1976; Waters, Vaughn, & Egeland, in press), have suggested that Group C babies may as newborns be constitutionally "difficult." Particularly if the mother's personality or life situation makes it hard for her to be sensitively responsive to infant cues, such a baby seems indeed likely to form an attachment relationship of anxious quality.

Mary D. Salter
Ainsworth

Contexts of Mother–Infant Interaction

Of the various contexts in which mother–infant interaction commonly takes place, the face-to-face situation has been the focus of most recent research. By many (e.g., Walters & Parke, 1965), interaction mediated by distance receptors and behaviors has been judged especially important in the establishment of human relationships. Microanalytic studies, based on frame-by-frame analysis of film records, show clearly that maternal sensitivity to infant behavioral cues is essential for successful pacing of face-to-face interaction (e.g., Brazelton, Koslowski, & Main, 1974; Stern, 1974). Telling evidence of the role of vision, both in the infant's development of attachment to the mother and in the mother's responsiveness to the infant, comes from Fraiberg's (1977) longitudinal study of blind infants.

So persuasive has been the studies of interaction involving distance receptors that interaction involving close bodily contact has been largely ignored. The evolutionary perspective of attachment theory attributes focal importance to bodily contact. Other primate species rely on the maintenance of close mother–infant contact as crucial for infant survival. Societies of hunter–gatherers, living much as the earliest humans did, are conspicuous for very much more mother–infant contact than are western societies (e.g., Konner, 1976). Blurton Jones (1972) presented evidence suggesting that humans evolved as a species in which infants are carried by the mother and are fed at frequent intervals, rather than as a species in which infants are left for long periods, are cached in a safe place, and are fed but infrequently. Bowlby (1969) pointed out that when attachment behavior is intensely activated it is close bodily contact that is specifically required. Indeed, Bell and Ainsworth (1972) found that even with the white, middle-class mothers of their sample, the most frequent and the most effective response to an infant's crying throughout the first year was to pick up the baby. A recent analysis of our longitudinal findings (Blehar, Ainsworth, & Main, Note 1) suggests that bodily contact is at least as important a context of interaction as face-to-face is, perhaps especially in the first few months of life. Within the limits represented by our sample, however, we found that it was *how* the mother holds her baby rather than *how much* she holds him or her that affects the way in which attachment develops.

In recent years the feeding situation has been neglected as a context for mother–infant interaction, except insofar as it is viewed as a setting for purely social, face-to-face interaction. Earlier, mother's gratification or frustration of infant interest to both psychoanalytically oriented and social-learning research, on the assumption that a mother's gratification or frustration of infant instinctual drives, or her role as a secondary reinforcer, determined the nature of the baby's tie to her. Such research yielded no evidence that methods of feeding significantly affected the course of infant development, although these negative findings seem almost certainly to reflect methodological deficiencies (Caldwell, 1964). In contrast, we have found that sensitive maternal responsiveness to infant signals relevant to feeding is closely related to the security or anxiety of attachment that eventually develops (Ainsworth & Bell, 1969). Indeed, this analysis seemed to redefine the meaning of "demand" feeding—letting infant behavioral cues determine not only when feeding is begun but also when it is terminated, how the pacing of feeding proceeds, and how new foods are introduced.

Our findings do not permit us to attribute overriding importance to any one context of mother–infant interaction. Whether the context is feeding, close bodily contact, face-to-face interaction, or indeed the situation defined by the infant's crying, mother–infant interaction provides the baby with opportunity to build up expectations of the mother and, eventually, a working model of her as more or less accessible and responsive. Indeed, our findings suggest that a mother who is sensitively responsive to signals in one context tends also to be responsive to signals in other contexts. . . .

Using the Mother as a Secure Base From Which to Explore

Attachment theory conceives of the behavioral system serving attachment as only one of several important systems, each with its own activators, terminators, predictable outcomes, and functions. During the prolonged period of human infancy, when the protective function of attachment is especially important, its interplay with exploratory behavior is noteworthy. The function of exploration is learning about the environment—which is particularly important in a species possessing much potential for adaptation to a wide range of environments. Attachment and exploration support each other. When attachment behavior is intensely activated, a baby tends to seek proximity contact rather than exploring; when attachment behavior is at low intensity a baby is free to respond to the pull of novelty. The presence of an attachment figure, particularly one who is believed to be accessible and responsive, leaves the baby open to stimulation that may activate exploration.

Nevertheless, it is often believed that somehow attachment may interfere with the development of independence. Our studies provide no support for such a belief. For example, Blehar et al. (Note 1) found that babies who respond positively to close bodily contact with their mothers also tend to respond positively to being put down again and to move off into independent exploratory play. Fostering the growth of secure attachment facilitates rather than hampers the growth of healthy self-reliance (Bowlby, 1973).

Response to Separation from Attachment Figures

Schaffer (1971) suggested that the crucial criterion for whether a baby has become attached to a specific figure is that he or she does not consider this figure interchangeable with any other figure. Thus, for an infant to protest the mother's departure or continued absence is a dependable criterion for attachment (Schaffer & Callender, 1959). This does not imply that protest is an invariable response to separation from an attachment figure under all circumstances;

the context of the separation influences the likelihood and intensity of protest. Thus there is ample evidence, which cannot be cited here, that protest is unlikely to occur, at least initially, in the case of voluntary separations, when the infant willingly leaves the mother in order to explore elsewhere. protest is less likely to occur if the baby is left with another attachment figure than if he or she is left with an unfamiliar person or alone. Being left in an unfamiliar environment is more distressing than comparable separations in the familiar environment of the home—in which many infants are able to build up expectations that reassure them of mother's accessibility and responsiveness even though she may be absent. Changes attributable to developmental processes affect separation protest in complex ways. Further research will undoubtedly be able to account for these shifts in terms of progressive cognitive achievements. . . .

Other Attachment Figures

Many have interpreted Bowlby's attachment theory as claiming that an infant can become attached to only one person—the mother. This is a mistaken interpretation. There are, however, three implications of attachment theory relevent to the issue of "multiple" attachments. First, as reported by Ainsworth (1967) and Schaffer and Emerson (1964), infants are highly selective in their choices of attachment figures from among the various persons familiar to them. No infant has been observed to have many attachment figures. Second, not all social relationships may be identified as attachments. Harlow (1971) distinguished between the infant–mother and peer–peer affectional systems, although under certain circumstances peers may become attachment figures in the absence of anyone more appropriate (see, e.g., Freud & Dann, 1951; Harlow, 1963). Third, the fact that a baby may have several attachment figures does not imply that they are all equally important. Bowlby (1969) suggested that they are not—that there is a principal attachment figure, usually the principal caregiver, and one or more secondary figures. Thus a hierarchy is implied. A baby may both enjoy and derive security from all of his or her attachment figures but, under certain circumstances (e.g., illness, fatigue, stress), is likely to show a clear preference among them.

In recent years there has been a surge of interest in the father as an attachment figure, as reported elsewhere in this issue. Relatively lacking is research into attachments to caregivers other than parents. Do babies become attached to their regular baby-sitters or to caregivers in day-care centers? Studies by Fleener (1973), Farran and Ramey (1977), and Ricciuti (1974) have suggested that they may but that the preference is nevertheless for the mother figure. Fox (1977) compared the mother and the *metapelet* as providers of security to kibbutz-reared infants in a strange situation, but surely much more research is needed into the behavior of infants and young children toward caregivers as attachment figures in the substitute-care environment.

... In comparison with anxiously attached infants, those who are securely attached as 1-year-olds are later more cooperative with and affectively more positive as well as less aggressive and/or avoidant toward their mothers and other less familiar adults. Later on, they emerge as more competent and more sympathetic in interaction with peers. In free-play situations they have longer bouts of exploration and display more intense exploratory interest, and in problem-solving situations they are more enthusiastic, more persistent, and better able to elicit and accept their mothers' help. They are more curious, more self-directed, more ego-resilient—and they usually tend to achieve better scores on both developmental tests and measures of language development. Some studies also reported differences between the two groups of anxiously attached infants, with the avoidant ones (Group A) continuing to be more aggressive, noncompliant, and avoidant, and the ambivalent ones (Group C) emerging as more easily frustrated, less persistent, and generally less competent.

Conclusion

It is clear that the nature of an infant's attachment to his or her mother as a 1-year-old is related both to earlier interaction with the mother and to various aspects of later development. The implication is that the way in which the infant organizes his or her behavior toward the mother affects the way in which he or she organizes behavior toward other aspects of the environment, both animate and inanimate. This organization provides a core of continuity in development despite changes that come with developmental acquisitions, both cognitive and socioemotional.

NOTE

1. Blehar, M. C., Ainsworth, M. D. S., & Main, M. *Mother–infant interaction relevant to close bodily contact.* Monograph in preparation, 1979.

REFERENCES

Ainsworth, M. D. S. *Infancy in Uganda: Infant care and the growth of love.* Baltimore, Md.: Johns Hopkins Press, 1967.

Ainsworth, M. D. S. Attachment as related to mother–infant interaction. In J. S. Rosenblatt, R. A. Hinde, C. Beer, & M. Busnel (Eds.), *Advances in the study of behavior* (Vol. 9). New York: Academic Press, 1979.

Ainsworth, M. D. S., & Bell, S. M. Some contemporary patterns of mother–infant interaction in the feeding situation. In A. Ambrose (Ed.), *Stimulation in early infancy.* London: Academic Press, 1969.

Ainsworth, M. D. S., Blehar, M. C., Waters, E., & Wall, S. *Patterns of attachment: A psychological study of the strange situation.* Hillsdale, N.J.: Erlbaum, 1978.

Bell, S. M., & Ainsworth, M. D. S. Infant crying and maternal responsiveness. *Child Development,* 1972, *43,* 1171–1190.

Blurton Jones, N. G. Comparative aspects of mother–child contact. In N. G. Blurton Jones (Ed.), *Ethological studies of child behavior.* London: Cambridge University Press, 1972.

Bowlby, J. *Attachment and loss: Vol. 1. Attachment.* New York: Basic Books, 1969.

Bowlby, J. *Attachment and loss: Vol. 2. Separation: Anxiety and anger.* New York: Basic Books, 1973.

Brazelton, T. B., Koslowski, B., & Main, M. The origins of reciprocity: The early mother–infant interaction. In M. Lewis & L. A. Rosenblum (Eds.), *The effect of the infant on its caregiver.* New York: Wiley, 1974.

Caldwell, B. M. The effects of infant care. In M. L. Hoffman & L. W. Hoffman (Eds.), *Review of child development research* (Vol. 1). New York: Russell Sage Foundation, 1964.

Connell, D. B. *Individual differences in attachment: An investigation into stability, implications, and relationships to the structure of early language development.* Unpublished doctoral dissertation, Syracuse University, 1976.

Farran, D. C., & Ramey, C. T. Infant day care and attachment behavior toward mother and teachers. *Child Development,* 1977, *48,* 1112–1116.

Fleener, D. E. Experimental production of infant-maternal attachment behaviors. *Proceedings of the 81st Annual Convention of the American Psychological Association,* 1973, *8,* 57–58. (Summary)

Fox, N. Attachment of kibbutz infants to mother. *Child Development,* 1977, *48,* 1228–1239.

Fraiberg, S. *Insights from the blind.* New York: Basic Books, 1977.

Freud, A., & Dann, S. An experiment in group upbringing. *Psychoanalytic Study of the Child,* 1951, *6,* 127–168.

Harlow, H. F. The maternal affectional system. In B. M. Foss (Ed.), *Determinants of infant behaviour* (Vol. 2) New York: Wiley, 1963.

Harlow, H. F. *Learning to love.* San Francisco: Albion, 1971.

Konner, M. J. Maternal care, infant behavior, and development among the !Kung. In R. B. Lee & I. DeVore (Eds.), *Kalahari hunter–gatherers.* Cambridge, Mass.: Harvard University Press, 1976.

Main, M. Avoidance in the service of proximity. In K. Immelmann, G. Barlow, M. Main, & L. Petrinovich (Eds.), *Behavioral development: The Bielefeld Interdisciplinary Project.* New York: Cambridge University Press, in press.

Ricciuti, H. N. Fear and the development of social attachments in the first year of life. In M. Lewis & L. A. Rosenblum (Eds.), *The origins of fear.* New York: Wiley, 1974.

Schaffer, H. R. *The growth of sociability.* London: Penguin Books, 1971.

Schaffer, H. R., & Callender, W. M. Psychological effects of hospitalization in infancy. *Pediatrics,* 1959, *25,* 528–539.

Schaffer, H. R., & Emerson, P. E. The development of social attachments in infancy. *Monographs of the Society for Research in Child Development,* 1964, *3* (Serial No. 94).

Stayton, D. J., & Ainsworth, M. D. S. Individual differences in infant responses to brief, everyday separations as related to other infant and maternal behaviors. *Developmental Psychology,* 1973, *9,* 226–235.

Stern, D. N. Mother and infant at play: The dyadic interaction involving facial, vocal, and gaze behaviors. In M. Lewis & L. A. Rosenblum (Eds.), *The effect of the infant on its caregiver.* New York: Wiley, 1974.

Walters, R. H., & Parke, R. D. The role of the distance receptors in the development of social responsiveness. In L. P. Lipsitt & C. C. Spiker (Eds.), *Advances in child development and behavior.* New York: Academic Press, 1965.

Walters, E., Vaughn, B. E., & Egeland, B. R. Individual differences in infant–mother attachment relationships at age one: Antecedents in neonatal behavior in an urban economically disadvantaged sample. *Child Development,* in press.

3.3 LAWRENCE KOHLBERG

The Child as a Moral Philosopher

The development of the awareness of ethical behavior, or moral development, is an important part of a child's socialization. Psychologists are therefore interested in how an individual acquires moral reasoning. One important theory, based on three levels of moral thinking, was proposed by Lawrence Kohlberg.

Kohlberg (1927–1987) spent a considerable part of his career studying moral development. He is particularly well known for his 1969 book *Stages in the Development of Moral Thought and Action*.

This selection from "The Child as a Moral Philosopher," which was published in 1968 in *Psychology Today*, gives a very readable account of Kohlberg's theory of moral development. In addition to outlining his theory, Kohlberg describes the results of some cross-cultural research that confirm the generality of his data. Note that the original data were collected only on boys. As you read this selection, consider whether the results are applicable to both sexes or only to males.

Key Concept: moral development

*H*ow can one study morality? Current trends in the fields of ethics, linguistics, anthropology and cognitive psychology have suggested a new approach which seems to avoid the morass of semantical confusions, value-bias and cultural relativity in which the psychoanalytic and semantic approaches to morality have foundered. New scholarship in all these fields is now focusing upon structures, forms and relationships that seem to be common to all societies and all languages rather than upon the features that make particular languages or cultures different.

For 12 years, my colleagues and I studied the same group of 75 boys, following their development at three-year intervals from early adolescence through young manhood. At the start of the study, the boys were aged 10 to 16. We have now followed them through to ages 22 to 28. In addition, I have explored moral development in other cultures—Great Britain, Canada, Taiwan, Mexico and Turkey.

Inspired by Jean Piaget's pioneering effort to apply a structural approach to moral development, I have gradually elaborated over the years of my study a typological scheme describing general structures and forms of moral thought which can be defined independently of the specific content of particular moral decisions or actions.

The typology contains three distinct levels of moral thinking, and within each of these levels distinguishes two related stages. These levels and stages may be considered separate moral philosophies, distinct views of the socio-moral world.

We can speak of the child as having his own morality or series of moralities. Adults seldom listen to children's moralizing. If a child throws back a few adult cliches and behaves himself, most parents—and many anthropologists and psychologists as well—think that the child has adopted or internalized the appropriate parental standards.

Actually, as soon as we talk with children about morality, we find that they have many ways of making judgments which are not "internalized" from the outside, and which do not come in any direct and obvious way from parents, teachers or even peers.

MORAL LEVELS

The *preconventional* level is the first of three levels of moral thinking; the second level is *conventional*, and the third *postconventional* or autonomous. While the preconventional child is often "well-behaved" and is responsive to cultural labels of good and bad, he interprets these labels in terms of their physical consequences (punishment, reward, exchange of favors) or in terms of the physical power of those who enunciate the rules and labels of good and bad.

This level is usually occupied by children aged four to 10, a fact long known to sensitive observers of children. The capacity of "properly behaved" children of this age to engage in cruel behavior when there are holes in the power structure is sometimes noted as tragic (*Lord of the Flies, High Wind in Jamaica*), sometimes as comic (Lucy in *Peanuts*).

The second or *conventional* level also can be described as conformist, but that is perhaps too smug a term. Maintaining the expectations and rules of the individual's family, group or nation is perceived as valuable in its own right. There is a concern not only with *conforming* to the individual's social order but in *maintaining*, supporting and justifying this order.

The *postconventional* level is characterized by a major thrust toward autonomous moral principles which have validity and application apart from authority of the groups or persons who hold them and apart from the individual's identification with those persons or groups.

Within each of these three levels there are two discernible stages. At the preconventional level we have:

Stage 1: Orientation toward punishment and unquestioning deference to superior power. The physical consequences of action regardless of their human meaning or value determine its goodness or badness.

Stage 2: Right action consists of that which instrumentally satisfies one's own needs and occasionally the needs of others. Human relations are viewed in terms like those of the marketplace. Elements of fairness, of reciprocity and equal sharing are present, but they are always interpreted in a physical, pragmatic way. Reciprocity is a matter of "you scratch my back and I'll scratch yours" not of loyalty, gratitude or justice.

And at the conventional level we have:

Stage 3: Good-boy–good-girl orientation. Good behavior is that which pleases or helps others and is approved by them. There is much conformity to stereotypical images of what is majority or "natural" behavior. Behavior is often judged by intention—"he means well" becomes important for the first time, and is overused, as by Charlie Brown in *Peanuts.* One seeks approval by being "nice."

Stage 4: Orientation toward authority, fixed rules and the maintenance of the social order. Right behavior consists of doing one's duty, showing respect for authority and maintaining the given social order for its own sake. One earns respect by performing dutifully.

At the postconventional level, we have:

Stage 5: A social-contract orientation, generally with legalistic and utilitarian overtones. Right action tends to be defined in terms of general rights and in terms of standards which have been critically examined and agreed upon by the whole society. There is a clear awareness of the relativism of personal values and opinions and a corresponding emphasis upon procedural rules for reaching consensus. Aside from what is constitutionally and democratically agreed upon, right or wrong is a matter of personal "values" and "opinion." The result is an emphasis upon the "legal point of view," but with an emphasis upon the possibility of *changing* law in terms of rational considerations of social utility, rather than freezing it in the terms of Stage 4 "law and order." Outside the legal realm, free agreement and contract are the binding elements of obligation. This is the "official" morality of American government, and finds its ground in the thought of the writers of the Constitution.

Stage 6: Orientation toward the decisions of conscience and toward self-chosen *ethical principles* appealing to logical comprehensiveness, universality and consistency. These principles are abstract and ethical (the Golden Rule, the categorical imperative); they are not concrete moral rules like the Ten Commandments. Instead, they are universal principles of *justice,* of the *reciprocity* and *equality* of human rights, and of respect for the dignity of human beings as *individual persons.* . . .

MORAL REASONS

In our research, we have found definite and universal levels of development in moral thought. In our study of 75 American boys from early adolescence on, these youths were presented hypothetical moral dilemmas, all deliberately philosophical, some of them found in medieval works of casuistry.

On the basis of their reasoning about these dilemmas at a given age, each boy's stage of thought could be determined for each of 25 basic moral concepts or aspects. One such aspect, for instance, is "Motive Given for Rule Obedience or Moral Action." In this instance, the six stages look like this:

1. Obey rules to avoid punishment.
2. Conform to obtain rewards, have favors returned, and so on.
3. Conform to avoid disapproval, dislike by others.
4. Conform to avoid censure by legitimate authorities and resultant guilt.
5. Conform to maintain the respect of the impartial spectator judging in terms of community welfare.
6. Conform to avoid self-condemnation.

In another of these 25 moral aspects, the value of human life, the six stages can be defined thus:

1. The value of a human life is confused with the value of physical objects and is based on the social status or physical attributes of its possessor.
2. The value of a human life is seen as instrumental to the satisfaction of the needs of its possessor or of other persons.
3. The value of a human life is based on the empathy and affection of family members and others toward its possessor.
4. Life is conceived as sacred in terms of its place in a categorical moral or religious order of rights and duties.
5. Life is valued both in terms of its relation to community welfare and in terms of life being a universal human right.
6. Belief in the sacredness of human life as representing a universal human value of respect for the individual.

I have called this scheme a typology. This is because about 50 per cent of most people's thinking will be at a single stage, regardless of the moral dilemma involved. We call our types *stages* because they seem to represent an *invariant developmental sequence.* "True" stages come one at a time and always in the same order.

All movement is forward in sequence, and does not skip steps. Children may move through these stages at varying speeds, of course, and may be found half in and half out of a particular stage. An individual may stop at any give stage and at any age, but if he continues to move, he must move in accord with these steps. Moral reasoning of the conventional or Stage 3–4 kind never occurs before the preconventional Stage-1 and Stage-2 thought has taken place. No adult in Stage 4 has gone through Stage 6, but all Stage-6 adults have gone at least through 4.

While the evidence is not complete, my study strongly suggests that moral change fits the stage pattern just described. (The major uncertainty is whether all Stage 6s go through Stage 5 or whether these are two alternate mature orientations.) . . .

ACROSS CULTURES

When I first decided to explore moral development in other cultures, I was told by anthropologist friends that I would have to throw away my culture-bound moral concepts and stories and start from scratch learning a whole new set of values for each new culture. My first try consisted of a brace of villages, one Atayal (Malaysian aboriginal) and the other Taiwanese.

My guide was a young Chinese ethnographer who had written an account of the moral and religious patterns of the Atayal and Taiwanese villages. Taiwanese boys in the 10–13 age group were asked about a story involving theft of food. A man's wife is starving to death but the store owner won't give the man any food unless he can pay, which he can't. Should he break in and steal some food? Why? Many of the boys said, "He should steal the food for his wife because if she dies he'll have to pay for her funeral and that costs a lot."

My guide was amused by these responses, but I was relieved: they were of course "classic" Stage-2 responses. In the Atayal village, funerals weren't such a big thing, so the Stage-2 boys would say, "He should steal the food because he needs his wife to cook for him."

This means that we need to consult our anthropologists to know what content a Stage-2 child will include in his instrumental exchange calculations, or what a Stage-4 adult will identify as the proper social order. But one certainly doesn't have to start from scratch. What made my guide laugh was the difference in form between the children's Stage-2 thought and his own, a difference definable independently of particular cultures. . . .

TRADING UP

In summary, the nature of our sequence is not significantly affected by widely varying social, cultural or religious conditions. The only thing that is affected is the *rate* at which individuals progress through this sequence.

Why should there be such a universal invariant sequence of development? In answering this question, we need first to analyze these developing social concepts in terms of their internal logical structure. At each stage, the same basic moral concept or aspect is defined, but at each higher stage this definition is more differentiated, more integrated and more general or universal. When one's concept of human life moves from Stage 1 to Stage 2 the value of life becomes more differentiated from the value of property, more integrated (the value of life enters an organizational hierarchy where it is "higher" than property so that one steals property in order to save life) and more universalized (the life of any sentient being is valuable regardless of status or property). The same advance is true at each stage in the hierarchy. Each step of development then is a better cognitive organization than the one before it, one which takes account of everything present in the previous stage, but making new distinctions and organizing them into a more comprehensive or more equilibrated structure. The fact that this is the case has been demonstrated by a series of studies indicating that children and adolescents comprehend all stages up to their own, but not more than one stage beyond their own. And importantly, *they prefer this next stage.*

We have conducted experimental moral discussion classes which show that the child at an earlier stage of development tends to move forward when confronted by the views of a child one stage further along. In an argument between a Stage-3 and Stage-4 child, the child in the third stage tends to move toward or into Stage 4, while the Stage-4 child understands but does not accept the arguments of the Stage-3 child.

Moral thought, then, seems to behave like all other kinds of thought. Progress through the moral levels and stages is characterized by increasing differentiation and increasing integration, and hence is the same kind of progress that scientific theory represents. Like acceptable scientific theory—or like *any* theory or structure of knowledge—moral thought may be considered partially to generate its own data as it goes along, or at least to expand so as to contain in a balanced, self-consistent way a wider and wider experiential field. The raw data in the case of our ethical philosophies may be considered as conflicts between roles, or values, or as the social order in which men live.

3.4 JANET SHIBLEY HYDE

Children's Understanding of Sexist Language

Sexism in the English language (for example, the use of the pronoun *he* to refer to both sexes) has important implications for our daily lives. However, empirical research on the consequences of this bias has occurred slowly. In examining this problem, psychologists have become interested in how children learn to interpret gender-neutral pronouns, as shown in this selection by Janet Shibley Hyde.

Hyde (b. 1948) received her Ph.D. from the University of California at Berkeley in 1972. She taught at Bowling Green State University and Denison University before going to the University of Wisconsin, where she is currently a professor of psychology. She is interested in gender issues, and she has written several books, including *Half the Human Experience: The Psychology of Women,* 3rd ed. (D.C. Heath, 1985).

Hyde's article "Children's Understanding of Sexist Language," from which this selection is taken, was published in 1984 in the American Psychological Association's journal *Developmental Psychology.* In addition to providing the results of research on how children interpret sexist language, it is a good example of the research article format. Note that in Hyde's experiment, significantly more students wrote a story about females when they were cued beforehand with "he or she" rather than with "he" alone. In a second experiment not included in this selection, Hyde found that when a fictitious, gender-neutral occupation was described, children rated the ability of women to do the job significantly higher when "she" was used than when "he" was used.

Do not worry about Hyde's specific statistical analyses, but remember that a *p* (probability) value that is .05 or smaller is significant (which means that there is a real difference between groups). Psychologists use such statistical techniques to help them generalize from their subjects to a larger population.

Key Concept: children's understanding of sexist language

*B*eginning a little more than a decade ago, the feminist movement raised a number of issues, including equal pay for equal work and availability of day care. One of those issues was sexism in language—the notion that the English language contains sex bias, particularly in usages such as "he" and "man" to refer to everyone (e.g., Martyna, 1980).

Concern over sexism in language raises a number of interesting questions for which the psychologist can provide empirical answers. How do people process gender-neutral uses of "he?" How do they interpret that pronoun when they hear or read it? And how does that processing affect other factors such as memory, stereotyping, or attitudes?

Moulton, Robinson, and Elias (1978) conducted an important first empirical study on sex bias in language use. College students were asked to make up a story about a fictional character who fit the following theme: "In a large coeducational institution the average student will feel isolated in ___ introductory courses." One third of the students received the pronoun "his" in the blank, one third received "his or her," and one third received "their." (Some students instead received a sentence concerning personal appearance, but the coeducational-institution cue is most relevant to the present study because it is explicitly gender neutral.) There was a strong tendency for male subjects to write stories about male characters and for female subjects to write about female characters. But strikingly, over all conditions, when the pronoun "his" was used, 35% of the stories were about females, compared with 46% for "their" and 56% female stories for "his or her." Thus, this study demonstrated that, although "his" may be gender-neutral in a grammatical sense, it is not gender neutral in a psychological sense. Even when the rest of the sentence explicitly provides a gender-neutral context, subjects more often think of a male when the pronoun is "his." . . .

In theoretical accounts and empirical investigations of gender-role development, the roles of imitation and reinforcements (Bandura & Walters, 1963; Mischel, 1966) and level of cognitive development (Kohlberg, 1966) have received great attention. In contrast, the role of language in gender-role development has been virtually ignored. The foregoing studies of adults raise some important questions for the developmental psychologist. How do children process sexist language, specifically gender-neutral "he?" Does their processing change with age, and does it differ from adults' processing? Is language a contributor to gender-role development, and can it be integrated into theories of gender-role development? . . .

A more complete statement of the cognitive approach is Bem's Gender Schema Theory (1981; see also Martin & Halverson, 1981). Bem argued that children learn a gender schema, a set of associations linked with maleness and femaleness in our society. This schema in turn organizes perception and affects the processing of information. Sex typing occurs because the self-concept becomes assimilated to the gender schema. Her studies with college students provided evidence consistent with the processing of information according to a gender schema, based on measures of clustering in free-recall and reaction times. Although she provided no data for children, she cited two studies, the results of which are consistent with the existence of gender-schematic processing in children as early as 6 years of age (Kail & Levine, 1976; Liben & Signorella, 1980). Martin and Halverson (1983) have also demonstrated, with 5- and 6-year-olds, that children distort information in sex-inconsistent pictures to make them sex consistent, a result that is congruent with the Gender Schema Theory. According to Bem, there are numerous inputs into the formation of the gender schema, and one of these is language, although she did not pursue this point empirically.

Two lines of thought, then—concern over sexist language as a social issue and a concern for a theoretical understanding of inputs into gender-role development—combine to raise a number of questions. How do children, compared with adults, process sexist language, specifically gender-neutral "he?" What is the effect on children of the use of gender-neutral "he"—does it contribute to the sex-typing process? Does it contribute to stereotyping, for example, stereotyping of occupations? Does it affect the formation of the gender schema? If so, what specific aspects of the gender schema might be affected—stereotyping of occupations, or perhaps more diffuse aspects, such as the relative status attached to the male and female roles, or the relative status of the self as a male or female?

The purpose of Experiment 1 was to replicate the Moulton et al. study with college students, and to extend it to first, third, and fifth graders, to assess age differences in responses to gender-neutral "he." Several other tasks were included in order to gain a more complete understanding of the nature of the responses. A fill-in task was used, and subjects were questioned for their understanding of the grammatical rule underlying the use of gender-neutral "he."

EXPERIMENT 1

Method

Subjects A total of 310 subjects participated: 60 first graders (23 boys, 37 girls, 5–8* to 7–8, M = 6–7), 67 third graders (34 boys, 33 girls, 7–8 to 10–2, M = 8–11), 59 fifth graders (26 boys, 33 girls, 9–8 to 12–0, M = 10–10), and 124 college students (57 men, 67 women, 17–11 to 21–9, M = 19–3). College students participated in order to fulfill the requirements for introductory psychology. The parents of all elementary subjects had returned signed consent forms for their children to participate. The elementary school children were drawn from three elementary schools, two middle-class, the other working-class to lower class.

Procedure All elementary school children were interviewed individually, half by a male interviewer, half by a female.

STORIES. After a brief warm up, the interviewer said "I'm going to tell you a little bit about a kid, and then I want you to make up a story about that child and tell it to me, and I'll write it down. When a kid goes to school, ___

*[Age 5–8 means 5 years, 8 months.—Ed.]

often feels excited on the first day." One third of the subjects received "he" for the blank, one third "they" and one third "he or she." The cue sentence was designed as an age-appropriate parallel to the neutral sentence used by Moulton et al. The interviewers recorded the basic content of the story, including the character's name. Later in the interview (at the end of the correct-sentences task), subjects were explicitly asked "Is (name of their character) a boy or a girl? Why did you make up your story about a ___?"

FILL-IN SENTENCES.   Next, children were questioned in several ways to determine their understanding of gender-neutral masculine pronoun use. First they were asked to complete a fill-in-the-blank task. In each case, the interviewer read the following sentences (or allowed the child to read it if he or she wanted to and was able):

1. If a kid likes candy, ___ might eat too much.
2. Most parents want ___ kids to get good grades.
3. When a kid plays football, ___ likes to play with friends.
4. When a kid learns to read, ___ can do more at school.

CORRECT SENTENCES.   Children were then asked to correct sentences with pronouns. They were told, "Now I'm going to read you some sentences and I want you to tell me if they're right or wrong, and if they're wrong, what's wrong with them. For example, if I say 'he goed to the store,' would that be right or wrong? Why?"

5. When a baby starts to walk ___ often falls down. Right or wrong? Why?
6. Usually a kid wants to be just like ___ own parents. Right or wrong? Why?
7. The average kid learns to read before ___ can write. Right or wrong? Why?
8. The average kid likes to play football with ___ friends. Right or wrong? Why?

Each child randomly received one of the following four pronouns replacing the blank: his (or he), they (or their), he or she (or his or her), or her (she).

RULE KNOWLEDGE.   Subjects were asked "When you use 'he' in a sentence, does it always mean it's a boy? For example, when I say 'When a kid goes to school, he often feels excited on the first day,' does that mean the kid is a boy?" If the child answered no, then he or she was asked what it did mean.

COLLEGE STUDENTS.   College students were tested in groups using a printed form. The form said:

Your task is to make up a story creating a fictional character who fits the following theme. Please do not write about yourself.

In a large coeducational institution the average student will feel isolated in ___ introductory courses.

One third received "his" for the blank, one third "his or her," and one third "their."

When subjects had completed the task, they were told to turn the papers over and answer the following questions briefly:

When a person uses "he" or "his" in a sentence, does it always mean it's a male? For example, if I say "In a large coeducational institution the average student will feel isolated in his introductory courses," does that mean that the student is a male? If your answer is no, then what does the "he" or "his" mean?

Results

Sex of Character in Story   The results, tabulated as percentage of stories written about female characters, are shown in Figure 1. The data were analyzed using a four-way chi-square* (Sex of Subject × Sex of Character in Story × Pronoun × Grade). Following the recommendation of Everitt (1977) the first test carried out was for the mutual independence of all four variables (or equivalently, whether sex of subject, pronoun, and grade showed a three-way interaction in affecting the dependent variable, sex of character). The results were highly significant, $x^2(40, N = 310) = 95.36$, $p < .001$ [N = number of subjects; p = probability that results were not due to random chance]. Once this test was significant, other specific hypotheses of interest could be tested (Everitt, 1977). In particular, the main effect [that is, examining one variable at a time,] for sex of subject was significant, $x^2(1, N = 310) = 35.54$, $p < .001$, with males overall telling 8% of their stories about females and females telling 38% female stories. The main effect for pronoun was also significant, $x^2(2, N = 310) = 28.81$, $p < .001$. When the pronoun was "he" or "his," overall 12% of the stories were about females; when it was "they" or "their," 18% were female, and when the pronoun was "his" or "her" ("he" or "she"), 42% of the stories were about females. The main effect of grade level was not significant, $x^2(3, N = 310) = 5.34$, although it must be remembered that grade level interacted significantly with sex of subject and pronoun as noted above. The nature of this interaction can be seen in Figure 1. Note that not a single first-grade boy told a story about a female. Third-grade boys produced no female stories when the pronoun was "he" or "they," but nearly 30% of their stories were about females in response to "his" or "her."

Correct Sentences   Overall, children (the correct-sentences task was not given to college students) judged most sentences to be correct (76%). Sentences with "he" inserted were judged wrong 19% of the time, whereas sentences with "she" were judged wrong 28% of the time. The children's judgments interacted with the sex typing of the sentence. For example, in the sentence about football,

---

*[Chi-square is a statistical test.—Ed.]

FIGURE 1 *Percentage of Stories About Female Characters Written Under the "His," "Their," and "His or Her" Pronoun Conditions, for Male and Female Subjects at the Three Grade Levels*

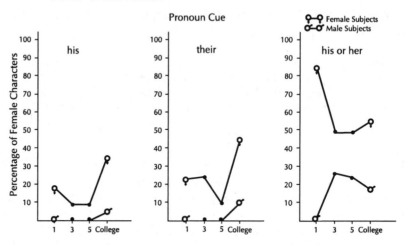

"he" was judged wrong 6% of the time, but "she" was judged wrong 39% of the time. This effect in turn showed age trends. "She" in the football sentence was judged wrong by 18% of the first graders and by 67% of the fifth graders. . . .

Fill-In Sentences . . . At all grade levels, the great majority of children supplied "he" or "his" in the sentences, with the exception of Sentence 2, in which "their" was correct, and was correctly supplied. In the remaining three singular sentences, the sex typing of the sentence was varied, "candy" being gender-neutral, "football" masculine, and "read" feminine. In fact, "he" was supplied so uniformly and frequently that the sex typing of the sentence had little impact. The most important sentence is the first, in which the cue is explicitly gender neutral (referring to candy), yet 72% of first graders, 88% of third graders, and 76% of fifth graders provided the pronoun "he" for the blank.

Rule Knowledge Knowledge of the rule that, in gender-neutral contexts, "he" refers to both males and females was tested by asking "When you use 'he' in a sentence, does it always mean it's a boy? For example, when I say 'when a kid goes to school, he often feels excited on the first day,' does that mean the kid is a boy?" If the subject responded "no" and indicated that it could be a boy or girl, the subject was scored as knowing the rule. Knowledge of the rule increased with age: 28% of first graders, 32% of third graders, 42% of fifth graders, and 84% of college students gave responses indicating they knew the rule. An additional 6% of college students gave "feminist" responses indicating that they knew the rule but disagreed with it—for example, "Yes, he refers to males, so one should use 'he or she' to be clear that everyone is included." . . .

Janet Shibley
Hyde

In general, the results from the college students in Experiment 1 replicate those of Moulton et al. (1978), although with even lower percentages of female stories (39% in Moulton et al.'s study vs. 30% in the present study). As Moulton et al. found, females are more likely to write stories about female characters than males are. The pronoun "his" yielded the lowest percentage of female stories, and "his or her" yielded the highest percentage. If "his" were gender neutral in a psychological sense, then approximately 50% of stories would be about females, yet college students created only 21% of their stories about females in response to "his." Thus the conclusion from the present data is the same as the conclusion of Moulton et al. (1978): "His" is not gender neutral in a psychological sense.

The data for the children are equally striking. The tendency for first, third, and fifth graders to create male characters when the pronoun is "he" is even stronger than it is for college students. Only 7% of elementary school children's stories were about females when the pronoun was "he." . . .

The strong tendency for children to tell stories about male characters in response to the "he" cue becomes more understandable when one looks at the data on the children's knowledge of the grammatical rule. Few know the rule and the majority apparently believe that "he" always means the person is a male.

The data from the fill-in task indicate that elementary school children, and particularly third and fifth graders, have already learned to supply "he" in a singular, gender-neutral context, although the correct-sentences task indicates that they cannot articulate why they do so. The results of the fill-in task are quite similar to those of Martyna (1978) with college students completing sentences. . . .

Therefore, it seems reasonable to conclude that (a) the majority of elementary school children have learned to supply "he" in gender-neutral contexts, and (b) the majority of elementary school children do not know the rule that "he" in gender-neutral contents refers to both males and females, and have a strong tendency to think of males in creating stories from "he" cues. The chain of concepts for them, then, is that (a) the typical person is a "he"; and (b) "he" refers only to males. Logically then, might they not conclude (c) the typical person is a male?

We know that by first grade, girls have less self-confidence and lower expectations for success than do boys (Block, 1976; Crandall, 1969, 1978). A speculation as to one of the causes of that phenomenon arises from the present studies, namely that language may be a contributor. That is, if first graders routinely use "he" to refer to everyone without knowing the grammatical rule behind the use, might they not begin to attach greater status and normativeness to the male, and correspondingly devalue the female? If Bem (1981) is correct that self-concept is assimilated to the gender schema, could low self-confidence in females be related to aspects of the gender schema that have been shaped by sexist language? These are important questions deserving research. . . .

In summary, it is clear that the tendency for subjects to think of males when they hear "he" in a gender-neutral context (story-telling data) is present from first grade through the college years. . . . The contributions of language to sex role development are deserving of considerably more attention, both theoretical and empirically. We must find out how children think about sexist language and other gender-related features of language, and how these features influence the developing gender schema.

REFERENCES

Bandura, A., & Walters, R. H. (1963). *Social learning and personality development.* New York: Holt, Rinehart & Winston.

Bem, S. L. (1981). Gender schema theory: A cognitive account of sex typing. *Psychological Review, 88.* 354–364.

Block, J. H. (1976). Issues, problems, and pitfalls in assessing sex differences: A critical review of *The Psychology of Sex Differences. Merrill-Palmer Quarterly, 22,* 283–308.

Crandall, V. C. (1969). Sex differences in expectancy of intellectual and academic reinforcement. In C. P. Smith (Ed.), *Achievement related motives in children.* New York: Russell Sage.

Crandall, V. C. (1978, August). *Expecting sex differences and sex differences in expectancies: A developmental analysis.* Paper presented at the meeting of the American Psychological Association, Toronto.

Everitt, B. S. (1977). *The analysis of contingency tables.* London: Chapman and Hall.

Kail, R. V., & Levine, L. E. (1976). Encoding processes and sex-role preferences. *Journal of Experimental Child Psychology, 21,* 256–263.

Kohlberg, L. (1966). A cognitive-developmental analysis of children's sex-role concepts and attitudes. In E. E. Maccoby (Ed.), *The development of sex differences* (pp. 82–172). Stanford, CA: Stanford University Press.

Liben, L. S., & Signorella, M. L. (1980). Gender-related schemata and constructive memory in children. *Child Development, 51,* 11–18.

Martin, C. L., & Halverson, C. F. (1981). A schematic processing model of sex-typing and stereotyping in children. *Child Development, 52,* 1119–1134.

Martin, C. L., & Halverson, C. F. (1983). The effects of sex-typing schemas on young children's memory. *Child Development, 54,* 563–574.

Martyna, W. (1978, Winter). What does "he" mean? Use of the generic masculine. *Journal of Communication, 28,* 131–138.

Martyna, W. (1980). Beyond the "he/man" approach: The case for nonsexist language. *Signs, 5,* 482–493.

Mischel, W. (1966). A social-learning view of sex differences in behavior. In E. E. Maccoby (Ed.), *The development of sex differences.* Stanford, CA: Stanford University Press.

Moulton, J., Robinson, G. M., & Elias, C. (1978). Psychology in action: Sex bias in language use: "Neutral" pronouns that aren't. *American Psychologist, 33,* 1032–1036.

3.5 ELEANOR E. MACCOBY

Gender and Relationships: A Developmental Account

Psychologists have shown increasing interest in gender differences during the past two decades. Much of the research that has been conducted has focused on individual differences, such as cognitive abilities, mathematical problem-solving skills, emotional expression, and verbal skills. Leading developmental psychologist Eleanor E. Maccoby has argued that focusing on individual differences obscures important dimensions of gender differences in social relationships.

Maccoby (b. 1917) earned her Ph.D. in experimental psychology from the University of Michigan in 1950. She worked in the Laboratory of Human Development at Harvard University until 1958 and then moved to Stanford University, where she is currently a professor emeritus. Among her many publications is the classic book *The Psychology of Sex Differences* (Stanford University Press, 1974), coauthored by Carol Jacklin.

This selection is from "Gender and Relationships: A Developmental Account," which was published in *American Psychologist* in 1990. In it, Maccoby argues that behavioral sex differences are minimal when children are tested individually but that they appear in social situations. One important finding is that children prefer same-sex play partners and often segregate themselves in social settings. Note how the distinctive interactive styles that develop in same-sex groups are carried over into mixed-sex group interactions. How can a better understanding of these gender differences help in everyday social interactions?

Key Concept: gender and social relationships

*H*istorically, the way we psychologists think about the psychology of gender has grown out of our thinking about individual differences. We are accustomed to assessing a wide variety of attributes and skills and giving scores to individuals based on their standing relative to other individuals in a sample population. On most psychological attributes, we see wide variation among individuals, and a major focus of research has been the effort to identify correlates or sources of this variation. Commonly, what we have done is to classify individuals by some antecedent variable, such as age or some aspect of their environment, to determine how much of the variance among individuals in their performance on a given task can be accounted for by this so-called *antecedent* or *independent* variable. Despite the fact that hermaphrodites exist, almost every individual is either clearly male or clearly female. What could be more natural for psychologists than to ask how much variance among individuals is accounted for by this beautifully binary factor?

Fifteen years ago, Carol Jacklin and I put out a book summarizing the work on sex differences that had come out of the individual differences perspective (Maccoby & Jacklin, 1974). We felt at that time that the yield was thin. That is, there were very few attributes on which the average values for the two sexes differed consistently. Furthermore, even when consistent differences were found, the amount of variance accounted for by sex was small, relative to the amount of variation within each sex. Our conclusions fitted in quite well with the feminist zeitgeist of the times, when most feminists were taking a minimalist position, urging that the two sexes were basically alike and that any differences were either illusions in the eye of the beholder or reversible outcomes of social shaping. Our conclusions were challenged as having both overstated the case for sex differences (Tieger, 1980) and for having understated it (Block, 1976).

In the last 15 years, work on sex differences has become more methodologically sophisticated, with greater use of meta analyses to reveal not only the direction of sex differences but quantitative estimates of their magnitude. In my judgment, the conclusions are still quite similar to those Jacklin and I arrived at in 1974: There are still some replicable sex differences, of moderate magnitude, in performance on tests of mathematical and spatial abilities, although sex differences in verbal abilities have faded. Other aspects of intellectual performance continue to show gender equality. When it comes to attributes in the personality-social domain, results are particularly sparse and inconsistent. Studies continue to find that men are more often agents of aggression than are women (Eagly, 1987; Huston, 1985; Maccoby & Jacklin, 1980). Eagly (1983, 1987) reported in addition that women are more easily influenced than men and that men are more altruistic in the sense that they are more likely to offer help to others. In general, however, personality traits measured as characteristics of individuals do not appear to differ systematically by sex (Huston, 1985). This no doubt reflects in part the fact that male and female persons really are much alike, and their lives are governed mainly by the attributes that all persons in a given culture have in common. Nevertheless, I believe that the null findings coming out of comparisons of male and female individuals on personality measures are partly illusory. That is, they are an artifact of our historical reliance on an individual differences perspective. Social behavior, as many have pointed out, is never a function of the individual alone. It is a function of the interaction between two or more persons. Individuals behave differently with different partners. There are certain important ways in which gender is implicated in social behavior—ways that may be obscured or missed altogether when behavior is summed across all categories of social partners.

An illustration is found in a study of social interaction between previously unacquainted pairs of young children (mean age, 33 months; Jacklin & Maccoby, 1978). In some pairs, the children had same-sex play partners; in others, the pair was made up of a boy and a girl. Observers recorded the social behavior of each child on a time-sampling basis. Each child received a score for total social behavior directed toward the partner. This score included both positive and negative behaviors (e .g., offering a toy and grabbing a toy; hugging and pushing; vocally greeting, inviting, protesting, or prohibiting). There was no overall sex difference in the amount of social behavior when this was evaluated without regard to sex of partner. But there was a powerful interaction between sex of the subject and that of the partner: Children of each sex had much higher levels of social behavior when playing with a same-sex partner than when playing with a child of the other sex. This result is consistent with the findings of Wasserman and Stern (1978) that when asked to approach another child, children as young as age three stopped farther away when the other child was of the opposite sex, indicating awareness of gender similarity or difference, and wariness toward the other sex.

The number of time intervals during which a child was simply standing passively watching the partner play with the toys was also scored. There was no overall sex difference in the frequency of this behavior, but the behavior of girls was greatly affected by the sex of the partner. With other girls, passive behavior seldom occurred; indeed, in girl-girl pairs it occurred less often than it did in boy-boy pairs. However when paired with boys, girls frequently stood on the sidelines and let the boys monopolize the toys. Clearly, the little girls in this study were not more passive than the little boys in any overall, trait-like sense. Passivity in these girls could be understood only in relation to the characteristics of their interactive partners. It was a characteristic of girls in cross-sex dyads. This conclusion may not seem especially novel because for many years we have known that social behavior is situationally specific. However, the point here is that interactive behavior is not just situationally specific, but that it depends on the gender category membership of the participants. We can account for a good deal more of the behavior if we know the gender mix of dyads, and this probably holds true for larger groups as well.

An implication of our results was that if children at this early age found same-sex play partners more compatible, they ought to prefer same-sex partners when they entered group settings that included children of both sexes. There were already many indications in the literature that children do have same-sex playmate preferences, but there clearly was a need for more systematic attention to the degree of sex segregation that prevails in naturally occurring children's groups at different ages. As part of a longitudinal study of children from birth to age six, Jacklin and I did time-sampled behavioral observation of approximately 100 children on their preschool playgrounds, and again two years later when the children were playing during school recess periods (Maccoby & Jacklin, 1987). Same-sex playmate preference was clearly apparent in preschool when the children were approximately 4½. At this age, the children were spending nearly 3 times as much time with same-sex play partners as with children of the other sex. By age 6½, the preference had grown much stronger. At this time, the children were spending 11 times as much time with same-sex as with opposite-sex partners.

Elsewhere we have reviewed the literature on playmate choices (Maccoby, 1988; Maccoby & Jacklin, 1987), and here I will simply summarize what I believe the existing body of research shows:

1. Gender segregation is a widespread phenomenon. It is found in all the cultural settings in which children are in social groups large enough to permit choice.
2. The sex difference in the gender of preferred playmates is large in absolute magnitude, compared to sex differences found when children are observed or tested in nonsocial situations.
3. In a few instances, attempts have been made to break down children's preferences for interacting with other same-sex children. It has been found that the preferences are difficult to change.
4. Children choose same-sex playmates spontaneously in situations in which they are not under pressure from adults to do so. In modern co-educational schools, segregation is more marked in situations that have not been structured by adults than in those that have (e.g., Eisenhart & Holland, 1983). Segregation is situationally specific, and the two sexes can interact comfortably under certain conditions, for example, in an absorbing joint task, when structures and roles are set up by adults, or in nonpublic settings (Thorne, 1986).
5. Gender segregation is not closely linked to involvement in sex-typed activities. Preschool children spend a great deal of their time engaged in activities that are gender neutral, and segregation prevails in these activities as well as when they are playing with dolls or trucks.
6. Tendencies to prefer same-sex playmates can be seen among three-year-olds and at even earlier ages under some conditions. But the preferences increase in strength between preschool and school and are maintained at a high level between the ages of 6 and at least age 11.
7. The research base is thin, but so far it appears that a child's tendency to prefer same-sex playmates has little to do with that child's standing on measures of individual differences. In particular, it appears to be unrelated to measures of masculinity or femininity and also to measures of gender schematicity (Powlishta, 1989).

Why do we see such pronounced attraction to same-sex peers and avoidance of other-sex peers in childhood? [E]vidence point[s] to two factors that seem to be important in the preschool years (Maccoby, 1988). The first is the rough-and-tumble play style characteristic of boys and their orientation toward issues of competition and dominance. These aspects of male–male interaction appear to be somewhat aversive to most girls. At least, girls are made wary by male play styles. The second factor of importance is that girls find it difficult to influence boys. Some important work by Serbin and colleagues (Serbin, Sprafkin, Elman, & Doyle, 1984) indicates that between the ages of 3½ and 5½, children greatly increase the frequency of their attempts to influence their play partners. This indicates that children are learning to integrate their activities with those of others so as to be able to carry out coordinated activities. Serbin and colleagues found that the increase in influence attempts by girls was almost entirely an increase in making polite suggestions to others, whereas among boys the increase took the form of more use of direct demands. Furthermore, during this formative two-year period just before school entry, boys were becoming less and less responsive to polite suggestions, so that the style being progressively adopted by girls was progressively less effective with boys. Girls' influence style was effective with each other and was well adapted to interaction with teachers and other adults.

Eleanor E. Maccoby

These asymmetries in influence patterns were presaged in our study with 33-month-old children: We found then that boys were unresponsive to the vocal prohibitions of female partners (in that they did not withdraw), although they would respond when a vocal prohibition was issued by a male partner. Girls were responsive to one another and to a male partner's prohibitions. Fagot (1985) also reported that boys are "reinforced" by the reactions of male peers—in the sense that they modify their behavior following a male peer's reaction—but that their behavior appears not to be affected by a female's response.

My hypothesis is that girls find it aversive to try to interact with someone who is unresponsive and that they begin to avoid such partners. Students of power and bargaining have long been aware of the importance of reciprocity in human relations. Pruitt (1976) said, "Influence and power are omnipresent in human affairs. Indeed, groups cannot possibly function unless their members can influence one another" (p. 343). From this standpoint, it becomes clear why boys and girls have difficulty forming groups that include children of both sexes.

Why do little boys not accept influence from little girls? Psychologists almost automatically look to the nuclear family for the origins of behavior patterns seen in young children. It is plausible that boys may have been more reinforced for power assertive behavior by their parents, and girls more for politeness, although the evidence for such differential socialization pressure has proved difficult to come by. However, it is less easy to imagine how or why parents should reinforce boys for being unresponsive to *girls*. Perhaps it is a matter of observational learning: Children may have observed that between their two parents, their fathers are more influential than their mothers. I am skeptical about such an explanation. In the first place, mothers exercise a good deal of managerial authority within the households in which children live, and it is common for fathers to defer to their judgment in matters concerning the children. Or, parents form a coalition, and in the eyes of the children they become a joint authority, so that it makes little difference to them whether it is a mother or a father who is wielding authority at any given time. Furthermore, the asymmetry in children's cross-sex influence with their peers appears to have its origins at quite an early age—earlier, I would suggest, than children have a very clear idea about the connection between their own sex and that of the same-sex parent. In other words, it seems quite unlikely that little boys ignore girls' influence attempts because little girls remind them of their mothers. I think we simply do not know why girls' influence styles are ineffective with boys, but the fact that they are has important implications for a variety of social behaviors, not just for segregation.

Mere are some examples from recent studies. Powlishta (1987) observed preschool-aged boy–girl pairs competing for a scarce resource. The children were brought to a playroom in the nursery school and were given an opportunity to watch cartoons through a movie-viewer that could only be accessed by one child at a time. Powlishta found that when the two children were alone together in the playroom, the boys got more than their share of access to the movie-viewer. When there was an adult present, however, this was no longer the case. The adult's presence appeared to inhibit the boys' more power-assertive techniques and resulted in girls having at least equal access.

This study points to a reason why girls may not only avoid playing with boys but may also stay nearer to a teacher or other adult. Following up on this possibility, Greeno (1989) brought four-child groups of kindergarten and first-grade children into a large playroom equipped with attractive toys. Some of the quartets were all-boy groups, some all-girl groups, and some were made up of two boys and two girls. A female adult sat at one end of the room, and halfway through the play session, moved to a seat at the other end of the room. The question posed for this study was: Would girls move closer to the teacher when boys were present than when they were not? Would the sex composition of a play group make any difference to the locations taken up by the boys? The results were that in all-girl groups, girls actually took up locations *farther* from the adult than did boys in all-boy groups. When two boys were present, however, the two girls were significantly closer to the adult than were the boys, who tended to remain at intermediate distances. When the adult changed position halfway through the session, boys' locations did not change, and this was true whether there were girls present or not. Girls in all-girl groups tended to move in the opposite direction when the adult moved, maintaining distance between themselves and the adult; when boys were present, however, the girls tended to move *with* the adult, staying relatively close. It is worth noting, incidentally, that in all the mixed-sex groups except one, segregation was extreme; both boys and girls behaved as though there was only one playmate available to them, rather than three.

There are some fairly far-reaching implications of this study. Previous observational studies in preschools had indicated that girls are often found in locations closer to the teacher than are boys. These studies have been done in mixed-sex nursery school groups. Girls' proximity seeking toward adults has often been interpreted as a reflection of some general affiliative trait in girls and perhaps as a reflection of some aspect of early socialization that has bound them more closely to caregivers. We see in the Greeno study that proximity seeking toward adults was *not* a general trait in girls. It was a function of the gender composition of the group of other children present as potential interaction partners. The behavior of girls implied that they found the presence of boys to be less aversive when an adult was nearby. It was as though they realized that the rough, power-assertive behavior of boys was likely to be moderated in the presence of adults, and indeed, there is evidence that they were right.

We have been exploring some aspects of girls' avoidance of interaction with boys. Less is known about why boys avoid interaction with girls, but the fact is that they do. In fact, their cross-sex avoidance appears to be even stronger. Thus, during middle childhood both boys and girls spend considerable portions of their social play time in groups of their own sex. This might not matter much for future relationships were it not for the fact that fairly distinctive styles of interaction develop in all-boy and all-girl groups. Thus, the segregated play groups constitute powerful socialization environments in which children acquire distinctive interaction skills that are adapted to same-sex partners. Sex-typed modes of interaction become consolidated, and I wish to argue that the distinctive patterns developed by the two sexes at this time have implications for the same-sex and cross-sex relationships that individuals form as they enter adolescence and adulthood.

It behooves us, then, to examine in somewhat more detail the nature of the interactive milieus that prevail in all-boy and all-girl groups. Elsewhere I have reviewed some of the findings of studies in which these two kinds of groups have been observed (Maccoby, 1988). Here I will briefly summarize what we know.

The two sexes engage in fairly different kinds of activities and games (Huston, 1985). Boys play in somewhat larger groups, on the average, and their play is rougher (Humphreys & Smith, 1987) and takes up more space. Boys more often play in the streets and other public places; girls more often congregate in private homes or yards. Girls tend to form close, intimate friendships with one or two other girls, and these friendships are marked by the sharing of confidences (Kraft & Vraa, 1975). Boys' friendships, on the other hand, are more oriented around mutual interests in activities (Erwin, 1985). The breakup of girls' friendships is usually attended by more intense emotional reactions than is the case for boys.

For our present purposes, the most interesting thing about all-boy and all-girl groups is the divergence in the interactive styles that develop in them. In male groups, there is more concern with issues of dominance. Several psycholinguists have recorded the verbal exchanges that occur in these groups, and Maltz and Borker (1983) summarized the findings of several studies as follows: Boys in their groups are more likely than girls in all-girl groups to interrupt one another; use commands, threats, or boasts of authority; refuse to comply with another child's demand; give information; heckle a speaker; tell jokes or suspenseful stories; top someone else's story; or call another child names. Girls in all-groups, on the other hand, are more likely than boys to express agreement with what another speaker has just said, pause to give another girl a chance to speak, or when starting a speaking turn, acknowledge a point previously made by another speaker. This account indicates that among boys, speech serves largely egoistic functions and is used to establish and protect an individual's turf. Among girls, conversation is a more socially binding process.

In the past five years, analysts of discourse have done additional work on the kinds of interactive processes that are seen among girls, as compared with those among boys. The summary offered by Maltz and Borker has been both supported and extended. Sachs (1987) reported that girls soften their directives to partners, apparently attempting to keep them involved in a process of planning a play sequence, while boys are more likely simply to tell their partners what to do. Leaper (1989) observed children aged five and seven and found that verbal exchanges among girls more often take the form of what he called "collaborative speech acts" that involve positive reciprocity, whereas among boys, speech acts are more controlling and include more negative reciprocity. Miller and colleagues (Miller, Danaher, & Forbes, 1986) found that there was more conflict in boys' groups, and given that conflict had occurred, girls were more likely to use "conflict mitigating strategies," whereas boys more often used threats and physical force. Sheldon (1989) reported that when girls talk, they seem to have a double agenda: to be "nice" and sustain social relationships, while at the same time working to achieve their own individual ends. For boys, the agenda is more often the single one of self-assertion. Sheldon (1989) has noted that in interactions among themselves, girls are *not* unassertive. Rather, girls do successfully pursue their own ends, but they do so while toning down coercion and dominance, trying to bring about agreement, and restoring or maintaining group functioning. It should be noted that boys' confrontational style does not necessarily impede effective group functioning, as evidenced by boys' ability to cooperate with teammates for sports. A second point is that although researchers' own gender has been found to influence to some degree the kinds of questions posed and the answers obtained, the summary provided here includes the work of both male and female researchers, and their findings are consistent with one another.

As children move into adolescence and adulthood, what happens to the interactive styles that they developed in their largely segregated childhood groups? A first point to note is that despite the powerful attraction to members of the opposite sex in adolescence, gender segregation by no means disappears. Young people continue to spend a good portion of their social time with same-sex partners. In adulthood, there is extensive gender segregation in workplaces (Reskin, 1984), and in some societies and some social-class or ethnic groups, leisure time also is largely spent with same-sex others even after marriage. The literature on the nature of the interactions that occur among same-sex partners in adolescence and adulthood is quite extensive and cannot be reviewed here. Suffice it to say in summary that there is now considerable evidence that the interactive patterns found in sex-homogeneous dyads or groups in adolescence and adulthood are very similar to those that prevailed in the gender-segregated groups of childhood (e.g., Aries, 1976: Carli, 1989: Cowan, Drinkard, & MacGavin, 1984; Savin-Williams, 1979).

How can we summarize what it is that boys and girls, or men and women, are doing in their respective groups that distinguishes these groups from one another? There have been a number of efforts to find the major dimensions that best describe variations in interactive styles. Falbo and Peplau (1980) have factor analyzed a battery of measures and have identified two dimensions: one called direct versus indirect, the other unilateral versus bilateral. Hauser et al. (1987) have distinguished what they called *enabling* interactive styles from *constricting* or *restrictive* ones, and I believe this distinction fits the styles of the two sexes especially well. A restrictive style is one that tends to derail the interaction—to inhibit the partner or cause the partner to withdraw, thus shortening the interaction or bringing it to an end. Examples are threatening a partner, directly contradicting or interrupting, topping the partner's story, boasting, or engaging in other forms of self-display. Enabling or facilitative styles are those, such as acknowledging another's comment or expressing agreement, that support whatever the partner is doing and tend to keep the interaction going. I want to suggest that it is because women and girls use more enabling styles that they are able to form more intimate and more integrated relationships. Also I think it likely that it is the male concern for turf and dominance—that is, with not showing weakness to other men and boys—that underlies their restrictive interaction style and their lack of self-disclosure.

*Eleanor E.
Maccoby*

REFERENCES

Aries, E. (1976). Interaction patterns and themes of male, female, and mixed groups. *Small Group Behavior, 7,* 7–18.

Block J. H. (1976). Debatable conclusions about sex differences. *Contemporary Psychology, 21,* 517–522.

Carli, L. L. (1989). Gender differences in interaction style and influence. *Journal of Personality and Social Psychology, 56,* 565–576.

Cowan, C., Drinkard, J., & MacGavin, L. (1984). The effects of target, age and gender on use of power strategies. *Journal of Personality and Social Psychology, 47,* 1391–1398.

Eagly, A. H. (1983). Gender and social influence. *American Psychologist, 38,* 971–981.

Eagly, A. H. (1987). *Sex differences in social behavior: A social role interpretation.* Hillsdale, NJ: Erlbaum.

Eisenhart, M. A., & Holland, D. C. (1983). Learning gender from peers: The role of peer group in the cultural transmission of gender. *Human Organization, 42,* 321–332.

Erwin. P. (1985). Similarity of attitudes and constructs in children's friendships. *Journal of Experimental Child Psychology, 40,* 470–485.

Fagot, B. I. (1985). Beyond the reinforcement principle: Another step toward understanding sex roles. *Developmental Psychology, 21,* 1097–1104.

Falbo, T., & Peplau, L. A. (1980). Power strategies in intimate relationships. *Journal of Personality and Social Psychology, 38,* 618–628.

Greeno, C. G. (1989). *Gender differences in children's proximity to adults.* Unpublished doctoral dissertation, Stanford University, Stanford, CA.

Hauser, S. T., Powers, S. I., Weiss-Perry, B., Follansbee, D. J., Rajapark, D., & Greene, W. M. (1987). *The constraining and enabling coding system manual.* Unpublished manuscript.

Humphreys, A. P., & Smith, P. K. (1987). Rough and tumble friendship and dominance in school children: Evidence for continuity and change with age in middle childhood. *Child Development, 58,* 201–212.

Huston, A. C. (1985). The development of sex-typing: Themes from recent research. *Developmental Review, 5,* 1–17.

Jacklin, C. N., & Maccoby, E. E. (1978). Social behavior at 33 months in same-sex and mixed-sex dyads. *Child Development, 49,* 557–569.

Kraft, L. W., & Vraa, C. W. (1975). Sex composition of groups and pattern of self-disclosure by high school females. *Psychological Reports, 37,* 733–734.

Leaper, C. (1989). *The sequencing of power and involvement in boys' and girls' talk.* Unpublished manuscript (under review), University of California, Santa Cruz.

Maccoby, E. E. (1988). Gender as a social category. *Developmental Psychology, 26,* 755–765.

Maccoby, E. E., & Jacklin, C. N. (1974). *The psychology of sex differences.* Stanford, CA: Stanford University Press.

Maccoby, E. E., & Jacklin, C. N. (1980). Sex differences in aggression: A rejoinder and reprise. *Child Development, 51,* 964–980.

Maccoby, E. E., & Jacklin, C. N. (1987). Gender segregation in childhood. In H. W. Reese (Ed.), *Advances in child development and behavior* (Vol. 20, pp. 239–288). New York: Academic Press.

Maltz, D. N., & Borker, R. A. (1983). A cultural approach to male-female miscommunication. In John A. Gumperz (Ed.), *Language and social identity* (pp. 195–216). New York: Cambridge University Press.

Miller, P., Danaher, D., & Forbes. D. (1986). Sex-related strategies for coping with interpersonal conflict in children aged five and seven. *Developmental Psychology, 22* 543–548.

Powlishta, K. K. (1987, April). *The social context of cross-sex interactions.* Paper presented at biennial meeting of the Society for Research in Child Development, Baltimore, MD.

Powlishta, K. K. (1989). *Salience of group membership: The case of gender.* Unpublished doctoral dissertation, Stanford University, Stanford,CA.

Pruitt, D. G. (1976). Power and bargaining in B. Seidenberg & A. Snadowsky (Eds.), Social psychology: An introduction (pp. 343–375). New York: Free Press.

Reskin, B. F. (Ed.). (1984). *Sex segregation in the workplace: Trends, explanations and remedies.* Washington, DC: National Academy Press.

Sachs, J. (1987). Preschool boys' and girls' language use in pretend play. In S. U. Phillips, S. Steele, & C. Tanz (Eds.), *Language, gender and sex in comparative perspective* (pp. 178–188). Cambridge, England: Cambridge University Press.

Savin-Williams, R. C. (1979). Dominance hierarchies in groups of early adolescents. *Child Development, 50,* 923–935.

Serbin, L. A., Sprafkin, C., Elman, M., & Doyle, A. (1984). The early development of sex differentiated patterns of social influence. *Canadian Journal of Social Science, 14,* 350–363.

Sheldon, A. (1989, April). *Conflict talk: Sociolinguistic challenges to self-assertion and how young girls meet them.* Paper presented at the biennial meeting of the Society for Research in Child Development, Kansas City.

Thorne, B. (1986). Girls and boys together, but mostly apart. In W. W. Hartup & L. Rubin (Eds.), *Relationships and development* (pp. 167–184). Hillsdale, NJ: Erlbaum.

Tieger, T. (1980). On the biological basis of sex differences in aggression. *Child Development, 51,* 943–963.

Wasserman, G. A., & Stern, D. N. (1978). An early manifestation of differential behavior toward children of the same and opposite sex. *Journal of Genetic Psychology, 133,* 129–137.

PART TWO

Perceptual Processes

On the Internet . . .

Sites appropriate to Part Two

A series of visual illusions created by Dr. David Landrigan, University of Massachusetts–Lowell.

> `http://aspen.uml.edu/~landrigad/ILLUSION.HTML`

The DreamLink Page, with theories and research techniques on dreaming.

> `http://www.iag.net/~hutchib/.dream/resources.html`

SleepNet provides resources and information on sleep disorders.

> `http://www.sleepnet.com/`

CHAPTER 4 Sensation and Perception

4.1 ELEANOR J. GIBSON AND RICHARD D. WALK

The "Visual Cliff"

Vision is an important sense for humans, and psychologists believe that knowledge of how visual perception develops in infants can help us understand its role in a child's adjustment. Psychologists have also shown interest in depth perception (the ability to perceive distance to an object) because it can shed light on the importance of heredity and environment in human development. Experimental psychologists Eleanor J. Gibson and Richard D. Walk developed the "visual cliff" described in this selection to study depth perception in human infants and young animals.

Gibson (b. 1910) earned her Ph.D. in experimental psychology from Yale University in 1938. She taught at Smith College until 1949 and then went to Cornell University, where she is currently a professor emeritus. Walk (b. 1920) received his Ph.D. in experimental psychology from Harvard University in 1951. He taught psychology at George Washington University until his retirement in 1991.

This selection is from "The 'Visual Cliff,' " which was published in *Scientific American* in 1960. The "visual cliff" that Gibson and Walk devised allowed them to test depth perception in infants as soon as they could crawl. As you read this selection, consider the degree to which heredity and experience might determine depth perception. Also, why do you think the experimenters tested animals in addition to humans?

Key Concept: the "visual cliff" and depth perception

*H*uman infants at the creeping and toddling stage are notoriously prone to falls from more or less high places. They must be kept from going over the brink by side panels on their cribs, gates on stairways and the vigilance of adults. As their muscular coordination matures they begin to avoid such accidents on their own. Common sense might suggest that the child learns to recognize falling-off places by experience—that is, by falling and hurting himself. But is experience really the teacher? Or is the ability to perceive and avoid a brink part of the child's original endowment?

Answers to these questions will throw light on the genesis of space perception in general. Height perception is a special case of distance perception: information in the light reaching the eye provides stimuli that can be utilized for the discrimination both of depth and or receding distance on the level. At what stage of development can an animal respond effectively to these stimuli? Does the onset of such response vary with animals of different species and habitats?

At Cornell University we have been investigating these problems by means of a simple experimental setup that we call a visual cliff. The cliff is a simulated one and hence makes it possible not only to control the optical and other stimuli (auditory and tactual, for instance) but also to protect the experimental subjects. It consists of a board laid across a large sheet of heavy glass which is supported a foot or more above the floor. On one side of the board a sheet of patterned material is placed flush against the undersurface of the glass, giving the glass the appearance as well as the substance of solidity. On the other side a sheet of the same material is laid upon the floor; this side of the board thus becomes the visual cliff.

We tested 36 infants ranging in age from six months to 14 months on the visual cliff. Each child was placed upon the center board, and his mother called him to her from the cliff side and the shallow side successively. All of the 27 infants who moved off the board crawled out on the shallow side at least once; only three of them crept off the brink onto the glass suspended above the pattern on the floor. Many of the infants crawled away from the mother when she called to them from the cliff side; others cried when she stood there, because they could not come to her without crossing an apparent chasm. The experiment thus demonstrated that most human infants can discriminate depth as soon as they can crawl.

The behavior of the children in this situation gave clear evidence of their dependence on vision. Often they would peer down through the glass on the deep side and then back away. Others would pat the glass with their hands, yet despite this tactual assurance of solidity would refuse to cross. It was equally clear that their perception of depth had matured more rapidly than had their locomotor abilities. Many supported themselves on the glass over the deep side as they maneuvered awkwardly on the board; some even backed out onto the glass as they started toward the mother on the shallow side. Were it not for the glass some of the children would have fallen off the board. Evidently infants should not be left close to a brink, no matter how well they may discriminate depth.

*Eleanor J.
Gibson and
Richard D. Walk*

This experiment does not prove that the human infant's perception and avoidance of the cliff are innate. Such an interpretation is supported, however, by the experiments with nonhuman infants. On the visual cliff we have observed the behavior of chicks, turtles, rats, lambs, kids, pigs, kittens and dogs. These animals showed various reactions, each of which proved to be characteristic of their species. In each case the reaction is plainly related to the role of vision in the survival of the species, and the varied patterns of behavior suggest something about the role of vision in evolution.

In the chick, for example, depth perception manifests itself with special rapidity. At an age of less than 24 hours the chick can be tested on the visual cliff. It never makes a "mistake" and always hops off the board on the shallow side. Without doubt this finding is related to the fact that the chick, unlike many other young birds, must scratch for itself a few hours after it is hatched.

Kids and lambs, like chicks, can be tested on the visual cliff as soon as they can stand. The response of these animals is equally predictable. No goat or lamb ever stepped onto the glass of the deep side, even at one day of age. When one of these animals was placed upon the glass on the deep side, it displayed characteristic stereotyped behavior. It would refuse to put its feet down and would back up into a posture of defense, its front legs rigid and its hind legs limp. In this state of immobility it could be pushed forward across the glass until its head and field of vision crossed the edge of the surrounding solid surface, whereupon it would relax and spring forward upon the surface.

At the Cornell Behavior Farm a group of experimenters has carried these experiments with kids and goats a step further. They fixed the patterned material to a sheet of plywood and were thus able to adjust the "depth" of the deep side. With the pattern held immediately beneath the glass, the animal would move about the glass freely. With the optical floor dropped more than a foot below the glass, the animal would immediately freeze into its defense posture. Despite repeated experience of the tactual solidity of the glass, the animals never learned to function without optical support. Their sense of security or danger continued to depend upon the visual cues that give them their perception of depth.

The rat, in contrast, does not depend predominantly upon visual cues. Its nocturnal habits lead it to seek food largely by smell, when moving about in the dark, it responds to tactual cues from the stiff whiskers (vibrissae) on its snout. Hooded rats tested on the visual cliff show little preference for the shallow side so long as they can feel the glass with their vibrissae. Placed upon the glass over the deep side, they move about normally. But when we raise the center board several inches, so that the glass is out of reach of their whiskers, they evince good visual depth-discrimination: 95 to 100 per cent of them descend on the shallow side.

Cats, like rats, are nocturnal animals, sensitive to tactual cues from their vibrissae. But the cat, as a predator, must rely more strongly on its sight. Kittens proved to have excellent depth-discrimination. At four weeks—about the earliest age that a kitten can move about with any facility—they invariably choose the shallow side of the cliff. On the glass over the deep side, they either freeze or circle aimlessly backward until they reach the center board.

The animals that showed the poorest performance in our series were the turtles. The late Robert M. Yerkes of Harvard University found in 1904 that aquatic turtles have somewhat poorer depth-discrimination than land turtles. On the visual cliff one might expect an aquatic turtle to respond to the reflections from the glass as it might to water and so prefer the deep side. They showed no such preference: 76 per cent of the aquatic turtles crawled off the board on the shallow side. The relatively large minority that choose the deep side suggests either that this turtle has poorer depth-discrimination than other animals, or that its natural habitat gives it less occasion to "fear" a fall.

All of these observations square with what is known about the life history and ecological niche of each of the animals tested. The survival of a species requires that its members develop discrimination of depth by the time they take up independent locomotion, whether at one day (the chick and the goat), three to four weeks (the rat and the cat) or six to 10 months (the human infant). That such a vital capacity does not depend on possibly fatal accidents of learning in the lives of individuals is consistent with evolutionary theory.

To make sure that no hidden bias was concealed in the design of the visual cliff we conducted a number of control experiments. In one of them we eliminated reflections from the glass by lighting the patterned surfaces from below the glass (to accomplish this we dropped the pattern below the glass on both sides, but more on one side than on the other). The animals—hooded rats—still consistently chose the shallow side. As a test of the role of the patterned surface we replaced it on either side of the centerboard with a homogeneous gray surface. Confronted with this choice, the rats showed no preference for either the shallow or the deep side. We also eliminated the optical difference between the two sides of the board by placing the patterned surface directly against the undersurface of the glass on each side. The rats then descended without preference to either side. When we lowered the pattern 10 inches below the glass on each side, they stayed on the board.

We set out next to determine which of two visual cues plays the decisive role in depth perception. To an eye above the center board the optical pattern on the two sides differs in at least two important respects. On the deep side distance decreases the size and spacing of the pattern elements projected on the retina. "Motion parallax," on the other hand, causes the pattern elements on the shallow side to move more rapidly across the field of vision when the animal moves its head, just as nearby objects seen from a moving car appear to pass by more quickly than distant ones. To eliminate the potential distance cue provided by pattern density we increased the size and spacing of the pattern elements on the deep side in proportion to its distance from the eye. With only the cue of motion parallax to guide them, adult rats still preferred the shallow side, though not so strongly as in the standard experiment. Infant rats chose the shallow side nearly 100 per cent of the time under both conditions, as did day-old chicks. Evidently both species can discriminate depth by differential motion alone, with no aid from texture density and probably little help from other cues. The perception of distance by binocular parallax, which doubtless plays an important part in human behavior, would not seem to have a significant role, for example, in the depth perception of chicks and rats.

Eleanor J. Gibson and Richard D. Walk

To eliminate the cue of motion parallax we placed the patterned material directly against the glass on either side of the board but used smaller and more densely spaced pattern-elements on the cliff side. Both young and adult hooded rats preferred the side with the larger pattern, which evidently "signified" a nearer surface. Day-old chicks, however, showed no preference for the larger pattern. It may be that learning plays some part in the preference exhibited by the rats, since the young rats were tested at a somewhat older age than the chicks. This supposition is supported by the results of our experiments with animals reared in the dark.

The effects of early experience and of such deprivations as dark-rearing represent important clues to the relative roles of maturation and learning in animal behavior. The first experiments along this line were performed by K. S. Lashley and James T. Russell at the University of Chicago in 1934. They tested light-reared and dark-reared rats on a "jumping stand" from which they induced animals to leap toward a platform placed at varying distances. Upon finding that both groups of animals jumped with a force closely correlated with distance, they concluded that depth perception in rats is innate. Other investigators have pointed out, however, that the dark-reared rats required a certain amount of "pretraining" in the light before they could be made to jump. Since the visual-cliff technique requires no pretraining, we employed it to test groups of light-reared and dark-reared hooded rats. At the age of 90 days both groups showed the same preference for the shallow side of the apparatus, confirming Lashley's and Russell's conclusion.

Recalling our findings in the young rat, we then took up the question of whether the dark-reared rats relied upon motion parallax or upon contrast in texture density to discriminate depth. When the animals were confronted with the visual cliff, cued only by motion parallax, they preferred the shallow side, as had the light-reared animals. When the choice was cued by pattern density, however, they departed from the pattern of the normal animals and showed no significant preference. The behavior of dark-reared rats thus resembles that of the day-old chicks, which also lack visual experience. It seems likely, therefore, that of the two cues only motion parallax is an innate cue for depth discrimination. Responses to differential pattern-density may be learned later.

One cannot automatically extrapolate these results to other species. But experiments with dark-reared kittens indicate that in these animals, too, depth perception matures independently of trial and error learning. In the kitten, however, light is necessary for normal visual maturation. Kittens reared in the dark to the age of 27 days at first crawled or fell off the center board equally often on the deep and shallow sides. Placed upon the glass over the deep side, they did not back in a circle like normal kittens but showed the same behavior that they had exhibited on the shallow side. Other investigators have observed equivalent behavior in dark-reared kittens; they bump into obstacles, lack normal eye movement and appear to "stare" straight ahead. These difficulties pass after a few days in the light. We accordingly tested the kittens every day. By the end of the week they were performing in every respect like normal kittens. They showed the same unanimous preference for the shallow side. Placed upon the glass over the deep side, they balked and circled backward to a visually secure surface. Repeated descents to the deep side, and placement upon the glass during their "blind" period, had not taught them that the deep side was "safe." Instead they avoided it more and more consistently. The initial blindness of dark-reared kittens makes them ideal subjects for studying the maturation of depth perception. With further study it should be possible to determine which cues they respond to first and what kinds of visual experience accelerate or retard the process of maturation.

From our first few years of work with the visual cliff we are ready to venture the rather broad conclusion that a seeing animal will be able to discriminate depth when its locomotion is adequate, even when locomotion begins at birth. But many experiments remain to be done, especially on the role of different cues and on the effects of different kinds of early visual experience.

4.2 KURT KOFFKA

Perception: An Introduction to the Gestalt-Theorie

Perception has always been a core topic in psychology. Today, scientists' understanding of perceptual principles is strongly influenced by the German Gestalt psychologists Max Wertheimer, Wolfgang Kohler, and Kurt Koffka.

Koffka (1886–1941) earned his Ph.D. from the University of Berlin in 1908 and then went to the University of Frankfurt, where he met the other Gestalt founders in 1910. In 1927 he became a professor at Smith College in Northampton, Massachusetts. Koffka was especially interested in studying the laws that govern our perceptions of the environment. Among his publications was the influential 1935 book *Principles of Gestalt Psychology.*

This selection is from Koffka's "Perception: An Introduction to the *Gestalt-Theorie*," which was published in *Psychological Bulletin* in 1922. The article was an attempt by the German psychologist to encourage American psychologists to support the Gestalt viewpoint. In it, Koffka discusses the relevance of sensation, association, and attention to psychology. Notice his reference to the American psychology of behaviorism. Although this paper was written 75 years ago, it touches on many of the same issues that are important to cognitive psychologists today. How important are association and attention to perception? Why do you think Koffka argued that Gestalt theory is more than a theory of perception? Do you agree?

Key Concept: Gestalt theory of perception

When it was suggested to me that I should write a general critical review of the work recently carried on in the field of perception, I saw an opportunity of introducing to American readers a movement in psychological thought which has developed in Germany during the last ten years. In 1912 Wertheimer stated for the first time the principles of a *Gestalt-Theorie* which has served as the starting point of a small number of German psychologists. Wherever this new method of thinking and working has come in touch with concrete problems, it has not only showed its efficiency, but has also brought to light startling and important facts, which, without the guidance of this theory, could not so easily have been discovered.

The *Gestalt-Theorie* is more than a theory of perception: it is even more than a mere psychological theory. Yet it originated in a study of perception, and the investigation of this topic has furnished the better part of the experimental work which has been done. Consequently, an introduction to this new theory can best be gained, perhaps, by a consideration of the facts of perception.

Since the new point of view has not yet won its way in Germany, it is but fair to state at the outset that the majority of German psychologists still stands aloof. However, much of the work done by other investigators contains results that find a place within the scope of our theory. Accordingly I shall refer to these results as well as to those secured by the *Gestalt*-psychologists proper; for I wish to demonstrate the comprehensiveness of our theory by showing how readily it embraces a number of facts hitherto but imperfectly explained. For the same reason I shall occasionally go farther back and refer to older investigations. On the other hand, I cannot hope to give a complete survey of the work on perception, and I shall therefore select my facts with reference to my primary purpose. . . .

When I speak of perception in the following essay, I do not mean a specific psychical function; all I wish to denote by this term is the realm of experiences which are not merely "imagined," "represented," or "thought of." Thus, I would call the desk at which I am now writing a perception, likewise the flavor of the tobacco I am now inhaling from my pipe, or the noise of the traffic in the street below my window. That is to say, I wish to use the term perception in a way that will exclude all theoretical prejudice; for it is my aim to propose a theory of these everyday perceptions which has been developed in Germany during the last ten years, and to contrast this theory with the traditional views of psychology. With this purpose in mind, I need a term that is quite neutral. In the current textbooks of psychology the term perception is used in a more specific sense, being opposed to sensation, as a more complex process. Here, indeed, is the clue to all the existing theories of perception which I shall consider in this introductory section, together with a glance at the fundamental principles of traditional psychology. Thus I find three concepts, involving three principles of psychological theory, in every current psychological system. In some systems these are the only fundamental concepts, while in others they are supplemented by additional conceptions; but for a long time the adequacy of these three has been beyond dispute. The three concepts to which I refer are those of *sensation, association,* and *attention*. I shall formulate the theoretical principles based upon these concepts and indicate their import in a radical manner so as to lay bare the methods of thinking which have been employed in their use. I am fully aware, of course, that most, if not all, the writers on this subject have tried to modify the assertions which I am about to make; but I maintain, nevertheless, that in working out concrete problems these principles have been employed in the manner in which I shall state them.

1. Sensation: All present or existential consciousness consists of a finite number of real, separable (though not necessarily separate) elements, each element

corresponding to a definite stimulus or to a special memory-residuum. Since a conscious unit is thus taken to be a bundle of such elements, Wertheimer, in a recent paper on the foundations of our new theory, has introduced the name "bundle-hypothesis" for this conception (7). These elements, or rather, some of them, are the sensations, and it is the first task of psychology to find out their number and their properties.

The elements, once aroused in the form of sensations, may also be experienced in the form of images. The images are also accepted as elements or atoms of psychological textures and are distinguishable from sensations by certain characteristic properties. They are, however, very largely a dependent class, since every image presupposes a corresponding sensation. Thus the concept of image, though not identical with that of sensation, rests upon the same principle, namely, the bundle-hypothesis.

In accordance with the method by which sensations have been investigated, it has been necessary to refer to the stimulus-side in defining the principle which underlies this concept. More explicitly, this relation of the sensation to its stimulus is expressed by a generally accepted rule, termed by Köhler the "constancy-hypothesis" (4); that the sensation is a direct and definite function of the stimulus. Given a certain stimulus and a normal sense-organ, we know what sensation the subject must have, or rather, we know its intensity and quality, while its "clearness" or its "degree of consciousness" is dependent upon still another factor, namely, *attention.*

What the stimulus is to the sensation, the residuum is to the image. Since each separate sensation-element leaves behind it a separate residuum, we have a vast number of these residua in our memory, each of which may be separately aroused, thus providing a certain independence of the original arrangement in which the sensations were experienced. This leads to the theory of the "association mixtures" (*associative Mischwirkungen*) propounded by G. E. Müller (5) and carried to the extreme in a paper by Henning (2).

2. Association: Even under our first heading we have met with the concept of memory. According to current teaching, the chief working principle of memory is association, although the purest of associationists recognize that it is not the only principle. It may suffice to point out in this connection that Rosa Heine (1) concludes from experiments performed in G. E. Müller's laboratory, that recognition is not based upon association; for she failed to detect in recognition any trace of that retroactive inhibition which is so powerful a factor in all associative learning. Likewise, Müller himself, relying upon experiments by L. Schlüter (6) acknowledges the possibility of reproduction by similarity. Yet, despite all this, association holds its position as the primary factor governing the coming and the going of our ideas, and the law of association is based upon the sensation-image concept. Our train of thought having been broken up into separate elements, the question is asked by what law does one element cause the appearance of another, and the answer is, association, the tie that forms between each element and all those other elements with which it has ever been in contiguity. As Wertheimer (7) again has pointed out, the core of this theory is this, that the necessary and sufficient cause for the formation and operation of an association is an original existential connection—the mere co-existence of a and b gives to each a tendency to reproduce the other. Meaning,

far from being regarded as one of the conditions of association, is explained by the working of associations, which in themselves are meaningless.

Another feature of this theory is its statistical nature. At every moment, endless associations are working, reinforcing and inhibiting each other. Since we can never have a complete survey of all the effective forces, it is impossible in any single case to make accurate prediction. As the special laws of association can be discovered by statistical methods only, so our predictions can be only statistical.

3. Attention: It is a recognized fact, that, clear and simple as association and sensation appear to be, there is a good deal of obscurity about the concept of attention. And yet, wherever there is an effect that cannot be explained by sensation or association, there attention appears upon the stage. In more complex systems attention is the makeshift, or the scapegoat, if you will, which always interferes with the working out of these other principles. If the expected sensation does not follow when its appropriate stimulus is applied, attention to other contents must have caused it to pass unnoticed, or if a sensation does not properly correspond to the stimulus applied, the attention must have been inadequate, thus leading us to make a false judgment. We meet with like instances over and over again which justify the following general statement, that attention must be added as a separate factor which not only influences the texture and the course of our conscious processes, but is also likely to be influenced by them.

Modern psychology has endeavored to give a physiological foundation to is psychological conceptions. Let us therefore glance at the physiological side of these three principles. The substratum of sensation (and image) is supposed to be the arousal of a separate and circumscribed area of the cortex, while the substratum for association is the neural connection established between such areas. Again attention holds an ambiguous position, for some see its essence as a facilitation and some as an inhibition of the nervous processes. Without going more into detail, let us examine the nature of this psycho-physical correspondence. Methodologically the physiological and the psychological aspects of these three principles are in perfect harmony; the cortex has been divided into areas, the immediate experience has been analyzed into elements, and connections are assumed to exist between brain areas as between the elements of consciousness. Furthermore, the nervous processes may be altered functionally and their corresponding psychological elements are subject to the functional factor of attention. Evidently the psychological and the physiological are interdependent, and are not sensation, association, and attention, factual? Do not cortical areas exist, and likewise nervous tracts, and the facilitation and inhibition of excitations? Certainly facts exist which have been interpreted in these ways, but we believe it can be proved that this interpretation is insufficient in the face of other and more comprehensive facts. Furthermore, we maintain that the insufficiency of the older theory cannot be remedied by supplementing the three principles, but that these must be sacrificed and replaced by other principles. . . .

Just a line at this point upon certain recent tendencies in American psychology. Behaviorism, excluding as it does all forms of consciousness from its realm, strictly speaking denies the use of these three principles altogether.

Therefore we do not find the terms attention and sensation in the behaviorist's writings, and even association has disappeared from the explanation in the sense of a tie that can be formed as an original act. And yet, as I have shown in a paper which discusses the fundamental differences between Wertheimer's theory and that of Meinong and Benussi (3), despite the restriction in his use of terms, the outfit of the Behaviorist is essentially the same as that of the traditional psychologist. He says "reaction" where the latter said "sensation," and in so doing includes the effector side of the process, but apart from this he builds his system in exactly the same manner, joining reflex arcs to reflex arcs entirely in accordance with the method of the "bundle-hypothesis."

REFERENCES

1. Heine, R. Über Wiederkennen und rückwirkende Hemmung. *Zeits. f. Psychol.*, 1914, **68**, 161–236.

2. Henning, H. Experimentelle Untersuchungen zur Denkpsychologie. I. Die assoziative Mischwirkung, das Vorstellen von noch nie Wahrgenommenem und deren Grenzen. *Zeits. f. Psychol.*, 1919, **81**, 1–96.

3. Koffka, K. The same. III. Zur Grundelgung der Wahrnehmungspsychologie. Eine Auseinandersetzung mit V. Benussi, von *K. Koffka*. *Zeits. f. Psychol.*, 1915, **73**, 11–90.

4. Köhler, W. Über unbemerkte Empfindungen und Urteilstäuschungen. *Zeits. f. Psychol.*, 1913, **66**, 51–80.

5. Müller, G. E. und Pilzecker, A. Experimentelle Beiträge zur Lehre vom Gedächtnis. *Erg. Bd.* **I**, *d. Zeits. f. Psychol.* Leipzig: Barth, 1900, pp. xiv+300.

6. Schlüter, L. Experimentelle Beiträge zur Prüfung der Auschauungs-und der Übersetzungsmethode bei der Einführung in einen fremdsprachlichen Wortschatz. *Zeits. f. Psychol.*, 1914, **68**, 1–114.

7. Wertheimer, M. Untersuchungen zur Lehre von der Gastalt. I. Prinzipielle Bemerkungen. *Psychol. Forsch.*, 1922, **1**, 47–58.

CHAPTER 5 Sleep and Consciousness

5.1 ERNEST R. HILGARD

Weapon Against Pain: Hypnosis Is No Mirage

Hypnosis has fascinated and frustrated psychologists for over 100 years. Many people have voiced skepticism over the purported uses of hypnosis, such as to reduce pain. One of the most complete scientific investigations of hypnosis has been conducted by Ernest R. Hilgard.

Hilgard (b. 1904) earned a degree in chemical engineering at Yale University and studied at Yale Divinity School before deciding on a career in psychology. He earned his Ph.D. in experimental psychology from Yale University in 1930. He taught at Yale University before taking a position at Stanford University, where he has remained since 1933. His many books include *Theories of Learning* (1948), *Introduction to Psychology* (1953), *Personality and Hypnosis* (1970), and *Psychology in America* (1987).

This selection is from "Weapon Against Pain: Hypnosis Is No Mirage," which was published in *Psychology Today* in 1974. It is a very readable account of some of the vast research that explores the properties of the altered state of consciousness known as hypnosis. As you read the selection, think about the possible uses of hypnosis in medical procedures, relaxation, and perhaps as a memory aid. Why do you think hypnosis has been widely criticized? What other applications for hypnosis can you think of?

Key Concept: hypnosis

*H*ypnosis works. Laboratory research to date allows us to say that with confidence, even as the clinical applications of hypnosis proliferate. From the pain-filled rooms of cancer patients to antismoking clinics, from dental surgeries to maternity wards, hypnosis is gaining ever wider acceptance as a weapon against pain. While there are many unanswered questions about how hypnosis works and whom it will work for; enough evidence is in to support it fully as a therapeutic tool.

Hypnosis has come a long way from the parlor magic of Franz Anton Mesmer and his theory of animal magnetism. But in part because of those lurid beginnings, and in part because of its association with charlatans, bad movies, and entertainers, hypnosis still is suspect in some quarters. Many psychologists argue that the hypnotic trance is a mirage. It would be unfortunate if this skeptical view were to gain such popularity that the benefits of hypnosis are denied to the numbers of those who could be helped. Consider, for example, the experience of women who give birth while in hypnotic trance. Obstetrician R. V. August delivered babies of 1,000 women from 1957 to 1960. Of the 850 women who gave birth under hypnosis, only 36 required chemical anesthesia in addition. And five of the women who relied solely on hypnoanesthesia delivered their babies by Caesarian section.

PHANTOM-LIMB PAIN   C. H. Harding reported successful treatment of migraine and vascular headaches with hypnotic suggestion. Of 90 patients he treated with four to seven sessions of hypnotic induction, 38 percent reported complete relief for periods of up to eight years. Thirty-two percent rated their relief as substantial. Only 11 of the 90 cases reported no relief from hypnotic treatment.

Hypnosis has also been used in the treatment of phantom-limb pain. About 57 percent of all amputees suffer from this peculiar affliction, which feels different from pain in the stump of the limb and is often extremely difficult to relieve. About 33 percent of these cases respond favorably to hypnotic suggestion. C. Cedercreutz and E. Uusitalo of Finland treated 37 cases of phantom-limb pain with hypnotic suggestion. Twenty patients lost all of their pain and another 10 improved so much that medication was no longer needed. Follow-up studies conducted from one to eight years after treatment revealed that eight patients were still totally pain-free and 10 others still showed some relief. The researchers concluded that, for phantom-limb pain, hypnosis is far better than other available treatments.

While hypnosis is used successfully in clinical settings, the skeptics argue that there is no true reduction in pain. Theodore Sarbin and his colleagues believe that a person adopts the role that is appropriate to his situation. When hypnotized, he plays the role of a hypnotized person, behaving as he believes a hypnotized person should. Similarly, Sarbin believes that reports by patients of pain relief indicate only a desire to please the therapist, to perform as he expects. The patient becomes so absorbed by the role, Sarbin believes, that in extreme cases it can lead to phenomena such as voodoo death.

HAND IMMOBILITY   Martin Orne, a psychologist at the University of Pennsylvania, found some truth in Sarbin's notion. He demonstrated hypnosis before two groups of students. Half of the students saw hypnotized subjects whose dominant hand was immobile; this fact was pointed out to the class as characteristic of the hypnotic state. The remaining students witnessed similar demonstrations except that the subject's hand did not become immobile. After the demonstration, members of each group were hypnotized; the hypnotist, however, did not know which demonstration a given student had witnessed. As expected, the students who had observed the model with hand immobility showed that characteristic while the other students did not.

These results are consistent with other studies that show the power of the experimental situation over the behavior of the subject. The efforts of the subject to please the experimenter, even when his demands are unreasonable, are so strong that Orne refers to the "demand characteristics" of the experimental situation. Critics of hypnosis feel that hypnotized subjects may simply be responding to the implied demands of the hypnotist. Response to demands does not lead Orne to reject hypnosis; his point is that the experimental evidence must be viewed critically. Nobody denies that hypnosis includes responses to suggestions, obvious or implicit.

One way to identify hypnosis as something unique would be to produce physiological evidence for the existence of the hypnotic state. It is difficult to prove whether or not a hypnotized person differs physiologically from one who is awake. Those who have been hypnotized report feeling quite different, and we know that at the deepest levels of hypnosis, a person may lose any further responsiveness to hypnotic suggestions. The EEG [electroencephalogram] patterns of hypnotized subjects are no different from those of their normal waking state, but they do differ from the patterns associated with sleep. We know that highly hypnotizable subjects produce more alpha waves in the normal waking state than do poor hypnotic subjects. In our laboratory we found a moderately strong correlation between the amount of alpha activity in a person's waking state and his susceptibility to hypnosis, but this correlation has to do with the potential for hypnotic response and not with the hypnotic state itself.

RIGHT AND LEFT LOOKERS

Other work suggests that a correlation exists between hypnotic suggestibility and hemispheric activity. When asked a question such as, "How many letters are in the word 'Washington'?" a person will typically look to the left or the right. About 75 percent of these eye movements will be to one side. Left-eye movements have been found to suggest that the brain's right hemisphere is dominant, while right-eye movements are associated with left-hemisphere dominance. Paul Bakan gave a test of hypnotic suggestibility to 46 undergraduate students and had them tested for eye movement. He found that left-lookers produced the highest hypnotic suggestibility scores, while the lowest scores came from right-lookers; his work, originally done in our laboratory, has been confirmed and extended here by Raquel and Ruben Gur.

Psychoactive drugs can also affect hypnotic suggestibility. Bernard Sjoberg found that LSD and mescaline increase suggestibility and that this effect lasts beyond the normal effects of the drug. We also know that hypnotic suggestibility is a regular function of age; it reaches a peak between eight and 11 years and then declines gradually. But none of the evidence concerning the physiological correlates of hypnosis proves conclusively that the hypnotic trance has distinctive physiological signs, such as the brain waves and rapid-eye movements associated with dreaming. A better question is whether or not hypnosis produces consequences that are real. We know, for example, that under hypnotic suggestion some people will do things they would otherwise not do. They will erase imaginary words from a blank blackboard, see and hear things that are not there, and *not* see and hear things that are there.

FREEZING WATER   To find out how real hypnotic effects are, much of the laboratory research has studied the hypnotic reduction of pain. It is possible to get objective measures of the degree of pain and to compare these with subjective reports of pain intensity. If people under hypnotic suggestion endure greater amounts of pain, and if they say they feel less pain than during the waking state, then hypnosis would seem to be genuine.

One technique for inducing pain in the laboratory is to immerse the volunteer's hand and forearm in freezing water. The subject rates the intensity of the pain he feels when awake, and after the hypnotic suggestion that his hand and arm are insensitive. We then compare the two ratings to determine if hypnotic suggestion reduces pain.

In one of our first experiments, we gave 54 volunteers a test of hypnotic suggestibility and then gave them the hypnotic suggestion that they would not feel pain. The subjects then rated the pain they felt during the ice-water test. Pain reduction was clearly related to hypnotic susceptibility. Of the highly hypnotizable subjects, 67 percent showed a 33 percent reduction in pain, while only 13 percent of the least hypnotizable subjects showed as much relief. At the same time, only seven percent of the highly suggestible volunteers showed 10 percent or less reduction in pain, while 56 percent of the subjects low in suggestibility showed this small amount of relief.

Our results were confirmed several years later by Michael Evans and Gordon Paul in another laboratory. They also found that ice-water pain could be reduced by hypnotic suggestion and that the amount of reduction increased with a person's susceptibility to hypnosis.

Evans and Paul conducted their experiment with college women. Each volunteer immersed her hand in the icy water for one minute. Then she rated the pain she had felt on a seven-point scale, ranging from pleasant to very painful. Later, each subject received one of four treatment procedures. One fourth of the volunteers were hypnotized and given the suggestion that they would not feel pain. Another group was hypnotized but not given the antipain suggestion. A third group was taught self-relaxation and given the suggestion that they would not feel pain. The last group learned self-relaxation but received no suggestion that their ability to feel pain would diminish. After she received one of the four sets of instructions, each woman again immersed her hand in the frigid water and rated the pain she felt. Evans and Paul compared this second rating with the first. Those who received the analgesic suggestion showed a greater reduction in pain than those who did not, but it made no difference whether the suggestion had been given under hypnosis or during the waking state, under self-relaxation.

Other studies of this sort have produced similar results, leading critics of hypnosis to decide that the results of suggested pain reduction are genuine, but that a prior induction of hypnosis is not necessary, and that therefore the concept of hypnosis is superfluous. However, these studies involve random selections of students, which make conclusions regarding the legitimacy of hypnosis of dubious value. . . .

CAREFUL FOCUS   Hypnotic induction seems to facilitate the use of imagination. During hypnosis, one woman pretended she was inside the *Venus de Milo* statue. Since she had no arms, she could feel no pain during the ice-water experiment. Another subject pretended he was somewhere else; since he was not in the experimental situation, he could not be hurt. Others imagine that they have been given an injection of an anesthetic; numbness spreads through their arms as the imaginary anesthetic dissipates.

It is not clear why imagination should be helpful in reducing pain. Hypnosis is often described as a state of heightened awareness in which attention is focused intensely on the suggestions of the hypnotist. Perhaps hypnotized subjects are able to focus attention so carefully on some imagined stimulus, such as those the hypnotist suggests, that competing stimuli are physiologically inhibited. All of us have had the experience of becoming so engrossed in a book, a conversation or some other activity that we did not hear our name being called. It is not just that we deny hearing our name; we actually do not hear it. This may not be so different from the experience of the hypnotic subject.

There is overwhelming evidence that some people get relief from pain by hypnotic suggestion; they are not merely withholding reports of suffering to please the hypnotist. The hundreds of patients who have received relief from pain through hypnotic suggestion do not need convincing. And those who may be helped in the future should not be denied the benefits of hypnosis simply because we do not yet understand precisely what hypnosis is or why it works. For now, it is enough to know that it does.

5.2 SIGMUND FREUD

The Dream as a Wish-Fulfilment

If you sleep eight hours per night, you spend approximately two of those hours dreaming. People have always been fascinated with dreams, and many have proposed theories to explain the functions and meaning of dreams. The most popular and well known dream theory was proposed by Sigmund Freud in 1900. Freud believed that dreams were the road to the elusive unconscious mind. His theory of dreams as wish fulfillments, which is examined in this selection, has sparked a great deal of controversy over the years.

Freud (1856–1939), a neurologist, received his M.D. in 1881 from Vienna University. He spent most of his life in Vienna, Austria, practicing medicine and studying mental disorders through clinical observation. As the father of psychoanalysis, Freud significantly influenced many areas of psychology, including personality, development, and clinical psychology.

In Freud's book *The Interpretation of Dreams* (1900), he presents his theory of the meaning of dreams. This selection is from chapter 3, "The Dream as a Wish-Fulfilment," of that book, and it illustrates one of the main points of Freud's dream theory. This selection allows you to see how Freud conceptualized dream interpretation as well as psychoanalysis. As you read this selection, think about how you interpret your own dreams.

Key Concept: Freud's theory of dreaming

When, after passing through a narrow defile, one suddenly reaches a height beyond which the ways part and a rich prospect lies outspread in different directions, it is well to stop for a moment and consider whither one shall turn next. We are in somewhat the same position after we have mastered this first interpretation of a dream. We find ourselves standing in the light of a sudden discovery. The dream is not comparable to the irregular sounds of a musical instrument, which, instead of being played by the hand of a musician, is struck by some external force; the dream is not meaningless, not absurd, does not presuppose that one part of our store of ideas is dormant while another part begins to awake. It is a perfectly valid psychic phenomenon, actually a wish-fulfilment; it may be enrolled in the continuity of the intelligible psychic activities of the waking state; it is built up by a highly complicated intellectual activity. But at the very moment when we are about to rejoice in this discovery a host of problems besets us. If the dream, as this theory defines it, represents a fulfilled wish, what is the cause of the striking and unfamiliar manner in which this fulfilment is expressed? What transformation has occurred in our dream-thoughts before the manifest dream, as we remember it on waking, shapes itself out of them? How has this transformation taken place? Whence comes the material that is worked up into the dream? What causes many of the peculiarities which are to be observed in our dream-thoughts; for example, how is it that they are able to contradict one another? . . . Is the dream capable of teaching us something new concerning our internal psychic processes, and can its content correct opinions which we have held during the day? I suggest that for the present all these problems be laid aside, and that a single path be pursued. We have found that the dream represents a wish as fulfilled. Our next purpose should be to ascertain whether this is a general characteristic of dreams, or whether it is only the accidental content of [a] particular dream . . . ; for even if we conclude that every dream has a meaning and psychic value, we must nevertheless allow for the possibility that this meaning may not be the same in every dream. The first dream . . . [may be] the fulfilment of a wish; another may turn out to be the realization of an apprehension; a third may have a reflection as its content; a fourth may simply reproduce a reminiscence. Are there, then, dreams other than wish-dreams; or are there none but wish-dreams?

It is easy to show that the wish-fulfilment in dreams is often undisguised and easy to recognize, so that one may wonder why the language of dreams has not long since been understood. There is, for example, a dream which I can evoke as often as I please, experimentally, as it were. If, in the evening, I eat anchovies, olives, or other strongly salted foods, I am thirsty at night, and therefore I wake. The waking, however, is preceded by a dream, which has always the same content, namely, that I am drinking. I am drinking long draughts of water; it tastes as delicious as only a cool drink can taste when one's throat is parched; and then I wake, and find that I have an actual desire to drink. The cause of this dream is thirst, which I perceive when I wake. From this sensation arises the wish to drink, and the dream shows me this wish as fulfilled. It hereby serves a function, the nature of which I soon surmise. I sleep well, and am not accustomed to being waked by a bodily need. If I succeed in appeasing my thirst by means of the dream that I am drinking, I need not wake up in order to satisfy that thirst. It is thus a *dream of convenience*. The dream takes the place of action, as elsewhere in life. Unfortunately, the need of water to quench the thirst cannot be satisfied by a dream, as can my thirst for revenge upon [some adversary], but the intention is the same. Not long ago I had the same dream in a somewhat modified form. On this occasion I felt thirsty before going to bed, and emptied the glass of water which stood on the little chest beside my bed. Some hours later, during the night, my thirst returned, with the consequent discomfort. In order to obtain water, I should have had to get up and fetch the glass which stood on my wife's bed-table. I thus quite appropriately dreamt that my wife was giving me a drink from a vase; this vase was an Etruscan cinerary urn, which I had brought home from Italy, and had since given away. But the water in it tasted so salty (apparently on account of the ashes) that I was forced to wake. It may be observed how conveniently the dream is capable of arranging matters. Since the fulfilment of a wish is its only purpose, it may be perfectly egoistic. Love of comfort is really not compatible with consideration for others. The introduction of the cinerary urn is probably once again the fulfilment of a wish; I regret that I no longer possess this vase; it, like the glass of water at my wife's side, is inaccessible to me. The cinerary urn is appropriate also in connection with the sensation of an increasingly salty taste, which I know will compel me to wake.

Such convenience-dreams came very frequently to me in my youth. Accustomed as I had always been to working until late at night, early waking was always a matter of difficulty. I used then to dream that I was out of bed and standing at the washstand. After a while I could no longer shut out the knowledge that I was not yet up; but in the meantime I had continued to sleep. The same sort of lethargy-dream was dreamed by a young colleague of mine, who appears to share my propensity for sleep. With him it assumed a particularly amusing form. The landlady with whom he was lodging in the neighbourhood of the hospital had strict orders to wake him every morning at a given hour, but she found it by no means easy to carry out his orders. One morning sleep was especially sweet to him. The woman called into his room: "Herr Pepi, get up; you've got to go to the hospital." Whereupon the sleeper dreamt of a room in the hospital, of a bed in which he was lying, and of a chart pinned over his head, which read as follows: "Pepi M., medical student, 22 years of age." He told himself in the dream: "If I am already at the hospital, I don't have to go there," turned over, and slept on. He had thus frankly admitted to himself his motive for dreaming.

Here is yet another dream of which the stimulus was active during sleep: One of my women patients, who had been obliged to undergo an unsuccessful operation on the jaw, was instructed by her physicians to wear by day and night a cooling apparatus on the affected cheek; but she was in the habit of throwing it off as soon as she had fallen asleep. One day I was asked to reprove her from doing so; she had again thrown the apparatus on the floor. The patient defended herself as follows: "This time I really couldn't help it; it was the result of a dream which I had during the night. In the dream I was in a box at the opera, and was taking a lively interest in the performance. But Herr Karl Meyer was lying in the sanatorium and complaining pitifully on account of pains in his jaw. I said to myself, 'Since I haven't the pains, I don't need the apparatus either'; that's why I threw it away." The dream of this poor sufferer reminds me of an expression which comes to our lips when we are in a disagreeable situation: "Well, I can imagine more amusing things!" The dream presents these "more amusing things!" Herr Karl Meyer, to whom the dreamer attributed her pains, was the most casual acquaintance of whom she could think.

It is quite as simple a matter to discover the wish-fulfilment in several other dreams which I have collected from healthy persons. A friend who was acquainted with my theory of dreams, and had explained it to his wife, said to me one day: "My wife asked me to tell you that she dreamt yesterday that she was having her menses. You will know what that means." Of course I know: if the young wife dreams that she is having her menses, the menses have stopped. I can well imagine that she would have liked to enjoy her freedom a little longer, before the discomforts of maternity began. It was a clever way of giving notice of her first pregnancy. Another friend writes that his wife had dreamt not long ago that she noticed milk-stains on the front of her blouse. This also is an indication of pregnancy, but not of the first one; the young mother hoped she would have more nourishment for the second child than she had for the first.

A young woman who for weeks had been cut off from all society because she was nursing a child who was suffering from an infectious disease dreamt, after the child had recovered, of a company of people in which Alphonse Daudet, Paul Bourget, Marcel Prévost and others were present; they were all very pleasant to her and amused her enormously. In her dream these different authors had the features which their portraits give them. M. Prévost, with whose portrait she is not familiar, looked like the man who had disinfected the sickroom the day before, the first outsider to enter it for a long time. Obviously the dream is to be translated thus: "It is about time now for something more entertaining than this eternal nursing."

Perhaps this collection will suffice to prove that frequently, and under the most complex conditions, dreams may be noted which can be understood only as wish-fulfilments, and which present their content without concealment. In most cases these are short and simple dreams, and they stand in pleasant contrast to the confused and overloaded dream-compositions which have almost exclusively attracted the attention of the writers on the subject. But it will repay us if we give some time to the examination of these simple dreams. The simplest dreams of all are, I suppose, to be expected in the case of children whose psychic activities are certainly less complicated than those of adults. Child psychology, in my opinion, is destined to render the same services to the psychology of adults as a study of the structure or development of the lower animals renders to the investigation of the structure of the higher orders of animals. Hitherto but few deliberate efforts have been made to make use of the psychology of the child for such a purpose.

The dreams of little children are often simple fulfilments of wishes, and for this reason are, as compared with the dreams of adults, by no means interesting. They present no problem to be solved, but they are invaluable as affording proof that the dream, in its inmost essence, is the fulfilment of a wish. I have been able to collect several examples of such dreams from the material furnished by my own children.

For two dreams, one that of a daughter of mine, at that time eight and a half years of age, and the other that of a boy of five and a quarter, I am indebted to an excursion to Hallstatt, in the summer of 1896. I must first explain that we were living that summer on a hill near Aussee, from which, when the weather was fine, we enjoyed a splendid view of the Dachstein. With a telescope we could easily distinguish the Simony hut. The children often tried to see it through the telescope—I do not know with what success. Before the excursion I had told the children that Hallstatt lay at the foot of the Dachstein. They looked forward to the outing with the greatest delight. From Hallstatt we entered the valley of Eschern, which enchanted the children with its constantly changing scenery. One of them, however, the boy of five, gradually became discontented. As often as a mountain came into view, he would ask: "Is that the Dachstein?" whereupon I had to reply: "No, only a foot-hill." After this question had been repeated several times he fell quite silent, and did not wish to accompany us up the steps leading to the waterfall. I thought he was tired. But the next morning he came to me, perfectly happy, and said: "Last night I dreamt that we went to the Simony hut." I understood him now; he had expected, when I spoke of the Dachstein, that on our excursion to Hallstatt he would climb the mountain, and would see at close quarters the hut which had been so often mentioned when the telescope was used. When he learned that he was expected to content himself with foot-hills and a waterfall he was disappointed, and became discontented. But the dream compensated him for all this. I tried to learn some details of the dream; they were scanty. "You go up steps for six hours," as he had been told.

On this excursion the girl of eight and a half had likewise cherished wishes which had to be satisfied by a dream. We had taken with us to Hallstatt our neighbour's twelve-year-old boy; quite a polished little gentleman, who, it seemed to me, had already won the little woman's sympathies. Next morning she related the following dream: "Just think, I dreamt that Emil was one of the family, that he said 'papa' and 'mamma' to you, and slept at our house, in the big room, like one of the boys. Then mamma came into the room and threw a handful of big bars of chocolate, wrapped in blue and green paper, under our beds." The girl's brothers, who evidently had not inherited an understanding of dream-interpretation, declared . . . : "That dream is nonsense." The girl defended at least one part of the dream, and from the standpoint of the theory of the neuroses it is interesting to learn which part it was that she defended: "That Emil was one of the family was nonsense, but that part about the bars of chocolate wasn't." It was just this latter part that was obscure to me, until my wife furnished the explanation. On the way home from the railway-station the children had stopped in front of a slot-machine, and had wanted exactly such bars of chocolate, wrapped in paper with a metallic lustre, such as the machine, in their experience, provided. But the mother thought, and rightly so, that the day had brought them enough wish-fulfilments, and therefore left this wish to be satisfied in the dream. This little scene had escaped me. That portion of the dream which had been condemned by my daughter I understood without any difficulty. I myself had heard the well-behaved little guest enjoining the children, as they were walking ahead of us, to wait until 'papa' or 'mamma' had come up. For the little girl the dream turned this temporary relationship into a permanent adoption. Her affection could not as yet conceive of any other way of enjoying her friend's company permanently than the adoption pictured in her dream, which was suggested by her brothers. Why the bars of chocolate were thrown under the bed could not, of course, be explained without questioning the child.

From a friend I have learned of a dream very much like that of my little boy. It was dreamed by a little girl of eight. Her father, accompanied by several children, had started on a walk to Dornbach, with the intention of visiting the Rohrer hut, but had turned back, as it was growing late, promising the children to take them some other time. On the way back they passed a signpost which pointed to the Hameau. The children now asked him to take them to the Hameau, but once more, and for the same reason, they had to be content with the promise that they should go there some other day. Next morning the little girl went to her father and told him, with a satisfied air: "Papa, I dreamed last night that you were with us at the Rohrer hut, and on the Hameau." Thus, in the dream her impatience had anticipated the fulfilment of the promise made by her father.

Another dream, with which the picturesque beauty of the Aussee inspired my daughter, at that time three and a quarter years of age, is equally straightforward. The little girl had crossed the lake for the first time, and the trip has passed too quickly for her. She did not want to leave the boat at the landing, and cried bitterly. The next morning she told us: "Last night I was sailing on the lake." Let us hope that the duration of this dream-voyage was more satisfactory to her.

My eldest boy, at that time eight years of age, was already dreaming of the realization of his fancies. He had ridden in a chariot with Achilles, with Diomedes as charioteer. On the previous day he had shown a lively interest in a book on the myths of Greece which had been given to his elder sister.

If it can be admitted that the talking of children in their sleep belongs to the sphere of dreams, I can relate the following as one of the earliest dreams in my collection: My youngest daughter, at that time nineteen months old, vomited one morning, and was therefore kept without food all day. During the night she was heard to call excitedly in her sleep: "Anna F(r)eud, *st'awbewy, wild st'awbewy, om'lette, pap!*" She used her name in this way in order to express the act of appropriation; the menu presumably included everything that would seem to her a desirable meal; the fact that two varieties of strawberry appeared in it was a demonstration against the sanitary regulations of the household, and was based on the circumstance, which she had by no means overlooked, that the nurse had ascribed her indisposition to an over-plentiful consumption of strawberries; so in her dream she avenged herself for this opinion which met with her disapproval.

When we call childhood happy because it does not yet know sexual desire, we must not forget what a fruitful source of disappointment and renunciation, and therefore of dream-stimulation, the other great vital impulse may be for the child. Here is a second example. My nephew, twenty-two months of age, had been instructed to congratulate me on my birthday, and to give me a present of a small basket of cherries, which at that time of the year were scarce, being hardly in season. He seemed to find the task a difficult one, for he repeated again and again: "Cherries in it," and could not be induced to let the little basket go out of his hands. But he knew how to indemnify himself. He had, until then, been in the habit of telling his mother every morning that he had dreamt of the "white soldier," an officer of the guard in a white cloak, whom he had once admired in the street. On the day after the sacrifice on my birthday he woke up joyfully with the announcement, which could have referred only to a dream: *"He[r] man eaten all the cherries!"*

What animals dream of I do not know. A proverb for which I am indebted to one of my pupils professes to tell us, for it asks the question: "What does the goose dream of?" and answers: "Of maize." The whole theory that the dream is the fulfilment of a wish is contained in these two sentences.

We now perceive that we should have reached our theory of the hidden meaning of dreams by the shortest route had we merely consulted the vernacular. Proverbial wisdom, it is true, often speaks contemptuously enough of dreams—it apparently seeks to justify the scientists when it says that "dreams are bubbles"; but in colloquial language the dream is predominantly the gracious fulfiller of wishes. "I should never have imagined that in my wildest dreams," we exclaim in delight if we find that the reality surpasses our expectations.

PART THREE

Learning and Cognitive Processes

On the Internet . . .

Sites appropriate to Part Three

This Theory Into Practice site provides links to descriptions of the major theories of learning.

        http://www.gwu.edu/~tip/theories.html

A positive reinforcement exercise developed by Professor Lyle K. Grant, Athabasca University, Alberta, Canada.

        http://server.bmod.athabascau.ca/html/prtut/
            reinpair.htm

This Upstream page provides resources on heredity and intelligence. Upstream is a Web site that contains essays, books, and links with the unifying theme "ideas that violate taboos or provoke fierce opposition."

        http://www.mosaic.co.za/gavan/Upstream/Issues/
            psychology/IQ/index.html

CHAPTER 6 Learning

6.1 JOHN B. WATSON AND ROSALIE RAYNER

Conditioned Emotional Reactions

The desire of early researchers to apply the techniques of classical and operant conditioning—two forms of behavioral learning involving stimulus association and reinforcement—to understand practical problems led to John B. Watson's well-known Little Albert experiment, which is discussed in this selection. This classic experiment of how Albert learned to fear a white rat—and other furry or rat-like stimuli—has been a favorite of students and instructors alike.

Watson (1878–1958), the founder of the school of behaviorism, received his Ph.D. from the University of Chicago in 1903, where he taught for five years before moving to the Johns Hopkins University. Rosalie Rayner (d. 1935) was an assistant in the psychology laboratory during the Little Albert experiment. Eventually, Rayner and Watson were married.

This selection is from "Conditioned Emotional Reactions," which was published in *Journal of Experimental Psychology* in 1920. Although the Little Albert experiment was originally intended as a pilot study and had some methodological flaws, it serves as a classic example of how conditioning can modify behavior. Watson and Rayner describe explicitly the procedures they used and the results they obtained. Unfortunately, Albert's mother removed him from the hospital after the experiment was conducted; hence, the experimenters could not develop a technique to remove the conditioned fear reaction from him. As you read this selection, try to remember how you learned to fear certain events as you were growing up.

Key Concept: conditioned emotional reactions in infants

*I*n recent literature various speculations have been entered into concerning the possibility of conditioning various types of emotional response, but direct experimental evidence in support of such a view has been lacking. If the theory advanced by Watson and Morgan to the effect that in infancy the original emotional reaction patterns are few, consisting so far as observed of fear, rage and love, then there must be some simple method by means of which the range of stimuli which can call out these emotions and their compounds is greatly increased. Otherwise, complexity in adult response could not be accounted for. These authors without adequate experimental evidence advanced the view that this range was increased by means of conditioned reflex factors. It was suggested there that the early home life of the child furnishes a laboratory situation for establishing conditioned emotional responses. The present authors have recently put the whole matter to an experimental test.

Experimental work has been done so far on only one child, Albert B. This infant was reared almost from birth in a hospital environment; his mother was a wet nurse in the Harriet Lane Home for Invalid Children. Albert's life was normal: he was healthy from birth and one of the best developed youngsters ever brought to the hospital, weighing twenty-one pounds at nine months of age. He was on the whole stolid and unemotional. His stability was one of the principal reasons for using him as a subject in this test. We felt that we could do him relatively little harm by carrying out such experiments as those outlined below.

At approximately nine months of age we ran him through the emotional tests that have become a part of our regular routine in determining whether fear reactions can be called out by other stimuli than sharp noises and the sudden removal of support. . . . In brief, the infant was confronted suddenly and for the first time successively with a white rat, a rabbit, a dog, a monkey, with masks with and without hair, cotton wool, burning newspapers, etc. A permanent record of Albert's reactions to these objects and situations has been preserved in a motion picture study. Manipulation was the most usual reaction called out. *At no time did this infant ever show fear in any situation.* These experimental records were confirmed by the casual observations of the mother and hospital attendants. No one had ever seen him in a state of fear and rage. The infant practically never cried.

Up to approximately nine months of age we had not tested him with loud sounds. The test to determine whether a fear reaction could be called out by a loud sound was made when he was eight months, twenty-six days of age. The sound was that made by striking a hammer upon a suspended steel bar four feet in length and three-fourths of an inch in diameter. The laboratory notes are as follows:

One of the two experimenters caused the child to turn its head and fixate her moving hand; the other, stationed back of the child, struck the steel bar a sharp blow. The child started violently, his breathing was checked and the arms were raised in a characteristic manner. On the second stimulation the same thing occurred, and in addition the lips began to pucker and tremble. On the third stimulation the child broke into a sudden crying fit. This is the first time an emotional situation in the laboratory has produced any fear or even crying in Albert.

We had expected just these results on account of our work with other infants brought up under similar conditions. It is worth while to call attention to the fact that removal of support (dropping and jerking the blanket upon which the infant was lying) was tried exhaustively upon this infant on the same occasion. It was not effective in producing the fear response. This stimulus is effective in younger children. At what age such stimuli lose their potency in producing fear is not known. Nor is it known whether less placid children ever lose their fear of them. This probably depends upon the training the child gets. It is well known that children eagerly run to be tossed into the air and caught. On the other hand it is equally well known that in the adult fear responses are called out quite clearly by the sudden removal of support, if the individual is walking across a bridge, walking out upon a beam, etc. There is a wide field of study here which is aside from our present point.

The sound stimulus, thus, at nine months of age, gives us the means of testing several important factors. I. Can we condition fear of an animal, *e.g.,* a white rat, by visually presenting it and simultaneously striking a steel bar? II. If such a conditioned emotional response can be established, will there be a transfer to other animals or other objects? . . .

I. The establishment of conditioned emotional responses. At first there was considerable hesitation upon our part in making the attempt to set up fear reactions experimentally. A certain responsibility attaches to such a procedure. We decided finally to make the attempt, comforting ourselves by the reflection that such attachments would arise anyway as soon as the child left the sheltered environment of the nursery for the rough and tumble of the home. We did not begin this work until Albert was eleven months, three days of age. Before attempting to set up a conditioned response we, as before, put him through all of the regular emotional tests. *Not the slightest sign of a fear response was obtained in any situation.*

The steps taken to condition emotional responses are shown in our laboratory notes.

11 Months 3 Days

1. White rat suddenly taken from the basket and presented to Albert. He began to reach for rat with left hand. Just as his hand touched the animal the bar was struck immediately behind his head. The infant jumped violently and fell forward, burying his face in the mattress. He did not cry, however.

2. Just as the right hand touched the rat the bar was again struck. Again the infant jumped violently, fell forward and began to whimper.

In order not to disturb the child too seriously no further tests were given for one week.

11 Months 10 Days

1. Rat presented suddenly without sound. There was steady fixation but no tendency at first to reach for it. The rat was then placed nearer, whereupon tentative reaching movements began with the right hand. When the rat nosed the infant's left hand, the hand was immediately withdrawn. He started to reach for the head of the animal with the forefinger of the left hand, but withdrew it suddenly before contact. It is thus seen that the two joint stimulations given the previous week were not without effect. He was tested with his blocks immediately afterwards to see if they shared in the process of conditioning. He began immediately to pick them up, dropping them, pounding them, etc. In the remainder of the tests the blocks were given frequently to quiet him and to test his general emotional state. They were always removed from sight when the process of conditioning was under way.
2. Joint stimulation with rat and sound. Started, then fell over immediately to right side. No crying.
3. Joint stimulation. Fell to right side and rested upon hands, with head turned away from rat. No crying.
4. Joint stimulation. Same reaction.
5. Rat suddenly presented alone. Puckered face, whimpered and withdrew body sharply to the left.
6. Joint stimulation. Fell over immediately to right side and began to whimper.
7. Joint stimulation. Started violently and cried, but did not fall over.
8. Rat alone. *The instant the rat was shown the baby began to cry. Almost instantly he turned sharply to the left, fell over on left side, raised himself on all fours and began to crawl away so rapidly that he was caught with difficulty before reaching the edge of the table.*

This was as convincing a case of a completely conditioned fear response as could have been theoretically pictured. In all seven joint stimulations were given to bring about the complete reaction. It is not unlikely had the sound been of greater intensity or of a more complex clang character that the number of joint stimulations might have been materially reduced. Experiments designed to define the nature of the sounds that will serve best as emotional stimuli are under way.

II. When a conditioned emotional response has been established for one object, is there a transfer? Five days later Albert was again brought back into the laboratory and tested as follows:

John B. Watson and Rosalie Rayner

11 Months 15 Days

1. Tested first with blocks. He reached readily for them, playing with them as usual. This shows that there has been no general transfer to the room, table, blocks, etc.
2. Rat alone. Whimpered immediately, withdrew right hand and turned head and trunk away.
3. Blocks again offered. Played readily with them, smiling and gurgling.
4. Rat alone. Leaned over to the left side as far away from the rat as possible, then fell over, getting up on all fours and scurrying away as rapidly as possible.
5. Blocks again offered. Reached immediately for them, smiling and laughing as before.
   The above preliminary test shows that the conditioned response to the rat had carried over completely for the five days in which no tests were given. The question as to whether or not there is a transfer was next taken up.
6. Rabbit alone. The rabbit was suddenly placed on the mattress in front of him. The reaction was pronounced. Negative responses began at once. He leaned as far away from the animal as possible, whimpered, then burst into tears. When the rabbit was placed in contact with him he buried his face in the mattress, then got up on all fours and crawled away, crying as he went. This was a most convincing test.
7. The blocks were next given him, after an interval. He played with them as before. It was observed by four people that he played far more energetically with them than ever before. The blocks were raised high over his head and slammed down with a great deal of force.
8. Dog alone. The dog did not produce as violent a reaction as the rabbit. The moment fixation occurred the child shrank back and as the animal came nearer he attempted to get on all fours but did not cry at first. As soon as the dog passed out of his range of vision he became quiet. The dog was then made to approach the infant's head (he was lying down at the moment). Albert straightened up immediately, fell over to the opposite side and turned his head away. He then began to cry.
9. The blocks were again presented. He began immediately to play with them.
10. Fur coat (seal). Withdrew immediately to the left side and began to fret. Coat put close to him on the left side, he turned immediately, began to cry and tried to crawl away on all fours.
11. Cotton wool. The wool was presented in a paper package. At the end the cotton was not covered by the paper. It was placed first on his feet. He kicked it away but did not touch it with his hands. When his hand was laid on the wool he immediately withdrew it but did not show the shock that the animals or fur coat produced in him. He then began to

play with the paper, avoiding contact with the wool itself. He finally, under the impulse of the manipulative instinct, lost some of his negativism to the wool.

12. Just in play W. put his head down to see if Albert would play with his hair. Albert was completely negative. Two other observers did the same thing. He began immediately to play with their hair. W. then brought the Santa Claus mask and presented it to Albert. He was again pronouncedly negative....

From the above results it would seem that emotional transfers do take place. Furthermore it would seem that the number of transfers resulting from an experimentally produced conditioned emotional reaction may be very large. In our observations we had no means of testing the complete number of transfers which may have resulted....

INCIDENTAL OBSERVATIONS

(a) Thumb sucking as a compensatory device for blocking fear and noxious stimuli. During the course of these experiments, ... it was noticed that whenever Albert was on the verge of tears or emotionally upset generally he would continually thrust his thumb into his mouth. The moment the hand reached the mouth he became impervious to the stimuli producing fear. Again and again while the motion pictures were being made at the end of the thirty-day rest period, we had to remove the thumb from his mouth before the conditioned response could be obtained. This method of blocking noxious and emotional stimuli (fear and rage) through erogenous stimulation seems to persist from birth onward....

(b) Equal primacy of fear, love and possibly rage. While in general the results of our experiment offer no particular points of conflict with Freudian concepts, one fact out of harmony with them should be emphasized. According to proper Freudians sex (or in our terminology, love) is the principal emotion in which conditioned responses arise which later limit and distort personality. We wish to take sharp issue with this view on the basis of the experimental evidence we have gathered. Fear is as primal a factor as love in influencing personality. Fear does not gather its potency in any derived manner from love. It belongs to the original and inherited nature of man. Probably the same may be true of rage although at present we are not so sure of this....

It is probable that many of the phobias in psychopathology are true conditioned emotional reactions either of the direct or the transferred type. One may possibly have to believe that such persistence of early conditioned responses will be found only in persons who are constitutionally inferior. Our argument is meant to be constructive. Emotional disturbances in adults cannot be traced back to sex alone. They must be retraced along at least three collateral lines—to conditioned and transferred responses set up in infancy and early youth in all three of the fundamental human emotions.

6.2   B. F. SKINNER

Shaping and Maintaining Operant Behavior

Reinforcement—an event that increases the probability that the behavior preceding it will be repeated—can have a profound effect on behavior, and we typically do things that lead to reinforcement. Much of what scientists originally discovered about the effects of reinforcement on animals has been applied to human behavior. The study of how reinforcement changes behavior is known as operant conditioning.

B. F. Skinner (1904–1990) was a pioneer in the study of operant conditioning. Skinner earned a B.A. in English from Hamilton College in 1926, but he decided he did not have anything important to say, so he went back to school and earned a Ph.D. in psychology from Harvard University in 1931. Indeed, he did have much to say, and he wrote numerous books, including *The Behavior of Organisms* (1938) and the fictional *Walden Two* (1948), in which Skinner describes a utopian society run in accordance with operant principles. In *Beyond Freedom and Dignity* (Alfred A. Knopf, 1971), he explains why it is important to understand how we control behavior in our day-to-day lives.

This selection is from chapter 6, "Shaping and Maintaining Operant Behavior," of Skinner's *Science and Human Behavior* (Free Press, 1953). Although Skinner's favorite subject for study was the pigeon, as illustrated in this selection, he believed that the laws of behavior apply to all organisms. Note how Skinner neatly applies the results of his animal research to human beings, as well as how clearly he defines the four intermittent schedules of reinforcement.

Key Concept: operant conditioning

THE CONTINUITY OF BEHAVIOR

Operant conditioning [a process in which reinforcement changes the frequency of a behavior] shapes behavior as a sculptor shapes a lump of clay. Although at some point the sculptor seems to have produced an entirely novel object, we can always follow the process back to the original undifferentiated lump, and we can make the successive stages by which we return to this condition as small as we wish. At no point does anything emerge which is very different from what preceded it. The final product seems to have a special unity or integrity of design, but we cannot find a point at which this suddenly appears. In the same sense, an operant [behavior generated by reinforcement consequences] is not something which appears full grown in the behavior of the organism. It is the result of a continuous shaping process.

The pigeon experiment demonstrates this clearly. "Raising the head" is not a discrete unit of behavior. It does not come, so to speak, in a separate package. We reinforce only slightly exceptional values of the behavior observed while the pigeon is standing or moving about. We succeed in shifting the whole range of heights at which the head is held, but there is nothing which can be accurately described as a new "response." A response such as turning the latch in a problem box appears to be a more discrete unit, but only because the continuity with other behavior is more difficult to observe. In the pigeon, the response of pecking at a spot on the wall of the experimental box seems to differ from stretching the neck because no other behavior of the pigeon resembles it. If in reinforcing such a response we simply wait for it to occur—and we may have to wait many hours or days or weeks—the whole unit appears to emerge in its final form and to be strengthened as such. There may be no appreciable behavior which we could describe as "almost pecking the spot."

The continuous connection between such an operant and the general behavior of the bird can nevertheless easily be demonstrated. It is the basis of a practical procedure for setting up a complex response. To get the pigeon to peck the spot as quickly as possible we proceed as follows: We first give the bird food when it turns slightly in the direction of the spot from any part of the cage. This increases the frequency of such behavior. We then withhold reinforcement until a slight movement is made toward the spot. This again alters the general distribution of behavior without producing a new unit. We continue by reinforcing positions successively closer to the spot, then by reinforcing only when the head is moved slightly forward, and finally only when the beak actually makes contact with the spot. We may reach this final response in a remarkably short time. A hungry bird, well adapted to the situation and to the food tray, can usually be brought to respond in this way in two or three minutes.

The original probability of the response in its final form is very low; in some cases it may even be zero. In this way we can build complicated operants which would never appear in the repertoire of the organism otherwise. By reinforcing a series of successive approximations, we bring a rare response to a very high probability in a short time. This is an effective procedure because it recognizes and utilizes the continuous nature of a complex act. The total act of turning toward the spot from any point the box, walking toward it, raising the head, and striking the spot may seem to be a functionally coherent unit of behavior; but it is constructed by a continual process of differential reinforcement from undifferentiated behavior, just as the sculptor shapes his figure from a lump of clay. When we wait for a single complete instance, we reinforce a similar sequence but far less effectively because the earlier steps are not optimally strengthened.

This account is inaccurate in one respect. We may detect a discontinuity between bringing the head close to the spot and pecking. The pecking movement usually emerges as an obviously preformed unit. There are two possible explanations. A mature pigeon will already have developed a well-defined pecking response which may emerge upon the present occasion. The history of this response might show a similar continuity if we could follow it. It is possible, however, that there is a genetic discontinuity, and that in a bird such as the pigeon the pecking response has a special strength and a special coherence as a form of species behavior. Vomiting and sneezing are human responses which probably have a similar genetic unity. Continuity with other behavior must be sought in the evolutionary process. But these genetic units are rare, at least in the vertebrates. The behavior with which we are usually concerned, from either a theoretical or practical point of view, is continuously modified from a basic material which is largely undifferentiated.

Through the reinforcement of slightly exceptional instances of his behavior, a child learns to raise himself, to stand, to walk, to grasp objects, and to move them about. Later on, through the same process, he learns to talk, to sing, to dance, to play games—in short, to exhibit the enormous repertoire characteristic of the normal adult. When we survey behavior in these later stages, we find it convenient to distinguish between various operants which differ from each other in topography and produce different consequences. In this way behavior is broken into parts to facilitate analysis. These parts are the units which we count and whose frequencies play an important role in arriving at laws of behavior. They are the "acts" into which, in the vocabulary of the layman, behavior is divided. But if we are to account for many of its quantitative properties, the ultimately continuous nature of behavior must not be forgotten. . . .

THE MAINTENANCE OF BEHAVIOR

One reason the term "learning" is not equivalent to "operant conditioning" is that traditionally it has been confined to the process of learning *how to do something*. In trial-and-error learning, for example, the organism learns how to get out of a box or how to find its way through a maze. It is easy to see why the acquisition of behavior should be emphasized. Early devices for the study of learning did not reveal the basic process directly. The effect of operant reinforcement is most conspicuous when there is a gross change in behavior. Such a chance occurs when an organism learns how to make a response which it did not or could not make before. A more sensitive measure, however, enables us to deal with cases in which the acquisition of behavior is of minor importance.

Operant conditioning continues to be effective even when there is no further change which can be spoken of as acquisition or even as improvement in skill. Behavior continues to have consequences and these continue to be important. If consequences are not forthcoming, extinction occurs. When we come to consider the behavior of the organism in all the complexity of its everyday life, we need to be constantly alert to the prevailing reinforcements, which maintain its behavior. We may, indeed, have little interest in how that behavior was first acquired. Our concern is only with its present probability of occurrence, which can be understood only through an examination of current contingencies of reinforcement. This is an aspect of reinforcement which is scarcely ever dealt with in classical treatments of learning.

INTERMITTENT REINFORCEMENT

In general, behavior which acts upon the immediate physical environment is consistently reinforced. We orient ourselves toward objects and approach, reach for, and seize them with a stable repertoire of responses which have uniform consequences arising from the optical and mechanical properties of nature. It is possible, of course, to disturb the uniformity. In a "house of mirrors" in an amusement park, or in a room designed to supply misleading cues to the vertical, well-established responses may fail to have their usual effects. But the fact that such conditions are so unusual as to have commercial value testifies to the stability of the everyday world.

A large part of behavior, however, is reinforced only intermittently. A given consequence may depend upon a series of events which are not easily predicted. We do not always win at cards or dice, because the contingencies are so remotely determined that we call them "chance." We do not always find good ice or snow when we go skating or skiing. Contingencies which require the participation of people are especially likely to be uncertain. We do not always get a good meal in a particular restaurant because cooks are not always predictable. We do not always get an answer when we telephone a friend because the friend is not always at home. We do not always get a pen by reaching into our pocket because we have not always put it there. The reinforcements characteristic of industry and education are almost always intermittent because it is not feasible to control behavior by reinforcing every response.

As might be expected, behavior which is reinforced only intermittently often shows an intermediate frequency of occurrence, but laboratory studies of various schedules have revealed some surprising complexities. Usually such behavior is remarkably stable and shows great resistance to extinction.* An experiment has already been mentioned in which more than 10,000 responses appeared in the extinction curve of a pigeon which had been reinforced on a special schedule. Nothing of the sort is ever obtained after continuous reinforcement. Since this is a technique for "getting more responses out of an organism" in return for a given number of reinforcements, it is widely used. Wages are paid in special ways and betting and gambling devices are designed to "pay off" on special schedules because of the relatively large return on the reinforcement in such a case. Approval, affection, and other personal favors are

*[Extinction is a decline in behavior frequency due to the withholding of reinforcement.—Ed.]

frequently intermittent, not only because the person supplying the reinforcement may behave in different ways at different times, but precisely because he may have found that such a schedule yields a more stable, persistent, and profitable return.

It is important to distinguish between schedules which are arranged by a system outside the organism and those which are controlled by the behavior itself. An example of the first is a schedule of reinforcement which is determined by a clock—as when we reinforce a pigeon every five minutes, allowing all intervening responses to go unreinforced. An example of the second is a schedule in which a response is reinforced after a certain number of responses have been emitted—as when we reinforce every fiftieth response the pigeon makes. The cases are similar in the sense that we reinforce intermittently in both, but subtle differences in the contingencies lead to very different results, often of great practical significance.

Interval Reinforcement

If we reinforce behavior at regular intervals, an organism such as a rat or pigeon will adjust with a nearly constant rate of responding, determined by the frequency of reinforcement. If we reinforce it every minute, the animal responds rapidly; if every five minutes, much more slowly. A similar effect upon probability of response is characteristic of human behavior. How often we call a given number on the telephone will depend, other things being equal, upon how often we get an answer. If two agencies supply the same service, we are more likely to call the one which answers more often. We are less likely to see friends or acquaintances with whom we only occasionally have a good time, and we are less likely to write to a correspondent who seldom answers. The experimental results are precise enough to suggest that in general the organism gives back a certain number of responses for each response reinforced. We shall see, however, that the results of schedules of reinforcement are not always reducible to a simple equating of input with output.

Since behavior which appears under interval reinforcement is especially stable, it is useful in studying other variables and conditions. The size or amount of each reinforcement affects the rate—more responses appearing in return for a larger reinforcement. Different kinds of reinforcers also yield different rates, and these may be used to rank reinforcers in the order of their effectiveness. The rate varies with the immediacy of the reinforcement: a slight delay between response and the receipt of the reinforcer means a lower over-all rate. Other variables which have been studied under interval reinforcement will be discussed in later chapters. They include the degree of deprivation and the presence or absence of certain emotional circumstances.

Optimal schedules of reinforcement are often of great practical importance. They are often discussed in connection with other variables which affect the rate. Reinforcing a man with fifty dollars at one time may not be so effective as reinforcing him with five dollars at ten different times during the same period. This is especially the case with primitive people where conditioned reinforcers have not been established to bridge the temporal span between a response and its ultimate consequence. There are also many subtle interactions between schedules of reinforcement and levels of motivation, immediacy of reinforcement, and so on.

If behavior continues to be reinforced at fixed intervals, another process intervenes. Since responses are never reinforced just after reinforcement, a change . . . eventually takes place in which the rate of responding is low for a short time after each reinforcement. The rate rises again when an interval of time has elapsed which the organism presumably cannot distinguish from the interval at which it is reinforced. These changes in rate are not characteristic of the effect of wages in industry, which would otherwise appear to be an example of a fixed-interval schedule. The discrepancy is explained by the fact that other reinforcing systems are used to maintain a given level of work. . . . Docking a man for time absent guarantees his presence each day by establishing a time-card entry as a conditioned reinforcer. The aversive reinforcement supplied by a supervisor or boss is, however, the principal supplement to a fixed-interval wage.

A low probability of response just after reinforcement is eliminated with what is called *variable-interval* reinforcement. Instead of reinforcing a response every five minutes, for example, we reinforce every five minutes *on the average*, where the intervening interval may be as short as a few seconds or as long as, say, ten minutes. Reinforcement occasionally occurs just after the organism has been reinforced, and the organism therefore continues to respond at that time. Its performance under such a schedule is remarkably stable and uniform. Pigeons reinforced with food with a variable interval averaging five minutes between reinforcements have been observed to respond for as long as fifteen hours at a rate of from two to three responses per second without pausing longer than fifteen or twenty seconds during the whole period. It is usually very difficult to extinguish a response after such a schedule. Many sorts of social or personal reinforcement are supplied on what is essentially a variable-interval basis, and extraordinarily persistent behavior is sometimes set up.

Ratio Reinforcement

An entirely different result is obtained when the schedule of reinforcement depends upon the behavior of the organism itself—when, for example, we reinforce every fiftieth response. This is reinforcement at a "fixed ratio"— the ratio of reinforced to unreinforced responses. It is a common schedule in education, where the student is reinforced for completing a project or a paper or some other specific amount of work. It is essentially the basis of professional pay and of selling on commission. In industry it is known as piecework pay. It is a system of reinforcement which naturally recommends itself to employers because the cost of the labor required to produce a given result can be calculated in advance.

Fixed-ratio reinforcement generates a very high rate of response provided the ratio is not too high. This should follow from the input-output relation alone. Any slight increase in rate increases the frequency of reinforcement with the result that the rate should rise still further. If no other factor intervened, the rate should reach the highest possible value. A limiting factor, which makes itself felt in industry, is simple fatigue. The high rate of responding and the long hours of work generated by this schedule can be dangerous to health. This is the main reason why piecework pay is usually strenuously opposed by organized labor.

Another objection to this type of schedule is based upon the possibility that as the rate rises, the reinforcing agency will move to a larger ratio. In the laboratory, after first reinforcing every tenth response and then every fiftieth, we may find it possible to reinforce only every hundredth, although we could not have used this ratio in the beginning. In industry, the employee whose productivity has increased as the result of a piecework schedule may receive so large a weekly wage that the employer feels justified in increasing the number of units of work required for a given unit of pay.

Under ratios of reinforcement which can be sustained, the behavior eventually shows a very low probability just after reinforcement, as it does in the case of fixed-interval reinforcement. The effect is marked under high fixed ratios because the organism always has "a long way to go" before the next reinforcement. Wherever a piecework schedule is used—in industry, education, salesmanship, or the professions—low morale or low interest is most often observed just after a unit of work has been completed. When responding begins, the situation is improved by each response and the more the organism responds, the better the chances of reinforcement become. The result is a smooth gradient of acceleration as the organism responds more and more rapidly. The condition eventually prevailing under high fixed-ratio reinforcement is not an efficient over-all mode of responding. It makes relatively poor use of the available time, and the higher rates of responding may be especially fatiguing.

The laboratory study of ratio reinforcement has shown that for a given organism and a given measure of reinforcement there is a limiting ratio beyond which behavior cannot be sustained. The result of exceeding this ratio is an extreme degree of extinction of the sort which we call abulia. Long periods of inactivity begin to appear between separate ratio runs. This is not physical fatigue, as we may easily show by shifting to another schedule. It is often called "mental" fatigue, but this designation adds nothing to the observed fact that beyond a certain high ratio of reinforcement the organism simply has no behavior available. In both the laboratory study of ratio reinforcement and its practical application in everyday life, the first signs of strain imposed by too high a ratio are seen in these breaks. Before a pigeon stops altogether—in complete "abulia"—it will often not respond for a long time after reinforcement. In the same way, the student who has finished a term paper, perhaps in a burst of speed at the end of the gradient, finds it difficult to start work on a new assignment.

Exhaustion can occur under ratio reinforcement because there is no self-regulating mechanism. In interval reinforcement, on the other hand, any tendency toward extinction is opposed by the fact that when the rate declines, the next reinforcement is received in return for fewer responses. The variable-interval schedule is also self-protecting: an organism will stabilize its behavior at a given rate under any length of interval.

We get rid of the pauses after reinforcement on a fixed-ratio schedule by adopting essentially the same practice as in variable-interval reinforcement: we simply vary the ratios over a considerable range around some mean value. Successive responses may be reinforced or many hundreds of unreinforced responses may intervene. The probability of reinforcement at any moment remains essentially constant and the organism adjusts by holding to a constant rate. This "variable-ratio reinforcement" is much more powerful than a fixed-ratio schedule with the same mean number of responses. A pigeon may respond as rapidly as five times per second and maintain this rate for many hours.

The efficacy of such schedules in generating high rates has long been known to the proprietors of gambling establishments. Slot machines, roulette wheels, dice cages, horse races, and so on pay off on a schedule of variable-ratio reinforcement. Each device has its own auxiliary reinforcements, but the schedule is the important characteristic. Winning depends upon placing a bet and in the long run upon the number of bets placed, but no particular payoff can be predicted. The ratio is varied by any one of several "random" systems. The pathological gambler exemplifies the result. Like the pigeon with its five responses per second for many hours, he is the victim of an unpredictable contingency of reinforcement. The long-term net gain or loss is almost irrelevant in accounting for the effectiveness of this schedule.

6.3 JOHN GARCIA AND ROBERT A. KOELLING

Relation of Cue to Consequence in Avoidance Learning

Since physiologist Ivan Pavlov first demonstrated classical conditioning techniques—in which the pairing of one stimulus with another stimulus and its response results in the first stimulus alone eliciting the response—many have believed that any stimulus and response could be paired to induce learning. When John Garcia first reported the specificity of this pairing in aversion learning, many psychologists were skeptical.

Garcia earned his Ph.D. in experimental psychology in 1965 from the University of California, Berkeley. He held positions at a number of institutions—including Harvard Medical School, Long Beach State College, and the U.S. Naval Radiological Defense Laboratory in San Francisco, California—before going to the University of California, Los Angeles, where he spent most of his professional career. Robert A. Koelling collaborated on a number of early research papers with Garcia.

This selection is from "Relation of Cue to Consequence in Avoidance Learning," which was published in *Psychonomic Science* in 1966. In it, Garcia and Koelling report an experiment in which rats were given flavored water (gustatory stimulus) accompanied by a flash of light and a clicking noise (audiovisual stimulus). The rats were then given either electric shock or a toxin/x-ray. Garcia and Koelling found that the electric shock only affected the audiovisual stimulus, whereas the toxin or x-ray only affected the gustatory stimulus. Thus, they concluded, conditioning only occurs when the appropriate pairing is made.

This selection might require you to carefully organize the various stimuli and reinforcers. The implications that conditioning is limited to specific associations is very important in learning. Later research demonstrated generalization of these results to humans. As you read this selection, consider why it is important to understand the nature of learning associations.

Key Concept: conditioned aversion learning

*A*n *audiovisual stimulus was made contingent upon the rat's licking at the water spout, thus making it analogous with a gustatory stimulus. When the audiovisual stimulus and the gustatory stimulus were paired with electric shock the avoidance reactions transferred to the audiovisual stimulus, but not the gustatory stimulus. Conversely, when both stimuli were paired with toxin or x-ray the avoidance reactions transferred to the gustatory stimulus, but not the audiovisual stimulus. Apparently stimuli are selected as cues dependent upon the nature of the subsequent reinforcer.*

A great deal of evidence stemming from diverse sources suggests an inadequacy in the usual formulations concerning reinforcement. Barnett (1963) has described the "bait-shy" behavior of wild rats which have survived a poisoning attempt. These animals utilizing olfactory and gustatory cues, avoid the poison bait which previously made them ill. However, there is no evidence that they avoid the "place" of the poisoning.

In a recent volume (Haley & Snyder, 1964) several authors have discussed studies in which ionizing radiations were employed as a noxious stimulus to produce avoidance reactions in animals. Ionizing radiation like many poisons produces gastrointestinal disturbances and nausea. Strong aversions are readily established in animals when distinctively flavored fluids are conditionally paired with x-rays. Subsequently, the gustatory stimulus will depress fluid intake without radiation. In contrast, a distinctive environmental complex of auditory, visual, and tactual stimuli does not inhibit drinking even when the compound stimulus is associated with the identical radiation schedule. This differential effect has also been observed following ingestion of a toxin and the injection of a drug (Garcia & Koelling, 1965).

Apparently this differential effectiveness of cues is due either to the nature of the reinforcer, i.e., radiation or toxic effects, or the peculiar relation which a gustatory stimulus has to the drinking response, i.e., gustatory stimulation occurs if and only if the animal licks the fluid. The environmental cues associated with a distinctive place are not as dependent upon a single response of the organism. Therefore, we made an auditory and visual stimulus dependent upon the animal's licking the water spout. Thus, in four experiments reported here "bright-noisy" water, as well as "tasty" water was conditionally paired with radiation, a toxin, immediate shock, and delayed shock, respectively, as reinforcers. Later the capacity of these response-controlled stimuli to inhibit drinking in the absence of reinforcement was tested.

METHOD

The apparatus was a light and sound shielded box (7 in. x 7 in. x 7 in.) with a drinking spout connected to an electronic drinkometer which counted each touch of the rat's tongue to the spout. "Bright-noisy" water was provided by connecting an incandescent lamp (5 watts) and a clicking relay into this circuit. "Tasty" water was provided by adding flavors to the drinking supply.

*John Garcia
and Robert A.
Koelling*

Each experimental group consisted of 10 rats (90 day old Sprague-Dawley males) maintained in individual cages without water, but *Purina Laboratory chow ad libidum.*

The procedure was: A. One week of habituation to drinking in the apparatus without stimulation. B. Pretests to measure intake of bright-noisy water and tasty water prior to training. C. Acquisition training with: (1) reinforced trials where these stimuli were paired with reinforcement during drinking, (2) nonreinforced trials where rats drank water without stimuli or reinforcement. Training terminated when there was a reliable difference between water intake scores on reinforced and nonreinforced trials. D. Post-tests to measure intake of bright-noisy water and tasty water after training.

In the x-ray study an audiovisual group and a gustatory group were exposed to an identical radiation schedule. In the other studies reinforcement was contingent upon the rat's response. To insure that both the audiovisual and the gustatory stimuli received equivalent reinforcement, they were combined and simultaneously paired with the reinforcer during acquisition training. Therefore, one group serving as its own control and divided into equal subgroups, was tested in balanced order with an audiovisual and a gustatory test before and after training with these stimuli combined.

One 20-min. reinforced trial was administered every three days in the x-ray and lithium chloride studies. This prolonged intertrial interval was designed to allow sufficient time for the rats to recover from acute effects of treatment. On each interpolated day the animals received a 20-min. nonreinforced trial. They were post-tested two days after their last reinforced trial. The x-ray groups received a total of three reinforced trials, each with 54 r of filtered 250 kv x-rays delivered in 20 min. Sweet water (1 gm saccharin per liter) was the gustatory stimulus. The lithium chloride group had a total of five reinforced trials with toxic salty water (.12 M lithium chloride). Non-toxic salty water (.12 M sodium chloride) which rats cannot readily distinguish from the toxic solution was used in the gustatory tests (Nachman, 1963).

The immediate shock study was conducted on a more orthodox avoidance schedule. Tests and trials were 2 min. long. Each day for four consecutive acquisition days, animals were given two nonreinforced and two reinforced trials in an NRRN, RNNR pattern. A shock, the minimal current required to interrupt drinking (0.5 sec. at 0.08-0.20 ma), was delivered through a floor grid 2 sec. after the first lick at the spout.

The delayed shock study was conducted simultaneously with the lithium chloride on the same schedule. Non-toxic salty water was the gustatory stimulus. Shock reinforcement was delayed during first trials and gradually increased in intensity (.05 to .30 ma) in a schedule designed to produce a drinking pattern during the 20-min. period which resembled that of the corresponding animal drinking toxic salty water.

RESULTS AND DISCUSSION

The results indicate that all reinforcers were effective in producing discrimination learning during the acquisition phase, but obvious differences occurred in the post-tests. The avoidance reactions produced by x-rays and lithium chloride are readily transferred to the gustatory stimulus but not to the audiovisual stimulus. The effect is more pronounced in the x-ray study, perhaps due to differences in dose. The x-ray animals received a constant dose while the lithium chloride rats drank a decreasing amount of the toxic solution during training. Nevertheless, the difference between post-test scores is statistically significant in both experiments ($p < 0.01$ by ranks test).

Apparently when gustatory stimuli are paired with agents which produce nausea and gastric upset, they acquire secondary reinforcing properties which might be described as "conditioned nausea." Auditory and visual stimulation do not readily acquire similar properties even when they are contingent upon the licking response.

In contrast, the effect of both immediate and delayed shock to the paws is in the opposite direction. The avoidance reactions produced by electric shock to the paws transferred to the audiovisual stimulus but not to the gustatory stimulus. As one might expect the effect of delayed shocks was not as effective as shocks where the reinforcer immediately and consistently followed licking. Again, the difference between post-test intake scores is statistically significant in both studies ($p < 0.01$ by ranks test). Thus, when shock which produces peripheral pain is the reinforcer, "conditioned fear" properties are more readily acquired by auditory and visual stimuli than by gustatory stimuli.

It seems that given reinforcers are not equally effective for all classes of discriminable stimuli. The cues, which the animal selects from the welter of stimuli in the learning situation, appear to be related to the consequences of the subsequent reinforcer. Two speculations are offered: (1) Common elements in the time-intensity patterns of stimulation may facilitate a cross modal generalization from reinforcer to cue in one case and not in another. (2) More likely, natural selection may have favored mechanisms which associate gustatory and olfactory cues with internal discomfort since the chemical receptors sample the materials soon to be incorporated into the internal environment. Krechevsky (1933) postulated such a genetically coded hypothesis to account for the predispositions of rats to respond systematically to specific cues in an insoluble maze. The hypothesis of the sick rat, as for many of us under similar circumstances, would be, "It must have been something I ate."

REFERENCES

Barnett, S. A. *The rat: a study in behavior.* Chicago: Aldine Press, 1963.

Garcia, J., & Koelling, R. A. A comparison of aversions induced by x-rays, toxins, and drugs in the rat. *Radiat. Res.,* in press, 1965.

Haley, T. J., & Snyder, R. S. (Eds.) *The response of the nervous system to ionizing radiation.* Boston: Little, Brown & Co., 1964.

Krechevsky, I. The hereditary nature of 'hypothesis'. *J. comp. Psychol.,* 1932, 16, 99–116.

Nachman, M. Learned aversion to the taste of lithium chloride and generalization to other salts. *J. comp. physiol. Psychol.,* 1963, 56, 343–349.

6.4 ALBERT BANDURA, DOROTHEA ROSS, AND SHEILA A. ROSS

Imitation of Film-Mediated Aggressive Models

Rising levels of crime and destructive aggression have been studied by psychologists for decades. One ongoing debate has focused on whether or not observation and imitation is a problem with regard to aggression that occurs in the media. Do children imitate the aggressive acts they observe in movies and on television? Through a series of studies, Albert Bandura and his colleagues have begun to answer this question.

Bandura (b. 1925), a leading theorist in observational learning, received his Ph.D. from the University of Iowa in 1952. Shortly afterward, he began his academic career at Stanford University, where he has remained. He has written many books, including *Aggression: A Social Learning Analysis* (Prentice Hall, 1973) and *Social Learning Theory* (Prentice Hall, 1977). Dorothea Ross and Sheila A. Ross both earned a Ph.D. in developmental psychology from Stanford University. Ross and Ross specialized in children's health and cognitive development prior to their retirement.

This selection is from "Imitation of Film-Mediated Aggressive Models," which was published in *Journal of Abnormal and Social Psychology* in 1963. It details Bandura et al.'s classic study on aggression imitation in standard research article format. Note the care with which the procedure was carried out. An important point for understanding the statistical results is that a probability (p) level less than .05 is significant and indicates a real difference among experimental conditions. Bandura et al.'s findings go against most of the research reported prior to the study, which maintained that film-mediated aggression reduces aggressive drives through a cathartic process. The research reported in this selection suggests that filmed aggression can facilitate aggression in children. What are the implications of this study for aggression and violence in movies and on television today?

Key Concept: observation learning of aggression

In a test of the hypothesis that exposure of children to film-mediated aggressive models would increase the probability of Ss' [Subjects—i.e., children] aggression to subsequent frustration, 1 group of experimental Ss observed real-life aggressive models, a 2nd observed these same models portraying aggression on film, while a 3rd group viewed a film depicting an aggressive cartoon character. Following the exposure treatment, Ss were mildly frustrated and tested for the amount of imitative and nonimitative aggression in a different experimental setting. The overall results provide evidence for both the facilitating and the modeling influence of film-mediated aggressive stimulation. In addition, the findings reveal that the effects of such exposure are to some extent a function of the sex of the model, sex of the child, and the reality cues of the model. . . .

A recent incident (San Francisco Chronicle, 1961) in which a boy was seriously knifed during a re-enactment of a switchblade knife fight the boys had seen the previous evening on a televised rerun of the James Dean movie, *Rebel Without a Cause*, is a dramatic illustration of the possible imitative influence of film stimulation. Indeed, anecdotal data suggest that portrayal of aggression through pictorial media may be more influential in shaping the form aggression will take when a person is instigated on later occasions, than in altering the level of instigation to aggression.

In an earlier experiment (Bandura & Huston, 1961), it was shown that children readily imitated aggressive behavior exhibited by a model in the presence of the model. A succeeding investigation (Bandura, Ross, & Ross, 1961), demonstrated that children exposed to aggressive models generalized aggressive responses to a new setting in which the model was absent. The present study sought to determine the extent to which film-mediated aggressive models may serve as an important source of imitative behavior.

Aggressive models can be ordered on a reality-fictional stimulus dimension with real-life models located at the realty end of the continuum, nonhuman cartoon characters at the fictional end, and films portraying human models occupying an intermediate position. It was predicted, on the basis of saliency and similarity of cues, that the more remote the model was from reality, the weaker would be the tendency for subjects to imitate the behavior of the model. . . .

To the extent that observation of adults displaying aggression conveys a certain degree of permissiveness for aggressive behavior, it may be assumed that such exposure not only facilitates the learning of new aggressive responses but also weakens competing inhibitory responses in subjects and thereby increases the probability of occurrence of previously learned patterns of aggression. It was predicted, therefore, that subjects who observed aggressive models would display significantly more aggression when subsequently frustrated than subjects who were equally frustrated but who had no prior exposure to models exhibiting aggression.

The subjects were 48 boys and 48 girls enrolled in the Stanford University Nursery School. They ranged in age from 35 to 69 months, with a mean age of 52 months.

Two adults, a male and a female, served in the role of models both in the real-life and the human film-aggression condition, and one female experimenter conducted the study for all 96 children.

General Procedure

Subjects were divided into three experimental groups and one control group of 24 subjects each. One group of experimental subjects observed real-life aggressive models, a second group observed these same models portraying aggression on film, while a third group viewed a film depicting an aggressive cartoon character. The experimental groups were further subdivided into male and female subjects so that half the subjects in the two conditions involving human models were exposed to same-sex models, while the remaining subjects viewed models of the opposite sex.

Following the exposure experience, subjects were tested for the amount of imitative and nonimitative aggression in a different experimental setting in the absence of the models.

The control group subjects had no exposure to the aggressive models and were tested only in the generalization situation.

Subjects in the experimental and control groups were matched individually on the basis of ratings of their aggressive behavior in social interactions in the nursery school. The experimenter and a nursery school teacher rated the subjects on four five-point rating scales which measured the extent to which subjects displayed physical aggression, verbal aggression, aggression toward inanimate objects, and aggression inhibition. The latter scale, which dealt with the subjects' tendency to inhibit aggressive reactions in the face of high instigation, provided the measure of aggression anxiety. Seventy-one percent of the subjects were rated independently by both judges so as to permit an assessment of interrater agreement. The reliability of the composite aggression score, estimated by means of the Pearson product-moment correlation, was .80. . . .

Experimental Conditions

Subjects in the Real-Life Aggressive condition were brought individually by the experimenter to the experimental room and the model, who was in the hallway outside the room, was invited by the experimenter to come and join in the game. The subject was then escorted to one corner of the room and seated at a small table which contained potato prints, multicolor picture stickers, and colored paper. After demonstrating how the subject could design pictures with the materials provided, the experimenter escorted the model to the opposite corner of the room which contained a small table and chair, a tinker toy set, a mallet, and a 5-foot inflated Bobo doll. The experimenter explained that this was the model's play area and after the model was seated, the experimenter left the experimental room.

The model began the session by assembling the tinker toys but after approximately a minute had elapsed, the model turned to the Bobo doll and spent the remainder of the period aggressing toward it with highly novel responses which are unlikely to be performed by children independently of the observation of the model's behavior. Thus, in addition to punching the Bobo doll, the model exhibited the following distinctive aggressive acts which were to be scored as imitative responses:

The model sat on the Bobo doll and punched it repeatedly in the nose.

The model then raised the Bobo doll and pommeled it on the head with a mallet.

Following the mallett aggression, the model tossed the doll up in the air aggressively and kicked it about the room. This sequence of physically aggressive acts was repeated approximately three times, interspersed with verbally aggressive responses such as, "Sock him in the nose . . . ," "Hit him down . . . ," "Throw him in the air . . . ," "Kick him . . . ," and "Pow."

Subjects in the Human Film-Aggression condition were brought by the experimenter to the semi-darkened experimental room, introduced to the picture materials, and informed that while the subjects worked on potato prints, a movie would be shown on a screen, positioned approximately 6 feet from the subject's table. The movie projector was located in a distant corner of the room and was screened from the subject's view by large wooden panels.

The color movie and a tape recording of the sound track was begun by a male projectionist as soon as the experimenter left the experimental room and was shown for a duration of 10 minutes. The models in the film presentations were the same adult males and females who participated in the Real-Life condition of the experiment. Similarly, the aggressive behavior they portrayed in the film was identical with their real-life performances.

For subjects in the Cartoon Film-Aggression condition, after seating the subject at the table with the picture construction material, the experimenter walked over to a television console approximately 3 feet in front of the subject's table, remarked, "I guess I'll turn on the color TV," and ostensibly tuned in a cartoon program. The experimenter then left the experimental room. The cartoon was shown on a glass lens screen in the television set by means of a rear projection arrangement screened from the subject's view by large panels. . . .

In both film conditions, at the conclusion of the movie the experimenter entered the room and then escorted the subject to the test room.

Aggression Instigation

In order to differentiate clearly the exposure and test situations subjects were tested for the amount of imitative learning in a different experimental room which was set off from the main nursery school building.

The degree to which a child has learned aggressive patterns of behavior through imitation becomes most evident when the child is instigated to aggression on later occasions. Thus, for example, the effects of viewing the movie, *Rebel Without a Cause*, were not evident until the boys were instigated to aggression the following day, at which time they re-enacted the televised switch-blade knife fight in considerable detail. For this reason, the children in the experiment, both those in the control group, and those who were exposed to the aggressive models, were mildly frustrated before they were brought to the test room.

Following the exposure experience, the experimenter brought the subject to an anteroom which contained a varied array of highly attractive toys. The experimenter explained that the toys were for the subject to play with, but, as soon as the subject became sufficiently involved with the play material, the experimenter remarked that these were her very best toys, that she did not let just anyone play with them, and that she had decided to reserve these toys for some other children. However, the subject could play with any of the toys in the next room. The experimenter and the subject then entered the adjoining experimental room. . . .

Test for Delayed Imitation

The experimental room contained a variety of toys, some of which could be used in imitative or nonimitative aggression, and others which tended to elicit predominantly nonaggressive forms of behavior. The aggressive toys included a 3-foot Bobo doll, a mallet and peg board, two dart guns, and a tether ball with a face painted on it which hung from the ceiling. The nonaggressive toys, on the other hand, included a tea set, crayons and coloring paper, a ball, two dolls, three bears, cars and trucks, and plastic farm animals. . . .

The subject spent 20 minutes in the experimental room during which time his behavior was rated in terms of predetermined response categories by judges who observed the session through a one-way mirror in an adjoining observation room. The 20-minute session was divided in 5-second intervals by means of an electric interval timer, thus yielding a total number of 240 response units for each subject. . . .

RESULTS

The mean imitative and nonimitative aggression scores for subjects in the various experimental and control groups are presented in Table 1.

Since the distributions of scores departed from normality and the assumption of homogeneity of variance could not be made for most of the measures, the Freidman two-way analysis of variance by ranks was employed for testing the significance of the obtained differences.

TABLE 1

Mean Aggression Scores for Subgroups of Experimental and Control Subjects

Response category	Experimental groups					
	Real-life aggressive		Human film aggressive		Cartoon film aggressive	Control group
	F Model	M Model	F Model	M Model		
Total aggression						
Girls	65.8	57.3	87.0	79.5	80.9	36.4
Boys	76.8	131.8	114.5	85.0	117.2	72.2
Imitative aggression						
Girls	19.2	9.2	10.0	8.0	7.8	1.8
Boys	18.4	38.4	34.3	13.3	16.2	3.9
Mallet aggression						
Girls	17.2	18.7	49.2	19.5	36.8	13.1
Boys	15.5	28.8	20.5	16.3	12.5	13.5
Sits on Bobo doll[a]						
Girls	10.4	5.6	10.3	4.5	15.3	3.3
Boys	1.3	0.7	7.7	0.0	5.6	0.6
Nonimitative aggression						
Girls	27.6	24.9	24.0	34.3	27.5	17.8
Boys	35.5	48.6	46.8	31.8	71.8	40.4
Aggressive gun play						
Girls	1.8	4.5	3.8	17.6	8.8	3.7
Boys	7.3	15.9	12.8	23.7	16.6	14.3

[a]This response category was not included in the total aggression score.

Total Aggression

The mean total aggression scores for subjects in the real-life, human film, cartoon film, and the control groups are 83, 92, 99, and 54 respectively. The results of the analysis of variance performed on these scores reveal that the main effect of treatment conditions is significant ($Xr^2 = p < .05$), confirming the prediction that exposure of subjects to aggressive models increases the probability that subjects will respond aggressively when instigated on later occasions. Further analyses of pairs of scores by means of the Wilcoxon matched-pairs signed-ranks test show that subjects who viewed the real-life models and the film-mediated models do not differ from each other in total aggressiveness but all three experimental groups expressed significantly more aggressive behavior than the control subjects. . . .

Albert Bandura et al.

In order to determine the influence of sex of model and sex of child on the expression of imitative and nonimitative aggression, the data from the experimental groups were combined and the significance of the differences between groups was assessed by t tests for uncorrelated means. In statistical comparisons involving relatively skewed distributions of scores the Mann-Whitney U test was employed.

Sex of subjects had a highly significant effect on both the learning and the performance of aggression. Boys, in relation to girls, exhibited significantly more total aggression ($t = 2.69$, $p < .01$), more imitative aggression ($t = 2.82$, $p < .005$), more aggressive gun play ($z = 3.38$, $p < .001$), and more nonimitative aggressive behavior ($t = 2.98$, $p < .005$). Girls, on the other hand, were more inclined than boys to sit on the Bobo doll but refrained from punching it ($z = 3.47$, $p < .001$).

The analyses also disclosed some influences of the sex of the model. Subjects exposed to the male model, as compared to the female model, expressed significantly more aggressive gun play ($z = 2.83$, $p < .005$). The most marked differences in aggressive gun play ($U = 9.5$, $p < .001$), however, were found between girls exposed to the female model ($M = 2.9$) and males who observed the male model ($M = 19.8$). Although the overall model difference in partially imitative behavior, Sits on Bobo, was not significant, Sex × Model subgroup comparisons yielded some interesting results. Boys who observed the aggressive female model, for example, were more likely to sit on the Bobo doll without punching it than boys who viewed the male model ($U = 33$, $p < .05$). Girls reproduced the nonaggressive component of the male model's aggressive pattern of behavior (i.e., sat on the doll without punching it) with considerably higher frequency than did boys who observed the same model ($U = 21.5$, $p < .02$). The highest incidence of partially imitative responses was yielded by the group of girls who viewed the aggressive female model ($M = 10.4$), and the lowest values by the boys who were exposed to the male model ($M = 0.3$). This difference was significant beyond the .05 significance level. These findings, along with the sex of child and sex of model differences reported in the preceding sections, provide further support for the view that the influence of models in promoting social learning is determined, in part, by the sex appropriateness of the model's behavior (Bandura et al., 1961). . . .

DISCUSSION

The results of the present study provide strong evidence that exposure to filmed aggression heightens aggressive reactions in children. Subjects who viewed the aggressive human and cartoon models on film exhibited nearly twice as much aggression than did subjects in the control group who were not exposed to the aggressive film content. . . .

Filmed aggression, not only facilitated the expression of aggression, but also effectively shaped the form of the subjects' aggressive behavior. The finding that children modeled their behavior to some extent after the film characters suggests that pictorial mass media, particularly television, may serve as an important source of social behavior. In fact, a possible generalization of responses originally learned in the television situation to the experimental film may account for the significantly greater amount of aggressive gun play displayed by subjects in the film condition as compared to subjects in the real-life and control groups. It is unfortunate that the qualitative features of the gun behavior were not scored since subjects in the film condition, unlike those in the other two groups, developed interesting elaborations in gun play (for example, stalking the imaginary opponent, quick drawing, and rapid firing), characteristic of the Western gun fighter.

REFERENCES

1. Bandura, A., & Huston, Aletha C. Identification as a process of incidental learning. *J. abnorm. soc. Psychol.*, 1961, **63,** 311–318.
2. Bandura, A., Ross, Dorothea, & Ross, Sheila A. Transmission of aggression through imitation of aggressive models. *J. abnorm. soc. Psychol.*, 1961, **63,** 575–582.
3. San Francisco Chronicle. "James Dean" knifing in South City. *San Francisco Chron.*, March 1, 1961, 6.

7.1 GEORGE A. MILLER

The Magical Number Seven, Plus or Minus Two: Some Limits on Our Capacity for Processing Information

Many people would like to have a better memory. Many psychologists have studied the limits of human memory, including George A. Miller, who has helped clarify the dimensions of short-term memory.

Miller (b. 1920), a cognitive psychologist, earned his Ph.D. in experimental psychology from Harvard University in 1946. He taught at Harvard before taking a position at Princeton University, where he spent most of his professional career. Miller has also served as president of the American Psychological Association (APA). Among his many publications is the influential 1951 book *Language and Communication*.

This selection is from "The Magical Number Seven, Plus or Minus Two: Some Limits on Our Capacity for Processing Information," which was published in *Psychological Review* in 1956. Do not let the jargon (e.g., bits, chunks) distract you from the main point of this article—that our memory system is limited, but we can extend the limit by including more information in the material we remember. The "seven, plus or minus two" in the title refers to the fact that we can usually recall about five to nine items shortly after we have memorized them. Think of how you could apply this concept as you are studying for a test. (Hint: reduce your notes to meaningful key points.)

Key Concept: short-term memory

My problem is that I have been persecuted by an integer. For seven years this number has followed me around, has intruded in my most private data, and has assaulted me from the pages of our most public journals. This number assumes a variety of disguises, being sometimes a little larger and sometimes a little smaller than usual, but never changing so much as to be unrecognizable. The persistence with which this number plagues me is far more than a random accident. There is, to quote a famous senator, a design behind it, some pattern governing its appearances. Either there really is something unusual about the number or else I am suffering from delusions of persecution. . . .

THE SPAN OF IMMEDIATE MEMORY

Let me summarize the situation in this way. There is a clear and definite limit to the accuracy with which we can identify absolutely the magnitude of a unidimensional stimulus variable. I would propose to call this limit the *span of absolute judgment,* and I maintain that for unidimensional judgments this span is usually somewhere in the neighborhood of seven. We are not completely at the mercy of this limited span, however, because we have a variety of techniques for getting around it and increasing the accuracy of our judgments. The three most important of these devices are (*a*) to make relative rather than absolute judgments; or, if that is not possible, (*b*) to increase the number of dimensions along which the stimuli can differ; or (*c*) to arrange the task in such a way that we make a sequence of several absolute judgments in a row.

The study of relative judgments is one of the oldest topics in experimental psychology, and I will not pause to review it now. [Consider] the second device, increasing the dimensionality. It seems that by adding more dimensions and requiring crude, binary, yes-no judgments on each attribute we can extend the span of absolute judgment from seven to at least 150. Judging from our everyday behavior, the limit is probably in the thousands, if indeed there is a limit. In my opinion, we cannot go on compounding dimensions indefinitely. I suspect that there is also a *span of perceptual dimensionality* and that this span is somewhere in the neighborhood of ten, but I must add at once that there is no objective evidence to support this suspicion. This is a question sadly needing experimental exploration.

Concerning the third device, the use of successive judgments, I have quite a bit to say because this device introduces memory as the handmaiden of discrimination. And, since mnemonic processes are at least as complex as are perceptual processes, we can anticipate that their interactions will not be easily disentangled.

Suppose that we start by simply extending slightly the experimental procedure that we have been using. Up to this point we have presented a single stimulus and asked the observer to name it immediately thereafter. We can extend this procedure by requiring the observer to withhold his response until we have given him several stimuli in succession. At the end of the sequence of stimuli he then makes his response. We still have the same sort of input-output situation that is required for the measurement of transmitted information. But now we have passed from an experiment on absolute judgment to what is traditionally called an experiment on immediate memory.

Before we look at any data on this topic I feel I must give you a word of warning to help you avoid some obvious associations that can be confusing. Everybody knows that there is a finite span of immediate memory and that for a lot of different kinds of test materials this span is about seven items in length. . . . [T]here is a span of absolute judgment that can distinguish about seven categories and . . . there is a span of attention that will encompass about six objects at a glance. What is more natural than to think that all three of these spans are different aspects of a single underlying process? And that is a fundamental mistake, as I shall be at some pains to demonstrate. This mistake is one of the malicious persecutions that the magical number seven has subjected me to.

My mistake went something like this. . . . [T]he invariant feature in the span of absolute judgment is the amount of information that the observer can transmit. There is a real operational similarity between the absolute judgment experiment and the immediate memory experiment. If immediate memory is like absolute judgment, then it should follow that the invariant feature in the span of immediate memory is also the amount of information that an observer can retain. If the amount of information in the span of immediate memory is a constant, then the span should be short when the individual items contain a lot of information and the span should be long when the items contain little information. For example, decimal digits are worth 3.3 bits apiece. We can recall about seven of them, for a total of 23 bits of information. Isolated English words are worth about 10 bits apiece. If the total amount of information is to remain constant at 23 bits, then we should be able to remember only two or three words chosen at random. In this way I generated a theory about how the span of immediate memory should vary as a function of the amount of information per item in the test materials.

The measurements of memory span in the literature are suggestive on this question, but not definitive. And so it was necessary to do the experiment to see. Hayes tried it out with five different kinds of test materials: binary digits, decimal digits, letters of the alphabet, letters plus decimal digits, and with 1,000 monosyllabic words. The lists were read aloud at the rate of one item per second and the subjects had as much time as they needed to give their responses. A procedure described by Woodworth was used to score the responses.

The results are shown by the filled circles in Fig. 1. Here the dotted line indicates what the span should have been if the amount of information in the span were constant. The solid curves represent the data. Hayes repeated the experiment using test vocabularies of different sizes but all containing only English monosyllables (open circles in Fig. 1). This more homogeneous test material did not change the picture significantly. With binary items the span is about nine and, although it drops to about five with monosyllabic English words, the difference is far less than the hypothesis of constant information would require. . . .

And so the outcome is perfectly clear. . . . [T]he span of absolute judgment and the span of immediate memory are quite different kinds of limitations that are imposed on our ability to process information. Absolute judgment is limited by the amount of information. Immediate memory is limited by the number of items. In order to capture this distinction in somewhat picturesque terms, I have fallen into the custom of distinguishing between *bits* of information and *chunks* of information. Then I can say that the number of bits of information is constant for absolute judgment and the number of chunks of information is constant for immediate memory. The span of immediate mem-

FIGURE 1

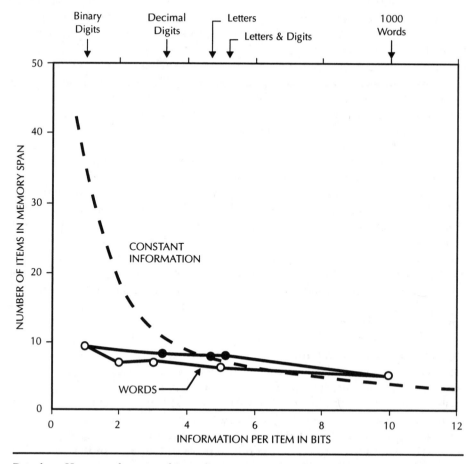

Data from Hayes on the span of immediate memory plotted as a function of the amount of information per item in the test materials.

ory seems to be almost independent of the number of bits per chunk, at least over the range that has been examined to date.

The contrast of the terms *bit* and *chunk* also serves to highlight the fact that we are not very definite about what constitutes a chunk of information. For example, the memory span of five words that Hayes obtained when each word was drawn at random from a set of 1000 English monosyllables might just as appropriately have been called a memory span of 15 phonemes, since each word had about three phonemes in it. Intuitively, it is clear that the subjects were recalling five words, not 15 phonemes, but the logical distinction is not immediately apparent. We are dealing here with a process of organizing or grouping the input into familiar units or chunks, and a great deal of learning has gone into the formation of these familiar units.

RECODING

In order to speak more precisely, therefore, we must recognize the importance of grouping or organizing the input sequence into units or chunks. Since the memory span is a fixed number of chunks, we can increase the number of bits of information that it contains simply by building larger and larger chunks, each chunk containing more information than before.

A man just beginning to learn radio-telegraphic code hears each *dit* and *dah* as a separate chunk. Soon he is able to organize these sounds into letters and then he can deal with the letters as chunks. Then the letters organize themselves as words, which are still larger chunks, and he begins to hear whole phrases. I do not mean that each step is a discrete process, or that plateaus must appear in his learning curve, for surely the levels of organization are achieved at different rates and overlap each other during the learning process. I am simply pointing to the obvious fact that the dits and dahs are organized by learning into patterns and that as these larger chunks emerge the amount of message that the operator can remember increases correspondingly. In the terms I am proposing to use, the operator learns to increase the bits per chunk.

In the jargon of communication theory, this process would be called *recoding*. The input is given in a code that contains many chunks with a few bits per chunk. The operator recodes the input into another code that contains fewer chunks with more bits per chunk. There are many ways to do this recoding, but probably the simplest is to group the input events, apply a new name to the group, and then remember the new name rather than the original input events. . . .

In my opinion the most customary kind of recoding that we do all the time is to translate into a verbal code. When there is a story or an argument or an idea that we want to remember, we usually try to rephrase it "in our own words." When we witness some event we want to remember, we make a verbal description of the event and then remember our verbalization. Upon recall we recreate by secondary elaboration the details that seem consistent with the particular verbal recoding we happen to have made. The well-known experiment by Carmichael, Hogan, and Walter on the influence that names have on the recall of visual figures is one demonstration of the process.

The inaccuracy of the testimony of eyewitnesses is well known in legal psychology, but the distortions of testimony are not random—they follow naturally from the particular recoding that the witness used, and the particular recoding he used depends upon his whole life history. Our language is tremendously useful for repackaging material into a few chunks rich in information. I suspect that imagery is a form of recoding, too, but images seem much harder to get at operationally and to study experimentally than the more symbolic kinds of recoding. . . .

SUMMARY

I have come to the end of the data that I wanted to present, so I would like now to make some summarizing remarks.

First, the span of absolute judgment and the span of immediate memory impose severe limitations on the amount of information that we are able to receive, process, and remember. By organizing the stimulus input simultaneously into several dimensions and successively into a sequence of chunks, we manage to break (or at least stretch) this informational bottleneck.

Second, the process of recoding is a very important one in human psychology and deserves much more explicit attention than it has received. In particular, the kind of linguistic recoding that people do seems to me to be the very lifeblood of the thought processes. Recoding procedures are a constant concern to clinicians, social psychologists, linguists, and anthropologists and yet, probably because recoding is less accessible to experimental manipulation than nonsense syllables or *T* mazes, the traditional experimental psychologist has contributed little or nothing to their analysis. Nevertheless, experimental techniques can be used, methods of recoding can be specified, behavioral indicants can be found. And I anticipate that we will find a very orderly set of relations describing what now seems an uncharted wilderness of individual differences. . . .

And finally, what about the magical number seven? What about the seven wonders of the world, the seven seas, the seven deadly sins, the seven daughters of Atlas in the Pleiades, the seven ages of man, the seven levels of hell, the seven primary colors, the seven notes of the musical scale, and the seven days of the week? What about the seven-point rating scale, the seven categories for absolute judgment, the seven objects in the span of attention, and the seven digits in the span of immediate memory? For the present I propose to withhold judgment. Perhaps there is something deep and profound behind all these sevens, something just calling out for us to discover it. But I suspect that it is only a pernicious, Pythagorean coincidence.

7.2 ENDEL TULVING

What Is Episodic Memory?

Ultimately, what we learn must enter our long-term memory, which appears to have an unlimited capacity and is relatively permanent. In the past two decades, psychologists have debated the structure of long-term memory with respect to the number of memory systems that exist. One theory comes from psychologist Endel Tulving, who supports a classification scheme that consists of three memory systems: procedural, semantic, and episodic.

Tulving (b. 1927) received his B.A. from the University of Toronto in 1953 and his Ph.D. in experimental psychology from Harvard University in 1957. He taught at Yale University before going to the University of Toronto in 1974, where he is currently a professor emeritus of psychology. He also serves as Tanenbaum Chair in Cognitive Neuroscience at Rotman Research Institute of Baycrest Centre in Toronto, Ontario, Canada. Tulving, a leader in the area of long-term memory, has many publications, including *Elements of Episodic Memory* (Oxford University Press, 1983).

This selection is from "What Is Episodic Memory?" which was published in the American Psychological Society's journal *Current Directions in Psychological Science* in 1993. In it, Tulving clarifies the distinction between episodic and semantic memory and discusses the characteristics of each. He points out that episodic memory is unique in that it requires the person to be aware of the past event that is remembered (he uses the term *autonoetic awareness*). As you read this selection, try to think of situations in which you have experienced episodic memory as distinct from semantic memory.

Key Concept: long-term memory

*F*ew problems in science are as difficult as those of working out the precise relation between two complex concepts that are deceptively similar. The relation between episodic and semantic memory belongs in this category. Intuition and rational thought reveal many similarities between these two kinds of memory and tempt us to think of the two as one. Yet, closer scrutiny reveals a number of fundamental differences. In this article, I discuss one such difference, namely, the nature of conscious awareness that characterizes retrieval of episodic and semantic information. . . .

EPISODIC AND SEMANTIC MEMORY SYSTEMS

In a nutshell, the theory [of episodic memory] holds that episodic and semantic memory are two of the five major human memory systems for which reasonably adequate evidence is now available. The other three systems are procedural, perceptual representation, and short-term memory.[1] Although each system serves particular functions that other systems cannot serve (the so-called criterion of functional incompatibility[2]), several systems usually interact in the performance of tasks in everyday life as well as in the memory laboratory.

Semantic memory registers and stores knowledge about the world in the broadest sense and makes it available for retrieval. If a person knows something that is in principle describable in the propositional form, that something belongs to the domain of semantic memory. Semantic memory enables individuals to represent and mentally operate on situations, objects, and relations in the world that are not present to the senses: The owner of a semantic memory system can think about things that are not here now.

Episodic memory enables a person to remember personally experienced events as such. That is, it makes it possible for a person to be consciously aware of an earlier experience in a certain situation at a certain time. Thus, the information of episodic memory could be said to concern the self's experiences in subjective space and time. In contrast, the information of semantic memory processes concerns objects and their relations in the world at large. The owner of an episodic memory system is not only capable of remembering the temporal organization of otherwise unrelated events, but is also capable of mental time travel: Such a person can transport at will into the personal past, as well as into the future, a feat not possible for other kinds of memory.

The relation between episodic and semantic memory is hierarchical: Episodic memory has evolved out of, but many of its operations have remained dependent on, semantic memory. A corollary is that semantic memory can operate (store and retrieve information) independently of episodic memory, but not vice versa. Episodic memory is not necessary for encoding and storing of information into semantic memory, although it may modulate such encoding and storage. Semantic memory develops earlier in childhood than episodic memory: Children are capable of learning facts of the world before they remember their own past experiences. Finally, whereas medial temporal lobe and diencephalic structures, among others, play a critical role in semantic memory, frontal lobe structures seem to be involved in subserving episodic memory.[3]

CONSCIOUS AWARENESS IN REMEMBERING

One idea that was not clearly articulated in the *Elements of Episodic Memory* concerned the nature of conscious awareness that accompanies the act of retrieval of information from the two systems. At that time, there was little objective evidence relevant to that problem. Some progress on this front has now been made, and I summarize some of it here.

The working hypothesis is that episodic and semantic memory differ fundamentally with respect to the nature of conscious awareness that accompanies retrieval of information. The act of remembering a personally experienced event, that is, consciously recollecting it, is characterized by a distinctive, unique awareness of reexperiencing here and now something that happened before, at another time and in another place. The awareness and its feeling-tone are intimately familiar to every normal human being. One seldom mistakes remembering for any other kind of experience—perceiving, imagining, dreaming, daydreaming, or just thinking about things one knows about the world.

I refer to the kind of conscious awareness that characterizes remembering one's past as *autonoetic* awareness, contrasting it with *noetic* awareness, which characterizes retrieval of information from semantic memory, and *anoetic* awareness, which accompanies expression of procedural knowledge.[4] . . .

"REMEMBER" AND "KNOW" JUDGMENTS

If amnesics can learn new facts and subsequently know them, in the absence of any autonoetic recollection of the sources of the facts, is it possible that normal people, too, know facts without remembering where or how they acquired them? Of course, it happens all the time. Every person knows hundreds and thousands of facts, without remembering the circumstances of their acquisition. This *source amnesia* that characterizes the learning in hypnotized people and amnesics, as well as older people, is well known to all of us. The phenomenon is simply more extreme in some of these special cases than in normal adults.

Gardiner and his collaborators have reported a number of studies on remembering versus knowing newly learned information in normal people.[5] The interesting feature of these studies is that the information in question is something that is usually associated with episodic memory, namely, occurrence of familiar words in a to-be-remembered list tested by recognition. In a typical experiment, subjects see a list of unrelated words, presented one at a time, on a single study trial, and then take a two-step test. In the test, they are shown both studied and nonstudied words and are asked to make a judgment about each word's presence in or absence from the study list and to indicate the basis of each positive recognition judgment.

Subjects are instructed that there are two ways in which they can tell that a word was in the study list: They either "remember" the event of the word's presentation in the study list or simply "know" on some basis that the item had appeared in the list, without remembering its occurrence.

In one experiment, for example, subjects studied a list of words under the conditions of either full or divided attention and were then tested as described. Division of attention reduced the proportion of "remembered" words (.50 vs. .38) but did not affect the proportion of words "known" to have been in the list (.21 vs. .20). Other experiments have examined the effect of other variables, such as levels of processing, generating versus reading the word at study, retention interval, word frequency, and age of subjects. These too have produced dissociations between the "remember" and "know" components of recognition memory. Yet other studies—done on brain-damaged subjects, or using psychoactive drugs, or recording event-related potentials—have begun to identify some of the neural correlates of "remember" and "know" judgments.[6]

There are other approaches to the study of awareness of source of information,[7] and correspondingly different ways of interpreting these experiments and their results. I prefer the hypothesis that "remember" judgments, based on autonoetic awareness, reflect the operation of the episodic system, whereas "know" judgments, based on noetic awareness, reflect the operation of the semantic system. Thus, subjects have two sources of information concerning the membership of words in a study list—episodic and semantic memory. When they retrieve this information from semantic memory, they appear to suffer source amnesia: They do not remember the particular event of encountering the word. In amnesic patients . . . , the source amnesia is more extensive, covering not just encounters with individual words, but personal encounters of all kinds.

CONCLUSION

Episodic memory is a neurocognitive memory system that enables people to remember past happenings. The *remembering* in this proposition is not a generic term designating all kinds of retrieval of stored information, but rather a specific concept that designates retrieval from episodic memory. For a rememberer to remember something means that he or she is autonoetically aware of a past happening in which he or she has participated. For an experimenter or theorist to study episodic memory means to study autonoetic awareness of past experiences, separately from noetic retrieval of the semantic contents of the remembered episodes.

NOTES

1. E. Tulving, Concepts of human memory, in *Memory; Organization and Locus of Change*, L. R. Squire, N. M. Weinberger, G. Lynch, and J. L. McGaugh, Eds. (Oxford University Press, New York, 1991).
2. D. F. Sherry and D. L. Schacter, The evolution of multiple memory systems, *Psychological Review, 94*, 439–454 (1987).
3. E. Tulving, Memory: Performance, knowledge, and experience, *European Journal of Cognitive Psychology, 1*, 3–26 (1989); A. P. Shimamura, J. J. Janowsky, and L. R. Squire, Memory for the temporal order of events in patients with frontal lobe lesions and amnesic patients, *Neuropsychologia, 28*, 803–813 (1990).
4. E. Tulving, Varieties of consciousness and levels of awareness in memory, in *Attention: Selection, Awareness and Control: A Tribute to Donald Broadbent*, A. Baddeley and L. Weiskrantz, Eds. (Oxford University Press, London, in press).
5. J. M. Gardiner and R. I. Java, Recognizing and remembering, in *Theories of Memory*, A. Collins, M. Conway, S. Gathercole, and P. Morris, Eds. (Erlbaum, Hillsdale, NJ, in press).

6. H. V. Curran, J. M. Gardiner, R. I. Java, and D. Allen, Effects of lorazepam upon recollective experience in recognition memory, *Psychopharmacology, 110,* 374–378 (1993); M. E. Smith, Neurophysiological manifestations of recollective experience during recognition memory judgments, *Journal of Cognitive Neuroscience, 5,* 1–13 (1993); T. A. Blaxton, *The role of temporal lobes in remembering visuospatial materials: Remembering and knowing,* manuscript submitted for publication (1993).

7. G. Mandler, P. Graf, and D. Kraft, Activation and elaboration effects in recognition and word priming, *The Quarterly Journal of Experimental Psychology, 38A,* 645–662 (1986); L. L. Jacoby, A process dissociation framework: Separating automatic from intentional uses of memory, *Journal of Memory and Language, 30,* 513–541 (1991); M. K. Johnson and W. Hirst, MEM: Memory subsystems as processes, in *Theories of Memory,* A. Collins, M. Conway, S. Gathercole, and P. Morris, Eds. (Erlbaum, Hillsdale, NJ, in press).

Leading Questions and the Eyewitness Report

Most people want to believe that they have perfect memories. Psychologists have discovered, however, that memory is subject to a wide variety of distortions. Elizabeth F. Loftus, for example, has studied how asking certain questions of eyewitnesses to an event affects their later recall of the incident.

Loftus (b. 1944) earned her Ph.D. in psychology from Stanford University in 1970. She is currently a professor of psychology at the University of Washington. Loftus is one of the leading legal consultants in the United States in the area of eyewitness testimony in trials. She has written several books, including *Eyewitness Testimony* (Harvard University Press, 1979), in which she describes how leading questions can have a permanent effect on the memory of a witness.

This selection from "Leading Questions and the Eyewitness Report," which was published in *Cognitive Psychology* in 1972, clearly demonstrates how easy it is to modify eyewitness memory. This selection consists of several different but related experiments, and for each one, the methods, the results, and a discussion section are provided. The chi-square (X^2) and the t-test are statistical tests used to determine significance (differences between conditions). A probability (p) less than .05 is significant. As you read this selection, consider the implications that Loftus's research has for everyday situations.

Key Concept: eyewitness memory

A total of 490 subjects, in four experiments, saw films of complex, fast-moving events, such as automobile accidents or classroom disruptions. The purpose of these experiments was to investigate how the wording of questions asked immediately after an event may influence responses to questions asked considerably later. It is shown that when the initial question contains either either true presuppositions (e.g., it postulates the existence of an object that did exist in the scene) or false presuppositions (e.g., postulates the existence of an object that did not exist), the likelihood is increased that subjects will later report having seen the presupposed object. The results suggest that questions asked immediately after an event can introduce new—not necessarily correct—information, which is then added to the memorial representation of the event, thereby causing its reconstruction or alteration.

Elizabeth F. Loftus

Although current theories of memory are derived largely from experiments involving lists of words or sentences, many memories occurring in everyday life involve complex, largely visual, and often fast-moving events. Of course, we are rarely required to provide precise recall of such experiences—though as we age, we often volunteer them—but on occasion such recall is demanded, as when we have witnessed a crime or an accident. Our theories should be able to encompass such socially important forms of memory. It is clearly of concern to the law, to police and insurance investigators, and to others to know something about the completeness, accuracy, and malleability of such memories.

When one has witnessed an important event, one is sometimes asked a series of questions about it. Do these questions, if asked immediately after the event, influence the memory of it that then develops? This paper first summarizes research suggesting that the wording of such initial questions can have a substantial effect on the answers given, and then reports four new studies showing that the wording of these initial questions can also influence the answers to different questions asked at some later time. The discussion of these findings develops the thesis that questions asked about an event shortly after it occurs may distort the witness' memory for that event.

ANSWERS DEPEND ON THE WORDING OF QUESTIONS

An example of how the wording of a question can affect a person's answer to it has been reported by Harris (1973). His subjects were told that "the experiment was a study in the accuracy of guessing measurements, and that they should make as intelligent a numerical guess as possible to each question" (p. 399). They were then asked either of two questions such as, "How tall was the basketball player?", or, "How short was the basketball player?" Presumably the former form of the question presupposes nothing about the height of the player, whereas the latter form involves a presupposition that the player is short. On the average, subjects guessed about 79 and 69 in. (190 and 175 mm), respectively. Similar results appeared with other pairs of questions. For example, "How long was the movie?", led to an average estimate of 130 min, whereas, "How short was the movie?" led to 100 min. While it was not Harris' central concern, his study clearly demonstrates that the wording of a question may affect the answer.

Past Personal Experiences

In one study (Loftus, unpublished), 40 people were interviewed about their headaches and about headache products under the belief that they were participating in market research on these products. Two of the questions were crucial to the experiment. One asked about products other than that currently being used, in one of two wordings:

(1a) In terms of the total number of products, how many other products have you tried? 1? 2? 3?

(1b) In terms of the total number of products, how many other products have you tried? 1? 5? 10?

The 1/2/3 subjects claimed to have tried an average of 3.3 other products, whereas the 1/5/10 subjects claimed an average of 5.2; $t(38) = 3.14$, $\sigma = .61$, $p < .01$.

The second key question asked about frequency of headaches in one of two ways:

(2a) Do you get headaches frequently, and, if so, how often?

(2b) Do you get headaches occasionally, and, if so, how often?

The "frequently" subjects reported an average of 2.2 headaches/wk, whereas the "occasionally" group reported only 0.7/wk; $t(38) = 3.19$, $\sigma = .47$, $p < .01$.

Recently Witnessed Events

Two examples from the published literature also indicate that the wording of a question put to a person about a recently-witnessed event can affect a person's answer to that question. In one study (Loftus, 1974; Loftus & Zanni, 1975), 100 students viewed a short file segment depicting a multiple-car accident. Immediately afterward, they filled out a 22-item questionnaire which contained six critical questions. Three of these asked about items that had appeared in the film whereas the other three asked about items not present in the film. For half the subjects, all the critical questions began with the words, "Did you see a . . ." as in, "Did you see a broken headlight?" For the remaining half, the critical questions began with the words, "Did you see the . . ." as in, "Did you see the broken headlight?"

Thus, the questions differed only in the form of the article, *the* or *a*. One uses "the" when one assumes the object referred to exists and may be familiar to the listener. An investigator who asks, "Did you see the broken headlight?" essentially says, "There was a broken headlight. Did you happen to see it?" His assumption may influence a witness' report. By contrast, the article "a" does not necessarily convey the implication of existence.

The results showed that witnesses who were asked "the" questions were more likely to report having seen something, whether or not it had really appeared in the film, than those who were asked "a" questions. Even this very subtle change in wording influences a witness' report.

In another study (Loftus & Palmer, 1974), subjects saw films of automobile accidents and then answered questions about the accidents. The wording of a question was shown to affect a numerical estimate. In particular, the question, "About how fast were the cars going when they smashed into each other?" consistently elicited a higher estimate of speed than when "smashed" was replaced by "collided," "bumped," "contacted," or "hit."

We may conclude that in a variety of situations the wording of a question about an event can influence the answer that is given. This effect has been observed when a person reports about his own experiences, about events he has recently witnessed, and when answering a general question (e.g., "How short was the movie?") not based on any specific witnessed incident.

QUESTION WORDING AND ANSWERS TO SUBSEQUENT QUESTIONS

Our concern in this paper is not on the effect of the wording of a question on its answer, but rather on the answers to other questions asked some time afterward. We will interpret the evidence to be presented as suggesting a memorial phenomenon of some importance.

In the present experiments, a key [set of] initial questions contains a *presupposition,* which is simply a condition that must hold in order for the question to be contextually appropriate. For example, the question, "How fast was the car going when it ran the stop sign?" presupposes that there was a stop sign. If a stop sign actually did exist, then in answering this question a subject might review, strengthen, or make more available certain memory representations corresponding to the stop sign. This being the case, the initial question might be expected to influence the answer to a subsequent question about the stop sign, such as the question, "Did you see the stop sign?" A simple extension of the argument of Clark and Haviland (in press) can be made here: When confronted with the initial question, "How fast was the car going when it ran the stop sign?", the subject might treat the presupposed information as if it were an address, a pointer, or an instruction specifying where information related to that presupposition may be found (as well as where new information is to be integrated into the previous knowledge). In the process the presupposed information may be strengthened.

What if the presupposition is false? In that case it will not correspond to any existing representation, and the subject may treat it as new information and enter it into his memory. Subsequently, the new "false" information may appear in verbal reports solicited from the subject.

To explore these ideas, subjects viewed films of complex, fast-moving events. Viewing of the film was followed by initial questions which contained presuppositions that were either true (Experiment 1) or false (Experiments 2–4). In Experiment 1, the initial questions either did or did not mention an object that was in fact present in the film. A subsequent question, asked a few minutes later, inquired as to whether the subject has seen the existing object. In

Experiments 2–4, the initial questions were again asked immediately after the film, whereas the subsequent questions were asked after a lapse of 1 wk.

EXPERIMENT 1

Method

One hundred and fifty University of Washington students, in groups of various sizes, were shown a film of a multiple-car accident in which one car, after failing to stop at a stop sign, makes a right-hand turn into the main stream of traffic. In an attempt to avoid a collision, the cars in the oncoming traffic stop suddenly and a five-car, bumper-to-bumper collision results. The film lasts less than 1 min, and the accident occurs within a 4-sec period.

At the end of the film, a 10-item questionnaire was administered. A diagram of the situation labeled the car that ran the stop sign as "A," and the cars involved in the collision as "B" through "F." The first question asked about the speed of Car A in one of two ways:

(1) How fast was Car A going when it ran the stop sign?

(2) How fast was Car A going when it turned right? Seventy-five subjects received the "stop sign" question and 75 received the "turned right" question. The last question was identical for all subjects: "Did you see a stop sign for Car A?" Subjects responded by circling "yes" or "no" on their questionnaires.

Results and Discussion

Fifty-three percent of the subjects in the "stop sign" group responded "yes" to the question, "Did you see a stop sign for Car A?", whereas only 35% in the "turn right" group claimed to have seen the stop sign; $x^2(1) = 4.98$, $p < .05$. The wording of a presupposition into a question about an event, asked immediately after that event has taken place, can influence the answer to a subsequent question concerning the presupposition itself, asked a very short time later, in the direction of conforming with the supplied information.

There are at least two possible explanations of this effect. The first is that when a subject answers the initial stop sign question, he somehow reviews, or strengthens, or in some sense makes more available certain memory representations corresponding to the stop sign. Later, when asked, "Did you see a stop sign . . . ?", he responds on the basis of the strengthened memorial representation.

A second possibility may be called the "construction hypothesis." In answering the initial stop sign question, the subject may "visualize" or "reconstruct " in his mind that portion of the incident needed to answer the question, and so, if he accepts the presupposition, he introduces a stop sign into his visualization whether or not it was in memory. When interrogated later about the existence of the stop sign, he responds on the basis of his earlier supplementation of the actual incident. In other words, the subject may "see" the stop sign that he has himself constructed. This would not tend to happen when the initial question refers only to the right turn.

The construction hypothesis has an important consequence. If a piece of true information supplied to the subject after the accident augments his memory, then, in a similar way, it should be possible to introduce into memory something that was not in fact in the scene, by supplying a piece of false information. For example, Loftus and Palmer (1974, Expt. 2) showed subjects a film of an automobile accident and followed it by questions about events that occurred in the film. Some subjects were asked "About how fast were the cars going when they smashed into each other?", whereas others were asked the same question with "hit" substituted for "smashed." On a retest 1 wk later, those questioned with "smashed" were more likely than those questioned with "hit" to agree that they had seen broken glass in the scene, even though none was present in the film. In the present framework, we assume that the initial representation of the accident the subject has witnessed is modified toward greater severity when the experimenter uses the term "smashed" because the question supplies a piece of new information, namely, that the cars did indeed *smash* into each other. On hearing the "smashed" question, some subjects may reconstruct the accident, integrating the new information into the existing representation. If so, the result is a representation of an accident in memory that is more severe than, in fact, it actually was. In particular, the more severe accident is more likely to include broken glass.

The presupposition that the cars smashed into each other may be additional information, but it can hardly be said to be false information. It is important to determine whether it is also true that false presuppositions can affect a witness' answer to a later question about that presupposition. Such a finding would imply that a false presupposition can be accepted by a witness, that the hypothesis of a strengthening of an existing memorial representation is untenable (since there should be no representation corresponding to nonexistent objects), and that the construction hypothesis discussed above is supported. Experiment 2 was designed to check this idea.

EXPERIMENT 2

Method

Forty undergraduate students at the University of Washington, again in groups of various sizes, were shown a 3-min videotape taken from the film *Diary of a Student Revolution*. The sequence depicted the disruption of a class by eight demonstrators; the confrontation, which was relatively noisy, resulted in the demonstrators leaving the classroom.

At the end of the videotape, the subjects received one of two questionnaires containing one key and nineteen filler questions. Half of the subjects were asked, "Was the leader of the four demonstrators who entered the classroom a male?", whereas the other half were asked, "Was the leader of the twelve demonstrators who entered the classroom a male?" The subjects responded by circling "yes" or "no."

One week later, all subjects returned and, without reviewing the videotape, answered a series of 20 new questions about the disruption. The subjects were urged to answer the questions from memory and not to make inference. The critical question here was, "How many demonstrators did you see entering the classroom?"

Results and Discussion

Subjects who had previously been asked the "12" question reported having seen an average 8.85 people 1 wk earlier, whereas those asked the "4" question recalled 6.40 people, $t(38) = 2.50$, $\sigma = .98$ $p < .01$. The actual number was, it will be recalled, eight. One possibility is that some fraction of the subjects remembered the number 12 or the number 4 from the prior questionnaire and were responding to the later question with that number, whereas the remainder had the correct number. An analysis of the actual responses given reveals that 10% of the people who had been interrogated with "12" actually responded "12," and that 10% of those interrogated with "4" actually responded with "4." A recalculation of the means, excluding those subjects in the "12" condition who responded "12" and those in the "4" condition who responded "4," still resulted in a significant difference between the two conditions (8.50 versus 6.67), $t(34) = 1.70$, $p < .05$. This analysis demonstrates that recall of the specific number given in the initial questionnaire is not an adequate alternative explanation of the present results.

The result shows that a question containing a false numerical presupposition can, on the average, affect a witness' answer to a subsequent question about that quantitative fact. The next experiment was designed to test whether the same is true for the existence of objects when the false presupposition concerns one that did not actually exist.

EXPERIMENT 3

Method

One hundred and fifty students at the University of Washington, in groups of various sizes, viewed a brief videotape of an automobile accident and then answered ten questions about the accident. The critical one concerned the speed of a white sports car. Half of the subjects were asked, "How fast was the white sports car going when it passed the barn while traveling along the country road?", and half were asked, "How fast was the white sports car going while traveling along the country road?" In fact, no barn appeared in the scene.

All of the subjects returned 1 wk later and, without reviewing the videotape, answered ten new questions about the accident. The final one was, "Did you see a barn?" The subjects responded by circling "yes" or "no" on their questionnaires.

Results and Discussion

Of the subjects earlier exposed to the question containing the false presupposition of a barn, 17.3% responded "yes" when later asked, "Did you see a barn?", whereas only 2.7% of the remaining subjects claimed to have seen it; $x^2(1) = 8.96, p < .01$. An initial question containing a false presupposition can, it appears, influence a witness' later tendency to report the presence of the nonexistent object corresponding to the presupposition.

The last experiment not only extends this finding beyond the single example, but asks whether or not the effect is wholly due to the word "barn" having occurred or not occurred in the earlier session. Suppose an initial question merely asks about, instead of presupposing, a nonexistent object; for example, "Did you see a barn?," when no barn existed. Presumably subjects will mostly respond negatively to such questions. But, what if that same question is asked again some time later? It is possible that a subject will reflect to himself, "I remember something about a barn, so I guess I must have seen one." If this were the case, then merely asking about a nonexistent object could increase the tendency to report the existence of that object at some later time, thereby accounting for the results of Expt III.

EXPERIMENT 4

Method

One hundred and fifty subjects from the University of Washington, run in groups of various sizes, viewed a 3-min 8 mm film clip taken from inside of an automobile which eventually collides with a baby carriage being pushed by a man. Following presentation of the film, each subject received one of three types of booklets corresponding to the experimental conditions. One hundred subjects received booklets containing five key and 40 filler questions. In the "direct" version, the key questions asked, in a fairly direct manner, about items that were not present in the film. One example was, "Did you see a school bus in the film?" In the "False presupposition" version, the key questions contained false presuppositions referring to an item that did not occur in the film. The corresponding example was, "Did you see the children getting on the school bus?" The third group of 50 subjects received only the 40 filler questions and no key questions. The goal of using so many filler items was to minimize the possibility that subjects would notice the false presuppositions.

All subjects returned 1 wk later and, without reviewing the film clip, answered 20 new questions about the incident. Five of these questions were critical: They were direct questions that had been asked a wk earlier in identical form, of only one of the three groups of subjects. The subjects responded to all questions by circling "yes" or "no" on their questionnaires.

Results and Discussion

... Overall, of those who had been exposed to questions including a false presupposition, 29.2% said "yes" to the key nonexistent items; of those who had been exposed to the direct questions, 15.6% said "yes" and of those in the control group, 8.4% said "yes."

For each question individually, the type of prior experience significantly influenced the percentage of "yes" responses, with all chi-square values having $p < .05$. Additional chi-square tests were performed to test for the significance of the differences between the pairs of groups. For each of the five questions, the differences were all significant between the control group and the group exposed to false presuppositions, all chi-square values having $p < .025$. Summing over all five questions, a highly significant chi-square resulted, $x^2(5) = 40.79$, $p < 001$. Similarly, over all five questions, the difference between the group exposed to direct questions and the group exposed to false presuppositions was significant, $x^2(5) = 14.73$, $p < .025$. The difference between the control group and the group exposed to direct questions failed to reach significance, $x^2(5) = 9.24$, $p > .05$.

REFERENCES

Clark, H. H., & Haviland, S. E. Psychological processes as linguistic explanation. In D. Cohen (Ed.), *The nature of explanation in linguistics.* Milwaukee: University of Wisconsin Press, in press.

Harris, R. J. Answering questions containing marked and unmarked adjectives and adverbs. *Journal of Experimental Psychology,* 1973, 97, 399–401.

Loftus, E. F. Reconstructing memory. The incredible eyewitness. *Psychology Today,* 1974, 8, 116–119.

Loftus, E. F., & Palmer, J. C. Reconstruction of automobile destruction: An example of the interaction between language and memory. *Journal of Verbal Learning and Verbal Behavior,* 1974, 13, 585–589.

Loftus, E. F., & Zanni, G. Eyewitness testimony: The influence of the wording of a question. *Bulletin of the Psychonomic Society,* 1975, 5, 86–88.

CHAPTER 8 Intelligence and Language

8.1 SANDRA SCARR AND RICHARD A. WEINBERG

The Minnesota Adoption Studies: Genetic Differences and Malleability

Because of ethical and methodological constraints, it is often difficult to conduct research on how heredity and environment affect human cognitive abilities such as intelligence. One research technique that has been used in this area is the adoption method. With this method, psychologists look at the cognitive similarities between adopted children and their adoptive parents, as well as their biological parents, thus distinguishing between likely genetic and environmental influences. The adoption method is evident in the Minnesota adoption studies, designed by Sandra Scarr and Richard A. Weinberg, part of which was used to investigate racial differences in intelligence.

Scarr (b. 1936) earned her Ph.D. in psychology from Harvard University in 1965. She has taught at Yale University and the University of Minnesota, and she has been teaching at the University of Virginia since 1983. Weinberg obtained his Ph.D. from the University of Minnesota in 1968, where he is currently a professor of child psychology.

This selection is from "The Minnesota Adoption Studies: Genetic Differences and Malleability," which was published in *Child Development* in 1983. In it, Scarr and Weinberg review two long-term adoption studies that were begun in 1974. As you read this selection, keep in mind that intelligence is influenced by many variables and that it is extremely difficult to isolate specific genetic and environmental factors. What do the results of these studies suggest about the relative importance of heredity and environment on intelligence?

Key Concept: intelligence, heredity, and adoption studies

*S*ocial sciences have been plagued by the controversy over nature and nurture, as though the conjunction were "or." At the core of the controversy is the idea that genetic variation fixes individual and group differences in human behavior. Opponents of the idea believe that genetic differences are antithetical to malleability or change in behavior. A common error underlying this belief is a failure to distinguish environmental and genetic sources of individual differences in behavior from the necessary roles of both genes and environments in behavioral development. One cannot assess the relative impact of heredity or environment in behavioral domains because everyone must have both a viable gene complement and an environment in which the genes can be expressed over development.

Behavioral differences among individuals, on the other hand, can arise in any population from genetic differences, from variations among their environments, or both. Imagine a population of genetically identical clones who are reared in family environments that vary from working to upper middle class. Any behavioral differences among the clones would necessarily arise from developing within those different environments. Next, imagine a genetically diverse human population reared in laboratory cages. All members experience exactly the same environments. Naturally, all differences among those individuals are accounted for by their genetic variability. Notice, however, that in the two fantasies the organisms all have both genes and environments for development (Scarr & Weinberg, 1980, p. 859). Because nearly all families share both genes and environments, it is usually impossible to know why individuals are similar or different from one another.

THE ADOPTION MODEL

The adoption of children with biological backgrounds that are different from both their adopting parents and each other provides an opportunity to evaluate the impact of environments on children's development. If differences among the child-rearing environments provided by families determine differences in children's development, then the differences among adopted children ought to be correlated with differences among their adoptive families. Theoretically, regressions of adopted-child outcomes on adoptive-family characteristics will provide genetically unbiased estimates of true environmental effects in the population from which they are drawn.

Unfortunately, adoptive families are selected by agencies for being above average in many virtues, including socioeconomic status [SES]. Children in adoptive families are reared in nondeprived, nonabusive environments. However, the fact that the SES range of adoptive families usually includes at least two-thirds of the U.S. white population makes results of adoption studies compelling.

Comparisons of adopted and biological relatives assume that the greater behavioral similarity usually found among biological relatives is a result of their greater genetic similarity. Critics of the adoption model assert to the contrary that important biases can creep into comparisons of genetically related and unrelated families through parental and child expectations of greater similarity among biological than adopted relatives. Fortunately for the adoption model, knowledge of adoptive or biological relatedness does not constitute a bias in comparisons of measured behavioral differences in biological and adoptive families, because there are no correlations between perceived and actual similarities in intelligence or personality (Scarr, Scarf, & Weinberg, 1980).

THE MINNESOTA ADOPTION STUDIES

Following in the tradition of Alice M. Leahy (1935), who conducted a pioneering adoption study in Minnesota, we launched two large adoption studies in 1974 for two quite different purposes. The Transracial Adoption Study was carried out from 1974 through 1976 in Minnesota to test the hypothesis that black and interracial children reared by white families (in the culture of the tests and the schools) would perform on IQ tests and school achievement measures as well as other adopted children (Scarr & Weinberg, 1976). A second investigation, the Adolescent Adoption Study, was conceived to assess the cumulative impact of differences in family environments on children's development at the end of the child-rearing period (Scarr & Weinberg, 1978; Scarr & Yee, 1980). In both studies, we examined the levels of intellectual and personality development, as well as the degree of resemblance among family members, by comparing adoptive and biological relatives. The focus of this review is on IQ and school achievement tests. . . .

TRANSRACIAL ADOPTION STUDY

Sample

The 101 transracial adoptive families included 176 adopted children, of whom 130 were socially classified as black. All of the adopted children were unrelated to the adoptive parents and to each other, with a few exceptions who

TABLE 1

Comparisons of Biological and Unrelated Parent-Child IQ Correlations in 101 Transracial Adoptive Families

	N (pairs)	r
Parents–unrelated children:		
Adoptive mother–adopted child	174	.21 (.23)[a]
Natural mother–own child of adoptive family[b]	217	.15
Adoptive father–adopted child	170	.27 (.15)[a]
Natural father–own child of adoptive family[b]	86	.19
Parents–biological children:		
Adoptive mother–own child	141	.34
Natural mother–adopted child[b]	135	.33
Adoptive father–own child	142	.39
Natural father–adopted child[b]	46	.43

[a]Early adopted only (*N* = 111).
[b]Educational level, not IQ scores.

were excluded from analyses. The sample also included 143 biological children of the adoptive parents. Among the adoptees, 111 were adopted in the first year of life and 65 after 12 months of age.

Results and Discussion

IQ Levels of Family Members. Both the parents and the biological children of the families scored in the bright average to superior range on age-appropriate IQ tests. The black and interracial adopted children were also found to score above the average of the white population, regardless of when they had been adopted. The black children adopted in the first 12 months of life scored on the average at IQ 110 (Scarr & Weinberg, 1976), 20 points above comparable children being reared in the black community. We interpreted the high IQ scores of the black and interracial children to mean that (*a*) genetic racial differences do not account for a major portion of the IQ performance difference between racial groups, and (*b*) black and interracial children reared in the culture of the tests and the schools perform as well as other adopted children in similar families (Burks, 1928; Horn, Loehlin, & Willerman, 1979; Leahy, 1935; Scarr & Weinberg, 1978). The adopted children scored 6 points below the natural children of the same families, however, as Burks (1928) and our second adoption study also found.

Parent-Child Correlations. Table 1 shows the correlations of the parents and children in the transracial adoption study. The adoptive families had adopted at least one black child, but there were also other adopted children and many biological offspring of these same parents. The children ranged in age from 4 to about 18. Because of the age range, children from 4 to 7 years

*Sandra Scarr
and Richard A.
Weinberg*

were given the Stanford-Binet (1973 norms), children from 8 to 16 the WISC, and older children and all parents the WAIS. The average age of the adopted children was 7, and of the natural children about 10. Table 1 gives the parent-child IQ correlations for all of the adopted children in the transracial adoptive families, regardless of when they had been adopted. The total sample of adopted children is just as similar to their adoptive parents as the early-adopted group is to theirs. The midparent–child IQ correlation for all adoptees is .29;[1] for the early adoptees it is .30. Mothers are equally similar to all adopted children, and fathers are more similar to the total sample than they are to the early-adopted children.

Table 1 also shows the correlations between all adopted children's IQ scores and their natural parents' educational levels. Because we did not have IQ assessments of the natural parents, education is used here as proxy. Despite this limitation, the correlations of natural parents' education with their adopted-away offspring's IQ scores are as high as the IQ correlations of biological parent–child pairs and exceed those of the adoptive parent–child IQ scores. The natural midparent–child correlation of .43 is significantly greater than the adopted midparent–child correlation of .29. . . .

The correlations between natural parents of adopted children and the biological children of the same adoptive families is an estimate of the effects of selective placement (entries 2 and 4 in Table 1). If agencies match educational and social class characteristics of the natural mothers with similar adoptive parents, then the resemblance between adoptive parents and children is enhanced by the genetic resemblance of natural and adoptive parents in intelligence. Selective placement also enhances the correlation between natural parents and their adopted-away offspring, because the adoptive parents carry out the genotype-environment correlation that would have characterized the natural parent–child pairs, had the children been retained by their natural parents. Thus, neither the adoptive parent–child correlations nor the natural parent–adopted child correlations deserve to be as high as they are (Scarr & Weinberg, 1977). From the comparison of biological and adoptive parent–child correlations, each corrected for selective placement, we estimated that 40%–70% of the IQ variance in this sample was due to genetic differences among the children.

Sibling Correlation. . . . [T]he sibling correlations reveal a different picture. Young siblings are similar to each other, whether genetically related to each other or not. The IQ correlations of adopted siblings [.44] are as high as those of the biological siblings reared together [.42]. Children reared in the same family environments and who are still under the major influence of their parents score at similar levels on IQ tests. The IQ correlations of the adopted siblings result in small part from their correlations in background, such as their natural mothers' educational levels (.16) and age at placement in the adoptive home (.37), which are in turn related to the present intellectual functioning of the children—the earlier the placement, the higher the IQ score. Age of placement is itself correlated with many other background characteristics of the child and is a complex variable (Scarr & Weinberg, 1976). But note that the correlation among the early adopted siblings is .39. Even among the families who had early adoptees, differences in family environments and selective placement account for a substantial resemblance between unrelated children. . . .

The major point is that the heritabilities (percentage of genetic variance) calculated from young-sibling data in the Minnesota Transracial Adoption Study are very different from those calculated from the parent–child data. As Christopher Jencks pointed out in his earlier book (1972), the correlations of unrelated young siblings reared together do not fit any biometrical model because they are too high. This study of young children confirms his point. Our second study, of older adolescents, however, does not.

ADOLESCENT ADOPTION STUDY

Sample

The adolescents in this study had spent an average of 18 years in their families—194 adopted children in 115 adoptive families and a comparison group of 237 biological children in 120 other families. All of the adoptees were placed in their families in the first year of life, the median being 2 months of age. From 1975 to 1977 both groups of children were 16–22 years old. Both samples of parents were of similar SES, from working to upper middle class, and of similar IQ levels on the WAIS. The IQ scores of parents in both adoptive and biological families averaged 115, approximately 1 SD [standard deviation] above the population mean. The biological children scored, on the average, an IQ of 113, and the adopted children 7 points lower at 106.

Results and Discussion

Parent–Child and Sibling Correlations. The parent–child IQ correlations in the biological families were what we were led to expect from the Transracial Adoption Study and others—about .40 when corrected for restriction of range in the parents' scores. The biological midparent–child correlation was .52. The adoptive parent–child correlations were lower than those of the younger adoptive parents and their children—about .13; the adoptive midparent–child correlation was only .14.

The adopted children's IQ scores were more closely correlated with the educational levels of their natural mothers (.28) and fathers (.43) than with those of their adoptive mothers (.09) and fathers (.11). In fact, adopted children's IQ scores were as highly correlated with their natural parents' education as were those of the adolescents in the biological sample (.17 and .26, respectively) (Scarr & Weinberg, 1980).

The IQ correlation of the biologically related siblings was .35, similar to that of the siblings in the Transracial Adoption Study. However, the IQ correlation of adopted children reared together for 18 years was zero! Unlike the younger siblings, who are of different races, these white adolescents reared together from infancy did not resemble their genetically unrelated siblings. The heritabilities calculated from the adolescent IQ data varied from .38 to .61, much like the parent–child data in the study of younger, transracial adoptees but unlike data on these younger siblings. . . .

Our interpretation of these results (Scarr & Weinberg, 1978) is that older adolescents are largely liberated from their families' influences and have made choices and pursued courses that are in keeping with their own talents and interests. Thus, the unrelated siblings have grown less and less alike. This hypothesis cannot be tested fully without longitudinal data on adopted siblings; to date all of the other adoption studies sampled much younger children, at the average age of 7 or 8. We can think of no other explanation for the markedly low correlations between the adopted siblings at the end of the child-rearing period, in contrast to the several studies of younger adopted siblings, who are embarrassingly similar.

DISCUSSION

We interpret the results of the two studies to mean that younger children, regardless of their genetic relatedness, resemble each other intellectually because they share a similar rearing environment. Older adolescents, on the other hand, resemble one another only if they share genes. Our interpretation is that older children escape the influences of the family and are freer to select their own environments. Parental influences are diluted by the more varied mix of adolescent experiences.

The results support the idea that older children and adolescents build their own niches, which can be seen as an active genotype-environment correlation (Plomin, DeFries, & Loehlin, 1977). Different people select different aspects of their environments that they find compatible. Choices of environments are influenced by genetic differences in what individuals enjoy and at which they are competent. Adopted children, not genetically related to their parents or to one another, build niches that are related to their own genotypes but not to those of their family members. Biologically related children also create niches that are correlated with their genotypes, but their choices are also correlated with those of their genetically related family members (see Scarr & McCartney, in this issue).

Malleability. What are the implications of these results for developmental plasticity? First, it is clear from the IQ scores of the transracially adopted children that they, like other adoptees, are responsive to the rearing environments in adoptive families, which as a group provide intellectual stimulation and exposure to the skills and knowledge sampled on IQ tests. The mean IQ scores of both samples of adoptees are above the average of age-mates, primarily because they benefit from their rearing environments.

Second, individual adoptees differ in their responses to the environmental advantages of adoptive families. Those with natural parents of higher educational levels, and by implication higher intellectual abilities, are more responsive to the rearing environments of adoptive families than are those with natural parents of more limited intellectual skills. Children adopted into families of adoptive parents at and above the average educational and IQ levels of adoptive parents score higher on the WAIS than children of comparable natural mothers adopted into families with less bright adoptive parents. . . . [T]he adolescents whose natural mothers and adoptive parents are both below average score 10.4 IQ points below those whose natural mothers and adoptive parents are both above average.

Individual differences among the adopted children at both younger and older ages are related to intellectual variation among adoptive parents and their biological parents, even though the average IQ of adoptees most likely exceeds that of their natural parents. Human beings are not infinitely plastic; malleability does not mean that given the same environment, all individuals will end up alike.

REFERENCES

Burks, B. S. The relative influence of nature and nurture upon mental development: A comparative study of foster parent–foster child resemblance and true parent–true child resemblance. *Yearbook of the National Society for the Study of Education*, 1928, **27**, 219–316.

Horn, J. M., Loehlin, J. C., & Willerman, L. Intellectual resemblance among adoptive and biological relatives: The Texas Adoption Project. *Behavior Genetics*, 1979, **9**, 177–207.

Jencks, C. *Inequality: A reassessment of the effects of family and schooling in America*. New York: Basic, 1972.

Leahy, A. M. Nature-nurture and intelligence. *Genetic Psychology Monographs*, 1935, **17**, 237–308.

Plomin, R., DeFries, J. C., & Loehlin, J. C. Genotype-environment interaction and correlation in the analysis of human behavior. *Psychological Bulletin*, 1977, **84**(2), 309–322.

Scarr, S., Scarf, E., & Weinberg, R. A. Perceived and actual similarities in biological and adoptive families: Does perceived similarity bias genetic influence? *Behavior Genetics*, 1980, **10**, 445–458.

Scarr, S., & Weinberg, R. A. IQ test performance of black children adopted by white families. *American Psychologist*, 1976, **31**, 726–739.

Scarr, S., & Weinberg, R. A. Intellectual similarities within families of both adopted and biological children. *Intelligence*, 1977, **1**, 170–191.

Scarr, S., & Weinberg, R. A. The influence of "family background" on intellectual attainment. *American Sociological Review*, 1978, **43**, 674–692.

Scarr, S., & Weinberg, R. A. Calling all camps! The war is over. *American Sociological Review*, 1980, **45**, 859–865.

Scarr, S., & Yee, D. Heritability and educational policy: Genetic and environmental effects on IQ, aptitude, and achievement. *Educational Psychologist*, 1980, **15**(1), 1–22.

NOTE

1. The midparent value is the average of the two parents' scores.

Listening to Speech in the First Year of Life: Experiential Influences on Phoneme Perception

The use of language is one of the defining characteristics of being human. Somehow during the first years of life, we learn to understand language and to use it to communicate with other people. Janet F. Werker and Renée N. Desjardins are two psychologists on the cutting edge of research designed to understand how infants learn to listen to speech.

Werker earned her Ph.D. in developmental psychology from the University of British Columbia in 1982. She was an assistant professor at Dalhousie University until 1986, when she returned to the University of British Columbia. Desjardins earned her M.A. in 1990 from the University of British Columbia. She was completing her Ph.D. there when this selection was written.

This selection is from "Listening to Speech in the First Year of Life: Experiential Influences on Phoneme Perception," which was published in *Current Directions in Psychological Science* in 1995. In it, Werker and Desjardins review research indicating that during the first year of life the infant moves from universal to language-specific phoneme recognition. Note the progression of the research, which is designed to determine when the ability to discriminate nonnative phonemes occurs. The researchers started with adolescents and gradually tested younger and younger children until they isolated the change in 6- to 12-month-old infants. As you read this selection, consider the implications of the research for parental communication with infants.

Key Concept: language development

173

The use of language to share thoughts, ideas, and feelings is a uniquely human characteristic. And to learn a language is one of the biggest challenges of infancy and early childhood. In order to be successful at this momentous task, the child must break down the speech stream, which consists of highly encoded and overlapping information, into smaller units such as clauses, phrases, and words. A yet smaller unit is the phoneme. Two words may differ by only one phoneme (e.g., *bat* vs. *pat*), yet this difference is enough to convey different meanings. Thus, a critical part of the language acquisition process is the ability to distinguish individual syllables on the basis of minimal differences in phonemes. In this review, we discuss the kinds of initial abilities infants bring to the task of phoneme perception, how these sensitivities are influenced by experience in a particular linguistic community, and whether events that occur during the prelinguistic period help prepare the child for the important task of language acquisition.

MAPPING THE CHANGES IN PHONEME PERCEPTION

Sensitive experimental techniques that were developed in the early 1970s allowed testing very young infants' speech perception abilities. These techniques revealed that infants can not only discriminate minimally distinctive phonemes, but can also distinguish phonemes from all the world's languages—including phonemes not used in their language-learning environment. In contrast, research with adults, using different techniques, had led scientists to believe that adults cannot readily discriminate all phonemic distinctions that are not used in their native language. Because adults typically perform better than infants at virtually any task given to them, this counterintuitive pattern of results was most intriguing. Our work was designed to explore the age at which experience first begins to influence phonemic perception and the mechanisms that might be responsible for this change.[1]

To explore the counterintuitive suggestion that infants discriminate non-native phonemes better than adults, we first compared the two groups directly. In order to do this, we needed a procedure that would be adaptable to both infants and adults. The procedure we chose is a category change procedure. In this task, the subject monitors a continuous background of syllables from one phonemic category (e.g., /ba/) and presses a button to signal when the stimuli change to a contrasting phonemic category (e.g., /da/). Correct button-presses are reinforced with the presentation of a flashing light (as feedback for older children and adults) or an electronically activated animal (as a reward for younger children). Incorrect button-presses are not reinforced, and misses are not signaled.

In the infant version of this procedure, called the conditioned head turn task, the infant sits on the parent's lap facing an experimental assistant who maintains the infant's interest by showing toys. The infant is conditioned to turn his or her head toward the sound source when he or she detects a change in the phonemic category. Correct head turns are reinforced with the illumination and activation of clapping and drumming toy animals inside a Plexiglas box. In addition, the experimental assistant claps and gives praise and encouragement. As is the case with children and adults, incorrect responses are not reinforced. In our laboratory, the criterion for successful discrimination is set at 9 out of 10 correct consecutive responses within a series of 25 trials, approximately half of which are control trials in which no change occurs.

In the first series of experiments, we compared infants and adults on their ability to discriminate two distinctions that are phonemic (i.e., can differentiate words) in Hindi but not in English and one that is phonemic in both Hindi and English. The Hindi-only contrasts were chosen to vary in their potential difficulty. The first contrast, /Ta/–/ta/, involves two phonemes that both sound like *t* to a native English speaker. The difference between them involves where the tongue is placed. For /Ta/, the tongue is curled back and the tip of the underside hits the roof of the mouth. This is called a retroflex consonant. For /ta/, the tip of the tongue is placed against the front teeth. This is called a dental consonant. An English speaker makes a /t/ by placing the tongue against the alveolar ridge directly behind the front teeth. This alveolar consonant is articulated at a place in between the dental and retroflex consonants.

The second contrast was a Hindi voicing contrast that also involves two phonemes that sound like *t* to an English speaker. In this case, the difference involves the timing and shape of the opening of the vocal cords. Hindi /tʰ/ and /dʰ/ involve a slightly different combination of timing and shape than is used in production of English phonemes. For linguistic and acoustic reasons, this voicing contrast is potentially easier to discriminate than the retroflex-dental contrast.

Subjects were also tested on the contrast between /ba/ and /da/, which is used in both Hindi and English. This contrast served as a control to ensure that the subjects understood (and, in the case of the infants, were willing to perform) the task.

In the first study done collaboratively with Richard Tees, John Gilbert, and Keith Humphrey, English-learning infants aged 6 to 8 months were compared with both English-speaking adults and Hindi-speaking adults. Virtually all subjects in all groups could discriminate the /ba/–/da/ contrast, and the English-learning infants and the Hindi-speaking adults could easily discriminate both Hindi contrasts. However, the English-speaking adults had difficulty discriminating the Hindi contrasts, and showed particular trouble with the difficult retroflex-dental distinction. A short training procedure (25 trials) was effective in raising the proportion of English-speaking adults who could discriminate the Hindi voicing contrast, but this amount of training did not improve adult performance on the retroflex-dental distinction.

This experiment confirmed what many researchers had expected. Testing using comparable procedures verified that infants discriminate nonnative phoneme contrasts better than adults. But we had no idea as to the age in development when the performance decrement occurs. An influential view at the time was Lenneberg's hypothesis that there is a "critical period" for language acquisition up to the onset of puberty. Extrapolating from this hypothesis led us to test children on the verge of adolescence, as well as two younger age groups. To our surprise, the results indicated that English-speaking children 12, 8, and even 4 years old perform as poorly as English-speaking adults on the Hindi contrasts not used in English. This effect was evident even though the 4-year-old children could easily discriminate the English contrast, and even though Hindi-learning children of age 4 discriminated both Hindi contrasts successfully when tested with the same procedure.

These results showing that language experience affects phoneme perception by age 4 led to additional tests of children between 6 months and 4 years old. A series of pilot tests led to a focus on the 1st year of life.

Infants between 6 and 12 months of age were tested on the difficult retroflex-dental contrast taken from Hindi, as well as on a new contrast taken from a Native Canadian language, Nthlakampx (one of the Interior Salish languages). The new contrast, glottalized velar /k'/ versus glottalized uvular /q'/, involves a difference in the position of the tongue in the back part of the vocal tract. English listeners hear these two sounds as "funny" *k*s. We found that although English-learning infants aged 6 to 8 months can discriminate both of these contrasts with ease, infants of 10 to 12 months, like English-speaking adults, fail to discriminate the difference in either non-English contrast. The same pattern of results was replicated in a study in which the same infants were tested at 6 to 8, 8 to 10, and 10 to 12 months of age. Thus, it appeared that the change occurs between 6 and 12 months of age. . . .

In a final manipulation, we tested a small number of 11- to 12-month-old infants who were being exposed to either Hindi or Nthlakampx in the home. Infants in each language group discriminated the contrast from their native language with ease, confirming that the change between 6 and 12 months reflects language-specific experience and is not just an age-related decrement in performance on difficult contrasts.

In a subsequent study, we tested English-learning infants using synthetically produced stimuli that varied in equal steps along a continuum from bilabial /ba/ to dental /da/ to retroflex /Da/. We found that English-learning infants aged 6 to 8 months can group stimuli according to the English boundary between labial and dental stimuli, and according to the Hindi boundary between retroflex and dental, but not according to an arbitrary boundary location that does not correspond to any known phonemic category. English-learning infants aged 10 to 12 months can group only according to the bilabial-dental boundary. These results confirm that the sensitivities shown by young infants prior to language-specific tuning are not arbitrary, but rather conform to potential phonemic categories. Also, with these synthetic stimuli, we replicated our finding that language-general perception shifts to language-specific perception between 6 and 12 months of age. . . .

SUMMARY

During the 1st year of life, long before uttering his or her first words, an infant makes remarkable progress toward mastering the sound structure of the native language. The biases and proclivities that allow the neonate to detect regularities in the speech stream are, by 1 year of age, exquisitely tuned to the properties of the native language. Our work documents the infant's movement from universal to language-specific phoneme perception. What we have described, however, represents only a part of the infant's remarkable journey toward becoming a native listener. The challenge for future work is to determine what makes the movement from language-general to language-specific perception possible, and how sensitivity to the various properties of the native language is linked to the functional task of language acquisition.

NOTE

1. For a review of the studies discussed in this introduction, see J. F. Werker, Becoming a native listener, *American Scientist, 77,* 54–59 (1989).

The Education of Sarah: A Chimp Learns the Language

One difference between humans and other animals is the ability to use language. Other primates cannot speak verbally as we do; however, a number of studies have been done to investigate the ability of nonhuman primates to learn to communicate with language. Researchers have seemingly taught primates to communicate through various means, such as with sign language or, as David Premack demonstrates in this selection, with plastic symbols.

Premack (b. 1925) earned his Ph.D. from the University of Minnesota and began his research with chimpanzees in 1954 at the Yerkes Laboratories for Primate Biology in Florida. He taught psychology at the University of California prior to teaching at the University of Pennsylvania, and he coauthored *The Mind of an Ape* (W. W. Norton, 1983) with his wife, Ann.

This selection is from "The Education of Sarah: A Chimp Learns the Language," which was published in *Psychology Today* in 1970. Although it is written in an informal, conversational style, it conveys the rigorous scientific research that Premack performed to examine language development in a chimpanzee. Each question about the chimp's ability and understanding is carefully tested. Research on teaching language to primates is controversial as well as difficult to conduct. Premack helps us understand how he went about investigating this fascinating phenomenon. As you read the selection, consider what criteria you would require to conclude that nonhuman primates can learn language.

Key Concept: teaching language to a chimpanzee

*I*n order to have a psychological theory of language, we must replace the structural emphasis of linguists with a functional emphasis. The general functions an organism carries out when it is engaged in language need to be separated from the specific form those functions take in man. Some aspects of human phonology and syntax might be unique to man, but it may be that the basic functions of language depend on other mechanisms—logic and semantics—that are more widely distributed.

The functional approach requires two things: 1) a list of functions, the behaviors an organism must show to give evidence of language; 2) a parallel list of strict training procedures, giving one way—preferably several ways—to produce each function. A training procedure is actually no more than an ordered series of steps, each small enough to be manageable by our languageless subject. It is not an explanation of how the organism learns the function; training procedure, at this stage, is a method in search of a theory. . . .

Our drawing board will be the chimpanzee, close to man phylogenetically, if not linguistically. Meet Sarah, age seven, who has been our eager and delightful subject for two years at the University of California, Santa Barbara.

Attempts to teach simians to talk have failed consistently; speech appears to be anatomically impossible for them. So we decided to establish a nonvocal language for Sarah. Each "word" is a metal-backed plastic bit, varying in shape, size, color and texture, that adheres to a magnetized slate. Words and sentences are placed on the slate vertically, simply because at first this seemed to be the style Sarah preferred.

Man & Dog.   The word is an essential unit of language. It reflects, among other things, the consensus that perceptual events can be divided into stable elements. In the occurrence "man bites dog," for instance, there are three clear units: someone doing the biting, the action of biting (as opposed to hitting or petting, perhaps), and something being bitten. Most functions of language serve to represent and distinguish the elements of experience.

But teaching first words to a totally naive animal is far different from introducing new words to a person who already has some language. The first step was to establish a simple social transaction between trainer and chimp—giving Sarah fruit—and it was this transaction that we set out to map with language.

At first, one of the trainers—Mary Morgan, Deborah Petersen, Randy Runk or Jim Olson—would place a banana on the table and watch benevolently as Sarah took it and ate it. This routine continued until one day the trainer introduced an element from the language system, a piece of colored plastic. The banana was now further back than usual, out of reach, while the plastic chip was easily within grasp. The trainer introduced Sarah to make a specific response with the "word": she had to place it on the language board before she got the banana. Sarah quickly learned to play this little game.

Variety.   Now we began to introduce new fruits and new plastic words for them. In each case Sarah had to put the plastic on the board before she could get the apple, orange, or other fruit.

Then we gave her two words but only one piece of fruit, to see whether she could match the correct word to the food. Sarah was generally successful in this task, but she could occasionally be using the "wrong" word as a request for the fruit not being offered. To detect this, we allowed her to choose between all possible pairs of fruits, and then between all possible pairs of plastic words. If her fruit preferences agreed with her word preferences, we reasoned, then she must know what word goes with what fruit. And she did.

Matches.   Next we began to change other aspects of the transaction, adding appropriate words. We varied the person giving the fruit. When Mary was present and the fruit was apple, Sarah had to write *Mary apple* on the board in order to get the food. If Randy was the donor, she had to write *Randy apple,* and so on. We used the same tests to see whether Sarah understood the association between persons and symbols and indeed Sarah did.

Sarah easily learned the fruit and donor classes. It was harder to vary the recipient of the fruit, since Sarah was understandably reluctant to write sentences calling for someone else to get the goodies. Similarly, the attempt to change the verb—*giving, cutting* or *inserting* the fruit—met with the same resistance: Sarah, childlike, only wanted to take it. These problems turned out to be practical matters, however; we handled them by arranging proper rewards. For example, when Sarah wrote *Mary give apple Randy,* thereby denying herself the apple, she got a tidbit she likes even more than apple. Altruism, properly rewarded, soon becomes quite reliable.

Classes.   The basic training procedure for the function *word* is thus very simple. We establish a transaction between chimp and trainer, and divide the event into perceptual classes: in this case donor, action, fruit, recipient. Then each class is rotated through a series of values, holding the other classes constant. With each variation a corresponding change is made in the language element. Ultimately, the whole transaction is mapped: Sarah can fully describe the event by writing *Mary give apple Sarah.*

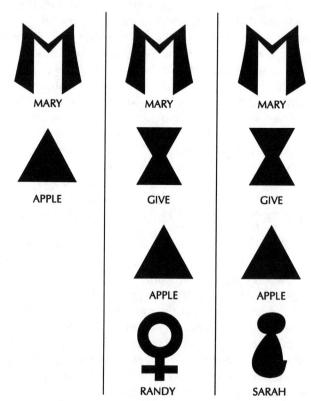

MARY   MARY   MARY

APPLE   GIVE   GIVE

APPLE   APPLE

RANDY   SARAH

But the chimp may produce a properly ordered string of words without understanding that the string is a sentence. Unlike a string of words, a sentence has internal organization—syntax—in which each word depends on all the others. Perhaps the simplest condition requiring syntax is the symmetrical two-term relation found in geometrical propositions (A on C but also C on A) and in some verbs of social behavior (X talks to Y but also Y talks to X). In cases of this kind, the A's and C's can be completely interchanged and the sentence will still have meaning; the only way to distinguish them is by the order of appearance.

By contrast, in closed relations there is a clear difference between items that appear in one position and those that appear in another. For example, *insert*, as a verb, involves a closed relation: we can insert fruit in dishes, but pieces of fruit do not insert us. If I were to give you three words—Sarah, banana, insert—you would know, regardless of their order, who does the inserting and what is to be inserted. We can therefore treat *insert* as a relation between two classes—inserters and insertables—that are defined by their physical or functional properties. This is an example of a semantic covariation rule, since as one class varies the other must also.

Order. We began Sarah's lesson in sentence structure with symmetrical relations, using the preposition *on*. To make sure that she was learning on a syntactic basis, we used sentences in which one order made as much sense as another. Colors provided a good example: *red on green* has no necessary edge over *green on red*—unlike *fly on horse*, which is notably more probable than the reverse. Thus if Sarah could learn to recognize when one color is *on* another, we might infer that she can understand one contribution of syntax, word order.

We had previously taught Sarah four colors: red, green, blue and yellow; each appeared on a two-inch-by-four-inch card. These four colors make 12 possible combinations: red on green, green on red, blue on yellow, etc. Training consisted of three steps: 1) teaching Sarah one pair of colors, in both orders; 2) seeing whether she could generalize to other sets of colors; 3) testing her ability to produce, as well as understand, the sentences.

Switch. First, Mary placed the red card on the table, put the words *green on red* on the board, handed Sarah the green card and induced her to place it on the red one. After she had done this several times and Sarah was getting the idea, Mary reversed the sentence: she put *red on green* on the board and gave Sarah the red card as the one to be placed on top. Sarah was soon adept at doing what either sentence called for.

In step two, the trainer wrote sentences with the 10 other possible combinations of colors, and Sarah's task was the same. If she wrote *yellow on blue*, Sarah had to place the yellow card on the blue one, and not vice-versa. She did just as well on the 10 new cases as she had on red and green, demonstrating that she had not simply memorized the training colors but could apply the preposition to new sentences.

In the last step, the trainer gave Sarah three words, two colors and *on*, and required her to put them on the board so as to correspond to her placement of the cards. If Mary put the blue card on the green one, Sarah had to write *blue on green.* Sarah was able to do this eight or nine times out of 10, her usual performance level. She has since been taught "side" and "front of," using essentially the same procedure.

Agent. Now consider the sentence, in chimp language, *Sarah insert banana pail apple dish*, which means that Sarah must put the banana in the pail and the apple in the dish. This example carries us beyond word order to a second contribution of syntax: hierarchical organization of a sentence. It would be impossible to carry out the instruction without understanding that banana goes with pail, apple with dish, that insert applies to both cases, and that Sarah is the agent of both actions.

Sarah's previous levels of comprehension would not permit her to understand this complicated instruction. Word knowledge alone, for instance, would tell her that she is to be the agent, that she must insert something; and that the objects are fruits and containers. But from here there would be great latitude as to what was inserted in what; the dish could end up in the pail as often as the banana. Only knowledge of the hierarchical organization of the sentence would insure the outcome we wanted.

Choice. Sarah's training on this problem again proceeded in three stages. First we taught her each of the four simple statements that could be derived from the target sentence:

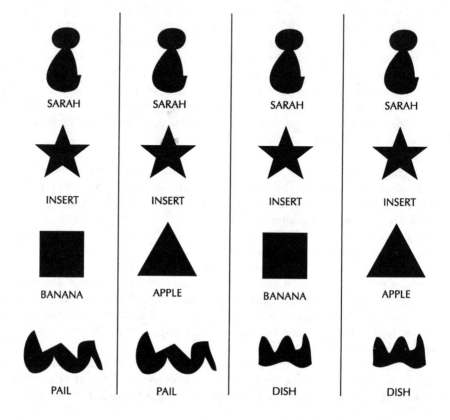

The trainer wrote each of these statements on the board, while offering Sarah a choice of fruits and containers, and required her to place the specified fruit in its proper container.

When Sarah had mastered this step, we gave her all possible pairs of the four statements, side by side. We included this step merely to accustom her to carrying out two acts of insertion, as required by the target sentence.

Finally, we combined all possible pairs of simple statements, this time one immediately above the other. . . .

Neither the deletion of the second use of *Sarah* nor the deletion of *insert* disrupted Sarah's performance. She carried out the instructions 80 to 90 per cent of the time, her usual level, even when we omitted the redundant words. Nor was she the least bit disturbed by our generalization tests. We substituted fruits (grape, apricot, orange); we replaced *insert* with *take out*; her performance remained highly accurate.

Outburst. To rule out the possibility that Sarah was using a semantic rule, such as "apply the container word to the fruit word immediately above it," we tried some modifications of the original sentence, such as *Sarah insert apple dish apple banana pail,* or *Sarah insert apple red dish apple banana green dish.* Although the last sentence was extremely difficult for her—judged by the emotional outbursts and the slow pace of her work—she was nevertheless able to do it. She put both apple and banana in the correct dish, proving that she could not simply be using a rule that said "apply container word to fruit word immediately above it."

Proving competence in syntax is, of course, a highly inferential matter. Still we feel justified in concluding that Sarah can understand some symmetrical and hierarchical sentence structures, and is therefore competent to some degree in the sentence function of language. . . .

Pairs. Sarah's language training had so far been a mapping of existing knowledge; words gave her labels for distinctions she could already perceive. Next we turned to metalinguistics, the function that uses language to teach language.

We taught Sarah the concept *is the name of* in the same way that we taught identity. We gave her a word *apple* and a real apple, and had her place the symbol *name of* between them. Likewise she had to put the symbol *not-name of* between incorrect pairs (word *banana* with apple). Soon Sarah was able to put the correct symbol between all sorts of word-object pairs.

Then we decided to see whether Sarah could use the concept *name of* in a more powerful way. If we taught her the name of a completely novel item, would she be able to use it in sentences thereafter?

We gave Sarah a new treat, figs. We placed a fig next to a plastic chip that was to be the word fig, and then put the newly learned symbol *name of* between them. We also put another plastic word by the fig, with *not-name of* between them. We gave Sarah a variety of tests ("Is *fig* the name of fig?" "What is *fig* to fig?"), and saw that she could clearly associate the word *fig* with the fruit.

To see whether Sarah could now use *fig* in a sentence, we gave her the real fruit and a number of words: the names of two other fruits, the name of fig, the word we told her was not the name of fig, and the familiar symbols *give, Sarah,* and *Mary.* We allowed Sarah to eat the fig when she wrote *Mary give fig Sarah.* To our delight she was highly successful on this test. She was equally good at learning other new words by this same metalinguistic procedure.

Condition. When does a piece of plastic become a word? We answer: when it is used as a word. For example, we consider a bit of blue plastic to be the name for apple because 1) it is the symbol used when Sarah requests apple, and 2) it is the answer Sarah gives to "what is the name for apple?" We can add that the plastic becomes a word when the properties ascribed to it are not those of the plastic, but those of the object it names.

We could see whether this condition was true for Sarah by use of matching-to-sample procedures. We gave her the apple and a pair of descriptive alternatives, and she had to tell us which of these was more like the apple. We began with four sets: red vs. green, round vs. square, square with stem vs. plain square, and plain circle vs. square with stem. Sarah gave consistent answers that tended to agree with those you and I would give.

Then we repeated the procedure exactly, but we replaced the real apple with the name for apple, a piece of blue plastic. Sarah assigned to the plastic the same properties that she had just ascribed to the apple: it was round, not square; red, not green, and so on. This is evidence that the chimp thinks of the word not as its literal form (blue plastic) but as the thing it represents (red apple).

Sarah's Turn. Our studies suggest that Sarah, who knows more than 120 words, has mastered ... important functions of language. This does not mean that she can produce all the functions of language, or that she can do everything a human can; but then, we have only been working with her a relatively short while.

To cynics who doubt that Sarah understands language, we can say only that she understands well enough to teach her teachers. During a preposition test one day, Sarah, who became restless, gave Mary what amounted to a sentence-completion test. Sarah put up a partial statement on one side of the language board (A is on . . .) and then arranged alternate answers on the other side. Sarah would point to each possible answer, and Mary's task (which took her a good while to figure out) was to nod when Sarah pointed to the right one. "The little devil would pass by the solution quickly and try to trick me into a mistake," Mary reported.

PART FOUR

Motivation and Emotion

On the Internet . . .

Sites appropriate to Part Four

The Perceptual Science Laboratory at the University of California, Santa Cruz, has put together this facial analysis page, which provides information and resources on researchers such as Paul Ekman.

```
http://mambo.ucsc.edu/psl/fan1.html
```

1001 Ways to Be Romantic® from World of Romance™ by Gregory J. P. Godek.

```
http://www.godek.com/1001.html
```

CHAPTER 9

Motivation

9.1 ABRAHAM H. MASLOW

A Theory of Human Motivation

Motivation, a core concept in psychology, has been studied from a wide variety of perspectives. One intriguing perspective is the humanistic theory, which proposes that there is a hierarchy of human needs that, when satisfied, leads to self-actualization, or the realization of one's potential.

Abraham H. Maslow (1908–1970), who first proposed the humanistic theory of motivation, earned his Ph.D. in experimental psychology from the University of Wisconsin in 1934. He taught at Brooklyn College and Brandeis University before going to the Laughlin Foundation in Menlo Park, California, in 1969. A leading proponent of the humanistic approach in psychology, Maslow wrote a number of books, including *Toward a Psychology of Being*, 2d ed. (Van Nostrand Reinhold, 1968) and *Motivation and Personality* (1954).

This selection is from "A Theory of Human Motivation," which was published in *Psychological Review* in 1943. In it, Maslow presents his original thinking in developing his "positive" humanistic theory. He perceives human needs as composing a hierarchy, with self-actualization—becoming what one is capable of becoming—as the ultimate need. Maslow writes in a straightforward style, but he deals with issues that are complex and that, in many ways, form the essence of being human. As you read this selection, consider what motivates you in your everyday life.

Key Concept: humanistic theory of motivation

*I*t is far easier to perceive and to criticize the aspects in motivation theory than to remedy them. Mostly this is because of the very serious lack of sound data in this area. I conceive this lack of sound facts to be due primarily to the absence of a valid theory of motivation. The present theory then must be considered to be a suggested program or framework for future research and must stand or fall, not so much on facts available or evidence presented, as upon researches yet to be done, researches suggested perhaps, by the questions raised in this paper.

THE BASIC NEEDS

The 'Physiological' Needs.   The needs that are usually taken as the starting point for motivation theory are the so-called physiological drives. Two recent lines of research make it necessary to revise our customary notions about these needs, first, the development of the concept of homeostasis, and second, the finding that appetites (preferential choices among foods) are a fairly efficient indication of actual needs or lacks in the body.

Homeostasis refers to the body's automatic efforts to maintain a constant, normal state of the blood stream. Cannon (1) has described this process for (1) the water content of the blood, (2) salt content, (3) sugar content, (4) protein content, (5) fat content, (6) calcium content, (7) oxygen content, (8) constant hydrogen-ion level (acid-base balance) and (9) constant temperature of the blood. Obviously this list can be extended to include other minerals, the hormones, vitamins, etc.

Young in a recent article (3) has summarized the work on appetite in its relation to body needs. If the body lacks some chemical, the individual will tend to develop a specific appetite or partial hunger for that food element.

Thus it seems impossible as well as useless to make any list of fundamental physiological needs for they can come to almost any number one might wish, depending on the degree of specificity of description. We can not identify all physiological needs as homeostatic. That sexual desire, sleepiness, sheer activity and maternal behavior in animals, are homeostatic, has not yet been demonstrated. Furthermore, this list would not include the various sensory pleasures (tastes, smells, tickling, stroking) which are probably physiological and which may become the goals of motivated behavior. . . .

It should be pointed out again that any of the physiological needs and the consummatory behavior involved with them serve as channels for all sorts of other needs as well. That is to say, the person who thinks he is hungry may actually be seeking more for comfort, or dependence, than for vitamins or proteins. Conversely, it is possible to satisfy the hunger need in part by other activities such as drinking water or smoking cigarettes. In other words, relatively isolable as these physiological needs are, they are not completely so.

Undoubtedly these physiological needs are the most prepotent of all needs [they exceed all others in power]. What this means specifically is, that in the human being who is missing everything in life in an extreme fashion, it is most likely that the major motivation would be the physiological needs rather than any others. A person who is lacking food, safety, love, and esteem would most probably hunger for food more strongly than for anything else. . . .

Obviously a good way to obscure the 'higher' motivations, and to get a lopsided view of human capacities and human nature, is to make the organism extremely and chronically hungry or thirsty. Anyone who attempts to make an emergency picture into a typical one, and who will measure all of man's goals and desires by his behavior during extreme physiological deprivation is certainly being blind to many things. It is quite true that man lives by bread alone—when there is no bread. But what happens to man's desires when there *is* plenty of bread and when his belly is chronically filled?

At once other (and 'higher') needs emerge and these, rather than physiological hungers, dominate the organism. And when these in turn are satisfied, again new (and still 'higher') needs emerge and so on. This is what we mean by saying that the basic human needs are organized into a hierarchy of relative prepotency.

One main implication of this phrasing is that gratification becomes as important a concept as deprivation in motivation theory, for it releases the organism from the domination of a relatively more physiological need, permitting thereby the emergence of other more social goals. The physiological needs, along with their partial goals, when chronically gratified cease to exist as active determinants or organizers of behavior. They now exist only in a potential fashion in the sense that they may emerge again to dominate the organism if they are thwarted. But a want that is satisfied is no longer a want. The organism is dominated and its behavior organized only by unsatisfied needs. If hunger is satisfied, it becomes unimportant in the current dynamics of the individual. . . .

The Safety Needs. If the physiological needs are relatively well gratified, there then emerges a new set of needs, which we may categorize roughly as the safety needs. All that has been said of the physiological needs is equally true, although in lesser degree, of these desires. The organism may equally well be wholly dominated by them. They may serve as the almost exclusive organizers of behavior, recruiting all the capacities of the organism in their service, and we may then fairly describe the whole organism as a safety-seeking mechanism. Again we may say of the receptors, the effectors, of the intellect and the other capacities that they are primarily safety-seeking tools. Again, as in the hungry man, we find that the dominating goal is a strong determinant not only of his current world-outlook and philosophy but also of his philosophy of the future. Practically everything looks less important than safety, (even sometimes the physiological needs which being satisfied, are now underestimated). A man, in this state, if it is extreme enough and chronic enough, may be characterized as living almost for safety alone.

Although in this paper we are interested primarily in the needs of the adult, we can approach an understanding of his safety needs perhaps more efficiently by observation of infants and children, in whom these needs are much more simple and obvious. One reason for the clearer appearance of the threat or danger reaction in infants, is that they do not inhibit this reaction at all, whereas adults in our society have been taught to inhibit it at all costs. Thus even when adults do feel their safety to be threatened we may not be able to see this on the surface. Infants will react in a total fashion and as if they were endangered, if they are disturbed or dropped suddenly, startled by loud noises, flashing light, or other unusual sensory stimulation, by rough handling, by general loss of support in the mother's arms, or by inadequate support. . . .

From these and similar observations, we may generalize and say that the average child in our society generally prefers a safe, orderly, predictable, organized world, which he can count on, and in which unexpected, unmanageable or other dangerous things do not happen, and in which, in any case, he has all-powerful parents who protect and shield him from harm. . . .

The healthy, normal, fortunate adult in our culture is largely satisfied in his safety needs. The peaceful, smoothly running, 'good' society ordinarily makes its members feel safe enough from wild animals, extremes of temperature, criminals, assault and murder, tyranny, etc. Therefore, in a very real sense, he no longer has any safety needs as active motivators. Just as a sated man no longer feels hungry, a safe man no longer feels endangered. If we wish to see these needs directly and clearly we must turn to neurotic or near-neurotic individuals, and to the economic and social underdogs. In between these extremes, we can perceive the expressions of safety needs only in such phenomena as, for instance, the common preference for a job with tenure and protection, the desire for a savings account, and for insurance of various kinds (medical, dental, unemployment, disability, old age).

Other broader aspects of the attempt to seek safety and stability in the world are seen in the very common preference for familiar rather than unfamiliar things, or for the known rather than the unknown. The tendency to have some religion or world-philosophy that organizes the universe and the men in it into some sort of satisfactorily coherent, meaningful whole is also in part motivated by safety-seeking. Here too we may list science and philosophy in general as partially motivated by the safety needs. . . .

The Love Needs. If both the physiological and the safety needs are fairly well gratified, then there will emerge the love and affection and belongingness needs, and the whole cycle already described will repeat itself with this new center. Now the person will feel keenly, as never before, the absence of friends, or a sweetheart, or a wife, or children. He will hunger for affectionate relations with people in general, namely, for a place in his group, and he will strive with great intensity to achieve this goal. He will want to attain such a place more than anything else in the world and may even forget that once, when he was hungry, he sneered at love. . . .

One thing that must be stressed at this point is that love is not synonymous with sex. Sex may be studied as a purely physiological need. Ordinarily sexual behavior is multi-determined, that is to say, determined not only by sexual but also by other needs, chief among which are the love and affection needs. Also not to be overlooked is the fact that the love needs involve both giving *and* receiving love.

The Esteem Needs. All people in our society (with a few pathological exceptions) have a need or desire for a stable, firmly based, (usually) high evaluation of themselves, for self-respect, or self-esteem, and for the esteem of others. By firmly based self-esteem, we mean that which is soundly based upon realty capacity, achievement and respect from others. These needs may be classified into two subsidiary sets. These are, first, the desire for strength, for achievement, for adequacy, for confidence in the face of the world, and for independence and freedom. Secondly, we have what we may call the desire for reputation or prestige (defining it as respect or esteem from other people), recognition, attention, importance or appreciation. . . .

Satisfaction of the self-esteem need leads to feelings of self-confidence, worth, strength, capability and adequacy of being useful and necessary in the world. But thwarting of these needs produces feelings of inferiority, of weakness and of helplessness. These feelings in turn give rise to either basic discouragement or else compensatory or neurotic trends. An appreciation of the necessity of basic self-confidence and an understanding of how helpless people are without it, can be easily gained from a study of severe traumatic neurosis (2).

The Need for Self-Actualization. Even is all these needs are satisfied, we may still often (if not always) expect that a new discontent and restlessness will soon develop, unless the individual is doing what he is fitted for. A musician must make music, an artist must paint, a poet must write, if he is to be ultimately happy. What a man *can* be, he *must* be. This need we may call self-actualization.

This term, first coined by Kurt Goldstein, is being used in this paper in a much more specific and limited fashion. It refers to the desire for self-fulfillment, namely, to the tendency for him to become actualized in what he is potentially. This tendency might be phrased as the desire to become more and more what one is, to become everything that one is capable of becoming.

The specific form that these needs will take will of course vary greatly from person to person. In one individual it may take the form of the desire to be an ideal mother, in another it may be expressed athletically, and in still another it may be expressed in painting pictures or in inventions. It is not necessarily a creative urge although in people who have any capacities for creation it will take this form.

The clear emergence of these needs rests upon prior satisfaction of the physiological, safety, love and esteem needs. We shall call people who are satisfied in these needs, basically satisfied people, and it is from these that we may expect the fullest (and healthiest) creativeness. Since, in our society, basically satisfied people are the exception, we do not know much about self-actualization, either experimentally or clinically. It remains a challenging problem for research.

The Preconditions for the Basic Need Satisfactions. There are certain conditions which are immediate prerequisites for the basic need satisfactions. Danger to these is reacted to almost as if it were a direct danger to the basic needs themselves. Such conditions as freedom to speak, freedom to do what one wishes so long as no harm is done to others, freedom to express one's self, freedom to investigate and seek for information, freedom to defend one's self,

justice, fairness, honesty, orderliness in the group are examples of such preconditions for basic need satisfactions. Thwarting in these freedoms will be reacted
to with a threat or emergency response. These conditions are not ends in themselves but they are *almost* so since they are so closely related to the basic needs,
which are apparently the only ends in themselves. These conditions are defended because without them the basic satisfactions are quite impossible, or at
least, very severely endangered.

If we remember that the cognitive capacities (perceptual, intellectual,
learning) are a set of adjustive tools, which have, among other functions, that
of satisfaction of our basic needs, then it is clear that any danger to them, any
deprivation or blocking of their free use, must also be indirectly threatening to
the basic needs themselves. Such a statement is a partial solution of the general
problems of curiosity, the search for knowledge, truth and wisdom, and the
ever-persistent urge to solve the cosmic mysteries. . . .

The Desires to Know and to Understand. So far, we have mentioned the
cognitive needs only in passing. Acquiring knowledge and systematizing the
universe have been considered as, in part, techniques for the achievement of
basic safety in the world, or, for the intelligent man, expressions of self-actualization. Also freedom of inquiry and expression have been discussed as preconditions of satisfactions of the basic needs. True though these formulation may
be, they do not constitute definitive answers to the question as to the motivation role of curiosity, learning, philosophizing, experimenting, etc. They are, at
best, no more than partial answers. . . .

FURTHER CHARACTERISTICS OF THE BASIC NEEDS

The Degree of Fixity of the Hierarchy of Basic Needs. We have spoken so far
as if this hierarchy were a fixed order but actually it is not nearly as rigid as we
may have implied. It is true that most of the people with whom we have
worked have seemed to have these basic needs in about the order that has been
indicated. However, there have been a number of exceptions. . . .

Degrees of Relative Satisfaction. So far, our theoretical discussion may
have given the impression that these five sets of needs are somehow in a
step-wise, all-or-none relationships to each other. We have spoken in such
terms as the following: "If one need is satisfied, then another emerges." This
statement might give the false impression that a need must be satisfied 100
percent before the next need emerges. In actual fact, most members of our
society who are normal, are partially satisfied in all their basic needs and
partially unsatisfied in all their basic needs at the same time. A more realistic
description of the hierarchy would be in terms of decreasing percentages of
satisfaction as we go up the hierarchy of prepotency. For instance, if I may
assign arbitrary figures for the sake of illustration, it is as if the average citizen
is satisfied perhaps 85 percent in his physiological needs, 70 percent in his

safety needs, 50 percent in his love needs, 40 percent in his self-esteem needs, and 10 percent in his self-actualization needs.

As for the concept of emergence of a new need after satisfaction of the prepotent need, this emergence is not a sudden saltatory phenomenon but rather a gradual emergence by slow degrees from nothingness. For instance, if prepotent need A is satisfied only 10 percent then need B may not be visible at all. However, as this need A becomes satisfied 25 percent, need B may emerge 5 percent, as need A becomes satisfied 75 percent need B may emerge 90 percent, and so on.

Unconscious Character of Needs. These needs are neither necessarily conscious nor unconscious. On the whole, however, in the average person, they are more often unconscious rather than conscious. It is not necessary at this point to overhaul the tremendous mass of evidence which indicates the crucial importance of unconscious motivation. It would by now be expected, on a priori grounds alone, that unconscious motivations would on the whole be rather more important than the conscious motivations. What we have called the basic needs are very often largely unconscious although they may, with suitable techniques, and with sophisticated people become conscious.

Cultural Specificity and Generality of Needs. This classification of basic needs makes some attempt to take account of the relative unity behind the superficial differences in specific desires from one culture to another. Certainly in any particular culture an individual's conscious motivational content will usually be extremely different from the conscious motivational content of an individual in another society. However, it is the common experience of anthropologists that people, even in different societies, are much more alike than we would think from our first contact with them, and that as we know them better we seem to find more and more of this commonness. We then recognize the most startling differences to be superficial rather than basic, *e.g.,* differences in style of hairdress, clothes, tastes in food, etc. Our classification of basic needs is in part an attempt to account for this unity behind the apparent diversity from culture to culture. No claim is made that it is ultimate or universal for all cultures. The claim is made only that it is relatively *more* ultimate, more universal, more basic, than the superficial conscious desires from culture to culture, and makes a somewhat closer approach to common-human characteristics. Basic needs are *more* common-human than superficial desires or behaviors.

Multiple Motivations of Behavior. These needs must be understood *not* to be *exclusive* or single determiners of certain kinds of behavior. An example may be found in any behavior that seems to be physiologically motivated, such as eating, or sexual play or the like. The clinical psychologists have long since found that any behavior may be a channel through which flow various determinants. Or to say it in another way, most behavior is multi-motivated. Within the sphere of motivational determinants any behavior tends to be determined by several or *all* of the basic needs simultaneously rather than by only one of them. The latter would be more an exception than the former. Eating may be partially for the sake of filling the stomach, and partially for the sake of comfort and amelioration of other needs. One may make love not only for pure sexual release, but also to convince one's self of one's masculinity, or to make a conquest, to feel powerful, or to win more basic affection. As an illustration, I may point out that it would be possible (theoretically if not practically) to analyze a single act of an individual and see in it the expression of his physiological needs, his safety needs, his love needs, his esteem needs and self-actualization. This contrasts sharply with the more naive brand of trait psychology in which one trait or one motive accounts for a certain kind of act, *i.e.*, an aggressive act is traced solely to a trait of aggressiveness. . . .

Goals as Centering Principle in Motivation Theory. It will be observed that the basic principle in our classification has been neither the instigation nor the motivated behavior but rather the functions, effects, purposes, or goals of the behavior. It has been proven sufficiently by various people that this is the most suitable point for centering in any motivation theory.

REFERENCES

1. CANNON, W. B. *Wisdom of the body.* New York: Norton, 1932.
2. KARDINER, A. *The traumatic neuroses of war.* New York: Hoeber, 1941.
3. YOUNG, P. T. The experimental analysis of appetite. *Psychol. Bull.*, 1941, 38, 129–164.

9.2 EDWARD L. DECI

Work: Who Does Not Like It and Why

Psychologists have always been interested in why people do what they do—in short, their motivation. Sometimes people do things for extrinsic or outside reasons (such as for money or for praise), and sometimes they do things for intrinsic or internal reasons (simply because they enjoy the activities). There are a number of situations, however, in which people are *expected* to work, such as in school or on the job. Teachers and employers are especially interested in work motivation. Edward L. Deci has spent much of his career trying to determine the influences on intrinsic and extrinsic motivation.

Deci (b. 1942) earned his Ph.D. in psychology from Carnegie-Mellon University in 1970. He is a professor of psychology at the University of Rochester, where he has been teaching since 1970. A leader in the study of intrinsic motivation, he has authored or coauthored a number of books, including *Intrinsic Motivation and Self-Determination in Human Behavior* (Plenum, 1985), with Richard M. Ryan.

This selection from "Work: Who Does Not Like It and Why," which was published in *Psychology Today* in 1972, is an informal discussion of the influences on intrinsic motivation and work. In this selection, Deci provides some practical advice to anyone who wants to enjoy what he or she does. In his later research, Deci found that self-determination is an important variable in intrinsic motivation. As you read this selection, notice how each experiment leads to the next one. Also, think about what you enjoy doing most and what motivates you to do it.

Key Concept: intrinsic motivation

I am fascinated with a child's unflagging curiosity. He explores everything; for him objects exist to be touched, smelled, tasted, and where possible, eaten. He learns, and learning excites and delights him. Yet by the time he reaches seventh grade, he is likely to complain that he doesn't like school and having to "learn stuff." And when he is out of school he may give up reading books entirely.

The work I have done over the last three years may account for some of this loss of curiosity. I began with the distinction that psychologists make between intrinsic and extrinsic motivation. When a person does a thing solely for the pleasure of the activity, we say that he is intrinsically motivated: the activity is its own reward. (I once spent a solid 12 hours doing a jigsaw puzzle. No one forced me; no one even knew that I had done it. I was intrinsically motivated.) By contrast, when a person does something for an outside reward— money, a better job—or to avoid a punishment—loss of money, censure—we say that he is extrinsically motivated.

Joy

Many psychologists have documented such intrinsically motivated acts as exploration and curiosity. Harry Harlow reports that monkeys will spend hours working on a puzzle for no apparent reward; they seem to like to work on the puzzle, much as I do. Robert W. White has suggested that man strives to deal effectively with his environment: we are, he says, intrinsically motivated to be creative, spontaneous and curious. Daniel Berlyne and other researchers have written about play, another intrinsic activity. In all, it is clear that human beings do many things for the simple joy of the activity.

Now consider a person who is involved in an intrinsically interesting task for which he is also receiving extrinsic rewards. This situation marks the child's development: he is eager to learn, but the school soon controls his learning with grades, threats of failure, gold stars, and so on. One must wonder what happens—whether extrinsic reinforcements increase a person's intrinsic motivation, decrease it, or leave it unchanged.

Puzzle

In quest of answers, I have observed hundreds of college students at work on an intrinsically interesting task. I used a popular puzzle called Soma, which consists of seven three-dimensional pieces, all variously shaped. We asked students to use the pieces to reproduce several configurations that were outlined on paper. Our pilot tests showed clearly that the students thought the puzzle was intrinsically interesting.

The outline for our series of experiments was the same. We gave each student four configurations to solve, allowing him 10 minutes for each puzzle. If he could not solve a puzzle in the allotted time, we stopped him and showed him the solution. After completing the four puzzles, the student remained alone in the experimental room, free to do what he wished: read magazines, solve more puzzles, or whatever. We reasoned that the students were intrinsically motivated if they continued to work on puzzles when they were alone, since there were other things they could do in that situation. Thus the additional amount of time they spent with the Soma game was our measure of their intrinsic motivation for that activity.

Edward L. Deci

Pay

Our first experiment looked at the effect of money. We told half of the 64 student subjects at the outset that they would receive one dollar for each correct solution; the most they could win, then, was four dollars (the average was over two dollars). The money reward was therefore contingent upon their performance. The other half of the students also worked on the four puzzles, but we did not pay them for the correct answer.

Money made a difference. Those students whom we had paid spent significantly less time with the puzzles when they were alone later than did those who had done the same puzzles for free. Once they got money for doing a fun game, their intrinsic motivation decreased; to an extent, they had become dependent on the external reward.

Buzzer

In a second experiment, Wayne Cascio and I sought to determine whether threats of punishment would have the same effect. We told half of the 32 students that if they were unable to solve a puzzle within 10 minutes a buzzer would sound, indicating that their time was up for that puzzle. We gave them a short sample blast of the noise, so they knew that it was truly obnoxious—to be avoided if at all possible. This group, then, worked on Soma partly to avoid a punishment, the buzzer. We found that these students, like those who had worked for money, were less intrinsically interested in the puzzle later than students who had not been threatened with the unpleasant sound. Actually, few students had to endure the punishment of the buzzer, since most were able to solve all the problems. So it seems to have been the *threat* of punishment that was critical in decreasing their intrinsic motivation.

Locus

In our third variation, we paid each student two dollars for participating in the experiment regardless of performance, instead of paying for each solution. This time they showed no change in degree of intrinsic motivation.

We can explain these findings in terms of locus of causality. That is, when a person does a thing for no apparent reward, he explains his behavior in terms of internal causes: *I am doing this because I like to*, he seems to say. When we give him external reasons, however, he begins to attribute his behavior to other causes: *I am doing this for the money, or to avoid punishments.* When we paid our students for each solution the locus of causality for their behavior shifted from internal motives to external ones. They readily came to perceive of the money as the reason for their behavior. However, when we did not tie payments directly to their performance—when we gave the flat fee to everyone—the students were less likely to think that the money was the reason for working. Doing the puzzles was not instrumental in getting the money, so they were less likely to think of the money as their reason for doing the puzzle.

A change in locus of causality is one of two processes that affect intrinsic motivation. The other concerns verbal feedback. We found, for instance, that if we rewarded a student for each correct solution with statements such as "good, that's very fast for that one," his intrinsic motivation increased markedly. The 48 students told us that they liked the puzzle more, and spent more free time working on it, than the 48 students whom we had not so praised.

Why did verbal rewards increase intrinsic motivation, while money rewards decreased it? The answer, we think, is that an intrinsically motivated activity is one that provides feelings of competence and self-determination for a person. I stayed with that 12-hour jigsaw partly out of furious resolve to beat the damned thing, and my success reinforced my feelings of competence. Verbal feedback does much the same thing: it reaffirms the individual's confidence in himself; it makes him feel competent and self-determining.

Pair

Thus external rewards have at least two functions: one is a controlling function that makes a person dependent on the reward; the other is a feedback function that affects his feelings of competence and self-determination. Money and threats are common controllers; we do not generally think of them as reassurance about our competence. Praise and compliments, however, make a person feel good. In this sense, verbal feedback from someone else may not differ phenomenologically from the feedback an individual gives himself; both help him feel that he is worthy and capable. Both, therefore, maintain one's intrinsic motivation.

Of course it is possible that a heavy dosage of verbal reward would make a person dependent on praise, just as he becomes dependent on money or threats; and it also is possible that this type of dependency too would decrease intrinsic motivation. So far, however, we can conclude that feedback rewards differ significantly from controlling rewards.

Offset

In our next experiment, we gave our subjects both money (one dollar per correct puzzle) and praise. Apparently, the two kinds of reward offset each other: this group showed the same level of intrinsic motivation that we found with students who received neither reward.

Finally, we wondered what would happen when feedback was negative. Cascio and I gave 32 students new puzzles that were much more difficult. They failed miserably at solving them; and later they were indeed less likely to spend time working on them than the 24 students who had worked on somewhat easier puzzles with higher success rates. The negative feelings associated with failure counteracted the positive feelings associated with the puzzle. Failure won: failing at a task, it seems, reduces our motive to stay with it. Similarly, Cascio and I found that negative verbal feedback also decreases intrinsic motivation.

Toy

Another area of social psychology that fits nicely with our research is that of insufficient justification. This line of theory suggests that when persons do not have sufficient external reasons to explain their actions, they develop internal reasons; attitudes change accordingly.

For example, Elliot Aronson and J. Merrill Carlsmith gave one group of children strong warnings against playing with a particular toy, and gave another group milder warnings. The first group had a clear, external reason for avoiding the attractive toy; hence they felt no need for internal justification for not playing with it. But the second group, those who were warned mildly, changed their attitudes toward the toy significantly: they decided that they really didn't want to play with the "dumb old thing" anyway. Since there were insufficient outside threats, they developed internal reasons. Jonathan Freedman reported similar findings. Children who developed internal reasons for not playing with the toy were less likely to play with the toy in a free situation even two months later. Intrinsic controls, it appears, have lasting effect.

Controls

When we apply the results of these experiments to the real world, we begin to see why curiosity and pleasure in learning decrease as the child grows up. When the child enters school he immediately becomes subject to numerous extrinsic controls. Teachers grade him, and warn him that he will fail if he does not do what he is told to do. Teachers determine what the child should learn, and at what pace he must learn it. Some parents compound the process by promising money or gifts for good marks. So the child begins to work for the grade, or the gift, or to avoid the consequences of failure. The result is a student who works only for external rewards.

John Holt has described this process beautifully. Children fail, he says, because they are afraid of punishment and bored by the dull and trivial tasks they must perform. The school provides little that is intrinsically interesting, and then teachers control the student's behavior in such a way that they destroy any intrinsic motivation that may sneak through.

Systems

Educators are not the only ones who want to know how to maintain intrinsic motivation. Organizations and businesses have become concerned. Managerial psychologists have begun to focus on factors that promote the worker's intrinsic motivation and ego-involvement with his job. They stress the kinds of work that promote creativity and they argue that workers should participate in the decision-making processes of the company.

Yet others look more at reward systems that tie money and other benefits to performance—sales commissions and piece-rate payments are examples. My research indicates, however, that such pay systems will *decrease* the intrinsic motivation that is aroused by the interesting jobs and sharing of decision-making. (Straight salaries, however, which are not directly tied to workers' performances, run less risk of this.)

Chaos

There are many individuals who argue that if we remove external controls, people will flounder about in their new-found freedom and abuse it. Lift curfews, say the administrators, and students will carouse all night. Lift threats, says the employer, and employees will stop working. Lift grades, says the parent, and my child will not strive for college.

In fact, they are probably right. The external controls which they have used have co-opted internal control, so the initial response to the breakdown of external controls can be chaotic or destructive behavior. However, I think that the internal control can be reestablished. Forced to rely on his own resources, a person establishes internal controls and limits. This is especially so if the administrators, the employers, and the parents are supportive.

Intrinsic motivation and internal controls have the advantage of being operative when no one is looking. More importantly, they help to maintain a person's sense of self-esteem and personal worth. Abraham Maslow, in *Eupsychian Management*, argues that internal controls also produce less anxiety and are more conducive to strong mental health than external controls are.

Level

It is clear to me that if we want individuals to enjoy what they do, to derive joy and satisfaction from their work as well as their play, we must do two things. We must create more activities that are inherently interesting and gratifying; and we must not use extrinsic rewards in a way that will lower the interest level of those activities that are intrinsically motivated. We should learn to give verbal support to our friends, colleagues and children, and not rely on tendencies to reward or threaten. External controls may get others to act the way we want them to, but such controls absolve them of the feeling of responsibility for those acts. Controlling others seems to insure that others will not control themselves.

9.3 DAVID M. BUSS

The Strategies of Human Mating

The focus of psychology has become increasingly multicultural in recent years as researchers look for universal laws of human behavior. The evolutionary approach to courtship and mate selection argues that men and women throughout the world have different reproductive strategies. David M. Buss of the University of Michigan, in collaboration with 50 other researchers around the world, surveyed over 10,000 men and women in 37 countries on their mating preferences. Buss has used the survey results to develop a theory of mate selection.

Buss received his Ph.D. in psychology from the University of California in 1981. He currently holds a position at the University of Texas at Austin, and he is director of the International Consortium of Personality and Social Psychologists. His evolutionary theory of human mate selection is detailed in his book *The Evolution of Desire: Strategies of Human Mating* (Basic Books, 1994).

This selection is from "The Strategies of Human Mating," which was published in *American Scientist* in 1994. In it, Buss outlines his theory and provides research results, obtained predominantly through surveys, that support the conclusion that, universally, men and women desire certain characteristics in a mate that are unique to each sex. How might an understanding of differences in sexual preference help men and women in their interpersonal relationships?

Key Concept: cross-cultural theory of mate selection

 W hat do men and women want in a mate? Is there anything consistent about human behavior when it comes to the search for a mate? Would a Gujarati of India be attracted to the same traits in a mate as a Zulu of South Africa or a college student in the midwestern United States?

As a psychologist working in the field of human personality and mating preferences, I have come across many attempts to answer such questions and provide a coherent explanation of human mating patterns. Some theories have suggested that people search for mates who resemble archetypical images of the opposite-sex parent (à la Freud and Jung), or mates with characteristics that are either complementary or similar to one's own qualities, or mates with whom to make an equitable exchange of valuable resources.

These theories have played important roles in our understanding of human mating patterns, but few of them have provided specific predictions that can be tested. Fewer still consider the origins and functions of an individual's mating preferences. What possible function is there to mating with an individual who is an archetypical image of one's opposite-sex parent? Most theories also tend to assume that the processes that guide the mating preferences of men and women are identical, and no sex-differentiated predictions can be derived. The context of the mating behavior is also frequently ignored; the same mating tendencies are posited regardless of circumstances.

Despite the complexity of human mating behavior, it is possible to address these issues in a single, coherent theory. David Schmitt of the University of Michigan and I have recently proposed a framework for understanding the logic of human mating patterns from the standpoint of evolutionary theory. Our theory makes several predictions about the behavior of men and women in the context of their respective sexual strategies. In particular, we discuss the changes that occur when men and women shift their goals from short-term mating (casual sex) to long-term mating (a committed relationship).

Some of the studies we discuss are based on surveys of male and female college students in the United States. In these instances, the sexual attitudes of the sample population may not be reflective of the behavior of people in other cultures. In other instances, however, the results represent a much broader spectrum of the human population. In collaboration with 50 other scientists, we surveyed the mating preferences of more than 10,000 men and women in 37 countries over a six-year period spanning 1984 through 1989. Although no survey, short of canvassing the entire human population, can be considered exhaustive, our study crosses a tremendous diversity of geographic, cultural, political, ethnic, religious, racial and economic groups. It is the largest survey ever on mate preferences.

What we found is contrary to much current thinking among social scientists, which holds that the process of choosing a mate is highly culture-bound. Instead, our results are consistent with the notion that human beings, like other animals, exhibit species-typical desires when it comes to the selection of a mate. These patterns can be accounted for by our theory of human sexual strategies.

COMPETITION AND CHOICE

Sexual-strategies theory holds that patterns in mating behavior exist because they are evolutionarily advantageous. We are obviously the descendants of people who were able to mate successfully. Our theory assumes that the sexual strategies of our ancestors evolved because they permitted them to survive and produce offspring. Those people who failed to mate successfully because they did not express these strategies are not our ancestors. One simple example is the urge to mate, which is a universal desire among people in all cultures and which is undeniably evolutionary in origin.

Although the types of behavior we consider are more complicated than simply the urge to mate, a brief overview of the relevant background should be adequate to understand the evolutionary logic of human mating strategies.

As with many issues in evolutionary biology, this background begins with the work of Charles Darwin.

Darwin was the first to show that mate preferences could affect human evolution. In his seminal 1871 treatise, *The Descent of Man and Selection in Relation to Sex,* Darwin puzzled over characteristics that seemed to be perplexing when judged merely on the basis of their relative advantage for the animal's survival. How could the brilliant plumage of a male peacock evolve when it obviously increases the bird's risk of predation? Darwin's answer was sexual selection, the evolution of characteristics that confer a reproductive advantage to an organism (rather than a survival advantage). Darwin further divided sexual selection into two processes: intrasexual competition and preferential mate choice.

Intrasexual competition is the less controversial of the two processes. It involves competition between members of the same sex to gain preferential access to mating partners. Characteristics that lead to success in these same-sex competitions—such as greater strength, size, agility, confidence or cunning—can evolve simply because of the reproductive advantage gained by the victors. Darwin assumed that this is primarily a competitive interaction between males, but recent studies suggest that human females are also very competitive for access to mates.

Preferential mate choice, on the other hand, involves the desire for mating with partners that possess certain characteristics. A consensual desire affects the evolution of characteristics because it gives those possessing the desired characteristics an advantage in obtaining mates over those who do not possess the desired characteristics. Darwin assumed that preferential mate choice operates primarily through females who prefer particular males. (Indeed, he even called this component of sexual selection *female choice.*)

Darwin's theory of mate-choice selection was controversial in part because Darwin simply assumed that females desire males with certain characteristics. Darwin failed to document how such desires might have arisen and how they might be maintained in a population.

The solution to the problem was not forthcoming until 1972, when Robert Trivers, then at Harvard University, proposed that the relative parental investment of the sexes influences the two processes of sexual selection. Specifically, the sex that invests more in offspring is selected to be more discriminating in choosing a mate, whereas the sex that invests less in offspring is more competitive with members of the same sex for sexual access to the high-investing sex. Parental-investment theory accounts, in part, for both the origin and the evolutionary retention of different sexual strategies in males and females.

Consider the necessary *minimum* parental investment by a woman. After internal fertilization, the gestation period lasts about nine months and is usually followed by lactation, which in tribal societies typically can last several years. In contrast, a man's minimum parental investment can be reduced to the contribution of sperm, an effort requiring as little time as a few minutes. This disparity in parental investment means that the replacement of a child who dies (or is deserted) typically costs more (in time and energy) for women than men. Parental-investment theory predicts that women will be more choosy and selective about their mating partners. Where men can provide resources, women should desire those who are able and willing to commit those resources to her and her children.

SEXUAL STRATEGIES

Our evolutionary framework is based on three key ingredients. First, human mating is inherently strategic. These strategies exist because they solved specific problems in human evolutionary history. It is important to recognize that the manifestation of these strategies need not be through conscious psychological mechanisms. Indeed, for the most part we are completely unaware of *why* we find certain qualities attractive in a mate. A second component of our theory is that mating strategies are context-dependent. People behave differently depending on whether the situation presents itself as a short-term or long-term mating prospect. Third, men and women have faced different mating problems over the course of human evolution and, as a consequence, have evolved different strategies.

. . . [S]exual strategies theory consists of nine hypotheses. We can test these hypotheses by making several predictions about the behavior of men and women faced with a particular mating situation. Even though we make only a few predictions for each hypothesis, it should be clear that many more predictions can be derived to test each hypothesis. We invite the reader to devise his or her own tests of these hypotheses.

Hypothesis 1: Short-term mating is more important for men than women. This hypothesis follows from the fact that men can reduce their parental investment to the absolute minimum and still produce offspring. Consequently, short-term mating should be a key component of the sexual strategies of men, and much less so for women. We tested three predictions based on this hypothesis in a sample of 148 college students (75 men and 73 women) in the midwestern United States.

First, we predict that men will express a greater interest in seeking a short-term mate than will women. We asked the students to rate the degree to which they were currently seeking a short-term mate (defined as a one-night stand or a brief affair) and the degree to which they were currently seeking a long-term mate (defined as a marriage partner). They rated their interests on a 7-point scale, where a rating of 1 corresponds to a complete lack of interest and a 7 corresponds to a high level of interest.

We found that although the sexes do not differ in their stated proclivities for seeking a long-term mate (an average rating of about 3.4 for both sexes), men reported a significantly greater interest (an average rating of about 5) in seeking a short-term sexual partner than did women (about 3). The results also showed that at any given time men are more interested in seeking a short-term mate rather than a long-term mate, whereas women are more interested in seeking a long-term mate than a short-term mate.

Second we predict that men will desire a greater number of mates than is desired by women. We asked the same group of college students how many sexual partners they would ideally like to have during a given time interval and during their lifetimes. In this instance men consistently reported that they desired a greater number of sex partners than reported by the women for every interval of time. For example, the average man desired about eight sex partners during the next two years, whereas the average woman desired to have one sex partner. In the course of a lifetime, the average man reported the desire to have about 18 sex partners, whereas the average woman desired no more that 4 or 5 sex partners.

A third prediction that follows from this hypothesis is that men will be more willing to engage in sexual intercourse a shorter period of time after first meeting a potential sex partner. We asked the sample of 148 college students the following question: "If the conditions were right, would you consider having sexual intercourse with someone you viewed as desirable if you had known that person for *(a time period ranging from one hour to five years)*?" For each of 10 time intervals the students were asked to provide a response ranging from –3 (definitely not) to 3 (definitely yes).

After a period of 5 years, the men and women were equally likely to consent to sexual relations, each giving a score of about 2 (probably yes). For all shorter time intervals, men were consistently more likely to consider sexual intercourse. For example, after knowing a potential sex partner for only one week, the average man was still positive about the possibility of having sex, whereas women said that they were highly unlikely to have sex with someone after knowing him for only one week.

The issue was addressed in a novel way by Russell Clark and Elaine Hatfield of the University of Hawaii. They designed a study in which college students were approached by an attractive member of the opposite sex who posed one of three questions after a brief introduction: "Would you go out on a date with me tonight?" "Would you go back to my apartment with me tonight?" or "Would you have sex with me tonight?"

Of the women who were approached, 50 percent agreed to the date, 6 percent agreed to go to the apartment and none agreed to have sex. Many women found the sexual request from a virtual stranger to be odd or insulting. Of the men approached, 50 percent agreed to the date, 69 percent agreed to go back to the woman's apartment and 75 percent agreed to have sex. In contrast to women, many men found the sexual request flattering. Those few men who declined were apologetic about it, citing a fiancee or an unavoidable obligation that particular evening. Apparently, men are willing to solve the problem of partner number by agreeing to have sex with virtual strangers.

[Hypotheses 2 through 9, the discussions of which are not reprinted here, are as follows:

Hypothesis 2: Men seeking a short-term mate will solve the problem of identifying women who are sexually accessible.

Hypothesis 3: Men seeking a short-term mate will minimize commitment and invest-ment.

Hypothesis 4: Men seeking a short-term mate will solve the problem of identifying fertile women.

Hypothesis 5: Men seeking a long-term mate will solve the problem of identifying reproductively valuable women.

Hypothesis 6: Men seeking a long-term mate will solve the problem of paternity confi-dence.

Hypothesis 7: Women seeking a short-term mate will prefer men willing to impart immediate resources.

Hypothesis 8: Women will be more selective than men in choosing a short-term mate.

Hypothesis 9: Women seeking a long-term mate will prefer men who can provide resources for her offspring.

As with Hypothesis 1, Buss makes and tests several predictions based on these hypothe-ses.—Ed.]

CONCLUSION

The results of our work and that of others provide strong evidence that the traditional assumptions about mate preferences—that they are arbitrary and culture-bound—are simply wrong. Darwin's initial insights into sexual selec-tion have turned out to be scientifically profound for people, even though he understood neither their functional-adaptive nature nor the importance of rela-tive parental investment for driving the two components of sexual selection.

Men and women have evolved powerful desires for particular charac-teristics in a mate. These desires are not arbitrary, but are highly patterned and universal. The patterns correspond closely to the specific adaptive problems that men and women have faced during the course of human evolutionary history. These are the problems of paternity certainty, partner number and reproductive capacity for men, and the problems of willingness and ability to invest resources for women.

It turns out that a woman's physical appearance is the most powerful predictor of the occupational status of the man she marries. A woman's ap-pearance is more significant than her intelligence, her level of education or even her original socioeconomic status in determining the mate she will marry. Women who possess the qualities men prefer are most able to translate their preferences into actual mating decisions. Similarly, men possessing what women want—the ability to provide resources—are best able to mate accord-ing to their preferences.

Some adaptive problems are faced by men and women equally: identifying mates who show a proclivity to cooperate and mates who show evidence of having good parenting skills. Men do not look at women simply as sex objects, nor do women look at men simply as success objects. One of our most robust observations was that both sexes place tremendous importance on mutual love and kindness when seeking a long-term mate.

David M. Buss

The similarities among cultures and between sexes implies a degree of psychological unity or species typicality that transcends geographical, racial, political, ethnic and sexual diversity. Future research could fruitfully examine the ecological and historical sources of diversity, while searching for the adaptive functions of the sexual desires that are shared by all members of our species.

Poor Fish

Scientists study animals both to better understand them and to provide insight into human behavior. The study of the behavior of animals, especially in a natural setting, is called "ethnology." In the 1930s Konrad Z. Lorenz became a leader of this approach. He often brought animals into his home so that he could carefully observe their behavior patterns.

Lorenz (1903–1989) received his M.D. in 1928 and his Ph.D. in 1933 from the University of Vienna. He spent his career at the University of Vienna and the Institute for the Physiology of Behavior. He is perhaps best known by American students for his work in the 1930s on imprinting in geese. He wrote a number of books, including *On Aggression* (Harcourt Brace Jovanovich, 1966) and *King Solomon's Ring: New Light on Animal Ways* (Thomas Y. Crowell, 1952). In 1973 the Nobel Prize for physiology was awarded to Lorenz, Niko Tinbergen, and Karl von Frisch for their work in animal behavior.

This selection is from chapter 4, "Poor Fish," in Lorenz's 1952 animal behavior book *King Solomon's Ring.* Lorenz was a delightful writer, and this selection shows how entertaining yet how educating he could be. Although he is describing the behavior of fish in this chapter, he is also writing about some fundamental principles of human behavior. As you read this selection, note the care with which he describes his subjects and the enjoyment with which he communicates with the reader.

Key Concept: animal behavior

*S*trange what blind faith is placed in proverbs, even when what they say is false or misleading. The fox is not more cunning than other beasts of prey and is much more stupid than wolf or dog, the dove is certainly not peaceful, and of the fish, rumour spreads only untruth: it is neither so cold-blooded as one says of dull people, nor is the "fish in water" nearly so happily situated as the converse saying would imply. In reality there is no other group of animals that, even in nature, is so plagued with infectious diseases as the fish. I have never yet known a newly caught bird, reptile or mammal bring an infectious disease into my animal population; but every newly acquired fish must, as a routine measure, go into the quarantine aquarium, otherwise you may bet a hundred to one that within a very short time the dreaded minute white spots, the sign of infection with the parasite *Ichthyophtirius multifiliis,* will appear on the fins of the previously installed aquarium dwellers.

And regarding the alleged cold-bloodedness of fishes; I am familiar with many animals and with their behaviour in the most intimate situations of their life, in the wild ecstasies of the fight and of love, but, with the exception of the wild canary, I know of no animal that can excel in hot-bloodedness a male stickleback, a Siamese fighting-fish or a cichlid. No animal becomes so completely transformed by love, none glows, in such a literal sense, with passion as a stickleback or fighting-fish. Who could reproduce in words, what artist in colour, that glowing red that makes the sides of the male stickleback glassy and transparent, the iridescent blue-green of its back whose colour and brilliance can only be compared with the illuminating power of neon lighting, or finally, the brilliant emerald green of its eyes? According to the rules of artistic taste, these colours should clash horribly, and yet what a symphony they produce, composed by the hand of nature.

In the fighting-fish, this marvel of colour is not continually present. For the little brown-grey fish that lies with folded fins in one corner of the aquarium reveals nothing of it for the moment. It is only when another fish, equally inconspicuous at first, approaches him and each sights the other, that they begin gradually to light up in all their incandescent glory. The glow pervades their bodies almost as quickly as the wire of an electric heater grows red. The fins unfold themselves like ornamental fans, so suddenly that one almost expects to hear the sound of an umbrella being opened quickly. And now follows a dance of burning passion, a dance which is not play but real earnest, a dance of life or death, of be-all or end-all. To begin with, strangely enough, it is uncertain whether it will lead to love overtures and mating, or whether it will develop, by an equally flowing transition, into a bloody battle. Fighting-fish recognize the sex of a member of their own species not simply by seeing it but by watching the way in which it responds to the severely ritualized, inherited, instinctive movements of the dancer.

The meeting of two previously unacquainted fighting-fish begins with a mutual "showing-off," a swaggering act of self-display in which every luminous colour-spot and every iridescent ray of the wonderful fins is brought into maximum play. Before the glorious male, the modestly garbed female lowers the flag—by folding her fins—and, if she is unwilling to mate, flees immediately. Should she be willing to mate, she approaches the male . . . in an attitude directly opposed to that of the swaggering male. And now begins a love ceremonial which, if it cannot compare in grandeur with the male war-dance, can emulate it in grace of movement.

When two males meet face to face, veritable orgies of mutual self-glorification take place. There is a striking similarity between the war-dance of these fish and the corresponding ceremonial dances of Japanese and other Indonesian peoples. In both man and fish the minutest detail of every movement is laid down by immutable and ancient laws, the slightest gesture has its own deeply symbolic meaning. There is a close resemblance between man and fish in the style and exotic grace of their movements of restrained passion.

The beautifully refined form of the movements betrays the fact that they have a long historical development behind them and that they owe their elaborateness to an ancient ritual. It is, however, not so obvious that though in man this ritual is a ceremony which has been handed down from generation to generation by a thousand-year-old tradition, in the fish it represents the result of an evolutional development of innate instinctive activities, at least a hundred times older. Genealogical research into the origin of such ritual expression, and the comparison of such ceremonies in related species are exceedingly illuminating. We know more of the evolutionary history of these movements than of all other instincts.

After this digression, let us return to the war-dance of the male fighting-fish. This has exactly the same meaning as the duel of words of the Homeric heroes, or of our Alpine farmers which, even today, often precedes the traditional Sunday brawl in the village inn. The idea is to intimidate one's opponent and at the same time to stimulate oneself to a state of fearlessness. In the fish, the long duration of these preliminaries, their ritual character and above all their great show of colour finery and fin development which at first only serve to subdue the opponent, mask, for the uninitiated, the seriousness of the situation. On account of their beauty, the fighters appear less malevolent than they really are and one is just as loth to ascribe to them embittered courage and contempt of death as one is to associate head-hunting with the almost effeminately beautiful Indonesian warriors. Nevertheless both are capable of fighting to the death. The battles of the fighting-fish often end in the death of one of the adversaries. When they are stimulated to the point of inflicting the first sword-thrust, it is only a matter of minutes till wide slits are gaping in their fins, which in a few more minutes are reduced to tatters. The method of attack of a fighting-fish, as of nearly all fish that fight, is literally the sword-thrust and not the bite. The fish opens its jaws so wide that all its teeth are directed forwards and, in this attitude, it rams them, with all the force of its muscular body, into the side of its adversary. The ramming of a fighting-fish is so strong and hard that its impact is clearly audible if, in the confusion of the fight, one of the antagonists happens to hit the glass side of the tank. The self-display-dance can last for hours but, should it develop into action, it is often only a matter of minutes before one of the combatants lies mortally wounded on the bottom.

The fights of our European sticklebacks are very different from those of the Siamese fighting-fish. In contrast to the latter, the stickleback, at mating time, glows not only when it sees an opponent or a female, but does so as long as it is in the vicinity of its nest, in its own chosen territory. The basic principle of his fighting is, "my home is my castle." Take his nest from a stickleback or remove him from the tank where he built it and put him with another male and he will not dream of fighting but, on the contrary, will make himself small and ugly. It would be impossible to use sticklebacks for exhibition battles as the Siamese have done, for hundreds of years, with fighting-fish. It is only when he has founded his home that the stickleback becomes physically capable of reaching a state of full sexual excitement; therefore, a real stickleback fight can only be seen when two males are kept together in a large tank where they are both building their nests. The fighting inclinations of a stickleback, at any given moment, are in direct proportion to his proximity to his nest. At the nest itself, he is a raging fury and with a fine contempt of death will recklessly ram the strongest opponent, or even the human hand. The further he strays from his headquarters in the course of his swimming, the more his courage wanes. When two sticklebacks meet in battle, it is possible to predict with a high degree of certainty how the fight will end: the one which is further from his nest will lose the match. In the immediate neighbourhood of his nest, even the smallest male will defeat the largest one, and the relative fighting potential of the individual is shown by the size of the territory which he can keep clear of rivals. The vanquished fish invariably flees homeward and the victor, carried away by his successes, chases the other furiously, far into its domain. The further the victor goes from home, the more his courage ebbs, while that of the vanquished rises in proportion. Arrived in the precincts of his nest, the fugitive gains new strength, turns right about and dashes with gathering fury at his pursuer. A new battle begins, which ends with absolute certainty in the defeat of the former victor, and off goes the chase again in the opposite direction. The pursuit is repeated a few times in alternating directions, swinging to and fro like a pendulum which at last reaches a state of equilibrium at a certain point. The line at which the fighting potentials of the individuals are thus equally balanced marks the border of their territories. This same principle is of great importance in the biology of many animals, particularly that of birds. Every bird lover has seen two male redstarts chasing each other in exactly the same manner.

Once on this borderline, both sticklebacks hesitate to attack. Taking on a peculiar threatening attitude, they incessantly stand on their heads and . . . they do it again and again. At the same time they turn broadside on towards each other and each erects threateningly the ventral spine on the side nearer his opponent. All the while they seem to be "pecking" at the bottom for food. In reality, however, they are executing a ritualized version of the activity normally used in nest-digging. If an animal finds the outlet for some instinctive action blocked by a conflicting drive, it often finds relief by discharging an entirely different instinctive movement. In this case, the stickleback, not quite daring to attack, finds an outlet in nest digging. This type of phenomenon, which is of great theoretical interest both from the physiological and psychological point of view, is termed in comparative ethology a "displacement activity."

Unlike the fighting-fish, the sticklebacks do not waste time by threatening before starting to fight, but will do so after or between battles. This, in itself, implies that they never fight to a finish, although from their method of fighting, the contrary might be expected. Thrust and counter-thrust follow each other so quickly that the eye of the observer can scarcely follow them. The large ventral spine, that appears so ominous, plays in reality quite a subordinate role. In older aquarium literature, it is often stated that these spines are used so effectively that one of the fighters may sink down dead, perforated by the spine of his opponent. Apparently the writers of these works have never tried to "perforate" a stickleback; for even a dead stickleback will slip from under the sharpest scalpel before one is able to penetrate its tough skin, even in places where it is not reinforced by bony armour. Place a dead stickleback on a soft surface—which certainly offers a much better resistance than water—and try to run it through with a sharp needle. You will be surprised at the force required to do so. Owing to the extreme toughness of the sticklebacks' skin, no serious wounds can be inflicted in their natural battles which, as compared with those of the fighting-fish, are absurdly harmless. Of course, in the confined space of a small tank, a stronger male stickleback may harry a weaker one to death, but rabbits and turtle doves, in analogous conditions, will do the same thing to each other.

The stickleback and the fighting-fish are as different in love as they are in fight, yet, as parents, they have much in common. In both species, it is the male and not the female that undertakes the building of the nest and the care of the young, and the future father only then begins to think of love when the cradle for the expected children is ready. But here the similarities end and the differences begin. The cradle of the stickleback lies, in a manner of speaking, under the floor, that of the fighting-fish above the ceiling: that is to say, the former digs a little hollow in the bottom and the latter builds his nest on the surface of the water; the one uses, for nest construction, plant strands and a special sticky kidney secretion, the other uses air and spittle. The castle-in-the-air of the fighting-fish, as also that of his nearer relations, consists of a little pile of air bubbles, stuck closely together, which protrudes somewhat over the water surface; the bubbles are coated with a tough layer of spittle and are very resistant. Already while building, the male radiates the most gorgeous colours, which gain in depth and iridescence when a female approaches. Like lightning, he shoots towards her and glowing, halts. If the female is prepared to accept him, she demonstrates it by investing herself with a characteristic, if modest colouring consisting of light grey vertical stripes on a brown background. With fins closely folded, she swims towards the male who, trembling with excitement, expands all his fins to breaking point and holds himself in such a position that the dazzling brilliance of his full broadside is presented to his bride. Next moment he swims off with a sweeping, gracefully sinuous movement, in the direction of the nest. The beckoning nature of this gesture is at once apparent even when seen for the first time. The essentially ritual nature of this swimming movement is easily understood: everything that enhances its optical effect is exaggerated in mimic, as the sinuous movements of the body or the waving of the tail fin, whereas all the means of making it mechanically effective are decreased. The movement says: "I am swimming away from you, hurry up and follow me!" At the same time, the fish swims neither fast nor far and turns back immediately to the female who is following . . . in his wake.

In this way the female is enticed under the bubble nest and now follows the wonderful love-play which resembles, in delicate grace, a minuet, but in general style, the trance dance of a Balinese temple dancer. In this love dance, by age-old law, the male must always exhibit his magnificent broadside to his partner, but the female must remain constantly at right angles to him. The male must never obtain so much as a glimpse of her flanks, otherwise he will immediately become angry and unchivalrous; for, standing broadsides means, in these fishes as in many others, aggressive masculinity and elicits instantaneously in every male a complete change of mood: hottest love is transformed to wildest hate. Since the male will not now leave the nest, he moves in circles round the female and she follows his every movement by keeping her head always turned towards him; the love-dance is thus executed in a small circle, exactly under the middle of the nest. Now the colours become more glowing, more frantic the movements, ever smaller the circles, until the bodies touch. Then, suddenly, the male slings his body tightly round the female, gently turns her on her back and, quivering, both fulfil the great act of reproduction. Ova and semen are discharged simultaneously.

The female remains, for a few seconds, . . . but the male has . . . things to attend to at once. The minute, glass-clear eggs are considerably heavier than water and sink at once to the ground. Now the posture of the bodies in spawning is such that the sinking eggs are bound to drift past the downward directed head of the male and thus catch his attention. He gently releases the female, glides downwards in pursuit of the eggs and gathers them up, one after the other, in his mouth. Turning upwards again, he blows the eggs into the nest. They now miraculously float instead of sinking. This sudden and amazing change of density is caused by a coating of buoyant spittle in which the male has enveloped every egg while carrying it in his mouth. He has to hurry in this work, for not only would he soon be unable to find the tiny, transparent globules in the mud, but, if he should delay a second longer, the female would wake from her trance and, also swimming after the eggs, would likewise proceed to engulf them. From these actions, it would appear, at first sight, that the female has the same intentions as her mate. But if we wait to see her packing the eggs in the nest, we will wait in vain, for these eggs will disappear, irrevocably swallowed. So the male knows very well why he is hurrying, and he knows, too, why he no longer allows the female near the nest when, after ten to twenty matings, all her eggs have been safely stored between the air bubbles.

*Konrad Z.
Lorenz*

CHAPTER 10 Emotion

Facial Expressions of Emotion: New Findings, New Questions

During the past two decades, researchers have discovered that facial expressions for a number of emotions are universally recognizable—that is, people from a wide variety of cultures will attribute certain facial expressions to the same emotions. More recently, psychologists have reported that facial muscular actions associated with specific emotions (such as frowning, which indicates sadness) cause changes in physiological arousal as well as enhance feelings of the emotion associated with the muscular movements. Paul Ekman has been at the cutting edge of research on facial expression of emotion.

Ekman (b. 1934) earned his Ph.D. from Adelphi University in 1958. He is currently a professor of psychology and the director of the Human Interaction Laboratory at the University of California at San Francisco. He has written a number of books, including *Emotion in the Human Face,* 2d ed. (Cambridge University Press, 1983) and *Telling Lies* (Berkeley, 1985).

This selection is from "Facial Expressions of Emotion: New Findings, New Questions," which was published in the American Psychological Society journal *Psychological Science* in 1992. In it, Ekman offers a glimpse of an active and relevant research program concerning observable facial expressions of emotion. In one part of the original article not included in this selection, Ekman demonstrates that there are differences among smiles and that it is possible to distinguish a smile of enjoyment from other kinds of smiling (such as a smile of embarrassment). As you read this selection, consider how easy it is to detect a person's emotions by observing his or her facial expressions. Does Ekman's evidence suggest that it is possible to modify your emotional state by exercising certain facial muscles?

Key Concept: facial expression of emotion

*T*his paper focuses on the evidence and issues regarding observable facial expression of emotion. . . . I will focus on two new findings and one set of studies dating back 20 years. I will begin with those older studies, of universals in facial expression, because they provide the background for the newer research and also because there is renewed controversy about universals, as well as some new findings and a number of unanswered questions.

UNIVERSAL FACIAL EXPRESSIONS

From 1920 through 1960 many influential psychologists maintained that facial expressions are socially learned and culturally variable, with no fixed relationship between an expression and what it signifies. In the early 1970s there were two challenges: a critical reevaluation of the experiments which had supported that position (Ekman, Friesen, & Ellsworth, 1972) and, more important, new data. Izard and also Friesen and I conducted similar studies of literate cultures, working independently but at the same time. Izard's work and ours was influenced by Tomkins's writings on emotion (1962) and his advice on the conduct of the research we performed.

In each culture subjects chose the emotion terms which fit photographs of posed Caucasian facial expressions. Although Izard (1971) and I (Ekman, Sorenson, & Friesen, 1969) showed different photographs, gave our subjects somewhat different lists of emotion terms, and examined people in different cultures, we both obtained consistent evidence of agreement across more than a dozen Western and non-Western literate cultures in the labeling of enjoyment, anger, fear, sadness, disgust, and surprise facial expressions.

In order to rule out the possibility that such agreement could be due to members of every culture having learned expressions from a shared mass media input, Friesen and I (Ekman, 1972; Ekman & Friesen, 1971; Ekman et al., 1969) also studied a visually isolated preliterate culture in New Guinea. We replicated our findings for literate cultures, as did Heider and Rosch a few years later in another visually isolated culture in what is now West Irian. Although surprise expressions were distinguished from anger, sadness, disgust, and enjoyment expressions in both preliterate cultures, surprise was not distinguished from fear expressions in one of these cultures. Friesen and I also reversed the research design and found that when New Guineans posed facial expressions they were understandable to Western observers (Ekman & Friesen, 1971).

To reconcile these findings of universality with the many reports by cultural anthropologists of dissimilar facial expressions, we (Ekman & Friesen, 1969) postulated *display rules* to refer to what we presume each culture teaches its members about the management of expression in social contexts. Cultural differences in display rules could explain how universal expressions might be modified to create, on occasion, the appearance of culture-specific facial expressions of emotion. We tested this idea in a study comparing the spontaneous expressions shown by Japanese and Americans when they were alone, and presumably no display rules should operate, and when they were with another person (Ekman, 1972; Friesen, 1972). As predicted, there was no difference between cultures in the expressions shown in response to films of unpleasant scenes when the subjects thought they were alone. However, when an authority figure was present the Japanese more than the Americans masked negative expressions with the semblance of smile.

We, like Izard, interpreted the evidence in terms of universal facial expressions as posited by Tomkins (1962) and (much earlier) by Darwin (1872). Consistent with an evolutionary view of expression were other reports of similarities in expression in other primates and in early appearance developmentally. Recently, there have been some challenges to that interpretation. Lutz and White (1986) cited anthropologists who regard emotions as social constructions and reported cultures in which the emotions proposed as universal are neither named nor expressed. Unfortunately, such reports are not substantiated by quantitative methods nor protected against the potential for bias or error when the information is obtained by the single observer who formulated the hypothesis under study. Ortony and Turner (1990) provided a different challenge, speculating that it is only the components of expressions, not the full emotional expressions, which are universal: but see my rebuttal (Ekman, in press-a) and one by Izard (in press).

A new line of studies has found consistent evidence of cultural differences in the perception of the strength of an emotion rather than of which emotion is shown in a facial expression. Japanese make less intense attributions than do Americans (Ekman et al., 1987) regardless of whether the person showing the emotion is Japanese or American, male or female (Matsumoto & Ekman, 1989). This difference appears to be specific to the interpretation of facial expressions of emotions, since it was not found in the judgment of either nonfacial emotional stimuli or facial nonemotional stimuli (Matsumoto & Kudoh, 1991).

A number of empirical questions remain about universals in facial expression. Although there is evidence of more than one different expression for each emotion (up to five visibly different expressions for some emotions) in Western cultures, we do not know how many of those different expressions which signal a single emotion are shown universally (Ekman & Friesen, 1975, 1978). Nor is there certain knowledge about whether there are other emotions in addition to anger, fear, disgust, sadness, enjoyment, and surprise that have universal expressions. There is some evidence, although it is contradictory, for universal facial expressions for contempt, interest, shame, and guilt. Little is known also about cross-cultural differences in display rules, as a function of sex, role, age, and social context (but see recent work by Matsumoto, in press). These and other questions about universals have recently been reviewed (Ekman, 1989b).

FACIAL ACTION GENERATES EMOTION PHYSIOLOGY

Most emotion theorists emphasize the involuntary nature of emotional experience, ignoring those instances when people choose to generate an emotion through reminiscence or by adopting the physical actions associated with a particular emotion (e.g., speaking more softly to deintensify anger or smiling to generate enjoyment). Facial expression from this vantage point is seen as one of a number of emotional responses that are generated centrally when an emotion is called forth by, for example, an event, memory, or image.

A new role for facial expression was found in my collaborative study with Levenson and Friesen (Ekman, Levenson, & Friesen, 1983). Voluntarily performing certain facial muscular actions generated involuntary changes in autonomic nervous system (ANS) activity. We did not ask subjects to pose emotions, but instead to follow muscle-by-muscle instructions to create on their faces one of the expressions which had been found to be universal. For example, rather than ask a subject to pose anger we said: "Pull your eyebrows down and together; raise your upper eyelids and tighten your lower eyelids; narrow your lips and press them together." Different patterns of ANS activity occurred when subjects made the muscular movements which had been found universally for the emotions of anger, fear, sadness, and disgust.

This work has since been replicated in three more experiments (Levenson, Carstensen, Frisen, & Ekman, 1991; Levenson, Ekman, & Friesen, 1990), and a number of possible artifacts which could have been responsible for this phenomenon have been ruled out. The findings were again obtained in a very different culture—the Minangkabau of Sumatra, Indonesia, who are fundamentalist Moslem and matrilineal—suggesting that this phenomenon may be pan-cultural (Ekman, 1989a).

It appears that the specific patterns of ANS activity that were generated by making the different facial expressions are not unique to this task, but are the same as are found in more conventional emotion-arousing tasks. This lack of specificity confirms my proposal (Ekman, 1984, in press-b) that emotions are characterized by patterned changes in both expression and physiology, changes which are distinctive for each emotion, and which are not (in large part) specific to the means by which the emotion was aroused. This latter point is most readily noted with facial expression, which can signal that someone is angry, for example, without providing any clue as to what made the person angry.

When subjects followed our instructions to make these facial expressions, most reported not simply a physiological change but the experience of an emotion. In response to an open-ended question about what emotions, sensations, or memories they experienced, there were few reports of memories or sensations, while on 78% of the trials the subjects reported feeling an emotion. More information on this point, on the issue of generality, and on the details of the emotion-specific patterns of ANS activity can be found in . . . Levenson et al. (1990).

Before turning to the question of *how* voluntarily making different facial configurations generates different patterns of physiology, let me broaden our focus to consider central nervous system (CNS), not just ANS, physiology. In a study employing the same muscle-by-muscle instructions used to study ANS activity, subjects created the various facial configurations while left and right frontal, temporal, and parietal electroencephalographic (EEG) activity was measured. Different patterns of EEG activity occurred when subjects made the muscular movements which had been found universally for the emotions of happiness, anger, fear, sadness, and disgust (Davidson & Ekman, 1991; Ekman & Davidson, 1991).

In an unpublished research Friesen, Levenson, and I have formulated nine different explanations of how voluntary facial action generates emotion-specific physiology. Here I will indicate only three broad divisions among these explanations, leaving out the specific details relevant to subdistinctions within each of these divisions. The first explanation, which is the one we endorse, posits a central, hard-wired connection between the motor cortex and other areas of the brain involved in directing the physiological changes which occur during emotion. The second group of explanations proposes that such a connection is learned, not hard-wired. Such learning could be common to all members of our species or culture-specific. (Our findings in Indonesia raise questions but cannot rule out the viability of the culture-specific variation.) The third set of explanations emphasizes peripheral feedback from the facial actions themselves, rather than a central connection between the brain areas which direct those facial movements and other brain areas. This view includes variations in terms of whether feedback comes from the muscles, the skin, or temperature changes and whether it is hard-wired or requires learning. This explanation is consistent with the view of Izard (in press), Laird (Laird, 1971; Duclos et al., 1989), Tomkins (1962), and Zajonc (1985).

For now, there is no clear empirical basis for a definitive choice among these explanations. Through studies of people with facial paralysis who have no possibility of peripheral facial action or feedback we hope to challenge the third category of explanations, but this work is not yet complete, and the results may not be unambiguous. . . .

OTHER ISSUES ABOUT EXPRESSION

In closing let me mention three major questions about observable facial expressions. Every student who examines expression itself, not its recognition, must be impressed with individual differences in the speed, magnitude, and duration of expression as well as variations in which facial expression of emotion occurs in response to a particular event. It is not known whether such differences are consistent across emotions or situations, or over time. We also do not know whether a facial activity is a necessary part of any emotional experience. Under what circumstances, and with what kinds of people, might there be evidence of physiological changes relevant to emotion and the subjective experience of emotion with no evidence of visible expression or nonvisible electromyographic facial activity? Another issue requiring study is whether personality traits, moods, and psychopathology have facial markers or are second-order inferences drawn from the occurrence of facial expressions of emotion.

REFERENCES

Darwin, C. (1972). *The expression of the emotions in man and animals.* New York: Philosophical Library.

Davidson, R. J., & Ekman, P. (1991). *Differences in regional brain activity among different emotions.* Unpublished manuscript.

Duclos, S. E., Laird, J. D., Schneider, E., Sexter, M., Stern, L., & Van Leighten, O. (1989). Emotion-specific effects of facial expressions and postures on emotional experience. *Journal of Personality and Social Psychology, 57,* 100–108.

Ekman, P. (1972). Universals and cultural differences in facial expressions of emotion. In J. Cole (Ed.), *Nebraska symposium on motivation, 1971* (pp. 207–283). Lincoln: University of Nebraska Press.

Ekman, P. (1984). Expression and the nature of emotion. In K. Scherer & P. Ekman (Eds.), *Approaches to emotion* (pp. 319–344). Hillsdale, NJ: Erlbaum.

Ekman, P. (1989a). The argument and evidence about universals in facial expressions of emotion. In H. Wagner & A. Manstead (Eds.), *Handbook of social psychophysiology* (pp. 143–164). Chichester, England: Wiley.

Ekman, P. (1989b, January). *A cross cultural study of emotional expression, language and physiology.* Symposium conducted at the annual meeting of the American Association for the Advancement of Science, San Francisco.

Ekman, P. (in press-a). Are there basic emotions? A reply to Ortony and Turner. *Psychological Review.*

Ekman, P. (in press-b). An argument for basic emotions. *Cognition and Emotion.*

Ekman, P., & Davidson, R. J. (1991). *Hemispheric activation in different types of smiles.* Unpublished manuscript.

Ekman, P., & Friesen, W. V. (1969). The repertoire of nonverbal behavior: Categories, origins, usage, and coding. *Semiotica, 1,* 49–98.

Ekman, P., & Friesen, W. V. (1971). Constants across cultures in the face and emotion. *Journal of Personality and Social Psychology, 17,* 124–129.

Ekman, P., & Friesen, W. V. (1975). *Unmasking the face: A guide to recognizing emotions from facial clues.* Englewood Cliffs, NJ: Prentice-Hall.

Ekman, P., & Friesen, W. V. (1978). *The Facial Action Coding System: A technique for the measurement of facial movement.* Palo Alto, CA: Consulting Psychologists Press.

Ekman, P., Friesen, W. V., & Ellsworth, P. (1972). *Emotion in the human face: Guidelines for research and an integration of findings.* New York: Pergamon Press.

Ekman, P., Friesen, W. V., O'Sullivan, M., Chan, A., Diacoyanni-Tarlatzis, I., Heider, K., Krause, R., LeCompte, W. A., Pitcairn, T., Ricci-Bitti, P. E., Scherer, K. R., Tomita, M., & Tzavaras, A. (1987). Universals and cultural differences in the judgments of facial expressions of emotion. *Journal of Personality and Social Psychology, 53,* 712–717.

Ekman, P., Levenson, R. W., & Friesen, W. V. (1983). Autonomic nervous system activity distinguishes between emotions. *Science, 221,* 1208–1210.

Ekman, P., Sorenson, E. R., & Friesen, W. V. (1969). Pan-cultural elements in facial displays of emotions. *Science, 164,* 86–88.

Friesen, W. V. (1972). *Cultural differences in facial expression in a social situation: An experimental test of the concept of display rules.* Unpublished doctoral dissertation, University of California, San Francisco.

Izard, C. E. (1971). *The face of emotion.* New York: Appleton-Century-Crofts.

Izard, C. E. (in press). Basic emotions, relation among emotions and emotion-cognition relation. *Psychological Review.*

Laird, J. D. (1974). Self-attribution of emotion: The effects of expressive behavior on the quality of emotional experience. *Journal of Personality and Social Psychology, 29,* 475–486.

Levenson, R. W., Carstensen, L. L., Friesen, W. V., & Ekman, P. (1991). Emotion, physiology, and expression in old age. *Psychology and Aging, 6,* 28–35.

Levenson, R. W., Ekman, P., & Friesen, W. V. (1990). Voluntary facial action generates emotion-specific autonomic nervous system activity. *Psychophysiology, 27,* 363–384.

Lutz, C., & White, G. M. (1986). The anthropology of emotions. *Annual Review of Anthropology, 15,* 405–436.

Matsumoto, D. (in press). Cultural similarities and differences in display rules. *Motivation and Emotion.*

Matsumoto, D., & Ekman, P. (1989). American-Japanese cultural differences in rating the intensity of facial expressions of emotion. *Motivation and Emotion, 13,* 143–157.

Matsumoto, D., & Kudoh, T. (1991). *Cultural differences in judgments of emotion and other personal attributes: What's in a smile?* Manuscript submitted for publication.

Ortony, A., & Turner, T. J. (1990). What's basic about basic emotions? *Psychological Review, 97,* 315–331.

Tomkins, S. S. (1962). *Affect, imagery, consciousness: Vol. 1. The positive affects.* New York: Springer.

Zajonc, R. B. (1985). Emotion and facial efference: A theory reclaimed. *Science, 228,* 15–21.

10.2 MARVIN ZUCKERMAN

Dimensions of Sensation Seeking

People differ in their preferences for sensory stimulation. Some enjoy high levels of arousal, whereas others avoid excess sources of stimulation. Psychologist Marvin Zuckerman has been investigating personality characteristics and sensation-seeking tendencies for nearly three decades. His Sensation Seeking Scale has been widely used to identify individual differences in sensory stimulation preferences.

Zuckerman (b. 1928) earned his Ph.D. in clinical psychology from New York University in 1954. He served as a research associate at the Albert Einstein Medical Center, and in 1969 he joined the faculty at the University of Delaware, where he is currently a professor of psychology. He is the author of *Behavioral Expressions and Biosocial Bases of Sensation Seeking* (Cambridge University Press, 1994).

This selection is from "Dimensions of Sensation Seeking," which was published in *Journal of Consulting and Clinical Psychology* in 1971. In it, Zuckerman describes the four dimensions of sensation seeking: thrill and adventure seeking, experience seeking, disinhibition, and boredom susceptibility. Zuckerman found that men and women alike showed the first three dimensions, while the fourth was more prominent in men. The development of the Sensation Seeking Scale is an ongoing project, which is why Zuckerman refers to Form I and Form II of the scale early in the selection. As you read this selection, consider the extent to which you exhibit the characteristics of each dimension. How might awareness of an individual's sensation-seeking tendencies be helpful?

Key Concept: sensation seeking

*T*he author (Zuckerman, 1969) has proposed a theory of sensory deprivation based on the construct "optimal level of stimulation." The Sensation Seeking Scale (SSS) was developed in an earlier attempt to assess individual differences in optimal levels of stimulation or arousal. It was postulated that the need for change, variety, and itensity of stimulation would manifest itself in many aspects of behavior, including sensory, social, and thrill-seeking types of activity.

Form I of the SSS consisted of 50 forced-choice items written to reflect individual differences in the hypothesized trait. At that time the main interest was in a general trait measure. The form was given to 268 male and 277 female undergraduates at Brooklyn College. . . . Form II of the SSS (Zuckerman, Kolin, Price, & Zoob, 1964) consisted of 34 forced-choice items, including the 22 items in the SSS General M–F subscale. The article cited describes the development of the scale, its reliability, and some validity data. . . .

A study by Farley (1967) suggested that the general SSS might include more than one simple factor. Zuckerman and Link (1968) rotated the factors obtained in the factor analyses of the Brooklyn College sample. The results suggested that additional factors labeled Thrill Seeking, Social Sensation Seeking, Visual Sensation Seeking, and Antisocial Sensation Seeking might be identifiable in males. Only the first two factors were definable in females. However, Form I did not include enough items to define any but the first factor clearly. For this reason, it was decided to write new items in an attempt to define the dimensions of sensation seeking.

METHOD

Additional forced-choice items were written on the basis of the factors suggested by the preliminary results in the study by Zuckerman and Link (1968). Items were also written to tap another hypothesized factor not considered in Form I: sexual sensation seeking. Form III was an experimental form consisting of the original 50 items in Form I plus 63 new items, for a total of 113 forced-choice items. This form was given to 160 male and 172 female undergraduates at Temple University and later to 41 male and 51 female undergraduates at the University of North Carolina. The second sample was obtained to check the reliabilities of scales developed from the factor analyses of the Temple University sample. . . .

RESULTS AND DISCUSSION

Four interpretable factors were found in both sex groups and were tentatively labeled Thrill and Adventure Seeking, Experience Seeking, Disinhibition, and Boredom Susceptibility. Boredom Susceptibility was the fourth factor in males, but emerged as the sixth factor in the females. The correlations between the factor loadings in the males and females were as follows: Thrill and Adventure Seeking, .75; Experience Seeking, .83; Disinhibition, .81; and Boredom Susceptibility, .37. The first three of these factors showed good factor reliability across the sexes, but the fourth factor, Boredom Susceptibility, was not as consistent in its structure. It was more clearly identified by item content of significantly loading items in the male group than in the female group.

One of the new factors, Thrill and Adventure Seeking, was expected on the basis of earlier analyses by Farley (1967) and Zuckerman and Link (1968). The other three factors seemed to cut across the predicted factors which were used as the basis for writing new items. However, a perusal of the content of the items in these factors seemed to yield a good post hoc rationale for them. The stability of three of the four factors across sex groups indicated that they are not accidental.

The Thrill and Adventure Seeking factor consists of items (Table 1) which express a desire to engage in outdoor sports or other activities involving elements of speed or danger.

The Experience Seeking factor might be termed a "hippie" factor (Table 2). Its essence is "experience for its own sake." The factor includes items indicating wanderlust, exhibitionism in dress and behavior, the use of marijuana and hallucinatory drugs, associating with unusual and unconventional persons, a liking of modern, arousing music and art, and flouting of "irrational" authority.

The Disinhibition factor might also be labeled "swinger." It consists of items (Table 3) which express the loss of social inhibitions: heavy social drinking, variety in sexual partners, "wild parties," and gambling. It is interesting

TABLE 1

Thrill and Adventure Seeking Items and Loadings

| Form IV Item No. | Item Loading[a] | | Sensation Seeking Item Choice[b] |
	Male	Female	
1B	35	40	I enjoy many of the rides in amusement parks.
10A	46	36	I often wish I could be a mountain climber.
21B	52	30	I sometimes like to do things that are a little frightening.
29A	67	66	I would like to take up the sport of water-skiing.
31A	72	59	I would like to try surfboard riding.
35B	63	37	I would like to learn to fly an airplane.
37A	63	39	I would like to go scuba diving.
40A	44	50	I like to drive in open convertibles.
43A	65	35	I would like to try parachute jumping.
49B	52	46	Sometimes I like to swim far out from the shore.
53A	51	47	I like to dive off the high board.
67B	54	46	I would like to drive or ride on a motorcycle.
69B	55	41	I would like to sail a long distance in a small but seaworthy sailing craft.
71B	57	55	I think I would enjoy the sensations of skiing very fast down a high mountain slope.

[a] Orthogonal loadings, decimals omitted. All items except 21 and 67 also loaded significantly for males and females in oblique rotations.
[b] Other choices not shown here.

TABLE 2

Experience Seeking Items and Loadings

Form IV Item No.	Item Loading[a]		Sensation Seeking Item Choice[b]
	Male	Female	
3A	41	65	I would like to hitchhike across the country.
8B	38	36	I sometimes use "four-letter words" to express my feelings or to shock someone.
13A	34	36	I like to dress in unusual styles.
14B	35	50	I would like to travel to strange, out of the way places like the upper Amazon or Antarctica.
18A	61	59	I have tried marijuana or would like to.
19B	61	44	I would like to try some of the new drugs that produce hallucinations.
33A	38	42	I would like to take off on a trip with no preplanned or definite routes or timetable.
34B	47	47	I would like to make friends in some of the "far-out" groups like artists or "hippies."
36B	58	60	I like to see men wearing beards.
38A	53	54	I would like to meet some persons who are homosexual (men or women).
39A	39	38	I would prefer modern jazz or classical music to more popular or light classical music.
45B	36	35	I like to listen to new and unusual kinds of music.
46A	36	48	I prefer friends who are excitingly unpredictable.
47B	51	47	I like to have new and exciting experiences and sensations even if they are a little frightening, unconventional, or illegal.
50A	38	50	I often enjoy flouting irrational authority.
51B	51	44	I often find beauty in the "clashing" colors and irregular forms of modern paintings.
56A	35	42	I sometimes like to do "crazy" things just to see the effects on others.
68B	45	51	People should dress in individual ways even if the effects are sometimes strange.

[a] Orthogonal loadings, decimals omitted. All items except 13 also loaded significantly for males and females in oblique rotations.
[b] Other choices not shown here.

that the one item which this factor had in common with the Experience Seeking factor was one in which alcohol and marijuana were given as alternate ways of "getting high." The item was assigned to the Disinhibition factor because of somewhat higher loadings.

The Boredom Susceptibility factor in males contains items (Table 4) indicating a dislike of repetition of experience, routine work, predictable, dull, or boring people, a preference for exciting people and variety, and a restlessness when things are unchanging. . . .

At present, one can only speculate on the possible validity of the new scales. The Thrill and Adventure subscale seems to be related to arousal seek-

TABLE 3

225

Disinhibition Items and Loadings

Item Loadings[a]			
Form IV Item No.	*Male*	*Female*	*Sensation Seeking Item Choice*[b]
4B	35	35	I like to gamble for money.
6A	54	52	I like "wild" uninhibited parties.
22B	41	50	I enjoy the company of real "swingers."
23B	44	50	I often like to get high (drinking liquor or smoking marijuana).
26B	38	32	It's normal to get bored after a time with the same sexual partner.
30A	38	32	Most adultery happens because of sheer boredom.
54A	44	32	I like to date members of the opposite sex who are physically exciting.
55B	37	49	Keeping the drinks full is the key to a good party.
59A	44	36	A person should have considerable sexual experience before marriage.
60B	42	42	I could conceive of myself seeking pleasures around the world with the "jet set."
61A	40	50	I like people who are sharp and witty even if they do sometimes insult others.
62A	48	37	Almost everything enjoyable is illegal or immoral.
64B	40	52	I enjoy watching many of the "sexy" scenes in movies.
66A	43	33	I feel best after taking a couple of drinks.

[a] Orthogonal loadings, decimals omitted. All items except 26 also loaded significantly for males and females in oblique rotations.
[b] Other choices not shown here.

ing through kinesthetic and autonomic sensations produced by speed and danger. One of the items states "I sometimes like to do things that are a little frightening." All of the activities involved are socially acceptable. This factor dominated the General scale used in the previous research and may explain the restlessness of high scorers in sensory deprivation (Hocking & Robertson, 1969; Zuckerman et al., 1966).

The Experience Seeking subscale is broader in scope. It describes the seeking of more moderate arousal through the mind and all of the senses. There is a need for varied experience and nonconformity to established ways. Drug taking is accepted as a way of seeking new experiences. The experience seeker may be one of the rare types who enjoys short-term sensory deprivation because of the fantasies, hallucinations, dreams, and self-contemplation experiences. He has the capacity to become aroused without external stimulation.

Disinhibition seems to be one of the sensation seeking modes of the "older" generation, although it is probably still favored by the majority of young males as well. There were no sex differences on the Experience Seeking subscale, but males scored far higher than females on Disinhibition. Alcohol, rather than drugs, is favored because it affects the loosening of social inhibi-

TABLE 4

Boredom Susceptibility Items and Loadings

	Item Loadings[a]		
Form IV Item No.	*Male*	*Female*	*Sensation Seeking Item Choice*[b]
7A	31	39	I can't standing watching a movie that I've seen before.
9B	32	16	Although it is sometimes necessary, I usually dislike routine kinds of work.
12A	54	35	I get bored seeing the same old faces.
16B	42	17	When you can predict almost everything a person will do and say he or she must be a bore.
17A	53	27	I usually don't enjoy a movie or play where I can predict what will happen in advance.
20B	34	07	I would have preferred living in the unsettled days of our history.
24A	35	07	A person should change jobs from time to time simply to avoid getting into a rut.
25B	38	04	I like to try new foods that I have never tasted before.
27B	30	31	Looking at someone's home movie or travel slides bores me tremendously.
28A	31	06	I like to try new brands on the chance of finding something different or better.
32A	32	04	I find people who disagree with my beliefs more stimulating than people who agree with me.
46A	41	10	I prefer friends who are excitingly unpredictable.
52B	33	52	I get restless if I have to stay around home for any length of time.
57B	38	06	The worst social sin is to be a bore.
58B	36	10	I wish I didn't have to waste so much of a day sleeping.
63A	33	03	A good painting should shock or jolt the senses.
65B	32	14	I enjoyed a heated intellectual argument even if people sometimes get upset.
70A	33	38	I have no patience with dull or boring persons.

[a] Orthogonal loadings, decimals omitted. Items 12, 16, 17, 25, 46, 57, and 58 also loaded significantly for males in oblique rotations.

tions. Although the physiological effect of alcohol is depression, the initial effects are often described as "getting high" because of the euphoria which often accompanies the initial lowering of inhibition. Sexual sensation and variety seeking is also involved in this factor, while it is absent in the Experience Seeking factor. This is not because the experience seekers are inhibited, but because they tend to disparage the "swinger" type of casual, impersonal sex, and they emphasize "love."

Boredom Susceptibility incorporates the need for change and variety more than any of the other factors. Rather than the seeking of sensation or experience, it seems to involve a high aversion to conditions of "sameness." This factor is one which we would expect to be more highly related to satiation tendencies, and the one which might predict slide-viewing behavior more than we have been able to do with the General scale.

FARLEY, F. H. Social desirability and dimensionality in the Sensation Seeking Scale. *Acta Psychologica*, 1967, **26,** 89–96.

HOCKING, J., & ROBERTSON, M. The Sensation Seeking Scale as a predictor of need for stimulation during sensory restriction. *Journal of Consulting and Clinical Psychology*, 1969, **33,** 367–369.

ZUCKERMAN, M. Theoretical formulations: I. In J. Zubek (Ed.), *Sensory deprivation: Fifteen years of research.* New York: Appleton-Century-Crofts, 1969.

ZUCKERMAN, M., KOLIN, E. A., PRICE, L., & ZOOB, I. Development of a Sensation-Seeking Scale. *Journal of Consulting Psychology*, 1964, 28, 477–482.

ZUCKERMAN, M., LINK, K. Construct validity for the Sensation-Seeking Scale. *Journal of Consulting and Clinical Psychology*, 1968, 32, 420–426.

The Ingredients of Love

Love is one of the most important human emotions. Although it has been the subject of countless poems and works of art, it has only recently become the focus of research by psychologists. Researchers recognize that there are different kinds of love, making it difficult to generalize the results of love studies. In an attempt to make such a generalization, Yale University psychologist Robert J. Sternberg has proposed a triangular theory of love in which love consists of intimacy, passion, and decision/commitment.

Sternberg (b. 1949) earned his Ph.D. from Stanford University in 1975. He has been very influential in psychology in the cognitive area of intelligence and in the emotional area of love. The American Psychological Association awarded him the Distinguished Scientific Award for Early Career Contribution to Psychology in 1981. Sternberg has written much about his research on love, including his book *The Triangle of Love: Intimacy, Passion, and Commitment* (Basic Books, 1988).

This selection is from chapter 2, "The Ingredients of Love," of Sternberg's *Triangle of Love*. In it, Sternberg describes, in an informal, practical style, how the three ingredients intimacy, passion, and commitment combine to form eight possible kinds of love. He provides many examples, some of which should seem familiar to you. Sternberg's objective is to help you more fully understand the characteristics of love. As you read this selection, evaluate Sternberg's theory of love. Are there any other ingredients that he may have left out of his theory?

Key Concept: love

A substantial body of evidence suggests that the components of intimacy, passion, and commitment play a key role in love over and above other attributes. Even before I collected the first bit of data to test my theory, I had several reasons for choosing these three components as the building blocks for it.

First, many of the other aspects of love prove, on close examination, to be either parts or manifestations of these three components. Communication, for example, is a building block of intimacy, as is caring or compassion. Were one to subdivide intimacy and passion and commitment into their own subparts, the theory would eventually contain so many elements as to become unwieldy.

There is no one, solely correct fineness of division. But a division into three components works well in several ways. . . .

Second, my review of the literature on couples in the United States, as well as in other lands, suggested that, whereas some elements of love are fairly time-bound or culture-specific, the three I propose are general across time and place. The three components are not equally weighted in all cultures, but each component receives at least some weight in virtually any time or place.

Third, the three components do appear to be distinct, although, of course, they are related. You can have any one without either or both of the others. In contrast, other potential building blocks for a theory of love—for example, nurturance and caring—tend to be difficult to separate, logically as well as psychologically.

Fourth, . . . many other accounts of love seem to boil down to something similar to my own account, or a subset of it. If we take away differences in language and tone, the spirit of many other theories converges with mine.

Finally, and perhaps most important, the theory works. . . .

INTIMACY

In the context of the triangular theory, intimacy refers to those feelings in a relationship that promote closeness, bondedness, and connectedness. My research with Susan Grajek . . . indicates that intimacy includes at least ten elements:

1. *Desiring to promote the welfare of the loved one.* The lover looks out for the partner and seeks to promote his or her welfare. One may promote the other's welfare at the expense of one's own—but in the expectation that the other will reciprocate when the time comes.
2. *Experiencing happiness with the loved one.* The lover enjoys being with his or her partner. When they do things together, they have a good time and build a store of memories upon which they can draw in hard times. Furthermore, good times shared will spill over into the relationship and make it better.
3. *Holding the loved one in high regard.* The lover thinks highly of and respects his or her partner. Although the lover may recognize flaws in the partner, this recognition does not detract from the overall esteem in which the partner is held.
4. *Being able to count on the loved one in times of need.* The lover feels that the partner is there when needed. When the chips are down, the lover can call on the partner and expect that he or she will come through.
5. *Having mutual understanding with the loved one.* The lovers understand each other. They know each other's strengths and weaknesses and how to respond to each other in a way that shows genuine empathy for the loved one's emotional states. Each knows where the other is "coming from."
6. *Sharing oneself and one's possessions with the loved one.* One is willing to give of oneself and one's time, as well as one's things, to the loved one.

Although all things need not be joint property, the lovers share their property as the need arises. And, most important, they share themselves.

7. *Receiving emotional support from the loved one.* The lover feels bolstered and even renewed by the loved one, especially in times of need.
8. *Giving emotional support to the loved one.* The lover supports the loved one by empathizing with, and emotionally supporting, him or her in times of need.
9. *Communicating intimately with the loved one.* The lover can communicate deeply and honestly with the loved one, sharing innermost feelings.
10. *Valuing the loved one.* The lover feels the great importance of the partner in the scheme of life.

These are only some of the possible feelings one can experience through the intimacy of love; moreover, it is not necessary to experience all of these feelings in order to experience intimacy. To the contrary, our research indicates that you experience intimacy when you sample a sufficient number of these feelings, with that number probably differing from one person and one situation to another. You do not usually experience the feelings independently, but often as one overall feeling. . . .

Intimacy probably starts in self-disclosure. To be intimate with someone, you need to break down the walls that separate one person from another. It is well known that self-disclosure begets self-disclosure: if you want to get to know what someone else is like, let him or her learn about you. But self-disclosure is often easier in same-sex friendships than in loving relationships, probably because people see themselves as having more to lose by self-disclosure in a loving relationship. And odd as it may sound, there is actually evidence that spouses may be less symmetrical in self-disclosure than are strangers, again probably because the costs of self-disclosure can be so high in love. . . .

Intimacy, then, is a foundation of love, but a foundation that develops slowly, through fits and starts, and is difficult to achieve. Moreover, once it starts to be attained, it may, paradoxically, start to go away because of the threat it poses. It poses a threat in terms not only of the dangers of self-disclosure but of the danger one starts to feel to one's existence as a separate, autonomous being. Few people want to be "consumed" by a relationship, yet many people start to feel as if they are being consumed when they get too close to another human being. The result is a balancing act between intimacy and autonomy which goes on throughout the lives of most couples, a balancing act in which a completely stable equilibrium is often never achieved. But this in itself is not necessarily bad: the swinging back and forth of the intimacy pendulum provides some of the excitement that keeps many relationships alive.

PASSION

The passion component of love includes what Elaine Hatfield and William Walster refer to as a "state of intense longing *for union* with the other." Passion is largely the expression of desires and needs—such as for self-esteem, nurturance, affiliation, dominance, submission, and sexual fulfillment. The strengths of these various needs vary across persons, situations, and kinds of loving relationship. For example, sexual fulfillment is likely to be a strong need in romantic relationships but not in filial ones. These needs manifest themselves through psychological and physiological arousal, which are often inseparable from each other.

Passion in love tends to interact strongly with intimacy, and often they fuel each other. For example, intimacy in a relationship may be largely a function of the extent to which the relationship meets a person's need for passion. Conversely, passion may be aroused by intimacy. In some close relationships with members of the opposite sex, for example, the passion component develops almost immediately; and intimacy, only after a while. Passion may have drawn the individuals into the relationship in the first place, but intimacy helps sustain the closeness in the relationship. In other close relationships, however, passion, especially as it applies to physical attraction, develops only after intimacy. Two close friends of the opposite sex may find themselves eventually developing a physical attraction for each other once they have achieved a certain emotional intimacy. . . .

Most people, when they think of passion, view it as sexual. But any form of psychophysiological arousal can generate the experience of passion. For example, an individual with a high need for affiliation may experience passion toward an individual who provides him or her with a unique opportunity to affiliate. For example, Debbie grew up in a broken home, with no extended family to speak of, and two parents who were constantly at war with each other and eventually divorced when she was an adolescent. Debbie felt as though she never had a family, and when she met Arthur, her passion was kindled. What he had to offer was not great sex but a large, warm, closely knit family that welcomed Debbie with open arms. Arthur was Debbie's ticket to the sense of belongingness she had never experienced but had always craved, and his ability to bring belongingness into her life aroused her passion for him. . . .

For other people, the need for submission can be the ticket to passion. . . . Social workers are often frustrated when, after months spent getting a battered woman to leave her husband, the woman ultimately goes back to the batterer. To some observers, her return may seem incomprehensible; to others, it may seem like a financial decision. But often it is neither. Such a woman has had the misfortune to identify abuse with being loved and, in going back to the abuse, is returning to what is, for her, love as she has learned it.

These patterns of response have been established through years of observation and sometimes first-hand experience, which cannot be easily undone by a social worker or anyone else in a few months. Probably the strangest learning mechanism for the buildup of passionate response is the mechanism of *intermittent reinforcement*, the periodic, sometimes random rewarding of a particular response to a stimulus. If you try to accomplish something, and sometimes are rewarded for your efforts and sometimes not, you are being intermittently reinforced. Oddly enough, intermittent reinforcement is even more powerful at developing or sustaining a given pattern of behavior than is continuous reinforcement. You are more likely to lose interest in or desire for something, and to become bored, if you are always rewarded when you seek it than if you are sometimes rewarded, but sometimes not. Put another way, sometimes the fun is in wanting something rather than in getting it. And if you are never rewarded for a given pattern of behavior, you are likely to give up on it ("extinguish," as learning theorists would say), if only because of the total frustration you experience when you act in that particular way.

Passion thrives on the intermittent reinforcement that is intense at least in the early stages of a relationship. When you want someone, sometimes you feel as if you are getting closer to him or her, and sometimes you feel you are not—an alternation that keeps the passion aroused. . . .

DECISION AND COMMITMENT

The decision/commitment component of love consists of two aspects—one short-term and one long-term. The short-term aspect is the decision to love a certain other, whereas the long-term one is the commitment to maintain that love. These two aspects of the decision/commitment component of love do not necessarily occur together. The decision to love does not necessarily imply a commitment to that love. Oddly enough, the reverse is also possible, where there is a commitment to a relationship in which you did not make the decision, as in arranged marriages. Some people are committed to loving another without ever having admitted their love. Most often, however, a decision precedes the commitment both temporally and logically. Indeed, the institution of marriage represents a legalization of the commitment to a decision to love another throughout life.

While the decision/commitment component of love may lack the "heat" or "charge" of intimacy and passion, loving relationships almost inevitably have their ups and downs, and in the latter, the decision/commitment component is what keeps a relationship together. This component can be essential for getting through hard times and for returning to better ones. In ignoring it or separating it from love, you may be missing exactly that component of a loving relationship that enables you to get through the hard times as well as the easy ones. Sometimes, you may have to trust your commitment to carry you through to the better times you hope are ahead.

The decision/commitment component of love interacts with both intimacy and passion. For most people, it results from the combination of intimate involvement and passionate arousal; however, intimate involvement or passionate arousal can follow from commitment, as in certain arranged marriages or in close relationships in which you do not have a choice of partners. For example, you do not get to choose your mother, father, siblings, aunts, uncles, or cousins. In these close relationships, you may find that whatever intimacy or passion you experience results from your cognitive commitment to the relationship, rather than the other way around. Thus, love can start off as a decision.

The expert in the study of commitment is the UCLA psychologist Harold Kelley. . . . For Kelley, commitment is the extent to which a person is likely to stick with something or someone and see it (or him or her) through to the finish. A person who is committed to something is expected to persist until the goal underlying the commitment is achieved. A problem for contemporary relationships is that two members of a couple may have different ideas about what it means to stick with someone to the end or to the realization of a goal. These differences, moreover, may never be articulated. One person, for example, may see the "end" as that point where the relationship is no longer working, whereas the other may see the end as the ending of one of the couple's lives. In a time of changing values and notions of commitment, it is becoming increasingly common for couples to find themselves in disagreement about the exact nature and duration of their commitment to each other. When marital commitments were always and automatically assumed to be for life, divorce was clearly frowned upon. Today, divorce is clearly more acceptable than it was even fifteen years ago, in part because many people have different ideas about how durable and lasting the marital commitment need be.

Difficulties in mismatches between notions of commitment cannot always be worked out by discussing mutual definitions of it, because these may change over time and differently for the two members of a couple. Both may intend a life-long commitment at the time of marriage, for example; but one of them may have a change of mind—or heart—over time. . . .

KINDS OF LOVING

How do people love, and what are some examples of ways in which they love? A summary of the various kinds of love captured by the triangular theory is shown in table 1.

TABLE 1

Taxonomy of Kinds of Love

Kind of Love	Intimacy	Passion	Decision/ Commitment
Non-love	-	-	-
Liking	+	-	-
Infatuated love	-	+	-
Empty love	-	-	+
Romantic love	+	+	-
Companionate love	+	-	+
Fatuous love	-	+	+
Consummate love	+	+	+

Note: + = component present; - = component absent.

Intimacy Alone: Liking

... Liking results when you experience only the intimacy component of love without passion or decision/commitment. The term *liking* is used here in a nontrivial sense, to describe not merely the feelings you have toward casual acquaintances and passers-by, but rather the set of feelings you experience in relationships that can truly be characterized as friendships. You feel closeness, bondedness, and warmth toward the other, without feelings of intense passion or long-term commitment. Stated another way, you feel emotionally close to the friend, but the friend does not arouse your passion or make you feel that you want to spend the rest of your life with him or her.

It is possible for friendships to have elements of passionate arousal or long-term commitment, but such friendships go beyond mere liking. You can use the absence test to distinguish mere liking from love that goes beyond liking. If a typical friend whom you like goes away, even for an extended period of time, you may miss him or her but do not tend to dwell on the loss. You can pick up the friendship some years later, often in a different form, without even having thought much about the friendship during the intervening years. When a close relationship goes beyond liking, however, you actively miss the other person and tend to dwell on or be preoccupied with his or her absence. The absence has a substantial and fairly long-term effect on your life. When the absence of the other arouses strong feelings of intimacy, passion, or commitment, the relationship has gone beyond liking.

Passion Alone: Infatuated Love

Tom met Lisa at work. One look at her was enough to change his life: he fell madly in love with her. Instead of concentrating on his work, which he hated, he would think about Lisa. She was aware of this, but did not much care for Tom. When he tried to start a conversation with her, she moved on as quickly as possible. . . .

Tom's "love at first sight" is infatuated love or, simply, infatuation. It results from the experiencing of passionate arousal without the intimacy and decision/commitment components of love. Infatuation is usually obvious, although it tends to be somewhat easier for others to spot than for the person who is experiencing it. An infatuation can arise almost instantaneously and dissipate as quickly. Infatuations generally manifest a high degree of psychophysiological arousal and bodily symptoms such as increased heartbeat or even palpitations of the heart, increased hormonal secretions, and erection of genitals. . . .

Decision/Commitment Alone: Empty Love

John and Mary had been married for twenty years, for fifteen of which Mary had been thinking about getting a divorce, but could never get herself to go through with it. . . .

Mary's kind of love emanates from the decision that you love another and are committed to that love even without having the intimacy or the passion associated with some loves. It is the love sometimes found in stagnant relationships that have been going on for years but that have lost both their original mutual emotional involvement and physical attraction. Unless the commitment to the love is very strong, such love can be close to none at all. Although in our society we see empty love generally as the final or near-final stage of a long-term relationship, in other societies empty love may be the first stage of a long-term relationship. As I have said, in societies where marriages are arranged, the marital partners start with the commitment to love each other, or to try to do so, and not much more. Here, *empty* denotes a relationship that may come to be filled with passion and intimacy, and thus marks a beginning rather than an end.

Intimacy + Passion: Romantic Love

Susan and Ralph met in their junior year of college. Their relationship started off as a good friendship, but rapidly turned into a deeply involved romantic love affair. They spent as much time together as possible, and enjoyed practically every minute of it. But Susan and Ralph were not ready to commit themselves permanently to the relationship: both felt they were too young to make any long-term decisions, and that until they at least knew where they would go after college, it was impossible to tell even how much they could be together. . . .

Ralph and Susan's relationship combines the intimacy and passion components of love. In essence, it is liking with an added element: namely, the arousal brought about by physical attraction. Therefore, in this type of love, the man and woman are not only drawn physically to each other but are also bonded emotionally. This is the view of romantic love found in classic works of literature, such as *Romeo and Juliet.* . . .

Intimacy + Commitment: Companionate Love

In their twenty years of marrige, Sam and Sara had been through some rough times. They had seen many of their friends through divorces, Sam through several jobs, and Sara through an illness that at one point had seemed as though it might be fatal. Both had friends, but there was no doubt in either of their minds that they were each other's best friend. When the going got rough, each of them knew he or she could count on the other. Neither Sam nor Sara felt any great passion in their relationship, but they had never sought out others. . . .

Sam and Sara's kind of love evolves from a combination of the intimacy and decision/commitment components of love. It is essentially a long-term, committed friendship, the kind that frequently occurs in marriages in which physical attraction (a major source of passion) has waned. . . .

Passion + Commitment: Fatuous Love

When Tim and Diana met at a resort in the Bahamas, they were each on the rebound. Tim's fiancée had abruptly broken off their engagement. . . . Diana was recently divorced, the victim of the "other woman." Each felt desperate for love, and when they met each other, they immediately saw themselves as a match made in heaven. . . . The manager of the resort, always on the lookout for vacation romances as good publicity, offered to marry them at the resort and to throw a lavish reception at no charge, other than cooperation in promotional materials. After thinking it over, Tim and Diana agreed. . . .

Fatuous love, as in the case of Tim and Diana, results from the combination of passion and decision/commitment without intimacy, which takes time to develop. It is the kind of love we sometimes associate with Hollywood, or with a whirlwind courtship, in which a couple meet one day, get engaged two weeks later, and marry the next month. This love is fatuous in the sense that the couple commit themselves to one another on the basis of passion without the stabilizing element of intimate involvement. Since passion can develop almost instantaneously, and intimacy cannot, relationships based on fatuous love are not likely to last.

Intimacy + Passion + Commitment: Consummate Love

Harry and Edith seemed to all their friends to be the perfect couple. And what made them distinctive from many such "perfect couples" is that they pretty much fulfilled the notion. They felt close to each other, they continued to have great sex after fifteen years, and they could not imagine themselves happy over the long term with anyone else. . . .

Consummate, or complete, love like Edith and Harry's results from the combination of the three components in equal measure. It is a love toward which many of us strive, especially in romantic relationships. Attaining consummate love is analogous, in at least one respect, to meeting your goal in a weight-reduction program: reaching your ideal weight is often easier than maintaining it. Attaining consummate love is no guarantee that it will last; indeed, one may become aware of the loss only after it is far gone. Consummate love, like other things of value, must be guarded carefully. . . .

The Absence of the Components: Non-Love

Jack saw his colleague Myra at work almost every day. They interacted well in their professional relationship, but neither was particularly fond of the other.

Neither felt particularly comfortable talking to the other about personal matters; and after a few tries, they decided to limit their conversations to business.

Non-love, as in the relationship of Jack and Myra, refers simply to the absence of all three components of love. Non-love characterizes many personal relationships, which are simply casual interactions that do not partake of love or even liking.

PART FIVE

Personality and Adjustment

On the Internet . . .

Sites appropriate to Part Five

The Personality Project site of William Revelle, director of the Graduate Program in Personality in the Department of Psychology at Northwestern University, with research references. Its server is not always available, so keep trying.

> http://fas.psych.nwu.edu/personality.html

This Mind Tools™ site provides useful information on stress management.

> http://www.gasou.edu/psychweb/mtsite/smpage.html

Psych Web's psychology self-help resources on the Internet has numerous adjustment and self-help resource links.

> http://www.gasou.edu/psychweb/resource/
>   selfhelp.htm

CHAPTER 11

Personality

11.1 SANDRA L. BEM

The Measurement of Psychological Androgyny

The past two decades have seen a significant increase in the efforts of psychologists to understand gender differences. An early milestone in this effort was Sandra Bem's development of the Bem Sex-Role Inventory (BSRI). The BSRI conceptualized two separate dimensions to determine the extent to which a person is masculine, feminine, or androgynous (having both masculine and feminine characteristics).

Bem (b. 1944) earned her Ph.D. in developmental psychology from the University of Michigan in 1968. She taught at Carnegie Mellon University and Stanford University before she went to Cornell University in 1978, where she is currently a professor of psychology. Her current research is presented in her book *The Lenses of Gender: Transforming the Debate on Sexual Inequality* (Yale University Press, 1993).

This selection is from "The Measurement of Psychological Androgyny," which was published in *Journal of Consulting and Clinical Psychology* in 1974. In it, Bem describes the rationale for androgyny and the selection procedure for the items in the BSRI. Remember that $p < .05$ means that the difference is significant, or large enough to accept as real.

Later research has found that the androgynous person tends to be the most psychologically healthy. Also, psychologists have recently begun to use the terms *instrumental* and *expressive* when referring to masculinity and femininity, respectively.

Key Concept: androgyny

Both in psychology and in society at large, masculinity and femininity have long been conceptualized as bipolar ends of a single continuum; accordingly, a person has had to be either masculine or feminine, but not both. This sex-role dichotomy has served to obscure two very plausible hypotheses: first, that many individuals might be "androgynous"; that is, they might be *both* masculine and feminine, *both* assertive and yielding, *both* instrumental and expressive—depending on the situational appropriateness of these various behaviors; and conversely, that strongly sex-typed individuals might be seriously limited in the range of behaviors available to them as they move from situation to situation. According to both Kagan (1964) and Kohlberg (1966), the highly sex-typed individual is motivated to keep his behavior consistent with an internalized sex-role standard, a goal that he presumably accomplishes by suppressing any behavior that might be considered undesirable or inappropriate for his sex. Thus, whereas a narrowly masculine self-concept might inhibit behaviors that are stereotyped as feminine, and a narrowly feminine self-concept might inhibit behaviors that are stereotyped as masculine, a mixed, or androgynous, self-concept might allow an individual to freely engage in both "masculine" and "feminine" behaviors.

The current research program is seeking to explore these various hypotheses, as well as to provide construct validation for the concept of androgyny (Bem, 1974). Before the research could be initiated, however, it was first necessary to develop a new type of sex-role inventory, one that would not automatically build in an inverse relationship between masculinity and femininity. This article describes that inventory.

The Bem Sex-Role Inventory (BSRI) contains a number of features that distinguish it from other, commonly used, masculinity–femininity scales, for example, the Masculinity–Femininity scale of the California Psychological Inventory (Gough, 1957). First, it includes both a Masculinity scale and a Femininity scale, each of which contains 20 personality characteristics. . . . Second, because the BSRI was founded on a conception of the sex-typed person as someone who has internalized society's sex-typed standards of desirable behavior for men and women, these personality characteristics were selected as masculine or feminine on the basis of sex-typed social desirability and not on the basis of differential endorsement by males and females as most other inventories have done. That is, a characteristic qualified as masculine if it was judged to be more desirable in American society for a man than for a woman, and it qualified as feminine if it was judged to be more desirable for a woman than for a man. Third, the BSRI characterizes a person as masculine, feminine, or androgynous as a function of the difference between his or her endorsement of masculine and feminine personality characteristics. A person is thus sex typed, whether masculine or feminine, to the extent that this difference score is high, and androgynous, to the extent that this difference score is low. Finally, the BSRI also includes a Social Desirability scale that is completely neutral with respect to sex. This scale now serves primarily to provide a neutral context for the Masculinity and Femininity scales, but it was utilized during the development of the BSRI to insure that the inventory would not simply be tapping a general tendency to endorse socially desirable traits. . . .

Both historically and cross-culturally, masculinity and femininity seem to have represented two complementary domains of *positive* traits and behaviors (Barry, Bacon, & Child, 1957; Erikson, 1964; Parsons & Bales, 1955). In general, masculinity has been associated with an instrumental orientation, a cognitive focus on "getting the job done"; and femininity has been associated with an expressive orientation, an affective concern for the welfare of others.

Accordingly, as a preliminary to item selection for the Masculinity and Femininity scales, a list was compiled of approximately 200 personality characteristics that seemed to the author and several students to be both positive in value and either masculine or feminine in tone. This list served as the pool from which the masculine and feminine characteristics were ultimately chosen. As a preliminary to item selection for the Social Desirability scale, an additional list was compiled of 200 characteristics that seemed to be neither masculine nor feminine in tone. Of these "neutral" characteristics, half were positive in value and half were negative.

Because the BSRI was designed to measure the extent to which a person divorces himself from those characteristics that might be considered more "appropriate" for the opposite sex, the final items were selected for the Masculinity and Femininity scales if they were judged to be more desirable in American society for one sex than for the other. Specifically, judges were asked to utilize a 7-point scale, ranging from 1 ("Not at all desirable") to 7 ("Extremely desirable"), in order to rate the desirability in American society of each of the approximately 400 personality characteristics mentioned above. (E.g., "In American society, how desirable is it for a man to be truthful?" "In American society, how desirable is it for a woman to be sincere?") Each individual judge was asked to rate the desirability of all 400 personality characteristics either "for a man" or "for a woman." No judge was asked to rate both. The judges consisted of 40 Stanford undergraduates who filled out the questionnaire during the winter of 1972 and an additional 60 who did so the following summer. In both samples, half of the judges were male and half were female.

A personality characteristic qualified as masculine if it was independently judged by both males and females in both samples to be significantly more desirable for a man than a woman ($p < .05$).[1] Similarly, a personality characteristic qualified as feminine if it was independently judged by both males and females in both samples to be significantly more desirable for a woman than for a man ($p < .05$). Of those characteristics that satisfied these criteria, 20 were selected for the Masculinity scale and 20 were selected for the Femininity scale. . . .

A personality characteristic qualified as neutral with respect to sex and hence eligible for the Social Desirability scale (*a*) if is was independently judged by both males and females to be no more desirable for one sex than for the other ($t < 1.2$, $p > .2$) and (*b*) if male and female judges did not differ significantly in their overall desirability judgments of that trait ($t < 1.2$, $p > .2$). Of these items that satisfied these several criteria, 10 positive and 10 negative personality characteristics were selected for the BSRI Social Desirability scale in accordance with Edwards' (1964) finding that an item must be quite positive or quite negative in tone if it is to evoke a social desirability response set. . . .

After all of the individual items had been selected, mean desirability scores were computed for the masculine, feminine, and neutral items for each of the 100 judges. . . . [F]or both males and females, the mean desirability of the masculine and feminine items was significantly higher for the "appropriate" sex than for the "inappropriate" sex, whereas the mean desirability of the neutral items were no higher for one sex than for the other. These results are, of course, a direct consequence of the criteria used for item selection.

Table 1 separates out the desirability ratings of the masculine and feminine items for male and female judges rating their *own* sex. These own-sex ratings seem to best represent the desirability of these various items as perceived by men and women when they are asked to describe *themselves* on the inventory. That is, the left-hand column of Table 1 represents the phenomenology of male subjects taking the test and the right-hand column represents the phenomenology of female subjects taking the test. As can be seen in Table 1, not only are "sex-appropriate" characteristics more desirable for both males and females than "sex-appropriate" characteristics, but the phenomenologies of male and female subjects are almost perfectly symmetric: that is, men and women are nearly equal in their perceptions of the desirability of sex-appropriate characteristics, sex-inappropriate characteristics, and the difference between them ($t < 1$ in all three comparisons).

SCORING

The BSRI asks a person to indicate on a 7-point scale how well each of the 60 masculine, feminine, and neutral personality characteristics describes himself. The scale ranges from 1 ("Never or almost never true") to 7 ("Always or almost always true") and is labeled at each point. On the basis of his responses, each person receives three major scores: a Masculinity score, a Femininity score and, most important, an Androgyny score. In addition, a Social Desirability score can also be computed.

The Masculinity and Femininity scores indicate the extent to which a person endorses masculine and feminine personality characteristics as self-de-

TABLE 1

Mean Social Desirability Ratings of the Masculine and Feminine Items for One's Own Sex

Item	Male Judges for a Man	Female Judges for a Woman
Masculine	5.59	3.46
Feminine	3.63	5.55
Difference	1.96	2.09
t	11.94*	8.88*

*$p < 001$.

scriptive. Masculinity equals the mean self-rating for all endorsed masculine items, and Femininity equals the mean self-rating for all endorsed feminine items. Both can range from 1 to 7. It will be recalled that these two scores are logically independent. That is, the structure of the test does not constrain them in any way, and they are free to vary independently.

The Androgyny score reflects the relative amounts of masculinity and femininity that the person includes in his or her self-description, and, as such, it best characterizes the nature of the person's total sex role. Specifically, the Androgyny score is defined as Students's t ratio for the difference between a person's masculine and feminine self-endorsement; that is, the Androgyny score is the difference between an individual's masculinity and femininity normalized with respect to the standard deviations of his or her masculinity and femininity scores. The use of a t ratio as the index of androgyny—rather than a simple difference score—has two conceptual advantages: first, it allows us to ask whether a person's endorsement of masculine attributes differs significantly from his or her endorsement of feminine attributes and, if it does ($|t| \geq$ 2.025, $df = 38$, $p < .05$), to classify that person as significantly sex typed; and second, it allows us to compare different populations in terms of the percentage of significantly sex-typed individuals present within each.[2]

It should be noted that the greater the absolute value of the Androgyny score, the more the person is sex typed or sex reversed, with high positive scores indicating femininity and high negative scores indicating masculinity. A "masculine" sex role thus represents not only the endorsement of masculine attributes but the simultaneous rejection of feminine attributes. Similarly, a "feminine" sex role represents not only the endorsement of feminine attributes but the simultaneous rejection of masculine attributes. In contrast, the closer the Androgyny score is to zero, the more the person is androgynous. An "androgynous" sex role thus represents the equal endorsement of both masculine and feminine attributes.

The Social Desirability score indicates the extent to which a person describes himself in a socially desirable direction on items that are neutral with respect to sex. It is scored by reversing the self-endorsement ratings for the 10 undesirable items and then calculating the subject's mean endorsement score across all 20 neutral personality characteristics. The Social Desirability score can thus range from 1 to 7, with 1 indicating a strong tendency to describe oneself in a socially undesirable direction and 7 indicating a strong tendency to describe oneself in a socially desirable direction. . . .

CONCLUDING COMMENT

It is hoped that the development of the BSRI will encourage investigators in the areas of sex differences and sex roles to question the traditional assumption that it is the sex-typed individual who typifies mental health and to begin focusing on the behavioral and societal consequences of more flexible sex-role self-concepts. In a society where rigid sex-role differentiation has already outlived its utility, perhaps the androgynous person will come to define a more human standard of psychological health.

NOTES

1. All significance levels in this article are based on two-tailed *t* tests.
2. A Statistical Package for the Social Sciences (SPSS) computer program for calculating individual *t* ratios is available on request from the author. In the absence of computer facilities, one can utilize the simple Androgyny difference score, Femininity–Masculinity, as the index of androgyny. Empirically, the two indices are virtually identical ($r = .98$), and one can approximate the *t*-ratio value by multiplying the Androgyny difference score by 2.322. This conversion factor was derived empirically from our combined normative sample of 917 students at two different colleges.

REFERENCES

BARRY, H., BACON, M. K., & CHILD, I. L. A cross-cultural survey of some sex differences in socialization. *Journal of Abnormal and Social Psychology*, 1957, 55, 327–332.

BEM, S. L. Sex-role adaptability: One consequence of psychological androgyny. *Journal of Personality and Social Psychology*, 1974, in press.

EDWARDS, A. L. The measurement of human motives by means of personality scales. In D. Levine (Ed.), *Nebraska symposium on motivation: 1964*. Lincoln: University of Nebraska Press, 1964.

ERIKSON, E. H. Inner and outer space: Reflections on womanhood. In R. J. Lifton (Ed.), *The woman in America*. Boston: Houghton Mifflin, 1964.

GOUGH, H. G. *Manual for the California Psychological Inventory*. Palo Alto, Calif.: Consulting Psychologists Press, 1957.

KAGAN, J. Acquisition and significance of sex-typing and sex-role identity. In M. L. Hoffman & L. W. Hoffman (Eds.), *Review of child development research*. Vol. 1. New York: Russell Sage Foundation, 1964.

KOHLBERG, L. A cognitive-developmental analysis of children's sex-role concepts and attitudes. In E. E. Maccoby (Ed.), *The development of sex differences*. Stanford, Calif.: Stanford University Press, 1966.

PARSONS, T., & BALES, R. F. *Family, socialization, and interaction process*. New York: Free Press of Glencoe, 1955.

11.2 JULIAN B. ROTTER

External Control and Internal Control

Psychologists do not agree on what determines personality, but many accept that reinforcement can shape behaviors that ultimately may influence personality. The social learning theory of personality suggests that behavior that is rewarded leads to the expectancy that the behavior will continue to produce rewards in the future. According to Julian B. Rotter's locus of control personality theory, which is based in the social learning theory, two personality types exist: People with an internal locus of control, who perceive that reinforcement is due to their own behavior; and people with an external locus of control, who perceive that reinforcement is independent of their behavior.

Rotter (b. 1916) earned his Ph.D. from Indiana University in 1941. He taught at several schools, including Ohio State University, before going to the University of Connecticut in 1963, where he is currently a professor of clinical psychology. Rotter's social learning theory (proposed in his 1954 book *Social Learning and Clinical Psychology*) has greatly influenced modern psychologists.

This selection is from "External Control and Internal Control," which was published in *Psychology Today* in 1971. It contains a straightforward description of Rotter's theory of personality as well as some fascinating applications. Note the development of Rotter's thinking as he describes how the idea of locus of control came to him. As you read this selection, think about the implications for people who have an internal or external locus of control. Which one, if either, do you think you have?

Key Concept: internal and external locus of control

*S*ome social scientists believe that the impetus behind campus unrest is youth's impatient conviction that they can control their own destinies, that they can change society for the better.

My research over the past 12 years has led me to suspect that much of the protest, outcry and agitation occurs for the opposite reason—because students feel they *cannot* change the world, that the system is too complicated and too much controlled by powerful others to be changed through the students' efforts. They feel more powerless and alienated today than they did 10 years ago, and rioting may be an expression of their hostility and resentment.

Dog

One of the most pervasive laws of animal learning is that a behavior followed by a reward tends to be repeated, and a behavior followed by a punishment tends not to be repeated. This seems to imply that reward and punishment act directly on behavior, but I think this formulation is too simplistic to account for many types of human behavior.

For example, if a dog lifts its leg at the exact moment that someone throws a bone over a fence, the dog may begin to lift its leg more often than usual when it is in the same situation—whether or not anyone is heaving a bone. Adult human beings are usually not so superstitious—a person who finds a dollar bill on the sidewalk immediately after stroking his hair is not likely to stroke his hair when he returns to the same spot.

It seemed to me that, at least with human beings who have begun to form concepts, the important factors in learning were not only the strength and frequency of rewards and punishments but also whether or not the person believed his behavior produced the reward or punishment.

According to the social-learning theory that I developed several years ago with my colleagues and students, rewarding a behavior strengthens an *expectancy* that the behavior will produce future rewards.

In animals, the expectation of reward is primarily a function of the strength and frequency of rewards. In human beings, there are other things that can influence the expectation of reward—the information others give us, our knowledge generalized from a variety of experiences, and our perceptions of causality in the situation.

Consider the ancient shell game. Suppose I place a pea under one of three shells and quickly shuffle the shells around the table. A player watches my movements carefully and then, thinking that he is using his fine perceptual skills, he tells me which shell the pea is under. If his choice is correct, he will likely choose the same shell again the next time he sees me make those particular hand movements. It looks like a simple case of rewarding a response.

But suppose I ask the subject to turn his back while I shuffle the shells. This time, even if his choice is rewarded by being correct, he is not so likely to select the same shell again, because the outcome seems to be beyond his control—just a lucky guess.

Chips

In 1957, E. Jerry Phares tried to find out if these intuitive differences between chance-learning and skill-learning would hold up in the laboratory.

Internal Control—External Control
A Sampler

Julian B. Rotter is the developer of a forced-choice 29-item scale for measuring an individual's degree of internal control and external control. This I-E test is widely used. The following are sample items taken from an earlier version of the test, but not, of course, in use in the final version. The reader can readily find for himself whether he is inclined toward internal control or toward external control, simply by adding up the choices he makes on each side

I more strongly believe that:	OR
Promotions are earned through hard work and persistence.	Making a lot of money is largely a matter of getting the right breaks.
In my experience I have noticed that there is usually a direct connection between how hard I study and the grades I get.	Many times the reactions of teachers seem haphazard to me.
The number of divorces indicates that more and more people are not trying to make their marriages work.	Marriage is largely a gamble.
When I am right I can convince others.	It is silly to think that one can really change another person's basic attitudes.
In our society a man's future earning power is dependent upon his ability.	Getting promoted is really a matter of being a little luckier than the next guy.
If one knows how to deal with people they are really quite easily led.	I have little influence over the way other people behave.
In my case the grades I make are the results of my own efforts; luck has little or nothing to do with it.	Sometimes I feel that I have little to do with the grades I get.
People like me can change the course of world affairs if we make ourselves heard.	It is only wishful thinking to believe that one can really influence what happens in society at large.
I am the master of my fate.	A great deal that happens to me is probably a matter of chance.
Getting along with people is a skill that must be practiced.	It is almost impossible to figure out how to please some people.

Phares would give each subject a small gray-colored chip and ask him to select one of 10 standard chips that had exactly the same shade of gray. The standards were all different but so similar in value that discrimination among them was very difficult. Phares told half of his subjects that matching the shades required great skill and that some persons were very good at it. He told the rest that the task was so difficult that success was a matter of luck. Before the experiment began, Phares arbitrarily decided which trials would be "right" and which would be "wrong"; the schedule was the same for everyone. He found that because of the difficulty of the task all subjects accepted his statements of right and wrong without question.

Phares gave each subject a stack of poker chips and asked him to bet on his accuracy before each trial as a measure of each subject's expectancy of success.

The subjects who thought that success depended on their own skills shifted and changed frequently—their bets would rise after success and drop after failure, just as reinforcement-learning theory would predict. But subjects who thought that a correct match was a matter of luck reacted differently. In fact, many of them raised their bets after failure and lowered them after success—the "gambler's fallacy." Thus, it appeared that traditional laws of learning could not explain some types of human behavior. . . .

I decided to study internal and external control (I-E), the beliefs that rewards come from one's own behavior or from external sources. The initial impetus to study internal-external control came both from an interest in individual differences and from an interest in explaining the way human beings learn complex social situations. There seemed to be a number of attitudes that would lead a person to feel that a reward was not contingent upon his own behavior, and we tried to build all of these attitudes into a measure of individual differences. A person might feel that luck or chance controlled what happened to him. He might feel that fate had preordained what would happen to him. He might feel that powerful others controlled what happened to him or he might feel that he simply could not predict the effects of this behavior because the world was too complex and confusing.

Scale

Phares first developed a test of internal-external control as part of his doctoral dissertation, and [William H.] James enlarged and improved on Phares' scale as part of his doctoral dissertation. Later scales were constructed with the important help of several of my colleagues including Liverant, Melvin Seeman and Crowne. In 1962 I developed a final 29-item version of the I-E scale and published it in *Psychological Monographs* in 1966. This is a forced-choice scale in which the subject reads a pair of statements and then indicates with which of the two statements he more strongly agrees. The scores range from zero (the consistent belief that individuals can influence the environment—that rewards come from *internal* forces) to 23 (the belief that all rewards come from *external* forces). . . .

Degree

One conclusion is clear from I-E studies: people differ in the tendency to attribute satisfactions and failures to themselves rather than to external causes, and these differences are relatively stable. For the sake of convenience most investigators divide their subjects into two groups—internals and externals—depending on which half of the distribution a subject's score falls into. This is not meant to imply that there are two personality types and that everyone can be classified as one or the other, but that there is a continuum, and that persons have varying degrees of internality or externality.

Many studies have investigated the differences between internals and externals. For example, it has been found that lower-class children tend to be external; children from richer, better-educated families tend to have more belief in their own potential to determine what happens to them. The scores do not seem to be related to intelligence, but young children tend to become more internal as they get older.

Esther Battle and I examined the attitudes of black and white children in an industrialized Ohio city. The scale we used consisted of five comic-strip cartoons; the subjects told us what they thought one of the children in the cartoon would say. We found that middle-class blacks were only slightly more external in their beliefs than middle-class whites but that among children from lower socioeconomic levels blacks were significantly more external than whites. Herbert Lefcourt and Gordon Ladwig also found that among young prisoners in a Federal reformatory, blacks were more external than whites.

Ute

It does not seem to be socioeconomic level alone that produces externality, however. Theodore Graves, working with Richard and Shirley L. Jessor, found that Ute Indians were more external than a group of Spanish-Americans, even though the Indians had higher average living standards than the Spanish-Americans. Since Ute tradition puts great emphasis on fate and unpredictable external forces, Graves concluded that internality and externality resulted from cultural training. A group of white subjects in the same community were more internal than either the Indians or the Spanish-Americans.

A measure of internal-external control was used in the well-known Coleman Report on Equality of Educational Opportunity. The experimenters found that among disadvantaged children in the sixth, ninth and 12th grades, the students with high scores on an achievement test had more internal attitudes than did children with low achievement scores.

One might expect that internals would make active attempts to learn about their life situations. To check on this, Seeman and John Evans gave the I-E scale to patients in a tuberculosis hospital. The internal patients knew more details about their medical conditions and they questioned doctors and nurses for medical feedback more often than did the external patients. The experimenters made sure that in their study there were no differences between the internals and externals in education, occupational status or ward placement. . . .

Bet

Highly external persons feel that they are at the mercy of the environment, that they are being manipulated by outside forces. When they *are* manipulated, externals seem to take it in stride. Internals are not so docile. For example, Crowne and Liverant set up an experiment to see how readily their subjects would go along with a crowd. In a simple . . . conformity experiment in which there is one true subject plus several stooges posing as subjects, Crowne and Liverant found that neither internals nor externals were more likely to yield to an incorrect majority judgment. But when the experimenters gave money to the subjects and allowed them to bet on their own judgments, the externals yielded to the majority much more often than did the internals. When externals did vote against the majority they weren't confident about their independence—they bet less money on being right than they did when they voted along with the crowd. . . .

Suspicion

Some externals, who feel they are being manipulated by the outside world, may be highly suspicious of authorities. With Herbert Hamsher and Jesse Geller, I found that male subjects who believed that the Warren Commission Report was deliberately covering up a conspiracy were significantly more external than male subjects who accepted the report.

To some degree externality may be a defense against expected failure but internals also have their defenses. In investigating failure defenses, Jay Efran studied high-school students' memories for tasks they had completed or failed. He found that the tendency to forget failures was more common in internal subjects than in external ones. This suggests that external subjects have less need to repress past failures because they have already resigned themselves to the defensive position that failures are not their responsibility. Internals, however, are more likely to forget or repress their failures.

Today's activist student groups might lead one to assume that our universities are filled with internals—people with strong belief in their ability to improve conditions and to control their own destinies. But scores on the same I-E test involving large numbers of college students in many localities show that between 1962 and 1971 there was a large increase in externality on college campuses. Today the average score on the I-E scale is about 11. In 1962 about 80 per cent of college students had more internal scores than this. The increase in externality has been somewhat less in Midwest colleges than in universities on the coasts, but there is little doubt that, overall, college students feel more powerless to change the world and control their own destinies now than they did 10 years ago.

Clearly, we need continuing study of methods to reverse this trend. Our society has so many critical problems that it desperately needs as many active, participating internal-minded members as possible. If feelings of external control, alienation and powerlessness continue to grow, we may be heading for a society of dropouts—each person sitting back, watching the world go by.

Julian B. Rotter

11.3   ROBERT R. McCRAE AND
PAUL T. COSTA, JR.

Validation of the Five-Factor Model of Personality Across Instruments and Observers

Over the years, there have been numerous attempts to classify personality traits. Little agreement was reached among psychologists until the five-factor model became popular. The five-factor model of personality was originally proposed in the early 1960s, but it did not become popular among psychologists until the 1980s. The five factors of this model are extraversion (sociability), agreeableness (friendliness), conscientiousness (dependability), emotional stability (versus neuroticism), and openness (liberalism). Psychologists do not all agree on the specific labels, but there is some consensus on the five areas of personality. Robert R. McCrae and Paul T. Costa, Jr., are among the leaders in the quest to understand these factors and how they can explain personality.

McCrae earned his Ph.D. from Boston University in 1976. He has since been an associate of the Gerontology Research Center of the National Institute of Aging, National Institutes of Health. Costa (b. 1942) received his Ph.D. from the University of Chicago in 1970. He is also with the National Institute on Aging, National Institutes of Health.

This selection is from "Validation of the Five-Factor Model of Personality Across Instruments and Observers," which was published in the American Psychological Association's *Journal of Personality and Social Psychology* in 1987. In it, McCrae and Costa describe the history and interpretation of each of the five factors in this model. In one part of the original article not included here, the authors report an experiment in which they used self-reports, peer ratings, and questionnaire scales to measure the five factors. The results of this study validated the five-factor model. As you read this selection, note which characteristics best describe your personality. Can you think of any other major factors of personality that might be included in this model?

Key Concept: five-factor model of personality

*P*erhaps in response to critiques of trait models (Mischel, 1968) and to rebuttals that have called attention to common inadequacies in personality research (Block, 1977), personologists in recent years have devoted much of their attention to methodological issues. . . . As a body, these studies have simultaneously increased the level of methodological sophistication in personality research and restored confidence in the intelligent use of individual difference models of personality.

Robert R. McCrae and Paul T. Costa, Jr.

In contrast, there has been relatively little interest in the substance of personality—the systematic description of traits. The variables chosen as vehicles for tests of methodological hypotheses often appear arbitrary. . . . Indeed, Kenrick and Dantchik (1983) complained that "catalogs of convenience" have replaced meaningful taxonomies of personality traits among "most of the current generation of social/personality researchers" (p. 299).

This disregard of substance is unfortunate because substance and method are ultimately interdependent. Unless methodological studies are conducted on well-defined and meaningful traits their conclusions are dubious; unless the traits are selected from a comprehensive taxonomy, it is impossible to know how far or in what ways they can be generalized.

Fortunately, a few researchers have been concerned with the problem of structure and have recognized the need for a consensus on at least the general outlines of a trait taxonomy (H. J. Eysenck & Eysenck, 1984; Kline & Barrett, 1983; Wiggins, 1979). One particularly promising candidate has emerged. The five-factor model—comprising extraversion or surgency, agreeableness, conscientiousness, emotional stability versus neuroticism, and culture—of Tupes and Christal (1961) was replicated by Norman in 1963 and heralded by him as the basis for "an adequate taxonomy of personality." Although it was largely neglected for several years, variations on this model have recently begun to reemerge (Amelang & Borkenau, 1982; Bond, Nakazato, & Shiraishi, 1975; Conley, 1985; Digman & Takemoto-Chock, 1981; Goldberg, 1981, 1982; Hogan, 1983; Lorr & Manning, 1978; McCrae & Costa, 1985b). . . .

THE NATURE OF THE FIVE FACTORS

. . . A growing body of research has pointed to the five-factor model as a recurrent and more or less comprehensive taxonomy of personality traits. Theorists disagree, however, in precisely how to conceptualize the factors themselves. It seems useful at this point to review each of the factors and attempt to define the clear elements as well as disputed aspects. . . .

Neuroticism Versus Emotional Stability

There is perhaps least disagreement about neuroticism, defined here by such terms as worrying, insecure, self-conscious, and temperamental. Although adjectives describing neuroticism are relatively infrequent in English (Peabody, 1984), psychologists' concerns with psychopathology have led to the

TABLE 1

80 Adjective Items From Peer Ratings

Adjectives	*Adjectives*

Neuroticism (N)
  Calm–worrying
  At ease–nervous
  Relaxed–high-strung
  Unemotional–emotional
  Even-tempered–temperamental
  Secure–insecure
  Self-satisfied–self-pitying
  Patient–impatient
  Not envious–envious/jealous
  Comfortable–self-conscious
  Not impulse ridden–impulse ridden
  Hardy–vulnerable
  Objective–subjective

Extraversion (E)
  Retiring–sociable
  Sober–fun loving
  Reserved–affectionate
  Aloof–friendly
  Inhibited–spontaneous
  Quiet–talkative
  Passive–active
  Loner–joiner
  Unfeeling–passionate
  Cold–warm
  Lonely–not lonely
  Task oriented–person oriented
  Submissive–dominant
  Timid–bold

Openness (O)
  Conventional–original
  Down to earth–imaginative
  Uncreative–creative
  Narrow interests–broad interests
  Simple–complex
  Uncurious–curious
  Unadventurous–daring
  Prefer routine–prefer variety
  Conforming–independent
  Unanalytical–analytical
  Conservative–liberal
  Traditional–untraditional
  Unartistic–artistic

Agreeableness vs. antagonism (A)
  Irritable–good natured
  Ruthless–soft hearted
  Rude–courteous
  Selfish–selfless
  Uncooperative–helpful
  Callous–sympathetic
  Suspicious–trusting
  Stingy–generous
  Antagonistic–acquiescent
  Critical–lenient
  Vengeful–forgiving
  Narrow-minded–open-minded
  Disagreeable–agreeable
  Stubborn–flexible
  Serious–cheerful
  Cynical–gullible
  Manipulative–straightforward
  Proud–humble

Conscientiousness vs. undirectedness (C)
  Negligent–conscientious
  Careless–careful
  Undependable–reliable
  Lazy–hardworking
  Disorganized–well organized
  Lax–scrupulous
  Weak willed–self-disciplined
  Sloppy–neat
  Late–punctual
  Impractical–practical
  Thoughtless–deliberate
  Aimless–ambitious
  Unstable–emotionally stable
  Helpless–self-reliant
  Playful–businesslike
  Unenergetic–energetic
  Ignorant–knowledgeable
  Quitting–persevering
  Stupid–intelligent
  Unfair–fair
  Imperceptive–perceptive
  Uncultured–cultured

development of innumerable scales saturated with neuroticism. Indeed, neuroticism is so ubiquitous an element of personality scales that theorists sometimes take it for granted.

A provocative view of neuroticism is provided by Tellegen (in press), who views it as negative emotionality, the propensity to experience a variety of negative affects, such as anxiety, depression, anger, and embarrassment. Virtually all theorists would concur in the centrality of negative affect to neuroticism; the question is whether other features also define it. Tellegen himself (in press) pointed out that his construct of negative emotionality has behavioral and cognitive aspects. Guilford included personal relations and objectivity in his emotional health factor (Guilford, Zimmerman, & Guilford, 1976), suggesting that mistrust and self-reference form part of neuroticism. We have found that impulsive behaviors, such as tendencies to overeat, smoke, or drink excessively, form a facet of neuroticism (Costa & McCrae, 1980), and *impulse-ridden* is a definer of the neuroticism factor in self-reports, although not in ratings. Others have linked neuroticism to irrational beliefs (Teasdale & Rachman, 1983; Vestre, 1984) or to poor coping efforts (McCrae & Costa, 1986).

What these behaviors seem to share is a common origin in negative affect. Individuals high in neuroticism have more difficulty than others in quitting smoking because the distress caused by abstinence is stronger for them. They may more frequently use inappropriate coping responses like hostile reactions and wishful thinking because they must deal more often with disruptive emotions. They may adopt irrational beliefs like self-blame because these beliefs are cognitively consistent with the negative feelings they experience. Neuroticism appears to include not only negative affect, but also the disturbed thoughts and behaviors that accompany emotional distress.

Extraversion or Surgency

Sociable, fun-loving, affectionate, friendly, and talkative are the highest loading variables on the extraversion factor. This is not Jungian extraversion (see Guilford, 1977), but it does correspond to the conception of H. J. Eysenck and most other contemporary researchers, who concur with popular speech in identifying extraversion with lively sociability.

However, disputes remain about which elements are central and which are peripheral to extraversion. Most writers would agree that sociability, cheerfulness, activity level, assertiveness, and sensation seeking all covary, however loosely. But the Eysencks have at times felt the need to distinguish between sociability and what they call impulsiveness (S. B. G. Eysenck & Eysenck, 1963; Revelle, Humphreys, Simon, & Gilliland, 1980). Hogan (1983) believed that the five-factor model was improved by dividing extraversion into sociability and assertiveness factors. In Goldberg's analyses, surgency (dominance and activity) were the primary definers of extraversion, and terms like warm–cold were assigned to the agreeableness–antagonism factor. Tellegen (in press) emphasized the complementary nature of neuroticism and extraversion by labeling his extraversion factor positive emotionality.

These distinctions do seem to merge at a high enough level of analysis (H. J. Eysenck & Eysenck, 1976; McCrae & Costa, 1983a), and sociability—the enjoyment of others' company—seems to be the core. What is essential to recall, however, is that liking people does not necessarily make one likable. Salesmen, those prototypic extraverts, are generally happier to see you than you are to see them.

Openness to Experience

The reinterpretation of Norman's culture as openness to experience was the focus of some of our previous articles (McCrae & Costa, 1985a, 1985b), and the replication of results in peer ratings was one of the purposes of the present article. According to adjective-factor results, openness is best characterized by original, imaginative, broad interests, and daring. In the case of this dimension, however, questionnaires may be better than adjectives as a basis for interpretation and assessment. Many aspects of openness (e.g., openness to feelings) are not easily expressed in single adjectives, and the relative poverty of the English-language vocabulary of openness and closedness may have contributed to confusions about this domain (McCrae & Costa, 1985a). We know from questionnaire studies that openness can be manifest in fantasy, aesthetics, feelings, actions, ideas, and values (Costa & McCrae, 1978, 1980), but only ideas and values are well represented in the adjective factor. Interestingly, questionnaire measures of openness give higher validity coefficients than do adjective-factor measures. . . .

Perhaps the most important distinction to be made here is between openness and intelligence. Open individuals tend to be seen by themselves and others as somewhat more intelligent. . . . However, joint factor analyses using Army Alpha intelligence subtests and either adjectives (McCrae & Costa, 1985b) or NEO Inventory scales (McCrae & Costa, 1985a) show that intelligence scales define a factor clearly separate from openness. Intelligence may in some degree predispose the individual to openness, or openness may help develop intelligence, but the two seem best construed as separate dimensions of individual differences.

Agreeableness Versus Antagonism

As a broad dimension, agreeableness–antagonism is less familiar than extraversion or neuroticism, but some of its component traits, like trust (Stark, 1978) and Machiavellianism (Christie & Geis, 1970), have been widely researched. The essential nature of agreeableness–antagonism is perhaps best seen by examining the disagreeable pole, which we have labeled antagonism. . . . [A]ntagonistic people seem always to set themselves against others. Cognitively they are mistrustful and skeptical; affectively they are callous and unsympathetic; behaviorally they are uncooperative, stubborn, and rude. It would appear that their sense of attachment or bonding with their fellow human beings is defective, and in extreme cases antagonism may resemble sociopathy (cf. H. J. Eysenck & Eysenck's, 1975, psychoticism).

An insightful description of antagonism in its neurotic form is provided by Horney's account of the tendency to move against people (1945, 1950). She theorized that a struggle for mastery is the root cause of this tendency and that variations may occur, including narcissistic, perfectionistic, and arrogant vindictive types. Whereas some antagonistic persons are overtly aggressive, other may be polished manipulators. The drive for mastery and the overt or inhibited hostility of antagonistic individuals suggests a resemblance to some formulations of Type A personality (Dembroski & MacDougall, 1983), and systematic studies of the relations between agreeableness–antagonism and measures of coronary-prone behavior should be undertaken.

Unappealing as antagonism may be, it is necessary to recognize that extreme scores on the agreeable pole may also be maladaptive. The person high in agreeableness may be dependent and fawning, and agreeableness has its neurotic manifestation in Horney's self-effacing solution of moving toward people.

Antagonism is most easily confused with dominance. Amelang and Borkenau (1982), working in German and apparently unaware of the Norman taxonomy, found a factor they called *dominance*. Among its key definers, however, were Hartnäckigkeit (*stubbornness*) and Erregbarkeit (*irritability*); scales that measure agreeableness and cooperation defined the opposite pole in their questionnaire factor. Clearly, this factor corresponds to antagonism. In self-reports (McCrae & Costa, 1985b), submissive–dominant is a weak definer of extraversion; from the peers' point of view, it is a definer of antagonism. The close etymological relationship of *dominant* and *domineering* shows the basis of the confusion.

Agreeableness–antagonism and conscientiousness–undirectedness are sometimes omitted from personality systems because they may seem too value laden. Indeed, the judgment of character is made largely along these two dimensions: Is the individual well or ill intentioned? Is he or she strong or weak in carrying out those intentions? Agreeableness–antagonism, in particular, has often been assumed to be an evaluative factor of others' perceptions rather than a veridical component of personality (e.g., A. Tellegen, personal communication, March 28, 1984).

However, the fact that a trait may be judged from a moral point of view does not mean that it is not a substantive aspect of personality. The consensual validation seen among peers and between peer-reports and self-reports demonstrates that there are some observable consistencies of behavior that underlie attributions of agreeableness and conscientiousness. They may be evaluated traits, but they are not mere evaluations.

Conscientiousness Versus Undirectedness

Conscientious may mean either governed by conscience or careful and thorough (Morris, 1976), and psychologists seem to be divided about which of these meanings best characterizes the last major dimension of personality. Amelang and Borkenau (1982) labeled their factor self-control versus impulsivity, and Conley (1985) spoke of impulse control. This terminology connotes an inhibiting agent, as Cattell (Cattell, Eber, & Tatsuoka, 1970) recognized when he named his Factor G *superego strength*. A conscientious person in this sense should be dutiful, scrupulous, and perhaps moralistic.

A different picture, however, is obtained by examining the adjectives that define this factor. In addition to conscientious and scrupulous, there are a number of adjectives that suggest a more proactive stance: hardworking, ambitious, energetic, persevering. Digman and Takemoto-Chock (1981) labeled this factor *will to achieve,* and it is notable that one of the items in the questionnaire measure of conscientiousness, "He strives for excellence in all he does," comes close to the classic definition of need for achievement (McClelland, Atkinson, Clark, & Lowell, 1953).

At one time, the purposefulness and adherence to plans, schedules, and requirements suggested the word *direction* as a label for this factor, and we have retained that implication in calling the opposite pole of conscientiousness *undirectedness.* In our view, the individual low in conscientiousness is not so much uncontrolled as undirected, not so much impulse ridden as simply lazy.

It seems probable that these two meanings may be related. Certainly individuals who are well organized, habitually careful, and capable of self-discipline are more likely to be able to adhere scrupulously to a moral code if they choose to—although there is no guarantee that they will be so inclined. An undirected individual may have a demanding conscience and a pervasive sense of guilt but be unable to live up to his or her own standards for lack of self-discipline and energy. In any case, it is clear that this is a dimension worthy of a good deal more empirical attention than it has yet received. Important real-life outcomes such as alcoholism (Conley & Angelides, 1984) and academic achievement (Digman & Takemoto-Chock, 1981) are among its correlates, and a further specification of the dimension is sure to be fruitful.

Some personality theorists might object that trait ratings, in whatever form and from whatever source, need not provide the best foundation for understanding individual differences. Experimental analysis of the psychophysiological basis of personality (H. J. Eysenck & Eysenck, 1984), examination of protypic acts and act frequencies (Buss & Craik, 1983), psychodynamic formulations (Horney, 1945), or behavioral genetics (Plomin, DeFries, & McClearn, 1980) provide important alternatives. But psychophysiological, behavioral, psychodynamic, and genetic explanations must eventually be related to the traits that are universally used to describe personality, and the five-factor model can provide a framework within which these relations can be systematically examined. The minor conceptual divergences noted in this article suggest the need for additional empirical work to fine-tune the model, but the broad outlines are clear in self-reports, spouse ratings, and peer ratings; in questionnaires and adjective factors; and in English and in German (Amelang & Borkenau, 1982; John, Goldberg, & Angleitner, 1984). Deeper causal analyses may seek to account for the structure of personality, but the structure that must be explained is, for now, best represented by the five-factor model.

REFERENCES

Amelang, M., & Borkenau, P. (1982). Über die faktorielle Struktur und externe Validität einiger Fragebogen-Skalen zur Erfasusng von Dimensionen der Extraversion und emotionalen Labilität [On the factor structure and external validity of some questionnaire scales measuring dimensions of extraversion and neuroticism]. *Zeitschrift für Differentielle und Diagnostische Psychologie, 3,* 119–146.

Block J. (1977). Advancing the psychology of personality: Paradigmatic shift or improving the quality of research? In D. Magnusson & N. S. Endler (Eds.), *Personality at the cross-roads: Current issues in interactional psychology* (pp. 37–63), Hillsdale, NJ: Erlbaum.

Bond, M. H., Nakazato, H., & Shiraishi, D. (1975). Universality and distinctiveness in dimensions of Japanese person perception. *Journal of Cross-Cultural Psychology, 6,* 346–357.

Buss, D. M., & Craik, K. H. (1983). The act frequency approach to personality. *Psychological Review, 90,* 105–126.

Cattell, R. B., Eber, H. W., & Tatsuoka, M. M. (1970). *The handbook for the Sixteen Personality Factor Questionnaire.* Champaign, IL: Institute for Personality and Ability Testing.

Christie, R., & Geis, R. L. (Eds.). (1970). *Studies in Machiavellianism.* New York: Academic Press.

Conley, J. J. (1985). Longitudinal stability of personality traits: A multitrait–multimethod–multioccasion analysis. *Journal of Personality and Social Psychology, 49,* 1266–1282.

Conley, J. J., & Angelides, M. (1984). *Personality antecedents of emotional disorders and alcohol abuse in men: Results of a forty-five year prospective study.* Manuscript submitted for publication.

Costa, P. T., Jr., & McCrae, R. R. (1978). Objective personality assessment. In M. Storandt, I. C. Siegler, & M. F. Elias (Eds.), *The clinical psychology of aging* (pp. 119–143). New York: Plenum Press.

Costa, P. T., Jr., & McCrae, R. R. (1980). Still stable after all these years: Personality as a key to some issues in adulthood and old age. In P. B. Baltes & O. G. Brim, Jr. (Eds.), *Life span development and behavior* (Vol. 3, pp. 65–102). New York: Academic Press.

Dembroski, T. M., & MacDougall, J. M. (1983). Behavioral and psychophysiological perspectives on coronary-prone behavior. In T. M. Dembroski, T. H. Schmidt, & G. Blumchen (Eds.), *Biobehavioral bases of coronary heart disease* (pp. 106–129). New York: Karger.

Digman, J. M., & Takemoto-Chock, N. K. (1981). Factors in the natural language of personality: Re-analysis, comparison, and interpretation of six major studies. *Multivariate Behavioral Research, 16,* 149–170.

Eysenck, H. J., & Eysenck, M. (1984). *Personality and individual differences.* London: Plenum Press.

Eysenck, H. J., & Eysenck, S. B. G. (1967). On the unitary nature of extraversion. *Acta Psychologica, 26,* 383–390.

Eysenck, H. J., & Eysenck, S. B. G. (1975). *Manual of the Eysenck Personality Questionnaire.* San Diego, CA: EdITS.

Eysenck, S. B. G., & Eysenck, H. J. (1963). On the dual nature of extraversion. *British Journal of Social and Clinical Psychology, 2,* 46–55.

Goldberg, L. R. (1981). Language and individual differences: The search for universals in personality lexicons. In L. Wheeler (Ed.), *Review of personality and social psychology* (Vol. 2, pp. 141–165). Beverly Hills, CA: Sage.

Goldberg, L. R. (1982). From ace to zombie: Some explorations in the language of personality. In C. D. Spielberger & J. N. Butcher (Eds.), *Advances in personality assessment* (Vol. 1, pp. 203–234). Hillsdale, NJ: Erlbaum.

Guilford, J. P. (1977). Will the real factor of extraversion–introversion please stand up? A reply to Eysenck. *Psychological Bulletin, 84,* 412–416.

Guilford, J. S. Zimmerman, W. S., & Guilford, J. P. (1976). *The Guilford–Zimmerman Temperament Survey handbook: Twenty-five years of research and application.* San Diego, CA: EdITS.

Hogan, R. (1983). Socioanalytic theory of personality. In M. M. Page (Ed.), *1982 Nebraska Symposium on Motivation: Personality—current theory and research* (pp. 55–89). Lincoln: University of Nebraska Press.

Horney, K. (1945). *Our inner conflicts.* New York: Norton.

Horney, K. (1950). *Neurosis and human growth.* New York: Norton.

John, O. P., Goldberg, L. R., & Angleitner, A. (1984). Better than the alphabet: Taxonomies of personality-descriptive terms in English, Dutch, and German. In H. J. C. Bonarius, G. L. M. van Heck, & N. G. Smid (Eds.), *Personality psychology in Europe: Theoretical and empirical developments.* Lisse, Switzerland: Swets & Zeitlinger.

Kenrick, D. T., & Dantchik, A. (1983). Interactionism, idiographics, and the social psychological invasion of personality. *Journal of Personality, 51,* 286–307.

Kline, P., & Barrett, P. (1983). The factors in personality questionnaires among normal subjects. *Advances in Behaviour Research and Therapy, 5,* 141–202.

Lorr, M., & Manning, T. T. (1978). Higher-order personality factors of the ISI. *Multivariate Behavioral Research, 13,* 3–7.

McClelland, D. C., Atkinson, J. W., Clark, R. A., & Lowell, E. L. (1953). *The achievement motive.* New York: Appleton-Century-Crofts.

McCrae, R. R., & Costa, P. T., Jr. (1983a). Joint factors in self-reports and ratings: Neuroticism, extraversion, and openness to experience. *Personality and Individual Differences, 4,* 245–255.

McCrae, R. R., & Costa, P. T., Jr. (1985a). Openness to experience. In R. Hogan & W. H. Jones (Eds.), *Perspectives in personality: Theory, measurement, and interpersonal dynamics* (Vol. 1). Greenwich, CT: JAI Press.

McCrae, R. R., & Costa, P. T., Jr. (1985b). Updating Norman's "adequate taxonomy": Intelligence and personality dimensions in natural language and in questionnaires. *Journal of Personality and Social Psychology, 49,* 710–721.

McCrae, R. R., & Costa, P. T., Jr. (1986). Personality, coping, and coping effectiveness in an adult sample. *Journal of Personality, 54,* 385–405.

Mischel, W. (1968). *Personality and assessment.* New York: Wiley.

Morris, W. (Ed.). (1976). *The American Heritage dictionary of the English language.* Boston: Houghton Mifflin.

Peabody, D. (1984). Personality dimensions through trait inferences. *Journal of Personality and Social Psychology, 46,* 384–403.

Plomin, R., DeFries, J. C., & McClearn, G. E. (1980). *Behavior genetics: A primer.* San Francisco: Freeman.

Revelle, W., Humphreys, M. S., Simon, L., & Gilliland, K. (1980). The interactive effect of personality, time of day, and caffeine: A test of the arousal model. *Journal of Experimental Psychology: General, 109,* 1–31.

Stark, L., (1978). Trust. In H. London & J. E. Exner, Jr. (Eds.), *Dimensions of personality* (pp. 561–599). New York: Wiley.

Teasdale, J. D., & Rachman, S. (Eds.). (1983). Cognitions and mood: Clinical aspects and applications [Special issue]. *Advances in Behaviour Research and Therapy, 5,* 1–88.

Tellegen, A. (in press). Structures of mood and personality and their relevance to assessing anxiety, with an emphasis on self-report. In A. H. Tuma & J. D. Maser (Eds.), *Anxiety and the anxiety disorders.* Hillsdale, NJ: Erlbaum.

Tupes, E. C., & Christal, R. E. (1961). Recurrent personality factors based on trait ratings. *USAF ASD Technical Report* (No. 61–97).

Vestre, N. D. (1984). Irrational beliefs and self-reported depressed mood. *Journal of Abnormal Psychology, 93*, 239–241.

Wiggins, J. S. (1979). A psychological taxonomy of trait-descriptive terms: The interpersonal domain. *Journal of Personality and Social Psychology, 37*, 395–412.

Robert R. McCrae and Paul T. Costa, Jr.

CHAPTER 12 Stress, Adjustment, and Health

12.1 HANS SELYE

The Evolution of the Stress Concept

Only in the past couple of decades have psychologists become convinced that psychological as well as physiological variables can produce stress. However, as far back as the 1930s, Canadian physiologist Hans Selye was studying stress through the general adaptation syndrome (GAS). The general adaptation syndrome, first identified by Selye, is a consistent series of bodily reactions to stress that can be divided into three stages: the alarm reaction stage, the stage of resistance, and the stage of exhaustion. The GAS serves as a model for investigating the long-term effects of stress on the body.

Selye (1907–1982) received his D.Sc. from McGill University in 1942 and later earned a Ph.D. and an M.D. He spent most of his professional career at the Institute of Experimental Medicine and Surgery at the University of Montreal. As an endocrinologist, he dedicated his life to understanding the hormonal reactions in the stress syndrome. Selye wrote over 30 books on stress, including *The Stress of Life* (1976) and *Stress Without Distress* (1974).

This selection is from "The Evolution of the Stress Concept," which was published in *American Scientist* in 1973. In it, Selye provides the history behind his famous general adaptation syndrome model of stress. Note how Selye's discoveries occurred in steps as he encountered different situations. As you read this selection, consider the definition of stress and how you measure the effects of stress in your life.

Key Concept: stress and the general adaptation syndrome

*E*verybody knows what stress is and nobody knows what it is. The word *stress*, like *success, failure,* or *happiness,* means different things to different people and, except for a few specialized scientists, no one has really tried to define it although it has become part of our daily vocabulary. . . .

Yet, how are we to cope with the stress of life if we cannot even define it? The businessman who is under constant pressure from his clients and employees alike, the air traffic controller who knows that a moment of distraction may mean death to hundreds of people, the athlete who desperately wants to win a race, and the husband who helplessly watches his wife slowly and painfully die of cancer—all suffer from stress. The problems they face are totally different, but medical research has shown that in many respects their bodies respond in a stereotyped manner with identical biochemical changes, meant fundamentally to cope with any type of increased demand upon the human machinery. The stress-producing factors—technically called *stressors*—are different, and yet they all produce essentially the same biologic stress response. This distinction between stressor and stress was perhaps the first important step in the scientific analysis of that most common biologic phenomenon that we all know only too well from personal experience.

But if we want to use what the laboratory has taught us about stress in formulating our own philosophy of life, if we want to avoid its bad effects and yet be able to enjoy the pleasures of accomplishment, we have to learn more about the nature and mechanism of stress. To succeed in this, we must concentrate on the fundamental technical data which the laboratory has given us as a basis for a scientific philosophy of conduct. Examination of the data seems to be the only way of finding purpose in life without having to fall back upon traditional beliefs whose acceptance depends primarily on indoctrination (1).

WHAT IS STRESS?

Stress is the nonspecific response of the body to any demand made upon it. In order to understand this definition we must first comprehend what is meant by "nonspecific." Each demand made upon our body is in a sense unique, that is, specific. When exposed to cold we shiver to produce more heat, and the blood vessels in our skin contract to diminish loss of heat from the body surface. When exposed to heat we sweat, because evaporation of perspiration from the surface of our skin has a cooling effect. When we eat so much sugar that the blood-sugar level rises above normal, we excrete some of it and try to activate chemical reactions which will enable us to store or burn up the rest so that the blood sugar may return to normal. A great muscular effort, such as running up many flights of stairs at full speed, makes increased demands upon our musculature and cardiovascular system: the muscles will need more energy to perform this unusual work; hence, the heart will beat more rapidly and strongly, and the blood pressure will rise to accelerate delivery of blood to the musculature.

Each drug and hormone has such specific actions: diuretics increase urine production; adrenalin augments the pulse rate and blood pressure, simultaneously increasing blood sugar, whereas insulin decreases blood sugar. Yet, no matter what kind of derangement is produced, all these agents have one thing in common: they also make an increased demand upon the body to readjust itself. This demand is nonspecific; it requires adaptation to a problem, regardless of what that problem may be. That is to say, in addition to their specific actions, all agents to which we are exposed produce a nonspecific increase in the need to perform certain adaptive functions and then to reestablish normalcy, which is independent of the specific activity that caused the rise in requirements. This nonspecific demand for activity as such is the essence of stress.

From the point of view of its stress-producing, or stressor, activity, it is even immaterial whether the agent or situation we face is pleasant or unpleasant; all that counts is the intensity of the demand for readjustment or adaptation. The mother who is suddenly told that her only son died in battle suffers a terrible mental shock; if years later it turns out that the news was false, and the son unexpectedly walks into her room alive and well, she experiences extreme joy. The *specific* results of the two events, sorrow and joy, are completely different, in fact, opposite to each other; yet their stressor effect—the *nonspecific* demand to readjust to an entirely new situation—may be the same.

It is difficult to see how such essentially different things as cold, heat, drugs, hormones, sorrow, and joy could provoke an identical biochemical reaction in the organism. Yet this is the case; it can now be demonstrated by highly objective quantitative biochemical determinations that certain reactions of the body are totally nonspecific and common to all types of exposure. . . .

WHAT STRESS IS NOT

Since the term stress has been used quite loosely, many confusing and often contradictory definitions have been formulated; hence, it will be useful to add a few remarks stating clearly what it is *not*. Stress is not simply nervous tension; stress reactions do occur in lower animals, which have no nervous system, and even in plants. Stress is not the nonspecific result of damage. We have seen that it is immaterial whether an agent is pleasant or unpleasant; its stressor effect depends merely on the intensity of the demand made upon the adaptive work of the body. As I have explained elsewhere (2), "normal activities—a game of tennis or even a passionate kiss—can produce considerable stress without causing conspicuous damage."

Stress is not something to be avoided. In fact, it is evident from the definition given earlier that it cannot be avoided; no matter what you do or what happens to you, there arises a demand to provide the necessary energy to perform the tasks required to maintain life and to resist and adapt to the changing external influences. Even while fully relaxed and asleep, you are under some stress: your heart must continue to pump blood, your intestines to digest last night's dinner, your muscles to move your chest to permit respiration; even your brain is not at complete rest while you are dreaming.

Complete freedom from stress is death. Contrary to public opinion, we must not—and indeed cannot—avoid stress, but we can meet it efficiently and enjoy it by learning more about its mechanism and adjusting our philosophy of life accordingly (1).

HISTORIC DEVELOPMENT

The concept of stress is very old; it must have occurred even to prehistoric man that the loss of vigor and feeling of exhaustion that overcame him after hard labor, prolonged exposure to cold or heat, loss of blood, agonizing fear, or any kind of disease had something in common. He may not have been consciously aware of this similarity in his response to anything that was just too much for him, but when the feeling came he must have realized that he had exceeded the limits of what he could reasonably handle, in other words that "he had had it."

Man soon must have discovered also that whenever faced with a prolonged and unaccustomed strenuous task—be it swimming in cold water, lifting rocks, or going without food—he passes through three stages: at first the experience is a hardship, then one gets used to it, and finally one cannot stand it any longer. . . .

How could different agents produce the same result? Is there a nonspecific adaptive reaction to change as such? In 1926, as a second-year medical student, I first came across this problem of a stereotyped response to any exacting task. I began to wonder why patients suffering from the most diverse diseases have so many signs and symptoms in common. Whether a man suffers from severe loss of blood, an infectious disease, or advanced cancer, he loses his appetite, his muscular strength, and his ambition to accomplish anything; usually the patient also loses weight, and even his facial expression betrays that he is ill. What is the scientific basis of what I thought of at the time as the "syndrome of just being sick"? Could the mechanism of this syndrome be analyzed by modern scientific techniques? Could it be reduced to its elements and expressed in the precise terms of biochemistry, biophysics, and morphology? Could this reaction be subject to scientific analysis?

It was not until 1936 that the problem presented itself again, now under conditions more suited to analysis. At that time, I was working in the biochemistry Department of McGill University, trying to find a new hormone in extracts of cattle ovaries. I injected the extracts into rats to see if their organs would show unpredictable changes that could not be attributed to any known hormone. Much to my satisfaction, the first and most impure extracts changed the rats in three ways: (1) the adrenal cortex became enlarged, (2) the thymus, spleen, lymph nodes, and all other lymphatic structures shrank, and (3) deep, bleeding ulcers appeared in the stomach and in the upper gut. Because the three types of change were closely interdependent they formed a definite syndrome. The changes varied from slight to pronounced, depending on the amount of extract I injected.

At first, I ascribed all these changes to a new sex hormone in the extract. But soon I found that all toxic substances—extracts of kidney, spleen, or even a toxin not derived from living tissue—produced the same syndrome. Gradually, my classroom concept of the "syndrome of just being sick" came back to me. I realized that the reaction I had produced with my impure extracts and toxic drugs was an experimental replica of this syndrome. Adrenal enlargement, gastrointestinal ulcers, and thymicolymphatic shrinkage were the omnipresent signs of damage to the body when under disease attack. The three changes thus became the objective indexes of stress and the basis for the development of the entire stress concept.

The reaction was first described in *Nature* (4 July 1936) as "A Syndrome Produced by Various Nocuous Agents" and, subsequently, it became known as the General Adaptation Syndrome (GAS) or biologic stress syndrome. In the same paper I also suggested the name *alarm reaction* for the initial response, arguing that it probably represents the somatic expression of a generalized "call to arms" of the body's defensive forces.

THE GENERAL ADAPTATION SYNDROME

The alarm reaction, however, was evidently not the entire response. Upon continued exposure to any noxious agent capable of eliciting this reaction, a stage of adaptation or resistance ensues. In other words, no organism can be maintained continuously in a state of alarm. If the agent is so drastic that continued exposure becomes incompatible with life, the animal dies during the alarm reaction within the first hours or days. If it can survive, this initial reaction is necessarily followed by the "stage of resistance." The manifestations of this second phase are quite different from—in many instances, the exact opposite of—those which characterize the alarm reaction. For example, during the alarm reaction, the cells of the adrenal cortex discharge their secretory granules into the bloodstream and thus become depleted of corticoid-containing lipid storage material; in the stage of resistance, on the other hand, the cortex becomes particularly rich in secretory granules. Whereas in the alarm reaction, there is hemoconcentration, hypochloremia, and general tissue catabolism, during the stage of resistance, there is hemodilution, hyperchloremia, and anabolism, with a return toward normal body weight.

Curiously, after still more exposure to the noxious agent, the acquired adaptation is lost again. The animal enters into a third phase, the "stage of exhaustion," which inexorably follows as long as the stressor is severe enough and applied for a sufficient length of time. Because of its great practical importance, it should be pointed out that the triphasic nature of the GAS gave us the first indication that the body's adaptability, or "adaptation energy," is finite since, under constant stress, exhaustion eventually ensues. We still do not know precisely what is lost, except that it is not merely caloric energy, since food intake is normal during the stage of resistance. Hence, one would think that once adaptation has occurred and ample energy is available, resistance should go on indefinitely. But just as any inanimate machine gradually wears out, so does the human machine sooner or later become the victim of constant wear and tear.

REFERENCES

1. H. Selye. In preparation. *Stress without Distress*. New York, Philadelphia: Lippincott.
2. H. Selye. 1956. *The Stress of Life*. New York: McGraw-Hill.

Little Hassles Can Be Hazardous to Health

There is no doubt that stress is harmful to mental and physical health. However, the common belief that major life changes cause the most severe stress was challenged in the early 1980s by Richard S. Lazarus, who emphasized the concept of daily hassles.

Lazarus (b. 1922) earned his Ph.D. in experimental psychology from the University of Pittsburgh in 1948. He taught at Johns Hopkins University and Clark University before accepting a position at the University of California, Berkeley in 1957, where he is currently a professor emeritus. Much of his professional career has focused on emotions and stress, as evidenced by his book *Emotion and Adaptation* (Oxford University Press, 1991).

This selection is from "Little Hassles Can Be Hazardous to Health," which was published in *Psychology Today* in 1981. In it, Lazarus defines *hassles* as the irritating or frustrating little incidents that happen every day, like spilling a drink, losing your car keys, having an argument, or being caught in a long line. He also discusses the pleasant uplifts that can occur. Note that the uplifts have a different effect on men than they do on women. As you read this selection, think about your daily hassles and uplifts. How do you generally respond to hassles in your life? How do you think you *should* respond?

Key Concept: hassles and stress

Modern research on the effects of stress has concentrated on the dramatic events of life: the death of a spouse or a friend, divorce, marriage, retirement, being fired. This research has largely ignored the effect of the minor but more frequent daily events that might be best described as hassles. Hassles, as I define them, are the irritating, frustrating, or distressing incidents that occur in our everyday transactions with the environment. They can take the form of disagreements, disappointments, accidents, or unpleasant surprises. They range from getting stuck in a traffic jam to losing a wallet; from an argument with a teenage son to a dispute with a superior or a subordinate at work.

Richard S.
Lazarus

I recently completed a year-long study of the effects of daily hassles with a group of my colleagues at the University of California at Berkeley: Allen Kanner, James Coyne, Catherine Schaefer, Anita DeLongis, and Gayle Dakof. We discovered that daily hassles are more closely linked to and may have a greater effect on our moods and our health than the major misfortunes of life. By keeping track of the accumulation of hassles, we found that their effects varied according to their frequency, intensity, and the reactions people had to them. We also kept track of the daily uplifts in the lives of our participants to see if pleasant or satisfying moments can counter the negative effects of daily hassles. To our surprise, we found that uplifts seemed to have a different effect on men and women.

While our findings may seem obvious to some readers, our work marks a significant shift in stress research. Most previous work in the field has operated under the premise that all major life changes—whether positive or negative—produce stress and that the more a person endures, the greater the potential for physical and mental illness. Our study raises serious doubts about that premise.

The preoccupation with major life events began in the mid-1960s with the pioneering work of Thomas Holmes and Richard Rahe at the University of Washington. Using interviews and health histories of several thousand people, Holmes and Rahe found a statistically significant relationship between the major events in their lives and their physical condition within the next year or two. The effect seemed to be cumulative: the more life changes, the greater the likelihood of a later illness. This finding applied both to positive events like marriage or promotion and to negative events like divorce or getting fired.

Holmes and Rahe developed a 43-item checklist of "recent life events" and gave each one a numerical value in "life change units" based on its estimated impact as a stressor. Death of a spouse, for example, they rated at 100 units; death of a close friend, at 37; a minor violation of the law, 11. People who have accumulated more than 300 life change units in the previous two years are supposedly more likely than others to suffer serious health problems.

In recent years the life events approach to stress research has come under increasing criticism on a number of different grounds:

- The particular events in the checklist may not be the most relevant ones for certain groups of people, such as students, working mothers, the poor, or the elderly.
- Simply adding up the life change units of major events fails to take into account the particular context of the changes, how the individual appraises them, and how well or how poorly he or she copes with them.
- The statistical correlation between life events scores and health outcomes, though positive, is relatively weak.
- The life events approach provides no clues to the specific processes by which the events have an impact on health; it tells us nothing about how the events are translated into the stresses of day-to-day living.
- Life events are built solely around the idea of change; yet much stress arises from chronic or repeated conditions of living—boredom, continuing tension in a family relationship, lack of occupational progress, isolation and loneliness, absence of meaning and commitment.

The Top Ten Hassles and Uplifts

HASSLES	*UPLIFTS*
1. Concern about weight	1. Relating well with your spouse or lover
2. Health of a family member	2. Relating well with friends
3. Rising prices of common goods	3. Completing a task
4. Home maintenance	4. Feeling healthy
5. Too many things to do	5. Getting enough sleep
6. Misplacing or losing things	6. Eating out
7. Yard work or outside home maintenance	7. Meeting responsibilities
8. Property, investment, or taxes	8. Visiting, phoning, or writing someone
9. Crime	9. Spending time with family
10. Physical appearance	10. Home pleasing to you

The impact of hassles on our physical and mental health depends to a great extent on their frequency, duration, and intensity. A person's response to a given hassle depends on a variety of other factors: personality, coping style, other resources, and how the rest of the day has gone. When someone is under pressure, petty problems that otherwise might be ignored—a broken shoelace, for example—can have a much greater effect that if they had occurred at less anxious times.

For that reason, the particular hassles cited by the people we surveyed are less important than their overall intensity and the individual reactions to them. And though our data do not yet allow us to say this, we suspect that some of the impact of hassles stems from their personal meaning and significance or from our ineptness in coping with certain interpersonal difficulties. As I pointed out in an interview with *Psychology Today* ("Positive Denial: The Case for Not Facing Reality," November 1979), "Psychological stress resides neither in the situation nor the person; it depends on a transaction between the two. It arises from how the person appraises an event and adapts to it."

The kind of hassles that affect a person's overall psychological economy have several possible sources. Major life events, in addition to their obvious or immediate impact, can create continuing hassles—a kind of "ripple effect." Divorce, for example, might force a man inexperienced at such tasks to make his own meals, do the laundry, or clean the house; it might force a woman to handle household finances or repair a leaky faucet for the first time.

Some hassles may recur because of a permanent but not always harmonious relationship in marriage or at work, such as sexual incompatibility with a spouse or personality conflict with a coworker. (There continuing hassles create the "chronic role strains" studied by Leonard Pearlin and Morton Lieberman at the University of Chicago.) Other hassles may occur not as a result of any major life change or permanent relationship, but from a momentary situation—an unexpected phone call, an uninvited guest, a flat tire.

Assessing the effect of daily hassles led us to consider the effect of uplifts, their positive psychological counterparts: pleasant, happy, or satisfying experiences like hearing good news, getting a good night's rest, solving a difficult problem. Just as negative stressors or hassles can cause physical and psychological changes that may result in illness, we think that uplifts may serve as emotional buffers against the same disorders.

There are several ways in which uplifts may help people cope with daily hassles. They may serve as breathers, sustainers, or restorers when psychological resources have been run down during stressful periods. They may help us recover from the effects of harm or loss. They may act as psychological protection against the effects of hassles or major life changes.

A group of us compiled a list of daily hassles and uplifts by citing common annoyances and pleasures that occur at work, among family and friends, or in other contexts. We got additional suggestions from patients enrolled in a regional group health insurance program. We converted our list into a hassles questionnaire. The questionnaire does not have a fixed or final form, for there are undoubtedly many common examples that could or should be on our list; and the list itself may not be appropriate for certain groups like young parents or the elderly.

We select our research sample of 100 people (48 men and 52 women), ages 45 to 64, from a much larger survey population in Alameda County, California. Our subjects were mainly white, middle-aged, middle-class, and Protestant, with above-average incomes and education. Most were married (86 percent) and relatively stable in employment history and residence. While we know that our sample is not representative of the general population, at this preliminary stage of our research we want to test our notions on a relatively small and homogeneous group. We hope to study more diverse groups in the future.

Participants in the study filled out a variety of questionnaires over the course of a year. At the beginning and end of the year they filled out a 24-item life events scale comparable to the Homes-Rahe scale. Each month they also filled out a 117-item hassle checklist and a 135-item uplift checklist. They marked the items that had occurred that month and rated the frequency and severity of the items on a 3-point scale.

To measure the effect of the hassles and uplifts, we had each person fill out physical- and mental-health questionnaires at the beginning and end of the year. We used a health-status questionnaire that covers a wide variety of chronic illnesses, like hypertension, and specific symptoms, like chest pains and measures of energy level. We also used the Hopkins Symptom Checklist, a 58-item psychological questionnaire that asks how often people have headaches, bad dreams, worries, poor appetite, crying spells, and so on. Each month, to measure fluctuations in mood, everyone filled out the Bradburn Morale Scale, a widely used index of emotions which asks whether a person is feeling lonely, angry, excited, pleased, bored, proud, restless, uneasy, and so on. Each month, the participants also kept a daily log of their emotions for four consecutive days.

As we expected, hassles turned out to be much better predictors of psychological and physical health than life events. The more frequent and intense the hassles people reported, the poorer their overall mental and physical health. While we found no significant relationship between life events that occurred during the study and the health of the participants at its end, we did find a moderate relationship between life events that occurred during the two and a half years *before* the study and people's health at the end. In short, we found that major events do have some long-term effects, but in the short term, hassles seem to have a much stronger impact on mental and physical health. . . .

When we added the information from the mood scales and daily logs of emotions to the data on hassles, we found that particularly for men, the more hassles and the more negative emotions, the worse a person's subsequent health. Our results strongly suggest that hassles trigger unpleasant emotions, which, in turn or in combination, have an adverse effect on health.

Contrary to our expectation, uplifts did not seem to have much buffer effect on the impact of hassles in this study. In fact, for women, uplifts seemed to have a negative effect on emotions and on psychological health.

At such an early stage in our research, we have no explanation that we can support with data for these surprising findings. In future studies we will continue to search for the positive functions that we still believe uplifts play in a person's psychological economy.

12.3 THOMAS H. HOLMES AND RICHARD H. RAHE

The Social Readjustment Rating Scale

Measuring and predicting the stress in people's lives has been a concern of psychologists for many years. This has been a difficult task because stress is interpreted in so many different ways—a good measure has been elusive. Psychiatrists Thomas H. Holmes and Richard H. Rahe were pioneers in the effort to effectively measure stress in humans.

Holmes and Rahe were both in the Department of Psychiatry at the University of Washington School of Medicine in Seattle, Washington, when their report "The Social Readjustment Rating Scale" was published. Holmes was also with the U.S. Navy's Medical Neuropsychiatric Research Unit in San Diego, California. His publications in the area of life changes and stress include *Life Change, Life Events, and Illness: Selected Papers* (Praeger, 1989), coauthored with Ella David. Rahe was with the U.S. Navy Medical Corps in Washington, D.C., before accepting his present position at the University of Nevada School of Medicine.

This selection is from "The Social Readjustment Rating Scale," which was published in *Journal of Psychosomatic Research* in 1967. In it, Holmes and Rahe describe how they developed a survey to measure how much stress a person has been exposed to recently. They also argue that a change in one's life (positive or negative) contributes most significantly to stress. Holmes and Rahe's approach looks mainly at major life changes, as opposed to minor daily hassles. As you read this selection, consider the amount of change that has occurred recently in your life.

Key Concept: life change stress

*I*n previous studies [1] it has been established that a cluster of social events requiring change in ongoing life adjustment is significantly associated with the time of illness onset. Similarly, the relationship of what has been called

275

'life stress,' 'emotional stress,' 'object loss,' etc. and illness onset has been demonstrated by other investigations [2–13]. It has been adduced from these studies that this clustering of social or life events achieves etiologic significance as a necessary but not sufficient cause of illness and accounts in part for the time of onset of disease.

Methodologically, the interview or questionnaire technique used in these studies has yielded only the *number* and *types* of events making up the cluster. Some estimate of the magnitude of these events is now required to bring greater precision to this area of research and to provide a quantitative basis for new epidemiological studies of diseases. This report defines a method which achieves this requisite.

METHOD

A sample of convenience composed of 394 subjects completed the paper and pencil test. (See Table 1 for characteristics of the sample.) The items were the 43 life events empirically derived from clinical experience. The following written instructions were given to each subject who completed the Social Readjustment Rating Questionnaire (SRRQ).

(A) Social readjustment includes the amount and duration of change in one's accustomed pattern of life resulting from various life events. As defined, social readjustment measures the intensity and length of time necessary to accommodate to a life event, *regardless of the desirability of this event.*

(B) You are asked to rate a series of life events as to their relative degrees of necessary readjustment. In scoring, *use all of your experience* in arriving at your answer. This means personal experience where it applies as well as what you have learned to be the case for others. Some persons accommodate to change more readily than others; some persons adjust with particular ease or difficulty to only certain events. Therefore, strive to give your opinion of the average degree of readjustment necessary for each event rather than the extreme.

(C) The mechanics of rating are these: Event 1, Marriage, has been given an arbitrary value of 500. As you complete each of the remaining events think to yourself, "Is this event indicative of more or less readjustment than marriage?" "Would the readjustment take longer or shorter to accomplish?" If you decide the readjustment is more intense and protracted, than choose a *proportionately larger* number and place it in the blank directly opposite the event in the column marked "VALUES." If you decide the event represents less and shorter readjustment than marriage then indicate how much less by placing a *proportionately smaller* number in the opposite blank. (If an event requires intense readjustment over a short time span, it may approximate in value an event requiring less intense readjustment over a long period of time.) If the event is equal in social readjustment to marriage, record the number 500 opposite the event. . . .

TABLE 1

*Pearson's Coefficient of Correlation Between Discrete Groups
in the Sample*

*Thomas H.
Holmes and
Richard H.
Rahe*

Group	No. in Group		Group	No. in Group	Coefficient of Correlation
Male	179	vs.	Female	215	0.965
Single	171	vs.	Married	223	0.960
Age < 30	206	vs.	Age 30–60	137	0.958
Age < 30	206	vs.	Age > 60	51	0.923
Age 30–60	137	vs.	Age > 60	51	0.965
1st Generation	19	vs.	2nd Generation	69	0.908
1st Generation	19	vs.	3rd Generation	306	0.929
2nd Generation	69	vs.	3rd Generation	306	0.975
< College	182	vs.	4 Years of College	212	0.967
Lower class	71	vs.	Middle class	323	0.928
White	363	vs.	Negro	19	0.820
White	363	vs.	Oriental	12	0.940
Protestant	241	vs.	Catholic	42	0.913
Protestant	241	vs.	Jewish	19	0.971
Protestant	241	vs.	Other religion	45	0.948
Protestant	241	vs.	No religious preference	47	0.926

RESULTS

The Social Readjustment Rating Scale (SRRS) is shown in Table 2. This table contains the magnitude of the life events which is derived when the mean score, divided by 10, of each item for the entire sample is calculated and arranged in rank order. That consensus is high concerning the relative order and magnitude of the means of items is demonstrated by the high coefficients of correlation (Pearsons's r) between the discrete groups contained in the sample. Table 1 reveals that all the coefficients of correlation are above 0.90 with the exception of that between white and Negro which was 0.82. Kendall's coefficient of concordance (W) for the 394 individuals was 0.477, significant at $p = <0.0005$.

DISCUSSION

Placed in historical perspective, this research evolved from the chrysalis of Psychobiology generated by Adolph Meyer [14]. His invention of the 'life chart,' a device for organizing the medical data as a dynamic biography, provided a unique method for demonstrating his schema of the relationship of biological, psychological, and sociological phenomena to the processes of health and disease in man. The importance of many of the life events used in this research was emphasized by Meyer: " . . . changes of habitat, of school entrance, graduations or changes or failures; the various jobs, the dates of

TABLE 2

Social Readjustment Rating Scale

Rank	Life Event	Mean Value
1	Death of spouse	100
2	Divorce	73
3	Marital separation	65
4	Jail term	63
5	Death of close family member	63
6	Personal injury or illness	53
7	Marriage	50
8	Fired at work	47
9	Marital reconciliation	45
10	Retirement	45
11	Change in health of family member	44
12	Pregnancy	40
13	Sex difficulties	39
14	Gain of new family member	39
15	Business readjustment	39
16	Change in financial state	38
17	Death of close friend	37
18	Change to different line of work	36
19	Change in number of arguments with spouse	35
20	Mortgage over $10,000	31
21	Foreclosure of mortgage or loan	30
22	Change in responsibilities at work	29
23	Son or daughter leaving home	29
24	Trouble with in-laws	29
25	Outstanding personal achievement	28
26	Wife begin or stop work	26
27	Begin or end school	26
28	Change in living conditions	25
29	Revision of personal habits	24
30	Trouble with boss	23
31	Change in work hours or conditions	20
32	Change in residence	20
33	Change in schools	20
34	Change in recreation	19
35	Change in church activities	19
36	Change in social activities	18
37	Mortgage or loan less than $10,000	17
38	Change in sleeping habits	16
39	Change in number of family get-togethers	15
40	Change in eating habits	15
41	Vacation	13
42	Christmas	12
43	Minor violations of the law	11

possibly important births and deaths in the family, and other fundamentally important environmental influences."[14].

More recently, in Harold G. Wolff's laboratory, the concepts of Pavlov, Freud, Cannon and Skinner were incorporated in the Meyerian schema. The research resulting from this synthesis adduced powerful evidence that 'stressful' life events, by evoking psychophysiologic reactions, played an important causative role in the natural history of many diseases [15–19]. Again, many of the life events denoted 'stressful' were those enumerated by Meyers. . . .

Beginning in this laboratory in 1949, the life chart device has been used systematically in over 5,000 patients to study the quality and quantity of life events empirically observed to cluster at the time of disease onset. . . . There are 2 categories of items: those indicative of the life style of the individual, and those indicative of occurrences involving the individual. Evolving mostly from ordinary, but some from extraordinary, social and interpersonal transactions, these events pertain to major areas of dynamic significance in the social structure of the American way of life. These include family constellation, marriage, occupation, economics, residence, group and peer relationships, education, religion, recreation and health.

During the developmental phase of this research the interview technique was used to assess the meaning of the events for the individual. As expected, the psychological significance and emotions varied widely with the patient. Also it will be noted that only some of the events are negative or 'stressful' in the conventional sense, i.e. are socially undesirable. Many are socially desirable and consonant with the American values of achievement, success, materialism, practicality, efficiency, future orientation, conformism and self-reliance.

There was identified, however, one theme common to all these life events. The occurrence of each usually evoked or was associated with some adaptive or coping behavior on the part of the involved individual. Thus, each item has been constructed to contain life events whose advent is either indicative of or requires a significant change in the ongoing life pattern of the individual. The emphasis is on change from the existing steady state and not on psychological meaning, emotion, or social desirability.

REFERENCES

1. Rahe R. H., Meyer M., Smith M., Kjaer G. and Holes T. H. Social stress and illness onset. *J. Psychosom. Res.* **8,** 35 (1964).

2. Graham D. T. and Stevenson I. Disease as response to life stress. In *The Psychological Basis of Medical Practice* (H. I. Lief, V. F. Lief and N. R. Lief, Eds.) Harper & Row, New York (1963).

3. Greene W. A., Jr., Psychological factors and reticulo-endothelial disease—I. Preliminary observations on a group of males with lymphomas and leukemias. *Psychosom. Med.* **16,** 220 (1954).

4. Greene W. A., Jr., Young L. E. and Swisher S. N. Psychological factors and reticulo-endothelial disease—II. Observations on a group of women with lymphomas and leukemias. *Psychosom. Med.* **18,** 284 (1956).

5. Greene W. A., Jr. and Miller G. Psychological factors and reticulo-endothelial disease—IV. Observations on a group of children and adolescents with leukemia: an interpretation of disease development in terms of the mother-child unit. *Psychosom. Med.* **20,** 124 (1958).

6. Weiss E., Dlin B., Rollin H. R., Fischer H. K. and Bepler C. R. Emotional factors in coronary occlusion. *A. M. A. Archs. Internal Med.* **99,** 628 (1957).

7. Fischer H. K., Dlin B., Winters W., Hagner S. and Weiss E. Time patterns and emotional factors related to the onset of coronary occlusion. [Abstract] *Psychosom. Med.* **24,** 516 (1962).

8. Kissen D. M. Specific psychological factors in pulmonary tuberculosis, *Hlth Bull. Edinburgh* **14,** 44 (1956).

9. Kissen D. M. Some psychosocial aspects of pulmonary tuberculosis. *Int. J. Soc. Psychiat.* **3,** 252 (1958).

10. Hawkins N. G., Davies R. and Holmes T. H. Evidence of psychosocial factors in the development of pulmonary tuberculosis. *Am. Rev. Tuberc. Pulmon. Dis.* **75,** 5 (1957).

11. Smith M. Psychogenic factors in skin disease, Medical Thesis, University of Washington, Seattle (1962).

12. Rahe R. H. and Holmes T. H. Social, psychologic and psychophysiologic aspects of inguinal hernia. *J. Psychosom. Res.* **8,** 487 (1965).

13. Kjaer G. Some psychosomatic aspects of pregnancy with particular reference to nausea and vomiting, Medical Thesis, University of Washington, Seattle (1959).

14. Lief A. (Ed.) *The Commonsense Psychiatry of Dr. Adolf Meyer,* McGraw-Hill, New York (1948).

15. Wolff H. G., Wolf S. and Hare C. C. (Eds.) *Life Stress and Bodily Disease,* Res. Publs. Ass. Res. Nerv. Ment. Dis. Vol. 29. Williams & Wilkins, Baltimore (1950).

16. Holmes T. H., Goodell H., Wolf S. and Wolff H. G. *The Nose. An Experimental Study of Reactions Within the Nose in Human Subjects During Varying Life Experiences,* Charles C. Thomas, Springfield, Illinois (1950).

17. Wolf S. *The Stomach.* Oxford University Press, New York 1965).

18. Wolf S., Cardon P. V., Shepard E. M., and Wolff H. G. *Life Stress and Essential Hypertension,* Williams & Wilkins, Baltimore (1955).

19. Grace W. J., Wolf S. and Wolff H. G. *The Human Colon,* Paul B. Hoeber, New York (1951).

PART SIX

Psychological Disorders

On the Internet . . .

Sites appropriate to Part Six

This Mental Health Infosource page provides information on psychological disorders.

> http://www.mhsource.com/disorders/disorders.html

This Austrian site contains a biography of Sigmund Freud and information on his influence and followers.

> http://austria-info.at/personen/freud/index.html

The American Psychological Association's public affairs office presents information on selecting a psychologist for therapy.

> http://www.apa.org/pubinfo/howto.html

CHAPTER 13 Abnormal Behavior

13.1 D. L. ROSENHAN

On Being Sane in Insane Places

Mental health workers have devised various classification schemes to help them diagnose abnormal behaviors. Although this may be beneficial in the vast majority of cases, some psychologists worry that misdiagnosis can result in inappropriate treatments or stigmatization and that mental health workers therefore need to be extremely careful about labeling mental patients. Social psychologist D. L. Rosenhan is a leading critic of the method in which patients are labeled in mental hospitals.

Rosenhan (b. 1929) earned his Ph.D. from Columbia University in 1958. He is currently a professor of psychology at Stanford University.

This selection is from "On Being Sane in Insane Places," which was published in *Science* in 1973. In it, Rosenhan describes his and others' experiences as pseudopatients (healthy people who secretly gained admission to mental hospitals as patients), and he discusses the implications of labeling mental patients as insane or as mentally ill. Rosenhan's article encouraged debate among mental health providers on diagnosis in clinical psychology that is still going on today. A readable article, it provides a good inside look at mental institutions as well as the labeling process. Although Rosenhan's research successfully persuaded psychologists to discuss the problems that come with diagnosing mental patients, some people have criticized the study as unethical. As you read this selection, consider what it must be like for mental patients to live in an institution.

Key Concept: labeling and the diagnosis of abnormal behavior

*I*f sanity and insanity exist, how shall we know them?

The question is neither capricious nor itself insane. However much we may be personally convinced that we can tell the normal from the abnormal, the evidence is simply not compelling. It is commonplace, for example, to read about murder trials wherein eminent psychiatrists for the defense are contradicted by equally eminent psychiatrists for the prosecution on the matter of the defendant's sanity. More generally, there are a great deal of conflicting data on the reliability, utility, and meaning of such terms as "sanity," "insanity," "mental illness," and "schizophrenia." Finally, as early as 1934, Benedict suggested that normality and abnormality are not universal (*1*). What is viewed as normal in one culture may be seen as quite aberrant in another. Thus, notions of normality and abnormality may not be quite as accurate as people believe they are.

To raise questions regarding normality and abnormality is in no way to question the fact that some behaviors are deviant or odd. Murder is deviant. So, too, are hallucinations. Nor does raising such questions deny the existence of the personal anguish that is often associated with "mental illness." Anxiety and depression exist. Psychological suffering exists. But normality and abnormality, sanity and insanity, and the diagnoses that flow from them may be less substantive than many believe them to be.

At its heart, the question of whether the sane can be distinguished from the insane (and whether degrees of insanity can be distinguished from each other) is a simple matter: do the salient characteristics that lead to diagnoses reside in the patients themselves or in the environments and contexts in which observers find them? . . . [T]he belief has been strong that patients present symptoms, that those symptoms can be categorized, and, implicitly, that the sane are distinguishable from the insane. More recently, however, this belief has been questioned. Based in part on theoretical and anthropological considerations, but also on philosophical, legal, and therapeutic ones, the view has grown that psychological categorization of mental illness is useless at best and downright harmful, misleading, and pejorative at worst. Psychiatric diagnoses, in this view, are in the minds of the observers and are not valid summaries of characteristics displayed by the observed.

Gains can be made in deciding which of these is more nearly accurate by getting normal people (that is, people who do not have, and have never suffered, symptoms of serious psychiatric disorders) admitted to psychiatric hospitals and then determining whether they were discovered to be sane and, if so, how. If the sanity of such pseudopatients were always detected, there would be prima facie evidence that a sane individual can be distinguished from the insane context in which he is found. Normality (and presumably abnormality) is distinct enough that it can be recognized wherever it occurs, for it is carried within the person. If, on the other hand, the sanity of the pseudopatients were never discovered, serious difficulties would arise for those who support traditional modes of psychiatric diagnosis. Given that the hospital staff was not incompetent, that the pseudopatient had been behaving as sanely as he had been outside of the hospital, and that it had never been previously suggested that he belonged in a psychiatric hospital, such an unlikely outcome would support the view that psychiatric diagnosis betrays little about the patient but much about the environment in which an observer finds him.

D. L. Rosenhan

This article describes such an experiment. Eight sane people gained secret admission to 12 different hospitals. Their diagnostic experiences constitute the data of the first part of this article; the remainder is devoted to a description of their experiences in psychiatric institutions. Too few psychiatrists and psychologists, even those who have worked in such hospitals, know what the experience is like. They rarely talk about it with former patients, perhaps because they distrust information coming from the previously insane. Those who have worked in psychiatric hospitals are likely to have adapted so thoroughly to the settings that they are insensitive to the impact of the experience. And while there have been occasional reports of researchers who submitted themselves to psychiatric hospitalization (3), these researchers have commonly remained in the hospitals for short periods of time, often with the knowledge of the hospital staff. It is difficult to know the extent to which they were treated like patients or like research colleagues. Nevertheless, their reports about the inside of the psychiatric hospital have been valuable. This article extends those efforts.

PSEUDOPATIENTS AND THEIR SETTINGS

The eight pseudopatients were a varied group. One was a psychology graduate student in his 20's. The remaining seven were older and "established." Among them were three psychologists, a pediatrician, a psychiatrist, a painter, and a housewife. Three pseudopatients were women, five were men. All of them employed pseudonyms, lest their alleged diagnoses embarrass them later. Those who were in mental health professions alleged another occupation in order to avoid the special attentions that might be accorded by staff, as a matter of courtesy or caution, to ailing colleagues. With the exception of myself (I was the first pseudopatient and my presence was known to the hospital administrator and chief psychologist and, so far as I can tell, to them alone), the presence of pseudopatients and the nature of the research program was not known to the hospital staffs.

The settings were similarly varied. In order to generalize the findings, admission into a variety of hospitals was sought. The 12 hospitals in the sample are located in five different states on the East and West coasts. Some were old and shabby, some were quite new. Some were research-oriented, others not. Some had good staff-patient ratios, others were quite understaffed. Only one was a strictly private hospital. All the others were supported by state or federal funds or, in one instance, by university funds.

After calling the hospital for an appointment, the pseudopatient arrived at the admissions office complaining that he had been hearing voices. Asked what the voices said, he replied that they were often unclear, but as far as he could tell they said "empty," "hollow," and "thud." The voices were unfamiliar and were of the same sex as the pseudopatient. The choice of these symptoms was occasioned by their apparent similarity to existential symptoms. Such symptoms were alleged to arise from painful concerns about the perceived meaninglessness of one's life. It is as if the hallucinating person were saying, "My life is empty and hollow." The choice of these symptoms was also determined by the *absence* of a single report of existential psychoses in the literature.

Beyond alleging the symptoms and falsifying name, vocation, and employment, no further alterations of person, history, or circumstances were made. The significant events of the pseudopatient's life history were presented as they had actually occurred. Relationships with parents and siblings, with spouse and children, with people at work and in school, consistent with the aforementioned exceptions, were described as they were or had been. Frustrations and upsets were described along with joys and satisfactions. These facts are important to remember. If anything, they strongly biased the subsequent results in favor of detecting sanity, since none of their histories or current behaviors were seriously pathological in any way.

Immediately upon admission to the psychiatric ward, the pseudopatient ceased simulating *any* symptoms of abnormality. In some cases, there was a brief period of mild nervousness and anxiety, since none of the pseudopatients really believed that they would be admitted so easily. Indeed their shared fear was that they would be immediately exposed as frauds and greatly embarrassed. Moreover, many of them had never visited a psychiatric ward; even those who had, nevertheless, had some genuine fears about what might happen to them. Their nervousness, then, was quite appropriate to the novelty of the hospital setting, and it abated rapidly.

Apart from that short-lived nervousness, the pseudopatient behaved on the ward as he "normally" behaved. The pseudopatient spoke to patients and staff as he might ordinarily. Because there is uncommonly little to do on a psychiatric ward, he attempted to engage others in conversation. When asked by staff how he was feeling, he indicated that he was fine, that he no longer experienced symptoms. He responded to instructions from attendants, to calls for medication (which was not swallowed), and to dining-hall instructions. Beyond such activities as were available to him on the admissions ward, he spent his time writing down his observations about the ward, its patients, and the staff. Initially these notes were written "secretly," but as it soon became clear that no one much cared, they were subsequently written on standard tablets of paper in such public places as the dayroom. No secret was made of these activities.

The pseudopatient, very much as a true psychiatric patient, entered a hospital with no foreknowledge of when he would be discharged. Each was told that he would have to get out by his own devices, essentially by convincing the staff that he was sane. The psychological stresses associated with hospitalization were considerable, and all but one of the pseudopatients desired to be discharged almost immediately after being admitted. They were, therefore, motivated not only to behave sanely, but to be paragons of cooperation. That their behavior was in no way disruptive is confirmed by nursing reports, which have been obtained on most of the patients. These reports uniformly indicate that the patients were "friendly," "cooperative," and "exhibited no abnormal indications."

D. L. Rosenhan

THE NORMAL ARE NOT DETECTABLY SANE

Despite their public "show" of sanity, the pseudopatients were never detected. Admitted, except in one case, with a diagnosis of schizophrenia, each was discharged with a diagnosis of schizophrenia "in remission." The label "in remission" should in no way be dismissed as a formality, for at no time during any hospitalization had any question been raised about any pseudopatient's simulation. Nor are there any indications in the hospital records that the pseudopatient's status was suspect. Rather, the evidence is strong that, once labeled schizophrenic, the pseudopatient was stuck with that label. If the pseudopatient was to be discharged, he must naturally be "in remission"; but he was not sane, nor, in the institution's view, had he ever been sane.

The uniform failure to recognize sanity cannot be attributed to the quality of the hospitals, for, although there were considerable variations among them, several are considered excellent. Nor can it be alleged that there was simply not enough time to observe the pseudopatients. Length of hospitalization ranged from 7 to 52 days, with an average of 19 days. The pseudopatients were not, in fact, carefully observed, but this failure clearly speaks more to traditions within psychiatric hospitals than to lack of opportunity.

Finally, it cannot be said that the failure to recognize the pseudopatients' sanity was due to the fact that they were not behaving sanely. While there was clearly some tension present in all of them, their daily visitors could detect no serious behavioral consequences—nor, indeed, could other patients. It was quite common for the patients to "detect" the pseudopatients' sanity. During the first three hospitalizations, when accurate counts were kept, 35 of a total of 118 patients on the admissions ward voiced their suspicions, some vigorously. "You're not crazy. You're a journalist, or a professor [referring to the continual note-taking]. You're checking up on the hospital." While most of the patients were reassured by the pseudopatient's insistence that he had been sick before he came in but was fine now, some continued to believe that the pseudopatient was sane throughout his hospitalization. The fact that the patients often recognized normality when staff did not raises important questions.

Failure to detect sanity during the course of hospitalization may be due to the fact that physicians operate with a strong bias toward what statisticians call the type 2 error (2). This is to say that physicians are more inclined to call a healthy person sick (a false positive, type 2) than a sick person healthy (a false negative, type 1). The reasons for this are not hard to find: it is clearly more dangerous to misdiagnose illness than health. Better to err on the side of caution, to suspect illness even among the healthy.

But what holds for medicine does not hold equally well for psychiatry. Medical illnesses, while unfortunate, are not commonly pejorative. Psychiatric diagnoses, on the contrary, carry with them personal, legal, and social stigmas (4). . . .

THE STICKINESS OF PSYCHODIAGNOSTIC LABELS

Beyond the tendency to call the healthy sick—a tendency that accounts better for diagnostic behavior on admission than it does for such behavior after a lengthy period of exposure—the data speak to the massive role of labeling in psychiatric assessment. Having once been labeled schizophrenic, there is nothing the pseudopatient can do to overcome this tag. The tag profoundly colors others' perceptions of him and his behavior. . . .

Once a person is designated abnormal, all of his other behaviors and characteristics are colored by that label. Indeed, that label is so powerful that many of the pseudopatients' normal behaviors were overlooked entirely or profoundly misinterpreted. . . .

All pseudopatients took extensive notes publicly. Under ordinary circumstances, such behavior would have raised questions in the minds of observers, as, in fact, it did among patients. Indeed, it seemed so certain that the notes would elicit suspicion that elaborate precautions were taken to remove them from the ward each day. But the precautions proved needless. The closest any staff member came to questioning these notes occurred when one pseudopatient asked his physician what kind of medication he was receiving and began to write down the response. "You needn't write it," he was told gently. "If you have trouble remembering, just ask me again."

If no questions were asked of the pseudopatients, how was their writing interpreted? Nursing records for three patients indicate that the writing was seen as an aspect of their pathological behavior. "Patient engages in writing behavior" was the daily nursing comment on one of the pseudopatients who was never questioned about his writing. Given that the patient is in the hospital, he must be psychologically disturbed. And given that he is disturbed, continuous writing must be a behavioral manifestation of that disturbance, perhaps a subset of the compulsive behaviors that are sometimes correlated with schizophrenia. . . .

A psychiatric label has a life and an influence of its own. Once the impression has been formed that the patient is schizophrenic, the expectation is that he will continue to be schizophrenic. When a sufficient amount of time has passed, during which the patient has done nothing bizarre, he is considered to be in remission and available for discharge. But the label endures beyond discharge, with the unconfirmed expectation that he will behave as a schizophrenic again. Such labels, conferred by mental health professionals, are as influential on the patient as they are on his relatives and friends, and it should not surprise anyone that the diagnosis acts on all of them as a self-fulfilling prophecy. Eventually, the patient himself accepts the diagnosis, with all of its surplus meanings and expectations, and behaves accordingly (5). . . . If it makes no sense to label ourselves permanently depressed on the basis of an occasional depression, then it takes better evidence than is presently available to label all patients insane or schizophrenic on the basis of bizarre behaviors or cognitions. It seems more useful, as Mischel (5) has pointed out, to limit our discussions to *behaviors*, the stimuli that provoke them, and their correlates. . . .

I may hallucinate because I am sleeping, or I may hallucinate because I have ingested a peculiar drug. These are termed sleep-induced hallucinations, or dreams, and drug-induced hallucinations, respectively. But when the stimuli to my hallucinations are unknown, that is called craziness, or schizophrenia—as if that inference were somehow as illuminating as the others. . . .

289

D. L. Rosenhan

SUMMARY AND CONCLUSIONS

It is clear that we cannot distinguish the sane from the insane in psychiatric hospitals. The hospital itself imposes a special environment in which the meanings of behavior can easily be misunderstood. The consequences to patients hospitalized in such an environment—the powerlessness, depersonalization, segregation, mortification, and self-labeling—seem undoubtedly counter-therapeutic.

I do not, even now, understand this problem well enough to perceive solutions. But two matters seem to have some promise. The first concerns the proliferation of community mental health facilities, of crisis intervention centers, of the human potential movement, and of behavior therapies that, for all of their own problems, tend to avoid psychiatric labels, to focus on specific problems and behaviors, and to retain the individual in a relatively nonpejorative environment. Clearly, to the extent that we refrain from sending the distressed to insane places, our impressions of them are less likely to be distorted. (The risk of distorted perceptions, it seems to me, is always present, since we are much more sensitive to an individual's behaviors and verbalizations than we are to the subtle contextual stimuli that often promote them. At issue here is a matter of magnitude. And, as I have shown, the magnitude of distortion is exceedingly high in the extreme context that is a psychiatric hospital).

The second matter that might prove promising speaks to the need to increase the sensitivity of mental health workers and researchers to the *Catch 22* position of psychiatric patients. Simply reading materials in this area will be of help to some such workers and researchers. For others, directly experiencing the impact of psychiatric hospitalization will be of enormous use. Clearly, further research into the social psychology of such total institutions will both facilitate treatment and deepen understanding.

REFERENCES AND NOTES

1. R. Benedict, *J. Gen. Psychol.* **10,** 59 (1934).
2. T. J. Scheff, *Being Mentally Ill: A Sociological Theory* (Aldine, Chicago, 1966).
3. A. Barry, *Bellevue Is a State of Mind* (Harcourt Brace Jovanovich, New York, 1971); . . .
4. J. Cumming and E. Cumming, *Community Ment. Health* **1,** 135 (1965); . . .
5. W. Mischel, *Personality and Assessment* (Wiley, New York, 1968).

Inhibitions, Symptoms and Anxiety

Anxiety is a part of everyone's life. Much of what psychologists know about anxiety has been shaped by the views of Sigmund Freud. Freud developed the psychoanalytic approach to psychological disorders, and anxiety was one of his cornerstones.

Freud (1856–1939), an Austrian neurologist, obtained his M.D. in 1881 from the University of Vienna. Through his medical practice, he began to study patients' mental disorders. In doing so, he employed his theory of psychoanalysis, which emphasizes past experiences and unconscious motivations as the determinants of personality.

This selection is from Freud's book *Inhibitions, Symptoms and Anxiety* (W. W. Norton, 1926). In it, Freud describes the symptoms of anxiety and discusses the functions of anxiety. He argues that anxiety is a reaction to danger and that it occurs whenever one perceives danger. Notice how he focuses on early experiences (e.g., birth) to explain the origins of anxiety. As you read this selection, think about what causes anxiety in your life. What do you think the function of anxiety might be?

Key Concept: anxiety disorders

*A*nxiety . . . is in the first place something that is felt. We call it an affective state, although we are also ignorant of what an affect is. As a feeling, anxiety has a very marked character of unpleasure. But that is not the whole of its quality. Not every unpleasure can be called anxiety, for there are other feelings, such as tension, pain or mourning, which have the character of unpleasure. Thus anxiety must have other distinctive features besides this quality of unpleasure. Can we succeed in understanding the differences between these various unpleasurable affects?

We can at any rate note one or two things about the feeling of anxiety. Its unpleasurable character seems to have a note of its own—something not very obvious, whose presence is difficult to prove yet which is in all likelihood there. But besides having this special feature which is difficult to isolate, we notice that anxiety is accompanied by fairly definite physical sensations which can be referred to particular organs of the body. As we are not concerned here with the physiology of anxiety, we shall content ourselves with mentioning a few representatives of these sensations. The clearest and most frequent ones are those connected with the respiratory organs and with the heart. They provide evidence that motor innervations—that is, processes of discharge—play a part in the general phenomenon of anxiety.

Analysis of anxiety-states therefore reveals the existence of (1) a specific character of unpleasure, (2) acts of discharge and (3) perceptions of those acts. The two last points indicate at once a difference between states of anxiety and other similar states, like those of mourning and pain. The latter do not have any motor manifestation; or if they have, the manifestation is not an integral part of the whole state but is distinct from it as being a result of it or a reaction to it. Anxiety, then, is a special state of unpleasure with acts of discharge along particular paths. In accordance with our general views we should be inclined to think that anxiety is based upon an increase of excitation which on the one hand produces the character of unpleasure and on the other finds relief through the acts of discharge already mentioned. But a purely physiological account of this sort will scarcely satisfy us. We are tempted to assume the presence of a historical factor which binds the sensations of anxiety and its innervations firmly together. We assume, in other words, that an anxiety-state is the reproduction of some experience which contained the necessary conditions for such an increase of excitation and a discharge along particular paths, and that from this circumstance the unpleasure of anxiety receives its specific character. In man, birth provides a prototypic experience of this kind, and we are therefore inclined to regard anxiety-states as a reproduction of the trauma of birth.

This does not imply that anxiety occupies an exceptional position among the affective states. In my opinion the other affects are also reproductions of very early, perhaps even pre-individual, experiences of vital importance; and I should be inclined to regard them as universal, typical and innate hysterical attacks, as compared to the recently and individually acquired attacks which occur in hysterical neuroses and whose origin and significance as mnemic symbols have been revealed by analysis. It would be very desirable, of course, to be able to demonstrate the truth of this view in a number of such affects—a thing which is still very far from being the case.

The view that anxiety goes back to the event of birth raises immediate objections which have to be met. It may be argued that anxiety is a reaction which, in all probability, is common to every organism, certainly every organism of a higher order, whereas birth is only experienced by the mammals; and it is doubtful whether in all of them, even, birth has the significance of a trauma. Therefore there can be anxiety without the prototype of birth. But this objection takes us beyond the barrier that divides psychology from biology. It may be that, precisely because anxiety has an indispensable biological function to fulfil as a reaction to a state of danger, it is differently contrived in different organisms. We do not know, besides, whether anxiety involves the same sensations and innervations in organisms far removed from man as it does in man himself. Thus there is no good argument here against the view that, in man, anxiety is modelled upon the process of birth.

If the structure and origin of anxiety are as described, the next question is: what is the function of anxiety and on what occasions is it reproduced? The answer seems to be obvious and convincing: anxiety arose originally as a reaction to a state of *danger* and it is reproduced whenever a state of that kind recurs.

This answer, however, raises further considerations. The innervations involved in the original state of anxiety probably had a meaning and purpose, in just the same way as the muscular movements which accompany a first hysterical attack. In order to understand a hysterical attack, all one has to do is to look for the situation in which the movements in question formed part of an appropriate and expedient action. Thus at birth it is probable that the innervation, in being directed to the respiratory organs, is preparing the way for the activity of the lungs, and, in accelerating the heartbeat, is helping to keep the blood free from toxic substances. Naturally, when the anxiety-state is reproduced later as an affect it will be lacking in any such expediency, just as are the repetitions of a hysterical attack. When the individual is placed in a new situation of danger it may well be quite inexpedient for him to respond with an anxiety-state (which is a reaction to an earlier danger) instead of initiating a reaction appropriate to the current danger. But his behavior may become expedient once more if the danger-situation is recognized as it approaches and is signalled by an outbreak of anxiety. In that case he can at once get rid of his anxiety by having recourse to more suitable measures. Thus we see that there are two ways in which anxiety can emerge: in an inexpedient way, when a new situation of danger has occurred, or in an expedient way in order to give a signal and prevent such a situation from occurring.

But what is a 'danger'? In the act of birth there is a real danger to life. We know what this means objectively; but in a psychological sense it says nothing at all to us. The danger of birth has as yet no psychical content. We cannot possibly suppose that the foetus has any sort of knowledge that there is a possibility of its life being destroyed. It can only be aware of some vast disturbance in the economy of its narcissistic libido. Large sums of excitation crowd in upon it, giving rise to new kinds of feelings of unpleasure, and some organs acquire an increased cathexis, thus foreshadowing the object-cathexis which will soon set in. What elements in all this will be made use of as the sign of a 'danger-situation'?

Unfortunately far too little is known about the mental make-up of a newborn baby to make a direct answer possible. I cannot even vouch for the validity of the description I have just given. It is easy to say that the baby will repeat its affect of anxiety in every situation which recalls the event of birth. The important thing to know is what recalls the event and what it is that is recalled.

All we can do is to examine the occasions on which infants in arms or somewhat older children show readiness to produce anxiety. In his book on the trauma of birth, Rank (1924) has made a determined attempt to establish a relationship between the earliest phobias of children and the impressions made on them by the event of birth. But I do not think he has been successful. His theory is open to two objections. In the first place, he assumes that the infant has received certain sensory impressions, in particular of a visual kind, at the time of birth, the renewal of which can recall to its memory the trauma of birth and thus evoke a reaction of anxiety. This assumption is quite unfounded and extremely improbable. It is not credible that a child should retain any but tactile and general sensations relating to the process of birth. If, later on, children show fear of small animals that disappear into holes or emerge from them, this reaction, according to Rank, is due to their perceiving an analogy. But it is an analogy of which they cannot be aware. In the second place, in considering these later anxiety-situations Rank dwells, as suits him best, now on the child's recollection of its happy intra-uterine existence, now on its recollection of the traumatic disturbance which interrupted that existence—which leaves the door wide open for arbitrary interpretation. There are, moreover, certain examples of childhood anxiety which directly traverse his theory. When, for instance, a child is left alone in the dark one would expect it, according to his view, to welcome the re-establishment of the intra-uterine situation; yet it is precisely on such occasions that the child reacts with anxiety. And if this is explained by saying that the child is being reminded of the interruption which the event of birth made in its intra-uterine happiness, it becomes impossible to shut one's eyes any longer to the far-fetched character of such explanations.

I am driven to the conclusion that the earliest phobias of infancy cannot be directly traced back to impressions of the act of birth and that so far they have not been explained. A certain preparedness for anxiety is undoubtedly present in the infant in arms. But this preparedness for anxiety, instead of being at its maximum immediately after birth and then slowly decreasing, does not emerge till later, as mental development proceeds, and lasts over a certain period of childhood. If these early phobias persist beyond that period one is inclined to suspect the presence of a neurotic disturbance, although it is not at all clear what their relation is to the undoubted neuroses that appear later on in childhood.

Only a few of the manifestations of anxiety in children are comprehensible to us, and we must confine our attention to them. They occur, for instance, when a child is alone, or in the dark, or when it finds itself with an unknown person instead of one to whom it is used—such as its mother. These three instances can be reduced to a single condition—namely, that of missing someone who is loved and longed for. But here, I think, we have the key to an understanding of anxiety and to a reconciliation of the contradictions that seem to beset it.

The child's mnemic image of the person longed for is no doubt intensely cathected, probably in a hallucinatory way at first. But this has no effect; and now it seems as though the longing turns into anxiety. This anxiety has all the appearance of being an expression of the child's feeling at its wits' end, as though in its still very undeveloped state it did not know how better to cope with its cathexis of longing. Here anxiety appears as a reaction to the felt loss of the object; and we are at once reminded of the fact that castration anxiety, too, is a fear of being separated from a highly valued object, and that the earliest anxiety of all—the 'primal anxiety' of birth—is brought about on the occasion of a separation from the mother.

But a moment's reflection takes us beyond this question of loss of object. The reason why the infant in arms wants to perceive the presence of its mother is only because it already knows by experience that she satisfies all its needs without delay. The situation, then, which it regards as a 'danger' and against which it wants to be safeguarded is that of non-satisfaction, of a *growing tension due to need*, against which it is helpless. I think that if we adopt this view all the facts fall into place. The situation of non-satisfaction in which the amounts of stimulation rise to an unpleasurable height without its being possible for them to be mastered psychically or discharged must for the infant be analogous to the experience of being born—must be a repetition of the situation of danger. What both situations have in common is the economic disturbance caused by an accumulation of amounts of stimulation which require to be disposed of. It is this factor, then, which is the real essence of the 'danger'. In both cases the reaction of anxiety sets in. (This reaction is still an expedient one in the infant in arms, for the discharge, being directed into the respiratory and vocal muscular apparatus, now calls its mother to it, just as it activated the lungs of the new-born baby to get rid of the internal stimuli.) It is unnecessary to suppose that the child carries anything more with it from the time of its birth than this way of indicating the presence of danger.

When the infant has found out by experience that an external, perceptible object can put an end to the dangerous situation which is reminiscent of birth, the content of the danger it fears is displaced from the economic situation on to the condition which determined that situation, viz., the loss of object. It is the absence of the mother that is now the danger; and as soon as that danger arises the infant gives the signal of anxiety, before the dreaded economic situation has set in. This change constitutes a first great step forward in the provision made by the infant for its self-preservation, and at the same time represents a transition from the automatic and involuntary fresh appearance of anxiety to the intentional reproduction of anxiety as a signal of danger.

13.3 MARTIN E. P. SELIGMAN

Depression

Depression is a very serious mental disorder, and a number of different theoretical explanations of depression have been proposed. In the mid-1970s, Martin E. P. Seligman proposed the learned helplessness model of depression. This theory suggests that when people come to feel that they have no control over a situation, they feel helpless and tend to give up; they passively accept adverse stimuli. This helplessness can lead to depression.

Seligman (b. 1942) received his Ph.D. in psychology in 1967 from the University of Pennsylvania, where he is currently a professor of psychology. In addition to depression, Seligman has also had an impact on psychology in the areas of learning theory, phobias, and personality and adjustment.

This selection is from chapter 5, "Depression," of Seligman's *Helplessness: On Depression, Development, and Death* (W. H. Freeman, 1975). In it, Seligman describes the causes of, consequences of, and treatments for learned helplessness. Note the emphasis Seligman places on common, everyday occurrences and their role in inducing helplessness. As you read this selection, consider how you react to frustrating situations.

Key Concept: learned helplessness

*L*earned helplessness is caused by learning that responding is independent of reinforcement; so the model suggests that the cause of depression is the belief that action is futile. What kind of events set off reactive depressions? Failure at work and school, death of a loved one, rejection or separation from friends and loved ones, physical disease, financial difficulty, being faced with insoluble problems, and growing old. There are many others, but this list captures the flavor.

I believe that what links these experiences and lies at the heart of depression is unitary: the depressed patient believes or has learned that he cannot control those elements of his life that relieve suffering, bring gratification, or provide nurture—in short, he believes that he is helpless. Consider a few of the precipitating events: What is the meaning of job failure or incompetence at school? Often it means that all of a person's efforts have been in vain, that his responses have failed to achieve his desires. When an individual is rejected by someone he loves, he can no longer control this significant source of gratification and support. When a parent or lover dies, the bereaved is powerless to elicit love from the dead person. Physical disease and growing old are helpless conditions par excellence; the person finds his own responses ineffective and is thrown upon the care of others.

Endogenous depressions [caused by internal factors], while not set off by an explicit helplessness-inducing event, also may involve the belief in helplessness. I suspect that a continuum of susceptibility to this belief may underlie the endogenous-reactive continuum. At the extreme endogenous end, the slightest obstacle will trigger in the depressive a vicious circle of beliefs in how ineffective he is. At the extreme reactive ends, a sequence of disastrous events in which a person is actually helpless is necessary to force the belief that responding is useless. . . .

Is depression a cognitive or an emotional disorder? Neither and both. Clearly, cognitions of helplessness lower mood, and a lowered mood, which may be brought about physiologically, increases susceptibility to cognitions of helplessness; indeed, this is the most insidious vicious circle in depression. In the end, I believe that the cognition-emotion distinction in depression will be untenable. Cognition and emotion need not be separable entities in nature simply because our language separates them. When depression is observed close up, the exquisite interdependence of feelings and thought is undeniable: one does not *feel* depressed without depressing thoughts, nor does one have depressing thoughts without feeling depressed. I suggest that it is a failure of language, not a failure of understanding, that has fostered the confusion about whether depression is a cognitive or an emotional disorder. . . .

In the last few years, many of my students have come to tell me that they felt depressed. Often they attributed their depression to their belief that life had no intrinsic meaning, that the Vietnam war would never end, that the poor and the black are oppressed, or that our leaders are corrupt. These are legitimate concerns and to devote so much thought and energy to them is certainly justifiable. But was the feeling, the actual depression, caused directly by these issues? Clearly, for a poor person, a black, or a student about to be drafted, these propositions could directly cause depression. But most of those I saw were neither poor, nor black, nor about to be drafted; these propositions were remote from their daily lives. Yet they said they were depressed about them—not just concerned or angry, but depressed. To me, this meant that they were feeling bad about something much closer to home, bad about themselves, their capacities, and their daily lives. Such existential depressions are rampant today, I daresay much more than when I was a student ten years ago.

At first it seems paradoxical. More of the good things of life are available now than ever before: more sex, more records, more intellectual stimulation, more books, more buying power. On the other hand, there have always been wars, oppression, corruption, and absurdity; the human condition has been pretty stable along these lines. Why should this particularly fortunate generation find itself especially depressed?

I think the answer may lie in the lack of contingency between the actions of these students and the good things, as well as the negative events, that came their way. These reinforcers came about less through the efforts of the young individuals who benefited from them, than because our society is affluent.

They have experienced a minimum of hard work followed by reward. From where does one get a sense of power, worth, and self-esteem? Not from what he owns, but from long experience watching his own actions change the world.

I am claiming, then, that not only trauma occurring independently of response, but noncontingent *positive* events, can produce helplessness and depression. After all, what is the evolutionary significance of mood? Presumably sentient organisms could just as well be constructed without mood—complex computers are. What selective pressure produced feeling and affect? It may be that the hedonic [pleasure] system evolved to goad and fuel instrumental action. I suggest that joy accompanies and motivates effective responding; and that in the absence of effective responding, an aversive state arises, which organisms seek to avoid. It is called depression. It is highly significant that when rats and pigeons are given a choice between getting free food and getting the same food for making responses, they choose to work. Infants smile at a mobile whose movements are contingent on their responses, but not at a noncontingent mobile. Do hunters hunt from a lust to kill or mountain climbers scale peaks for glory? I think not. These activities, because they entail effective instrumental responding, produce joy.

Dysphoria [a state of feeling unwell or unhappy] produced by the cessation of effective responding may explain "success depression." Not infrequently, when a person finally achieves a goal toward which he has been striving for years, depression ensues. Officials elected to public office after arduous campaigns, presidents of the American Psychological Association, successful novelists, and even men who land on the moon can become severely depressed soon after achieving the pinnacle. For a theory of depression by loss of reinforcers, these depressions are paradoxical, since successful individuals continue to receive most of their old reinforcers, plus more new reinforcers than ever before.

This phenomenon is not a paradox for the theory of helplessness. Depressed, successful people tell you that they are now rewarded not for what they're doing, but for who they are or what they *have* done. Having achieved the goal that they strove for, their rewards now come independently of any ongoing instrumental activity. . . .

In summary, I suggest that what produces self-esteem and a sense of competence, and protects against depression, is not only the absolute quality of experience, but the perception that one's own actions controlled the experience. To the degree that uncontrollable events occur, either traumatic or positive, depression will be predisposed and ego strength undermined. To the degree that controllable events occur, a sense of mastery and resistance to depression will result.

CURE OF DEPRESSION AND LEARNED HELPLESSNESS

Forced exposure to the fact that responding produces reinforcement is the most effective way of breaking up learned helplessness. Helplessness also dissipates in *time*. Furthermore, two physiological therapies seem to have an effect: electroconvulsive shock (ECS) broke up helplessness in three out of six dogs, and atropine cannulated to the septum broke it up in cats.

There is no scientifically established panacea for depression. Left alone, depression often dissipates in a few weeks or months; but there are therapies that are reported to alleviate depression and that are consistent with the theory of learned helplessness. According to this view, the central goal in successful therapy should be to have the patient come to believe that his responses produce the gratification he desires—that he is, in short, an effective human being. . . .

A. T. Beck's (1970, 1971) cognitive therapy is aimed at similar goals. In his view, successful manipulations change the negative cognitive set to a more positive one: he argues that the primary task of the therapist is to change the negative expectation of the depressed patient to a more optimistic one, in which the patient comes to believe that his responses will produce the outcomes he wants. . . .

Other therapies are claimed to be successful in alleviating depression and providing the patient with control over important outcomes. The "Tuscaloosa Plan" of a Veterans Administration hospital in Alabama puts severely depressed patients in an "anti-depression room." In this room the patient is subjected to an attitude of "kind firmness": He is told to sand a block of wood, and then reprimanded when he sands against the grain. He then sands with the grain, only to be reprimanded for that. Alternatively, he is told to begin counting about a million little seashells scattered about the room. This systematic harassment continues until the depressed patient finally tells the guard "Get off my back!" or says something like "I've counted my last seashell." He is then promptly let out of the room with apologies. The patient has been forced to emit one of the most powerful responses people have for controlling others—anger, and when this response is dragged out of his depleted repertoire, he is powerfully reinforced. This breaks up depression—lastingly.

Gradual exposure to the response-reinforcement contingencies of work reinforces active behaviors, and may be effective against depression. In a graded-task treatment of depression, E. P. Burgess (1968) first had her patients emit some minimal bit of behavior, like making a telephone call. She emphasizes that it is crucial that the patient succeed, rather than just start and give up. The task requirements were then increased, and the patient was reinforced for successfully completing the tasks by the attention and interest of the therapist. . . .

Individuals often adopt their own strategies for dealing with their own minor depressions. Asking for help and getting it or helping someone else (even caring for a pet) are two strategies that entail gaining control and may alleviate minor depressions. . . .

Many therapies . . . claim to be able to cure depression. But we do not yet have sufficient evidence from well-controlled studies to evaluate the effectiveness of any form of psychotherapy for depression. The evidence I have presented is selected: only those treatments that seem compatible with helplessness were discussed. It is possible that when other therapies work it is because they, too, restore the patient's sense of efficacy. What is needed now is experimental evidence isolating the effective variable in the psychological treatment of depression. It is also essential that untreated control groups be run, since depression dissipates in time, of its own accord.

PREVENTION OF DEPRESSION AND LEARNED HELPLESSNESS

Learned helplessness can be prevented if the subject first masters outcomes before being exposed to their uncontrollability. Can depression be prevented? Almost everyone loses control over some of the outcomes that are significant to him: parents die, loved ones reject him, failure occurs. Everyone becomes at least mildly and transiently depressed in the wake of such events, but why are some people hospitalized by depression for long periods, and others so resilient? . . .

The life histories of those individuals who are particularly resistant to depression, or resilient from depression, may have been filled with mastery; these people may have had extensive experience controlling and manipulating the sources of reinforcement in their lives, and may therefore see the future optimistically. Those people who are particularly susceptible to depression may have had lives relatively devoid of mastery; their lives may have been full of situations in which they were helpless to influence their sources of suffering and relief. . . .

A caveat is in order here, however. While it seems reasonable that extended experience with controllable outcomes will make a person more resilient from depression, how about the person who has met only with success? Is a person whose responses have always succeeded especially susceptible to depression when confronted with situations beyond his control? We all know of people who were stunningly successful in high school, but who collapsed on encountering their first failure in college. Everyone eventually confronts failure and anxiety; too much success with controlling reinforcers, just like too little, might not allow the development and use of responses for coping with failure.

Successful therapy should be preventative. Therapy must not focus just on undoing past problems; it should also arm the patient against future depressions. Would therapy for depression be more successful if it strove explicitly to provide the patient with a wide repertoire of coping responses that he could use at times when he found his usual responses ineffective?

CHAPTER 14

Therapy

14.1 TEODORO AYLLON

Intensive Treatment of Psychotic Behaviour by Stimulus Satiation and Food Reinforcement

Behavior therapy—the application of reinforcement and punishment to modify behavior—became popular in the 1960s. Today there are many kinds of behavior therapy (behavior modification) methods available.

Researcher Teodoro Ayllon (b. 1929) was instrumental in the development of behavior therapy: he was the first to demonstrate how reinforcement could be used to successfully treat mental patients. One of his best-known books is *The Token Economy: A Motivational System for Therapy and Rehabilitation* (1968), coauthored with Nathan Azrin, which describes an early study in behavior therapy in which the authors awarded tokens that were redeemable for privileges to mental patients who demonstrated desired behaviors.

This selection is from "Intensive Treatment of Psychotic Behaviour by Stimulus Satiation and Food Reinforcement," which was published in *Be-*

haviour Research and Therapy in 1963. It is based on a research project conducted by Ayllon at the Saskatchewan Hospital in Weyburn, Saskatchewan, Canada. This selection describes three experiments in behavior therapy that were conducted with one mental patient. Note that Ayllon focuses on one specific behavior at a time. As you read this selection, think about how you might use behavior modification techniques to eliminate unwanted traits in yourself or someone you know.

Key Concept: behavior therapy

INTRODUCTION

Until recently, the effective control of behaviour was limited to the animal laboratory. The extension of this control to human behaviour was made when Lindsley successfully adapted the methodology of operant conditioning to the study of psychotic behaviour (Lindsley, 1956). Following Lindsley's point of departure other investigators have shown that, in its essentials, the behaviour of mental defective individuals (Orlando and Bijou, 1960), stutterers (Flanagan, Goldiamond and Azrin, 1958), mental patients (Hutchinson and Azrin, 1961), autistic (Ferster and DeMyer, 1961), and normal children (Bijou, 1961; Azrin and Lindsley, 1956) is subject to the same controls.

Despite the obvious implications of this research for applied settings there has been a conspicuous lag between the research findings and their application. The greatest limitation to the direct application of laboratory principles has been the absence of control over the subjects' environment. Recently, however, a series of applications in a regulated psychiatric setting has clearly demonstrated the possibilities of behavioural modification (Ayllon and Michael, 1959; Ayllon and Haughton, 1962). Some of the behaviour studied has included repetitive and highly stereotyped responses such as complaining, pacing, refusal to eat, hoarding and many others.

What follows is a demonstration of behaviour techniques for the intensive individual treatment of psychotic behaviour. Specific pathological behaviour patterns of a single patient were treated by manipulating the patient's environment.

The Experimental Ward and Control Over the Reinforcement

This investigation was conducted in a mental hospital ward, the characteristics of which have been described elsewhere (Ayllon and Haughton, 1962). Briefly, this was a female ward to which only authorized personnel were allowed access. The ward staff was made up of psychiatric nurses and untrained aides who carried out the environmental manipulations under the direction of the experimenter. Using a time-sample technique, patients were observed daily every 30 minutes from 7:00 A.M. to 11:00 P.M.

The dining room was the only place where food was available and entrance to the dining room could be regulated. Water was freely available at a drinking fountain on the ward. None of the patients had ground passes or jobs outside the ward.

Subject

The patient was a 47-year-old female patient diagnosed as a chronic schizophrenic. The patient had been hospitalized for 9 years. Upon studying the patient's behaviour on the ward, it became apparent that the nursing staff spent considerable time caring for her. In particular, there were three aspects of her behaviour which seemed to defy solution. The first was stealing food. The second was the hoarding of the ward's towels in her room. The third undesirable aspect of her behaviour consisted in her wearing excessive clothing, e.g. a half-dozen dresses, several pairs of stockings, sweaters, and so on.

In order to modify the patient's behaviour systematically, each of these three types of behaviour (stealing food, hoarding, and excessive dressing) was treated separately.

EXPERIMENT I

Control of Stealing Food by Food Withdrawal

The patient had weighed over 250 pounds for many years. She ate the usual tray of food served to all patients, but, in addition, she stole food from the food counter and from other patients. Because the medical staff regarded her excessive weight as detrimental to her health, a special diet had been prescribed for her. However, the patient refused to diet and continued stealing food. In an effort to discourage the patient from stealing, the ward nurses had spent considerable time trying to persuade her to stop stealing food. As a last resort, the nurses would force her to return the stolen food.

To determine the extent of food stealing, nurses were instructed to record all behaviour associated with eating in the dining room. This record, taken for nearly a month, showed that the patient stole food during two thirds of all meals.

Procedure

The traditional methods previously used to stop the patient from stealing food were discontinued. No longer were persuasion, coaxing, or coercion used.

The patient was assigned to a table in the dining room, and no other patients were allowed to sit with her. Nurses removed the patient from the dining room when she approached a table other than her own, or when she picked up unauthorized food from the dining room counter. In effect, this procedure resulted in the patient missing a meal whenever she attempted to steal food.

Results

... [W]hen withdrawal of positive reinforcement (i.e. meal) was made dependent upon the patient's 'stealing', this response was eliminated in two weeks. Because the patient no longer stole food, she ate only the diet prescribed for her. The effective control of the stealing response is also indicated by the gradual reduction in the patient's body weight. At no time during the patient's 9 years of hospitalization had she weighed less than 230 pounds. . . . [A]t the conclusion of this treatment her weight stabilized at 180 pounds or 17 per cent loss from her original weight. At this time, the patient's physical condition was regarded as excellent.

Discussion

A principle used in the laboratory shows that the strength of a response may be weakened by the removal of positive reinforcement following the response (Ferster, 1958). In this case, the response was food-stealing and the reinforcer was access to meals. When the patient stole food she was removed from the dining room and missed her meal.

After one year of this treatment, two occasions of food stealing occurred. The first occasion, occurring after one year of not stealing food, took the nurses by surprise and, therefore the patient 'got away' with it. The second occasion occurred shortly thereafter. This time, however, the controlling consequences were in force. The patient missed that meal and did not steal again to the conclusion of this investigation.

Because the patient was not informed or warned of the consequences that followed stealing, the nurses regarded the procedure as unlikely to have much effect on the patient's behaviour. The implicit belief that verbal instructions are indispensable for learning is part of present day psychiatric lore. In keeping with this notion, prior to this behaviour treatment, the nurses had tried to persuade the patient to co-operate in dieting. Because there were strong medical reasons for her losing weight, the patient's refusal to follow a prescribed diet was regarded as further evidence of her mental illness.

EXPERIMENT II

Control of One Form of Hoarding Behaviour Through Stimulus Satiation

During the 9 years of hospitalization, the patient collected large numbers of towels and stored them in her room. Although many efforts had been made to discourage hoarding, this behaviour continued unaltered. The only recourse for the nursing staff was to take away the patient's towels about twice a week.

To determine the degree of hoarding behaviour, the towels in her room were counted three times a week, when the patient was not in her room. This count showed that the number of towels kept in her room ranged from 19 to 29 despite the fact that during this time the nurses continued recovering their towel supply from the patient's room.

Procedure

The routine removal of the towels from the patient's room was discontinued. Instead, a programme of stimulus satiation was carried out by the nurses. Intermittently, throughout the day, the nurses took a towel to the patient when she was in her room and simply handed it to her without any comment. The first week she was given an average of 7 towels daily, and by the third week this number was increased to 60.

Results

The technique of satiation eliminated the towel hoarding. Figure 1 shows the mean number of towels per count found in the patient's room. When the number of towels kept in her room reached the 625 mark, she started taking a few of them out. Thereafter, no more towels were given to her. During the next 12 months the mean number of towels found in her room was 1–5 per week. . . .

Discussion

The procedure used to reduce the amount of towel hoarding bears resemblance to satiation of a reinforcer. A reinforcer loses its effect when an excessive amount of that reinforcer is made available. Accordingly, the response maintained by that reinforcer is weakened. In this application, the towels constituted the reinforcing stimuli. When the number of towels in her room reached 625, continuing to give her towels seemed to make their collection aversive. The patient then proceeded to rid herself of the towels until she had virtually none.

During the first few weeks of satiation, the patient was observed patting her cheeks with a few towels, apparently enjoying them. Later, the patient was observed spending much of her time folding and stacking the approximately 600 towels in her room. A variety of remarks were made by the patient regarding receipt of towels. All verbal statements made by the patient were recorded by the nurse. The following represent typical remarks made during this experiment. First week: As the nurse entered the patient's room carrying a towel, the patient would smile and say, "Oh, you found it for me, thank you". Second week: When the number of towels given to patient increased rapidly, she told the nurses, "Don't give me no more towels. I've got enough". Third week: "Take them towels away. . . . I can't sit

FIGURE 1

305

A response, towel hoarding, is eliminated when the patient is given towels in excess. When the number of towels reaches 625 the patient starts to discard them. She continues to do so until the number found in her room averages 1–5 compared to the previous 20 towels per week.

here all night and fold towels". Fourth and fifth weeks: "Get these dirty towels out of here". Sixth week: After she had started taking the towels out of her room, she remarked to the nurse, "I can't drag any more of these towels, I just can't do it".

The quality of these remarks suggests that the initial effect of giving towels to the patient was reinforcing. However as the towels increased they ceased to be reinforcing, and presumably became aversive.

The ward nurses, who had undergone a three year training in psychiatric nursing, found it difficult to reconcile the procedure in this experiment with their psychiatric orientation. Most nurses subscribed to the popular psychiatric view which regards hoarding behaviour as a reflection of a deep 'need' for love and security. Presumably, no 'real' behavioural change was possible without meeting the patient's 'needs' first. Even after the patient discontinued hoarding towels in her room, some nurses predicted that the change would not last and that worse behaviour would replace it. Using a time-sampling technique the patient was under continuous observation for over a year after the termination of the satiation programme. Not once during this period did the patient return to hoarding towels. Furthermore, no other behaviour problem replaced hoarding.

EXPERIMENT III

Control of an Additional Form of Hoarding Through Food Reinforcement

Shortly after the patient had been admitted to the hospital she wore an excessive amount of clothing which included several sweaters, shawls, dresses, undergarments and stockings. The clothing also included sheets and towels wrapped around her body, and a turban-like head-dress made up of several towels. In addition, the patient carried two to three cups on one hand while holding a bundle of miscellaneous clothing, and a large purse on the other.

To determine the amount of clothing worn by the patient, she was weighed before each meal over a period of two weeks. By subtracting her actual body weight from that recorded when she was dressed, the weight of her clothing was obtained.

Procedure

The response required for reinforcement was stepping on a scale and meeting a predetermined weight. The requirement for reinforcement consisted of meeting a single weight (i.e. her body weight plus a specified number of pounds of clothing). Initially she was given an allowance of 23 pounds over her current body weight. This allowance represented a 2 pound reduction from her usual clothing weight. When the patient exceeded the weight requirement, the nurse stated in a matter-of-fact manner, "Sorry, you weigh too much, you'll have to weigh less". Failure to meet the required weight resulted in the patient missing the meal at which she was being weighed. Sometimes, in an effort to meet the requirement, the patient discarded more clothing than she was required. When this occurred the requirement was adjusted at the next weighing-time to correspond to the limit set by the patient on the preceding occasion.

Results

When food reinforcement is made dependent upon the removal of superfluous clothing the response increases in frequency. Figure 2 shows that the patient gradually shed her clothing to meet the more demanding weight requirement until she dressed normally. At the conclusion of this experiment her clothes weighed 3 pounds compared to the 25 pounds she wore before this treatment.

Some verbal shaping was done in order to encourage the patient to leave the cups and bundles she carried with her. Nurses stopped her at the dining room and said, "Sorry, no things are allowed in the dining room". No mention of clothing or specific items was made to avoid focusing undue attention upon

FIGURE 2

307

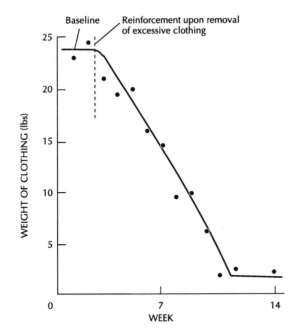

A response, excessive dressing, is eliminated when food reinforcement is made dependent upon removal of superfluous clothing. Once the weight of the clothing worn by the patient drops to 3 pounds it remains stable.

them. Within a week, the patient typically stepped on the scale without her bundle and assorted objects. When her weight was over the limit, the patient was informed that she weighed "too much". She then proceeded to take off a few clothes, stepped on the scale again, and upon meeting the weight requirement, gained access to the dining room. . . .

Discussion

According to the principle of reinforcement a class of responses is strengthened when it is followed by reinforcement. A reinforcer is such when it results in a response increase. In this application the removal of excessive clothing constituted the response and the reinforcer was food (i.e. access to meals). When the patient met the weight requirement she was reinforced by being given access to meals.

At the start of this experiment, the patient missed a few meals because she failed to meet the weight requirement, but soon thereafter she gradually discarded her superfluous clothing. First, she left behind odd items she had carried in her arms, such as bundles, cups and handbags. Next she took off the elaborate headgear and assorted capes or shawls she had worn over her shoulders. Although she had worn 18 pairs of stockings at one time, she eventually shed these also.

During the initial part of this experiment, the patient showed some emotional behaviour, e.g. crying, shouting and throwing chairs around. Because nurses were instructed to "ignore" this emotional behaviour, the patient obtained no sympathy or attention from them. The withholding of social reinforcement for emotional behaviour quickly led to its elimination.

At the conclusion of this behaviour treatment, the patient typically stepped on the scale wearing a dress, undergarments, a pair of stockings and a pair of light shoes. One of the behavioural changes concomitant with the current environmental manipulation was that as the patient began dressing normally she started to participate in small social events in the hospital. This was particularly new to the patient as she had previously remained seclusive spending most of the time in her room.

About this time the patient's parents came to visit her and insisted on taking her home for a visit. This was the first time during the patient's 9 years of hospitalization that her parents had asked to take her out. They remarked that previously they had not been interested in taking her out because the patient's excessive dressing in addition to her weight made her look like a "circus freak".

CONCLUSIONS

The research presented here was conducted under nearly ideal conditions. The variables manipulated (i.e. towels and food) were under full experimental control. Using a time-sample technique the patient was observed daily every 30 minutes from 7.00 A.M. to 11:00 P.M. Nurses and aides carried out these observations which were later analysed in terms of gross behaviour categories. These observations were in force for over a year during which time these three experiments were conducted. The results of these observations indicate that none of the three pathological behaviour patterns (i.e. food stealing, hoarding and excessive dressing) exhibited by the patient were replaced by any undesirable behaviour.

The patient displayed some emotional behaviour in each experiment, but each time it subsided when social reinforcement (i.e. attention) was not forthcoming. The patient did not become violent or seclusive as a consequence of these experiments. Instead, she became socially more accessible to patients and staff. She did not achieve a great deal of social success but she did begin to participate actively in social functions.

A frequent problem encountered in mental hospitals is overeating. In general this problem is solved by prescribing a reduction diet. Many patients, however, refuse to take a reduction diet and continue overeating. When confronted with this behaviour, psychiatric workers generally resort to two types of explanations.

One explanation of overeating points out that only with the active and sincere cooperation of the patient can weight reduction be accomplished. When the patient refuses to co-operate he is regarded as showing more signs of mental illness and all hopes of eliminating overeating come to an end.

Another type of explanation holds that overeating is not the behaviour to be concerned with. Instead, attention is focused on the psychological 'needs' of the patient. These 'needs' are said to be the cause of the observable behaviour, overeating. Therefore the emphasis is on the removal of the cause and not on the symptom or behaviour itself. Whatever theoretical merit these explanations may have, it is unfortunate that they fail to suggest practical ways of treating the behaviour itself. As a consequence, the patient continues to overeat often to the detriment of his health.

The current psychiatric emphasis on the resolution of the mental conflict that is presumably at the basis of the symptoms, is perhaps misplaced. What seems to have been forgotten is that behaviour problems such as those reported here, prevent the patient from being considered for discharge not only by the hospital personnel but also by the patient's relatives. Indeed, as far as the patient's relatives are concerned, the index of improvement or deterioration is the readily observable behaviour and not a detailed account of the mechanics of the mental apparatus.

Many individuals are admitted to mental hospitals because of one or more specific behaviour difficulties and not always because of a generalized 'mental' disturbance. For example, an individual may go into a mental hospital because he has refused to eat for several days, or because he talks to himself incessantly. If the goal of therapy were behavioural rehabilitation, these problems would be treated and normal eating and normal talking reinstated. However, the current emphasis in psychotherapy is on 'mental-conflict resolution' and little or no attention is given to dealing directly with the behavioural problems which prevent the patient from returning to the community.

REFERENCES

Ayllon, T. and Michael, J. (1959) The psychiatric nurse as a behavioural engineer. *J. exp. anal. Behav.* **2,** 323–334.

Ayllon, T. and Haughton, E. (1962) Control of the behaviour of schizophrenic patients by food. *J. Exp. anal. Behav.* **5,** 343–352.

Azrin, N. and Lindsley, O. (1956) The reinforcement of cooperation between children. *J. abnorm. (soc.) Psychol.* **52,** 100–102.

Bijou, S. (1961) Discrimination performance as a baseline for individual analysis of young children. *Child Develpm.* **32,** 160–163.

Ferster, C. B. (1958) Control of behaviour in chimpanzees and pigeons by time out from positive reinforcement. *Psychol. Monogr.* **72,** 1–38.

Ferster, C. and DeMyer, M. (1961) The development of performances in autistic children in an automatically controlled environment. *J. chron. Dis.* **13,** 312–345.

Flanagan, B., Goldiamond, I. and Azrin, N. (1958) Operant stuttering: The control of stuttering behaviour through response-contingent consequences. *J. exp. anal. Behav.* **56,** 49–56.

Hutchinson, R. R. and Azrin, N. H. (1961) Conditioning of mental hospital patients to fixed-ratio schedules of reinforcement. *J. exp. anal. Behav.* **4,** 87–95.

Lindsley, O. R. (1956) Operant conditioning methods applied to research in chronic schizophrenia. *Psychiat. Res. Rep.* **5,** 118–139.

Orlando, R. and Bijou, S. (1960) Single and multiple schedules of reinforcement in developmentally retarded children. *J. exp. anal. Behav.* **3,** 339–348.

14.2 CARL R. ROGERS

Some Hypotheses Regarding the Facilitation of Personal Growth

Insight therapy is designed to help people gain an understanding of who they are and why they feel the way they do. One popular type of insight therapy is person-centered therapy (formerly called "client-centered therapy"), which was founded by Carl R. Rogers. The main assumption of person-centered therapy is that everyone has the capacity to be psychologically healthy. The therapist's role is to provide a warm, nondirective atmosphere, to draw out the client's thoughts and feelings, and to help the client accept his or her true self.

Rogers (1902–1987), who helped develop the humanistic approach to psychology, earned his Ph.D. in clinical psychology from Columbia University in 1931. He taught at Ohio State University, the University of Chicago, and the University of Wisconsin before establishing the Center for Studies of the Person in La Jolla, California. Rogers wrote numerous books, including *Client-Centered Therapy* (Houghton Mifflin, 1951) and *A Way of Being* (Houghton Mifflin, 1980).

This selection is from chapter 2, "Some Hypotheses Regarding the Facilitation of Personal Growth," of *On Becoming a Person: A Therapist's View of Psychotherapy* (Houghton Mifflin, 1961). In this chapter, which is based on a talk that he gave at Oberlin College in Ohio in 1954, Rogers presents the core characteristics of the person-centered approach to therapy and tries to present his approach in an understandable fashion. As you read this selection, consider how the core characteristics of the person-centered relationship might be used to help foster personal growth in normal individuals.

Key Concept: person-centered therapy

To be faced by a troubled, conflicted person who is seeking and expecting help, has always constituted a great challenge to me. Do I have the knowledge, the resources, the psychological strength, the skill—do I have whatever it takes to be of help to such an individual?

For more than twenty-five years I have been trying to meet this kind of challenge. It has caused me to draw upon every element of my professional background: the rigorous methods of personality measurement which I first learned at Teachers' College, Columbia; the Freudian psychoanalytic insights and methods of the Institute for Child Guidance where I worked as interne; the continuing developments in the field of clinical psychology, with which I have been closely associated; the briefer exposure to the work of Otto Rank, to the methods of psychiatric social work, and other resources too numerous to mention. But most of all it has meant a continual learning from my own experience and that of my colleagues at the Counseling Center as we have endeavored to discover for ourselves effective means of working with people in distress. Gradually I have developed a way of working which grows out of that experience, and which can be tested, refined, and reshaped by further experience and by research.

A GENERAL HYPOTHESIS

One brief way of describing the change which has taken place in me is to say that in my early professional years I was asking the question, How can I treat, or cure, or change this person? Now I would phrase the question in this way: How can I provide a relationship which this person may use for his own personal growth?

It is as I have come to put the question in this second way that I realize that whatever I have learned is applicable to all of my human relationships, not just to working with clients with problems. It is for this reason that I feel it is possible that the learnings which have had meaning for me in my experience may have some meaning for you in your experience, since all of us are involved in human relationships.

Perhaps I should start with a negative learning. It has gradually been driven home to me that I cannot be of help to this troubled person by means of any intellectual or training procedure. No approach which relies upon knowledge upon training, upon the acceptance of something that is *taught*, is of any use. These approaches seem so tempting and direct that I have, in the past, tried a great many of them. It is possible to explain a person to himself, to prescribe steps which should lead him forward, to train him in knowledge about a more satisfying mode of life. But such methods are, in my experience, futile and inconsequential. The most they can accomplish is some temporary change, which soon disappears, leaving the individual more than ever convinced of his inadequacy.

The failure of any such approach through the intellect has forced me to recognize that change appears to come about through experience in a relationship. So I am going to try to state very briefly and informally, some of the essential hypotheses regarding a helping relationship which have seemed to gain increasing confirmation both from experience and research.

I can state the overall hypothesis in one sentence, as follows. If I can provide a certain type of relationship, the other person will discover within himself the capacity to use that relationship for growth, and change and personal development will occur.

THE RELATIONSHIP

But what meaning do these terms have? Let me take separately the three major phrases in this sentence and indicate something of the meaning they have for me. What is this certain type of relationship I would like to provide?

I have found that the more that I can be genuine in the relationship, the more helpful it will be. This means that I need to be aware of my own feelings, in so far as possible, rather than presenting an outward façade of one attitude, while actually holding another attitude at a deeper or unconscious level. Being genuine also involves the willingness to be and to express, in my words and my behavior, the various feelings and attitudes which exist in me. It is only in this way that the relationship can have *reality*, and reality seems deeply important as a first condition. It is only by providing the genuine reality which is in me, that the other person can successfully seek for the reality in him. I have found this to be true even when the attitudes I feel are not attitudes with which I am pleased, or attitudes which seem conducive to a good relationship. It seems extremely important to be *real*.

As a second condition, I find that the more acceptance and liking I feel toward this individual, the more I will be creating a relationship which he can use. By acceptance I mean a warm regard for him as a person of unconditional self-worth—of value no matter what his condition, his behavior, or his feelings. It means a respect and liking for him as a separate person, a willingness for him to possess his own feelings in his own way. It means an acceptance of and regard for his attitudes of the moment, no matter how negative or positive, no matter how much they may contradict other attitudes he has held in the past. This acceptance of each fluctuating aspect of this other person makes it for him a relationship of warmth and safety, and the safety of being liked and prized as a person seems a highly important element in a helping relationship.

I also find that the relationship is significant to the extent that I feel a continuing desire to understand—a sensitive empathy with each of the client's feelings and communications as they seem to him at that moment. Acceptance does not mean much until it involves understanding. It is only as I *understand* the feelings and thoughts which seem so horrible to you, or so weak, or so sentimental, or so bizarre—it is only as I see them as you see them, and accept them and you, that you feel really free to explore all the hidden nooks and frightening crannies of your inner and often buried experience. This *freedom* is an important condition of the relationship. There is implied here a freedom to explore oneself at both conscious and unconscious levels, as rapidly as one can dare to embark on this dangerous quest. There is also a complete freedom from any type of moral or diagnostic evaluation, since all such evaluations are, I believe, always threatening.

Thus the relationship which I have found helpful is characterized by a sort of transparency on my part, in which my real feelings are evident; by an acceptance of this other person as a separate person with value in his own right; and by a deep empathic understanding which enables me to see his private world through his eyes. When these conditions are achieved, I become a companion to my client, accompanying him in the frightening search for himself, which he now feels free to undertake.

I am by no means always able to achieve this kind of relationship with another, and sometimes, even when I feel I have achieved it in myself, he may be too frightened to perceive what is being offered to him. but I would say that when I hold in myself the kind of attitudes I have described, and when the other person can to some degree experience these attitudes, then I believe that change and constructive personal development will *invariably* occur—and I include the word "invariably" only after long and careful consideration.

THE MOTIVATION FOR CHANGE

So much for the relationship. The second phrase in my overall hypothesis was that the individual will discover within himself the capacity to use this relationship for growth. I will try to indicate something of the meaning which that phrase has for me. Gradually my experience has forced me to conclude that the individual has within himself the capacity and the tendency, latent if not evident, to move forward toward maturity. In a suitable psychological climate this tendency is released, and becomes actual rather than potential. It is evident in the capacity of the individual to understand those aspects of his life and of himself which are causing him pain and dissatisfaction, an understanding which probes beneath his conscious knowledge of himself into those experiences which he has hidden from himself because of their threatening nature. It shows itself in the tendency to reorganize his personality and his relationship to life in ways which are regarded as more mature. Whether one calls it a growth tendency, a drive toward self-actualization, or a forward-moving directional tendency, it is the mainspring of life, and is, in the last analysis, the tendency upon which all psychotherapy depends. It is the urge which is evident in all organic and human life—to expand, extend, become autonomous, develop, mature—the tendency to express and activate all the capacities of the organism, to the extent that such activation enhances the organism or the self. This tendency may become deeply buried under layer after layer of encrusted psychological defenses; it may be hidden behind elaborate façades which deny its existence; but it is my belief that it exists in every individual, and awaits only the proper conditions to be released and expressed.

THE OUTCOMES

I have attempted to describe the relationship which is basic to constructive personality change. I have tried to put into words the type of capacity which the individual brings to such a relationship. The third phrase of my general statement was that change and personal development would occur. It is my hypothesis that in such a relationship the individual will reorganize himself at both the conscious and deeper levels of his personality in such a manner as to cope with life more constructively, more intelligently, and in a more socialized as well as a more satisfying way.

Here I can depart from speculation and bring in the steadily increasing body of solid research knowledge which is accumulating. We know now that individuals who live in such a relationship even for a relatively limited number of hours show profound and significant changes in personality, attitudes, and behavior, changes that do not occur in matched control groups. In such a relationship the individual becomes more integrated, more effective. He shows fewer of the characteristics which are usually termed neurotic or psychotic, and more of the characteristics of the healthy, well-functioning person. He changes his perception of himself, becoming more realistic in his views of self. He becomes more like the person he wishes to be. He values himself more highly. He is more self-confident and self-directing. He has a better understanding of himself, becomes more open to his experience, denies or represses less of his experience. He becomes more accepting in his attitudes toward others, seeing others as more similar to himself.

In his behavior he shows similar changes. He is less frustrated by stress, and recovers from stress more quickly. He becomes more mature in his every-day behavior as this is observed by friends. He is less defensive, more adaptive, more able to meet situations creatively.

These are some of the changes which we now know come about in individuals who have completed a series of counseling interviews in which the psychological atmosphere approximates the relationship I described. Each of the statements made is based upon objective evidence. Much more research needs to be done, but there can no longer be any doubt as to the effectiveness of such a relationship in producing personality change.

14.3 AARON T. BECK

Principles of Cognitive Therapy

Aaron T. Beck developed cognitive therapy to help people with psychological disorders caused by negative, self-defeating thoughts and feelings. Cognitive therapists attempt to restructure these negative thoughts and modify the way people view the world. Beck originally developed cognitive therapy to treat depression, but recently he has extended it to the treatment of anxiety disorders.

Beck (b. 1921) earned his M.D. from the Yale University School of Medicine in 1946. He is currently a professor of psychiatry at the University of Pennsylvania. Beck's theories of depression and cognitive therapy have had a significant impact on clinical psychology. He has written a number of books in this area, including *Depression: Clinical, Experimental, and Theoretical Aspects* (1967) and *Anxiety Disorders and Phobias: A Cognitive Perspective* (Basic Books, 1985), coauthored with Gary Emery.

This selection is from chapter 9, "Principles of Cognitive Therapy," of Beck's *Cognitive Therapy and the Emotional Disorders* (International Universities Press, 1976). In it, Beck presents the basic concepts of cognitive therapy, and he provides several examples of how therapists apply these concepts in treating depressed patients. Note that cognitive therapy is effective only for those who are able to think and reason about their problems. Do you think the principles of cognitive therapy can be applied to everyday problems as well as to more serious psychological disorders?

Key Concept: cognitive therapy

We have seen that the common psychological disorders center around certain aberrations in thinking. The challenge to psychotherapy is to offer the patient effective techniques for overcoming his blindspots, his blurred perceptions, and his self-deceptions. A promising lead is provided by the observation that a person responds realistically and effectively to situations not related to his neurosis. His judgments and behavior in areas of experience beyond the boundaries of his specific vulnerability often reflect a high level of functioning. Furthermore, prior to the onset of illness, the neurotic frequently shows adequate development of his conceptual tools for dealing with the problems of living.

Psychological skills (integrating, labeling, and interpreting experience) can be applied to correcting the psychological aberrations. Since the central psychological problem and the psychological *remedy* are both concerned with the patient's thinking (or cognitions), we call this form of help cognitive therapy.

In the broadest sense, cognitive therapy consists of all the approaches that alleviate psychological distress through the medium of correcting faulty conceptions and self-signals. The emphasis on thinking, however, should not obscure the importance of the emotional reactions which are generally the immediate source of distress. It simply means that we get to the person's emotions through his cognitions. By correcting erroneous beliefs, we can damp down or alter excessive, inappropriate emotional reactions.

Many methods of helping a patient make more realistic appraisals of himself and his world are available. The "intellectual" approach consists of identifying the misconceptions, testing their validity, and substituting more appropriate concepts. Often the need for broad attitudinal change emerges with the patient's recognition that the rules he has relied on to guide his thinking and behavior have served to deceive and to defeat him.

The "experiential" approach exposes the patient to experiences that are in themselves powerful enough to change misconceptions. The interactions with other people in certain organized situations, such as encounter groups or conventional psychotherapy, may help a person to perceive others more realistically and consequently to modify his inappropriate maladaptive responses to them. In encounter groups, the interpersonal experiences may cut through maladaptive attitudes blocking the expression of intimate feelings. Similarly, a patient, in response to his psychotherapist's warmth and acceptance, often modifies his stereotyped conception of authority figures. Such a change has been labeled "corrective emotional experience" (Alexander, 1950). Sometimes the effectiveness of psychotherapy is implemented by motivating a patient to enter situations he had previously avoided because of his misconceptions.

The "behavioral" approach encourages the development of specific forms of behavior that lead to more general changes in the way the patient views himself and the real world. Practicing techniques for dealing with people who frighten him, as in "assertive training," not only enables him to regard other people more realistically but enhances his self-confidence. . . .

TARGETS OF COGNITIVE THERAPY

Cognitive techniques are most appropriate for people who have the capacity for introspection and for reflecting about their own thoughts and fantasies. This approach is essentially an extension and a refinement of what people have done to varying degrees since the early stages of their intellectual development. The particular techniques such as labeling objects and situations, setting up hypotheses, and weeding out and testing the hypotheses are based on skills that people apply automatically without being cognizant of the operations involved.

This kind of intellectual function is analogous to the formation of speech in which rules of pronunciation and grammatical construction are applied without consciousness of the rules or of their application. When an adult has to correct a speech disorder or attempts to learn a new language, then he has to concentrate on the formation of words and sentences. Similarly, when he has a problem in interpreting certain aspects of reality, it may be useful for him to focus on the rules he applies in making judgments. In examining a problem area, he finds that the rule is incorrect or that he has been applying it incorrectly.

Since making the incorrect judgments has probably become a deeply ingrained habit, which he may not be conscious of, several steps are required to correct it. First, he has to become aware of what he is thinking. Second, he needs to recognize what thoughts are awry. Then he has to substitute accurate for inaccurate judgments. Finally, he needs feedback to inform him whether his changes are correct. The same kind of sequence is necessary for making behavioral changes, such as improving form in a sport, correcting faults in playing an instrument, or perfecting techniques of persuasion.

To illustrate the process of cognitive change, let us take as a rather gross example a person who is afraid of all strangers. When we explore his reactions, we may find that he is operating under the rule, "All strangers are unfriendly or hostile." In this case, the rule is wrong. On the other hand, he may realize that strangers vary, but he may not have learned to discriminate among friendly strangers, neutral strangers, and unfriendly strangers. In such a case, his trouble is in applying the rule, that is, in converting the available information in a given situation into an appropriate judgment.

It is obvious that not all people who think erroneously need or want to get their thinking straightened out. When a person's erroneous ideation disrupts his life or makes him feel miserable, then he becomes a candidate for some form of help.

The troubles or problems that stimulate a person to seek help may be manifested by distress of a subjective nature (such as anxiety or depression), a difficulty in his overt behavior (such as disabling inhibition or overaggressiveness), or a deficiency in his responses (for example, inability to experience or express warm feelings). The kinds of thinking that underlie these problems may be summarized as follows.

Direct, Tangible Distortions of Reality

Distortions familiar to everybody are the thoughts of a paranoid patient who indiscriminately concludes when he sees other people (even people who are obviously friendly toward him): "Those people want to harm me." Or, as one patient once told me, "I killed President Kennedy."

Less obvious distortions of reality occur in all neuroses. For example, a depressed patient may say, "I have lost my ability to type, to read, to drive a car." However, when he becomes involved in the task, he may find his performance is still adequate. A depressed businessman complains that he is on the verge of bankruptcy, yet examination of his accounts indicates that he is completely solvent and, in fact, is prospering. The label "distortion of reality" is justified because an objective appraisal of the situation contradicts his appraisal.

Other examples of distortions that are relatively simple to check are ideas such as, "I am getting fat" or "I am a burden to my family." Some judgments require greater work to authenticate; for example, "Nobody likes me." The therapeutic sessions, particularly when the patient has been trained to report his automatic thoughts, provide an excellent laboratory for exposing distortions. The therapist may readily identify certain distortions, for instance, when a patient toward whom he has warm feelings reports the thought that he believes the therapist dislikes him.

Illogical Thinking

The patient's appraisal of reality may not be distorted, but his system of making inferences or drawing conclusions from his observations is at fault: He hears distant noise and concludes someone has fired a gun at him. In such instances, the basic premises may be erroneous or the logical processes may be faulty. A depressed patient observed that a faucet was leaking in a bathroom, that the pilot light was out in the stove, and that one of the steps in the staircase was broken. He concluded, "The whole house is deteriorating." The house was in excellent condition (except for these minor problems); he had made a massive overgeneralization. In the same way, patients who have difficulties as a result of their overt behavior often start from inaccurate premises. Someone who consistently alienates potential friends because of his overaggressiveness may operate according to the rule, "If I don't push people around, they will push me around." A timid, inhibited person may be indiscriminately applying the principle, "If I open my mouth, everybody will jump on me."

THE THERAPEUTIC COLLABORATION

Certain factors are important in practically all forms of psychotherapy, but are crucial in cognitive therapy. An obvious primary component of effective psychotherapy is genuine collaboration between the therapist and patient. Moving blindly in separate directions, as sometimes happens, frustrates the therapist and distresses the patient. It is important to realize that the dispenser of the service (the therapist) and the recipient (the patient) may envision the therapeutic relationship quite differently. The patient, for instance, may visualize therapy as a molding of a lump of clay by an omnipotent and omniscient God figure. To minimize such hazards, the patient and therapist should reach a consensus regarding what problem requires help, the goal of therapy, and how they plan to reach that goal. Agreement regarding the nature and duration of therapy is important in determining the outcome. One study has shown, for instance, that a discrepancy between the patient's expectations and the kind of therapy he actually receives militates against a successful outcome. On the other hand, preliminary coaching of the patient about the type of therapy selected appeared to enhance its effectiveness (Orne and Wender, 1968).

Furthermore, the therapist needs to be tuned in to the vicissitudes of the patient's problems from session to session. Patients frequently formulate an "agenda" of topics they want to discuss at a particular session; if the therapist disregards this, he may impose an unnecessary strain on the relationship. For instance, a patient who is disturbed by a recent altercation with his wife may be alienated by the therapist's rigid adherence to a predetermined format such as desensitizing him to his subway phobia.

It is useful to conceive of the patient-therapist relationship as a joint effort. It is not the therapist's function to try to reform the patient; rather, his role is working with the patient against "*it*," the patient's problem. Placing the emphasis on solving problems, rather than his presumed defects or bad habits, helps the patient to examine his difficulties with more detachment and makes him less prone to experience shame, a sense of inferiority, and defensiveness. The partnership concept helps the therapist to obtain valuable "feedback" about the efficacy of therapeutic techniques and further detailed information about the patient's thoughts and feelings. In employing systematic desensitization, for instance, I customarily ask for a detailed description of each image. The patient's report is often very informative and, on many occasions, reveals new problems that had not previously been identified. The partnership arrangement also reduces the patient's tendency to cast the therapist in the role of a superman. Investigators (Rogers, 1951; Truax, 1963) have found that if the therapist shows the following characteristics, a successful outcome is facilitated: genuine warmth, acceptance, and accurate empathy. By working with the patient as a collaborator, the therapist is more likely to show these characteristics than if he assumes a Godlike role.

ESTABLISHING CREDIBILITY

Problems often arise with regard to the suggestions and formulations offered by the therapist. Patients who view the therapist as a kind of superman are likely to accept his interpretations and suggestions as sacred pronouncements. Such bland ingestion of the therapist's hypotheses deprives the therapy of the corrective effect of critical evaluation by the patient.

A different type of problem is presented by patients who automatically react to the therapist's statements with suspicion or skepticism. Such a reaction is most pronounced in paranoid and severely depressed patients. In attempting to expose the distortions of reality, the therapist may become mired in the patient's deeply entrenched belief system. The therapist, therefore, must establish some common ground, find some point of agreement, and then attempt to extend the area of consensus from there. Depressed patients are often concerned that their emotional disorder will persist or get worse, and that they will not respond to therapy. If the therapist assumes a hearty optimistic attitude, the patient may decide that the therapist is either faking, doesn't really understand the gravity of the disorder, or is simply a fool. Similarly, trying to talk a paranoid patient out of his distorted views of reality may drive him to stronger belief in his paranoid ideas. Also, if the paranoid patient begins to regard the therapist as a member of the "opposition," he may assign the therapist a key role in his delusional system.

A more appropriate approach in establishing credibility is to convey a message such as: "You have certain ideas that upset you. They may or they may not be correct. Now let us examine some of them." By assuming a neutral stance, the therapist may then encourage the patient to express his distorted ideas and listen to them attentively. Later he sends up some "trial balloons" to determine whether the patient is ready to examine the evidence regarding these distortions. . . .

Many patients appear to agree with the therapist because of their fears of challenging him and their need to please him. A clue to such superficial consensus is provided by the patient who says, "I agree with you intellectually but not emotionally." Such a statement generally indicates that the therapist's comments or interpretations may seem logical to the patient, but that they do not penetrate the patient's basic belief system (Ellis, 1962). The patient continues to operate according to his faulty ideas. Moreover, strongly authoritative remarks that appeal to the patient's yearning for explanations for his misery may set the stage for disillusionment when the patient finds loopholes in the therapist's formulations. The therapist's confidence in his role as an expert requires a strong admixture of humility. Psychotherapy often involves a good deal of trial-and-error, experimenting with several approaches or formulations to determine which fit the best. . . .

In less extreme cases, it is possible to deal more directly with the irrational ideas. However, the therapist must assess the "latitude of acceptance" of the patient for statements challenging his distorted concepts. Being told that his ideas are wrong might antagonize the patient; but, he might respond favorably to a question such as "Is there another way of interpreting your wife's behavior?" As long as the therapist's attempts at clarification are within an acceptable range, the problem of a credibility gap is minimized.

PROBLEM REDUCTION

Many patients come to the therapist with a host of symptoms or problems. To solve each one of the problems in isolation from the others might very well take a lifetime. A patient may seek help for a variety of ailments such as headaches, insomnia, and anxiety, in addition to interpersonal problems. Identifying problems with similar causes and grouping them together is termed "problem reduction." Once the multifarious difficulties are condensed, the therapist can select the appropriate techniques for each group of problems.

Let us take as an example the patient with multiple phobias. A woman . . . was greatly handicapped by a fear of elevators, tunnels, hills, closed spaces, riding in an open car, riding in an airplane, swimming, walking fast or running, strong winds, and hot, muggy days. Treating each phobia separately with the technique of systematic desensitization might have required innumerable therapeutic sessions, However, it was possible to find a common denominator for her symptoms: an overriding fear of suffocation. She believed that each of the phobic situations presented substantial risk of deprivation of air and consequent suffocation. The therapy was focused directly on this central fear.

The principle of problem reduction is also applicable to a constellation of symptoms that comprise a specific disorder such as depression. By concentrating on certain key components of the disorder, such as low self-esteem or negative expectations, the therapy can produce improvement in mood, overt behavior, appetite, and sleeping pattern. One patient, for instance, revealed that whenever he was in a gratifying situation, he would get some kind of "kill-joy" thought: When he began to feel pleasure from listening to music, he would think, "This record will be over soon," and his pleasure would disappear. When he discovered that he was enjoying a movie, a date with a girl, or just walking, he would think: "This will end soon," and immediately his satisfaction was squelched. In this case, a thought pattern that he could not enjoy things because they would end became the focus of the therapy.

In another case the main focus was the patient's overabsorption in the negative aspects of her life and her selective inattention to positive occurrences. The therapy consisted of having her write down and report back positive experiences. She was surprised to find how many positive, gratifying experiences she had had and subsequently forgotten about.

Another form of problem reduction is the identification of the first link in a chain of symptoms. An interesting feature is that the first link may be a relatively small and easily eradicable problem that leads to consequences that are disabling. For analogy, a person may writhe with pain and be unable to walk, eat, talk at length, or perform minimal constructive activities—because of a speck in the eye. The "speck in the eye" syndrome probably occurs more frequently among psychiatric patients than is generally realized. Because of delay in identifying and dealing with the initial problem, however, the ensuing difficulties become deeply entrenched. A mother who was afraid to leave her children at home with a babysitter continued to be housebound long after the children reached maturity. . . .

LEARNING TO LEARN

. . . [I]t is not necessary for a psychotherapist to help a patient solve every problem that troubles him. Nor is it necessary to anticipate all the problems that may occur after the termination of therapy and to try to work them out in advance. The kind of therapeutic collaboration previously described is conducive to the patient's developing new ways to learn from his experiences and to solve problems. In a sense the patient is "learning to learn." This process has been labeled deutero-learning (Bateson, 1942).

The problem-solving approach to psychotherapy removes much of the responsibility from the therapist and engages the patient more actively in working on his difficulties. By reducing the patient's dependency on the therapist, this approach increases the patient's self-confidence and self-esteem. More important, perhaps, is the fact that the patient's active participation in defining the problem and considering various options yields more ample information than would otherwise be available. His participation in making the decision helps him implement it.

I have explained the problem-solving concept to patients in somewhat the following way: "One of the goals of therapy is to help you learn new ways of approaching problems. Then, as problems come up, you can apply the formulas that you have already learned. For instance, in learning arithmetic you simply learned the fundamental rules. It was not necessary to learn every single possible addition and subtraction. Once you had learned the operations, you could apply them to any arithmetic problem."

To illustrate "learning to learn," let us consider the practical and interpersonal problems that contribute to a patient's various symptoms. A woman, for instance, discovered she was constantly plagued with headaches, feelings of tension, abdominal pain, and insomnia. By focusing on her problems at work and at home, the patient was able to find some solutions for them and became less prone to experience symptoms. As was hoped, she was able to generalize these practical lessons to solving other problems of living, so that it was not necessary for us to work on all her problems in therapy. . . .

"Learning to learn" consists of much more than the patient's adopting a few techniques that can be used in a wide variety of situations. Basically, this approach attempts to remove obstacles that have prevented the patient from profiting from experience and from developing adequate ways of dealing with their internal and external problems. Most of the patients have been blocked in their psychosocial development by certain maladaptive attitudes and patterns of behavior. For instance, the woman with the numerous problems at work and at home had a characteristic response when she was confronted with sensitive interpersonal relations or new practical problems: "I don't know what to do." As a result of therapy, each successful experience tended to erode this negative attitude. Consequently, she was enabled to draw on her ingenuity in meeting and mastering completely different situations.

Patients generally try to avoid situations that cause them uneasiness. Consequently, they do not develop the trial-and-error techniques that are prerequisite to solving many problems. Or by staying out of difficult situations, they do not learn how to rid themselves of their tendency to distort or exaggerate. A person who stays close to home because he fears strangers does not learn how to test the validity of his fears or to discriminate between "safe" strangers and "dangerous" strangers. Through therapy he can learn to "reality-test" not only these fears but other fears as well.

The sense of mastery from solving one problem frequently inspires the patient to approach and solve other problems that he has long avoided. Thus, a bonus of successful therapy is not only freedom from the original problems, but a thorough psychological change that prepares him to meet new challenges.

Aaron T. Beck

REFERENCES

Alexander, F. (1950). *Psychomatic medicine: Its principles and applications.* New York: W. W. Norton.

Bateson, G. (1942). Social planning and the concept of deutero-learning in relation to the democratic way of life. In: *Science, philosophy, and religion* (2nd Symposium). New York: Harper.

Ellis, A. (1962). *Reason and emotion in psythotherapy.* New York: Lyle Stuart.

Orne, M. T., & Wender, P. H. (1968). Anticipatory socialization for psychotherapy: Method and rationale. *American Journal of Psychiatry, 124,* 1202–1212.

Rogers, C. R. (1951). *Client-centered therapy: Its current practice, implications, and theory.* Boston: Houghton Mifflin.

Truat, C. B. (1963). Effective ingredients in psychotherapy: an approach to unraveling the patient-therapist interaction. *Journal of Counseling Psychology, 10,* 256–263.

PART SEVEN

Social Processes

On the Internet . . .

Sites appropriate to Part Seven

Wesleyan University's social psychology network.

> http://www.wesleyan.edu/psyc/psyc260/home.html

This social cognition paper archive and information center is maintained by Eliot Smith, professor of psychological sciences at Purdue University.

> http://www.psych.purdue.edu/~esmith/scarch.html

CHAPTER 15 Social Psychology

15.1 LEON FESTINGER

An Introduction to the Theory of Dissonance

Psychologists have studied attitude development and attitude change for many years. In the late 1950s, Leon Festinger proposed a somewhat radical view (at the time) of attitude change. According to his theory of cognitive dissonance, people experience tension when they hold two inconsistent ideas, and this state creates a drive to reduce the dissonance, or tension.

Festinger (1919–1989) obtained his Ph.D. in psychology from the State University of Iowa in 1942. He taught at several universities, including Stanford University, before going to the New School for Social Research in New York City in 1968. Although Festinger contributed numerous theories to social psychology, none has had greater impact than his theory of cognitive dissonance.

This selection is from chapter 1, "An Introduction to the Theory of Dissonance," of Festinger's *A Theory of Cognitive Dissonance* (Stanford University Press, 1957). As well as providing a readable introduction to the development of dissonance, Festinger offers some possible techniques for reducing dissonance in everyday situations. As you read this selection, think about what variables influence cognitive dissonance in your daily life.

Key Concept: cognitive dissonance

*I*t has frequently been implied, and sometimes even pointed out, that the individual strives toward consistency within himself. His opinions and attitudes, for example, tend to exist in clusters that are internally consistent. Certainly one may find exceptions. . . . [S]omeone may think little children should be quiet and unobtrusive and yet may be quite proud when his child aggressively captures the attention of his adult guests. When such inconsistencies are found to exist, they may be quite dramatic, but they capture our interest primarily because they stand out in sharp contrast against a background of consistency. It is still overwhelmingly true that related opinions or attitudes are consistent with one another. Study after study reports such consistency among one person's political attitudes, social attitudes, and many others.

There is the same kind of consistency between what a person knows or believes and what he does. A person who believes a college education is a good thing will very likely encourage his children to go to college; a child who knows he will be severely punished for some misdemeanor will not commit it or at least will try not to be caught doing it. This is not surprising, of course; it is so much the rule that we take it for granted. Again what captures our attention are the exceptions to otherwise consistent behavior. A person may know that smoking is bad for him and yet continue to smoke; many persons commit crimes even though they know the high probability of being caught and the punishment that awaits them.

Granting that consistency is the usual thing, perhaps overwhelmingly so, what about these exceptions which come to mind so readily? Only rarely, if ever, are they accepted psychologically *as inconsistencies* by the person involved. Usually more or less successful attempts are made to rationalize them. Thus, the person who continues to smoke, knowing that it is bad for his health, may also feel (*a*) he enjoys smoking so much it is worth it; (*b*) the chances of his health suffering are not as serious as some would make out; (*c*) he can't always avoid every possible dangerous contingency and still live; and (*d*) perhaps even if he stopped smoking he would put on weight which is equally bad for his health. So, continuing to smoke is, after all, consistent with his ideas about smoking.

But persons are not always successful in explaining away or in rationalizing inconsistencies to themselves. For one reason or another, attempts to achieve consistency may fail. The inconsistency then simply continues to exist. Under such circumstances—that is, in the presence of an inconsistency—there is psychological discomfort.

The basic hypotheses . . . can now be stated. First, I will replace the word "inconsistency" with a term which has less of a logical connotation, namely, *dissonance*. I will likewise replace the word "consistency" with a more neutral term, namely, *consonance*. A more formal definition of these terms will be given shortly; for the moment, let us try to get along with the implicit meaning they have acquired as a result of the preceding discussion.

The basic hypotheses I wish to state are as follows:

1. The existence of dissonance, being psychologically uncomfortable, will motivate the person to try to reduce the dissonance and achieve consonance.

2. When dissonance is present, in addition to trying to reduce it, the person will actively avoid situations and information which would likely increase the dissonance.

Before proceeding to develop this theory of dissonance and the pressures to reduce it, it would be well to clarify the nature of dissonance, what kind of a concept it is, and where the theory concerning it will lead. The two hypotheses stated above provide a good starting point for this clarification. While they refer here specifically to dissonance, they are in fact very general hypotheses. In place of "dissonance" one can substitute other notions similar in nature, such as "hunger," "frustration," or "disequilibrium," and the hypotheses would still make perfectly good sense.

In short, I am proposing that dissonance, that is, the existence of nonfitting relations among cognitions, is a motivating factor in its own right. By the term *cognition* . . . I mean any knowledge, opinion, or belief about the environment, about oneself, or about one's behavior. Cognitive dissonance can be seen as an antecedent condition which leads to activity oriented toward dissonance reduction just as hunger leads to activity oriented toward hunger reduction. It is a very different motivation from what psychologists are used to dealing with but, as we shall see, nonetheless powerful. . . .

THE OCCURRENCE AND PERSISTENCE OF DISSONANCE

Why and how does dissonance ever arise? How does it happen that persons sometimes find themselves doing things that do not fit with what they know, or having opinions that do not fit with other opinions they hold? An answer to this question may be found in discussing two of the more common situations in which dissonance may occur.

1. New events may happen or new information may become known to a person, creating at least a momentary dissonance with existing knowledge, opinion, or cognition concerning behavior. Since a person does not have complete and perfect control over the information that reaches him and over events that can happen in his environment, such dissonances may easily arise. Thus, for example, a person may plan to go on a picnic with complete confidence that the weather will be warm and sunny. Nevertheless, just before he is due to start, it may begin to rain. The knowledge that it is now raining is dissonant with his confidence in a sunny day and with his planning to go to a picnic. Or, as another example, a person who is quite certain in his knowledge that automatic transmissions on automobiles are inefficient may accidentally come across an article praising automatic transmissions. Again, at least a momentary dissonance is created.

2. Even in the absence of new, unforeseen events or information, the existence of dissonance is undoubtedly an everyday condition. Very few things are all black or all white; very few situations are clear-cut enough so that opinions or behaviors are not to some extent a mixture of contradictions. Thus, a midwestern farmer who is a Republican may be opposed to his party's

position on farm price supports; a person buying a new car may prefer the economy of one model but the design of another; a person deciding on how to invest his money may know that the outcome of his investment depends upon economic conditions beyond his control. Where an opinion must be formed or a decision taken, some dissonance is almost unavoidably created between the cognition of the action taken and those opinions or knowledges which tend to point to a different action.

There is, then, a fairly wide variety of situations in which dissonance is nearly unavoidable. . . . If the hypotheses stated above are correct, then as soon as dissonance occurs there will be pressures to reduce it.

THE REDUCTION OF DISSONANCE

The presence of dissonance gives rise to pressures to reduce or eliminate the dissonance. The strength of the pressures to reduce the dissonance is a function of the magnitude of the dissonance. In other words, dissonance acts in the same way as a state of drive or need or tension. The presence of dissonance leads to action to reduce it just as, for example, the presence of hunger leads to action to reduce the hunger. Also, similar to the action of a drive, the greater the dissonance, the greater will be the intensity of the action to reduce the dissonance and the greater the avoidance of situations that would increase the dissonance.

In order to be specific about how the pressure to reduce dissonance would manifest itself, it is necessary to examine the possible ways in which existing dissonance can be reduced or eliminated. In general, if dissonance exists between two elements, this dissonance can be eliminated by changing one of those elements. The important thing is how these changes may be brought about. . . .

Changing a Behavioral Cognitive Element

When the dissonance under consideration is between an element corresponding to some knowledge concerning environment (environmental element) and a behavioral element, the dissonance can, of course, be eliminated by changing the behavioral cognitive element in such a way that it is consonant with the environmental element. . . . This method of reducing or eliminating dissonance is a very frequent occurrence. Our behavior and feelings are frequently modified in accordance with new information. If a person starts out on a picnic and notices that it has begun to rain, he may very well turn around and go home. There are many persons who do stop smoking if and when they discover it is bad for their health.

It may not always be possible, however, to eliminate dissonance or even to reduce it materially by changing one's action or feeling. The difficulty of changing the behavior may be too great, or the change, while eliminating some dissonances, may create a whole host of new ones.

Just as it is possible to change a behavioral cognitive element by changing the behavior which this element mirrors, it is sometimes possible to change an *environmental* cognitive element by changing the situation to which that element corresponds. This, of course, is much more difficult than changing one's behavior, for one must have a sufficient degree of control over one's environment—a relatively rare occurrence.

Changing the environment itself in order to reduce dissonance is more feasible when the social environment is in question than when the physical environment is involved. . . .

Whenever there is sufficient control over the environment, this method of reducing dissonance may be employed. For example, a person who is habitually very hostile toward other people may surround himself with persons who provoke hostility. His cognitions about the persons with whom he associates are then consonant with the cognitions corresponding to his hostile behavior. The possibilities of manipulating the environment are limited, however, and most endeavors to change a cognitive element will follow other lines. . . .

Adding New Cognitive Elements

It is clear that in order to eliminate a dissonance completely, some cognitive element must be changed. It is also clear that this is not always possible. But even if it is impossible to eliminate a dissonance, it is possible to reduce the total magnitude of dissonance by adding new cognitive elements. Thus, for example, if dissonance existed between some cognitive elements concerning the effects of smoking and cognition concerning the behavior of continuing to smoke, the total dissonance could be reduced by adding new cognitive elements that are consonant with the fact of smoking. In the presence of such dissonance, then, a person might be expected to actively seek new information that would reduce the total dissonance and, at the same time, to avoid new information that might increase the existing dissonance. Thus, to pursue the example, the person might seek out and avidly read any material critical of the research which purported to show that smoking was bad for one's health. At the same time he would avoid reading material that praised this research. (If he unavoidably came in contact with the latter type of material, his reading would be critical indeed.)

Actually, the possibilities for adding new elements which would reduce the existing dissonances are broad. Our smoker, for example, could find out all about accidents and death rates in automobiles. Having then added the cognition that the danger from smoking is negligible compared to the danger he runs driving a car, his dissonance would also have been somewhat reduced. Here the total dissonance is reduced by reducing the *importance* of the existing dissonance. . . .

Before moving on, it is worth while to emphasize again that the presence of pressures to reduce dissonance, or even activity directed toward such reduction, does not guarantee that the dissonance will be reduced. A person may not be able to find the social support needed to change a cognitive element, or he may not be able to find new elements which reduce the total dissonance. In fact, it is quite conceivable that in the process of trying to reduce dissonance, it might even be increased. This will depend upon what the person encounters while attempting to reduce the dissonance. The important point to be made so far is that in the presence of a dissonance, one will be able to observe the *attempts* to reduce it. If attempts to reduce dissonance fail, one should be able to observe symptoms of psychological discomfort, provided the dissonance is appreciable enough so that the discomfort is clearly and overtly manifested. . . .

AVOIDANCE OF DISSONANCE

The discussion thus far has focused on the tendencies to reduce or eliminate dissonance and the problems involved in achieving such reduction. Under certain circumstances there are also strong and important tendencies to avoid increases of dissonance or to avoid the occurrence of dissonance altogether. Let us now turn our attention to a consideration of these circumstances and the manifestations of the avoidance tendencies which we might expect to observe.

The avoidance of an increase in dissonance comes about, of course, as a result of the existence of dissonance. This avoidance is especially important where, in the process of attempting to reduce dissonance, support is sought for a new cognitive element to replace an existing one or where new cognitive elements are to be added. In both these circumstances, the seeking of support and the seeking of new information must be done in a highly selective manner. A person would initiate discussion with someone he thought would agree with the new cognitive element but would avoid discussion with someone who might agree with the element that he was trying to change. A person would expose himself to sources of information which he expected would add new elements which would increase consonance but would certainly avoid sources which would increase dissonance. . . .

The operation of a fear of dissonance may also lead to a reluctance to commit oneself behaviorally. There is a large class of actions that, once taken, are difficult to change. Hence, it is possible for dissonances to arise and to mount in intensity. A fear of dissonance would lead to a reluctance to take action—a reluctance to commit oneself. Where decision and action cannot be indefinitely delayed, the taking of action may be accompanied by a cognitive negation of the action. Thus, for example, a person who buys a new car and is very afraid of dissonance may, immediately following the purchase, announce his conviction that he did the wrong thing. Such strong fear of dissonance is probably relatively rare, but it does occur. Personality differences with respect to fear of dissonance and the effectiveness with which one is able to reduce dissonance are undoubtedly important in determining whether or not such avoidance of dissonance is likely to happen.

15.2 KENNETH L. DION AND
KAREN K. DION

Belief in a Just World and Physical Attractiveness Stereotyping

Many people believe in the just world hypothesis: good things happen to good people and bad things happen to bad people. In other words, people get what they deserve. When we hear about the plight of a crime victim, too often we feel that somehow the person deserved it. Likewise, often we believe that a physically attractive person must have many positive personality characteristics. Related to this phenomenon is Kenneth L. Dion and Karen K. Dion's research on social cognition processes, an important area of social psychology.

Kenneth Dion (b. 1944) and Karen Dion (b. 1945) earned their Ph.D.'s in psychology from the University of Minnesota in 1970. They are both professors of psychology at the University of Toronto in Canada, where they have been since 1970. Although they each study other areas in social psychology, they share an interest in stereotyping, especially stereotyping on the basis of physical and social cues.

This selection is from "Belief in a Just World and Physical Attractiveness Stereotyping," which was published in *Journal of Personality and Social Psychology* in 1987. In their experiment, Dion and Dion asked subjects to rate the personality traits of an attractive or an unattractive person. To analyze the data from their experiment, the authors use an analysis of variance (ANOVA), which is a statistical procedure for evaluating the differences among several variables. A probability level (p) of less than .05 is considered significant, meaning that a real difference was found. How susceptible do you think most people are to using attractiveness in judging a person's personality or ability? Why?

Key Concept: just world belief and physical attractiveness

Just-world theory provides a possible explanation of physical attractiveness stereotyping, in that believing in a just world should lead to a positive bias toward "winners," such as the physically attractive. Several hypotheses derived from this premise were tested by having adults complete the Just World Scale and rate the personality traits and expected life outcomes of an attractive or unattractive stimulus person. Predictions for the personality trait ratings were borne out for male but not for female stimulus persons: (a) Believers in a just world perceived the personalities of attractive, male stimulus persons as more socially desirable than nonbelievers and also attributed more socially desirable personalities to male stimulus persons who were attractive rather than unattractive; and (b) no effects were found for female stimulus persons. Predictions for the life-outcome ratings and differences in correlations between personality and life-outcome ratings as a function of belief in a just world were clearly supported. Implications for just-world theory, status-characteristics theory, and physical attractiveness stereotyping are discussed.

Dion, Berscheid, and Walster (1972) were among the first researchers to postulate and demonstrate a stereotype for physical attractiveness. They presented university students with college yearbook photographs of stimulus persons previously categorized by other judges as attractive, average looking, or unattractive. Each stimulus person was rated on a series of personality traits selected to provide an index of overall social desirability. The subjects also estimated the stimulus person's suitability for various roles (e.g., marital partner, parent, etc.) as well as his or her likelihood of finding success and happiness in different spheres of life.

The results revealed a pervasive bias in favor of physically attractive individuals. Attractive stimulus persons were perceived as having more socially desirable personalities in general than those who were unattractive. Furthermore, for every dimension of life success and satisfaction except parental competence, attractive stimulus persons were expected to fare better than their less attractive counterparts. Karen Dion and her colleagues summed up these findings by suggesting that in the eye of the beholder, "What is beautiful is good."

Since Dion et al.'s (1972) study, evidence of physical attractiveness stereotyping has been found in numerous studies (see Cash, 1981; Dion, 1986). Attractiveness has been shown to function as an evaluative cue for older as well as younger adults (Adams & Huston, 1975; Johnson & Pittenger, 1984), which suggests that attractiveness stereotyping occurs throughout adulthood. Among university students, attractiveness is such a powerful stereotypic cue that even having the experimenter emphasize that their attractiveness judgments are subjective and merely a matter of personal taste failed to weaken its impact on trait evaluations (Ellis, Olson, & Zanna, 1983). The attractiveness stereotype also has self-fulfilling properties (Snyder, Tanke, & Berscheid, 1977) because it biases the stereotype-holder's behavior toward an individual believed to be attractive or unattractive and elicits stereotype-confirming behavior from the target.

The important question of *why* perceivers rely on attractiveness in evaluating others is the focus of this article. To call the evaluative bias favoring attractive people a stereotype helps to describe the phenomenon but does not explain it. Our goal here is to explore Lerner's (1970, 1980) just-world theory as one possible explanation of physical attractiveness stereotyping. (Dion, 1986, discussed social learning and cognitive processes as bases of physical attractiveness stereotyping.) In essence, we propose that physical attractiveness stereotyping may partly reflect a person's belief in a just world.

According to Lerner, many of us believe, to some extent, in a just world "where people get what they deserve" and also "deserve what they get." This belief presumably enables people to view their environment as a safe, predictable place in which they can obtain desired ends and avoid unpleasant fates through foresight, ability, and effort. In essence, the belief in a just world is a naive faith or hope of a close connection between one's character and one's fate. Because good people are not supposed to suffer unfortunate fates, becoming aware of an innocent victim threatens one's belief in a just world by implying that the same thing could happen to oneself. Perceivers are assumed to go to considerable lengths to maintain and protect their faith in a just world in the face of discrepant information. . . .

Research on physical attractiveness stereotyping reveals a similar pattern. Attractive people are perceived as possessing better and more desirable personalities and as being more likely to obtain life's material and psychological benefits than are their less attractive counterparts. Rubin and Peplau (1975, pp. 67–68) suggested that the positive personality traits attributed to physically attractive people reflect a tendency by perceivers to see "the 'reward' of beauty" as being deserved. Going beyond this, however, might the "beautiful is good" stereotype itself partly reflect the belief in a just world, such that those who subscribe to this belief are more likely to stereotype on the basis of attractiveness than do those who do not? To explore this question, we conducted a study in which subjects (a) judged the personality and likely life outcomes of a stimulus person previously judged to be either attractive or unattractive and (b) completed a scale designed to measure their belief in a just world (Rubin & Peplau, 1975). . . .

METHOD

Subjects

One hundred forty-three patrons (i.e., people paying admission to see the exhibits) of the Ontario Science Centre volunteered for a study on social perception and attitudes. Most respondents also provided demographic information about themselves by answering some items at the top of the sheet containing the Just World Scale. Their responses help to describe the sample.

Women constituted approximately 60% of the sample. Subjects' ages ranged from 15 to 69 with a median of 33 years. A slight majority (54.4%) specified Canada as their country of residence, another sizable group indicated the United States (41.2%), and the remainder cited other countries (e.g., the United Kingdom, Israel, etc.). Our sample, then, was largely composed of adults from Canada and the United States, with a slightly greater representation of women than men.

Procedure

Upon being seated, subjects were presented with materials that included a photograph of a person to be judged, a sheet of scales for rating this stimulus person, and another sheet, titled "Opinion Inventory," that contained the Just World Scale. The order of completing the Just World Scale and rating the stimulus person was counterbalanced across subjects. After completing these tasks, subjects were thanked for their participation.

Just World Scale

The Just World Scale is a 20-item instrument, balanced for acquiescence response set, that Rubin and Peplau (1975) devised to measure the extent of an individual's belief in a just world. Both they and Lerner (1980, chapter 10) have described in detail the scale, its properties, and its correlates. These authors have also summarized the considerable evidence suggesting that the Just World Scale does indeed reflect individual differences in one's proneness to believe that the world is or is not a just place.

In completing the scale, respondents indicate their agreement or disagreement with statements that reflect a belief in a just world (e.g., "People who get 'lucky breaks' have usually earned their good fortune") or its opposite (e.g., "I've found that a person rarely deserves the reputation he has"). In this study, we used a 5-point Likert-type response format that ranged from *strongly disagree* to *strongly agree*, with *neither agree nor disagree* as a neutral midpoint. Responses to the items were scored with values ranging from 1 to 5 and keyed so that high scores indicate a stronger belief in a just world. . . .

As noted earlier, respondents were also asked to indicate their sex, country of residence, and age on the opinion inventory sheet. Analyses were performed to assess whether these dimensions correlated with the tendency to believe in a just world. Men and women did not differ in their just-world scores, $t(137) = 1.43$, *ns*. Similarly, a one-way analysis of variance (ANOVA) on just-world scores as a function of respondents' reported country of residence (i.e., Canada, United States, or other) showed no effects ($F < 1$). Age, however, correlated negatively with just-world scores, $r(135) = -19$, $p < .05$, which indicated a tendency for older persons to subscribe somewhat less to the belief in a just world. . . .

Kenneth L.
Dion and
Karen K. Dion

Stimulus persons were drawn from a pool of 280 individual photographs of previous visitors to the Ontario Science Centre, who had volunteered to have their photographs taken by a professional photographer and who had given written permission for their photo to be used in research by us. From this pool, 12 stimulus persons [six men and six women] varying in physical attractiveness were selected for use in this study. . . .

Ratings of Stimulus Persons

As in Dion et al.'s (1972) investigation, subjects rated the stimulus person on personality traits and also estimated the stimulus person's likelihood of finding success or happiness in various life spheres. The trait ratings incorporated a 7-point rating scale (scored 1 to 7), with higher scores representing more positive ratings. The 18 trait dimensions were as follows: poised–awkward, strong–weak, interesting–boring, self-assertive–submissive, sociable–unsociable, independent–dependent, warm–cold, desirable as a friend–undesirable as a friend, genuine–artificial, kind–cruel, exciting–dull, sophisticated–unsophisticated, sexually warm–sexually cold, sincere–insincere, sensitive–insensitive, well mannered–ill mannered, socially popular–socially unpopular, and polite–impolite. . . .

As mentioned earlier, subjects also estimated the likelihood of the stimulus person attaining each of nine desirable life objectives by using a six-category response format that ranged from *extremely unlikely* (1) to *extremely likely* (6). The life objectives included "will find total happiness," "will lead an exciting life," "will be an outstanding parent," "will be an understanding spouse," "will experience self-fulfillment," "will be successful in chosen occupation," "will have a high-status occupation," "will be popular with members of the opposite sex," and "will be popular with members of the same sex." Coefficient alpha for the life-outcome ratings was .851, which again indicated high internal consistency.

RESULTS

The attractiveness manipulation check and the dependent measures were analyzed in a 2 × 2 × 2 × 2 factorial ANOVA design with attractiveness of stimulus person, sex of stimulus person, sex of subject, and belief in a just world as independent variables. . . .

TABLE 1

Trait Ratings of the Stimulus Person

	Believers in a just world		Nonbelievers in a just world	
Stimulus person	Male stimulus person	Female stimulus person	Male stimulus person	Female stimulus person
Attractive	90.94	82.13	75.50	87.26
Unattractive	72.44	75.47	74.47	73.06

Dependent Measures

As noted earlier, two dependent measures were included in the present study: personality-trait ratings and life-outcome ratings of a stimulus person. In each case, given evidence of high internal consistency among items . . . , an overall composite index was created. For example, respondents' ratings of the stimulus person across 17 personality-trait dimensions were summed together to yield a social desirability index. A life-outcome index was created by summing respondents' ratings of the stimulus person across nine life objectives. Having described the key indexes, let us turn to the results of the ANOVA.

The social desirability index. Analysis of the social desirability index revealed two significant effects. As expected, an attractiveness main effect [significance in one variable] was obtained, $F(1, 123) = 13.69$, $p < .001$. Consistent with prior research, attractive stimulus persons were perceived as possessing more socially desirable personalities, in general, than were unattractive stimulus persons (Ms [means] = 83.99 vs. 73.83). The attractiveness main effect, however, was qualified by a three-way interaction among attractiveness of stimulus person, sex of stimulus person, and respondent's belief in a just world, $F(1, 123) = 4.67$, $p < .04$. The means underlying this interaction are presented in Table 1.

To determine which means differed significantly from one another, we used Cichetti's (1972) method for applying Tukey's multiple-range test to an ANOVA interaction table—a technique that focuses on unconfounded comparisons (i.e., pairs of means that differ on a single dimension, with other dimensions held constant). In the present case, a pair of means needed to differ by more than a critical value of 14.50 to attain significance at the .05 level. Two of the *unconfounded* comparisons shown in Table 1 met this criterion. First, believers in a just world perceived the personalities of attractive, male stimulus persons as being more socially desirable than did nonbelievers (Ms = 90.94 vs. 75.50). Second, believers in a just world attributed more socially desirable personalities to the male stimulus persons who were attractive rather than unattractive (Ms = 90.94 vs. 72.44, respectively). . . .

*Kenneth L.
Dion and
Karen K. Dion*

Life-outcome index. An ANOVA on the life-outcome index yielded only main effects for attractiveness of the stimulus person and respondents' belief in a just world, $Fs(1, 123) = 9.85$ and 5.40, $ps < .05$, respectively. Again, consistent with prior research, respondents attributed more positive life outcomes to an attractive stimulus person than to an unattractive one ($Ms = 36.66$ vs. 32.97). In addition, believers in a just world were more inclined to see the stimulus person as likely to experience positive life outcomes than were nonbelievers ($Ms = 36.01$ vs. 33.68).

Correlations of the indexes. Finally, the Pearson product-moment correlation [statistical measure of relatedness] between the social desirability index and the life-outcome index was .834 for believers in a just world and .615 for nonbelievers ($ps < .01$). As predicted, the correlation between the two indexes was significantly greater in the case of believers in a just world than for nonbelievers ($z = 2.85$, $p < .01$).

DISCUSSION

Overall, the preceding findings sustained our hypotheses reasonably well. As expected, the life-outcome ratings yielded a main effect for the stimulus person's attractiveness unqualified by higher order interactions with the respondents' belief in a just world. (Although we did not predict it, the fact that believers in a just world expected the stimulus persons to experience more positive life outcomes than nonbelievers accords with the greater optimism known to characterize those who think the world is a just place [Lerner, 1980].) Similarly, the prediction that the personality-trait ratings and life-outcome ratings of the stimulus person would be more highly correlated for believers in a just world than for nonbelievers was also clearly borne out.

The predicted interaction between respondents' belief in a just world and the stimulus person's level of attractiveness was confirmed for male stimulus persons. Specifically, believers in a just world perceived the personalities of male stimulus persons as being more socially desirable when the stimulus person was attractive rather than unattractive. As well, believers in a just world perceived the personalities of attractive, male stimulus persons as more socially desirable than did nonbelievers.

On the other hand, some findings did not accord with our just-world analysis of physical attractiveness stereotyping. Our predictions for the social desirability index were not borne out at all in the case of female stimulus persons. Believers in a just world did not perceive the personalities of attractive female stimulus persons as more socially desirable than unattractive ones. Nor did believers stereotype the personalities of female stimulus persons more strongly on the basis of physical attractiveness than did nonbelievers; in fact, though nonsignificant, the obtained trend was stronger in the case of nonbelievers (see Table 1)....

In summary, with a sample of Canadian and American respondents representing a broad spectrum of ages across adulthood, the present study has shown that the belief in a just world is an individual difference variable that moderates responsiveness to attractiveness as a stereotypic cue and status characteristic. The belief in a just world is associated with a tendency to rely on physical attractiveness, along with other status cues, in making judgments about a stimulus person. These findings provide further support to just-world theory by extending its scope to include attractiveness stereotyping, as well as by suggesting that the belief in a just world may influence an observer's perceptions and expectations even in the absence of a threat to their belief (Lerner & Miller, 1978). They also have relevance for status-characteristics theory because they suggest that some persons, such as those who believe in a just world, are more likely to respond to stereotypic cues and status characteristics than are others.

In conclusion, we suggest that isolating the moderators of physical attractiveness stereotyping in the form of personality and individual difference variables, situational factors, cultural dimensions, and cognitive processes is a meaningful approach for trying to understand why people stereotype on the basis of physical attractiveness (and other dimensions), especially when the research is guided, as in the present study, by clear theoretical rationales.

REFERENCES

Adams, G. R. & Huston, T. L. (1975). Social perception of middle-aged persons varying in physical attractiveness. *Developmental Psychology, 11*, 657–658.

Cash, T. F. (1981). Physical attractiveness: An annotated bibliography of theory and research in the behavioral sciences. JSAS: *Catalog of Selected Documents in Psychology, 11* 4. (Ms. No. 2370).

Cichetti, D. V. (1972). Extension of multiple-range tests to interaction tables in the analysis of variance. *Psychological Bulletin, 77*, 403–408.

Dion, K. K. (1986). Stereotyping based on physical attractiveness: Issues and conceptual perspectives. In C. P. Herman, M. P. Zanna, & E. T. Higgins (Eds.), *Appearance, stigma, and social behavior: The Ontario Symposium on Personality and Social Psychology* (Vol. 3, pp. 7–21). Hillsdale, NJ: Erlbaum.

Dion, K. K., Berscheid, E., and Walster, E. (1972). What is beautiful is good. *Journal of Personality and Social Psychology, 24*, 285–290.

Ellis, R. J., Olson, J. M., & Zanna, M. P. (1983). Stereotypic personality inferences following objective versus subjective judgments of beauty. *Canadian Journal of Behavioural Science, 15*, 35–42.

Johnson, D. F., & Pittenger, J. B. (1984). Attribution, the attractiveness stereotype, and the elderly. *Developmental Psychology, 20*, 1168–1172.

Lerner, M. J. (1970). The desire for justice and reactions to victims. In J. Macaulay & L. Berkowitz (Eds.), *Altruism and helping behavior* (pp. 205–229). New York: Academic Press.

Lerner, M. J. (1980). *The belief in a just world: A fundamental delusion.* New York: Plenum Press.

Lerner, M. J., & Miller, D. T. (1978). Just world research and the attribution process: Looking back and ahead. *Psychological Bulletin, 85,* 1030–1051.

Rubin, Z., & Peplau, L. A. (1975). Who believes in a just world? *Journal of Social Issues, 31*(3), 65–89.

Snyder, M., Tanke, E. D., & Berscheid, E. (1977). Social perception and interpersonal behavior: On the self-fulfilling nature of social stereotypes. *Journal of Personality and Social Psychology, 35,* 656–666.

Kenneth L. Dion and Karen K. Dion

Behavioral Study of Obedience

Obedience is a type of social influence in which an individual exhibits the behavior required by a command from someone else. We are taught as children to obey parents and teachers, and as we grow up we learn to obey employers, law enforcement officers, and a variety of other authority figures. One of the best-known studies on obedience was performed by Stanley Milgram at Yale University.

Milgram (1933–1984) studied under social psychologist Solomon E. Asch and earned his Ph.D. from Harvard University in 1960. He taught at Yale University and Harvard University before accepting a position at the Graduate Center of the City University of New York in 1967. Milgram, a very creative social psychologist, studied social communication, prejudice, interpersonal relationships, and obedience.

This selection is from "Behavioral Study of Obedience," which was published in *Journal of Abnormal and Social Psychology* in 1963. It presents the results of the first in a series of Milgram's obedience experiments, in which a large percentage of his subjects delivered what they believed to be the maximum level of electric shocks to "learners" (Milgram's confederates), despite the learners' screaming protests, because an authority figure told them to do so. This study has been a subject of controversy during the past three decades because of its ethical considerations as well as its social implications. As you read this selection, consider the extent to which you obey in today's society.

Key Concept: obedience

*O*bedience is as basic an element in the structure of social life as one can point to. Some system of authority is a requirement of all communal living, and it is only the man dwelling in isolation who is not forced to respond, through defiance or submission, to the commands of others. Obedience, as a determinant of behavior, is of particular relevance to our time. It has been

·reliably established that from 1933–45 millions of innocent persons were systematically slaughtered on command. Gas chambers were built, death camps were guarded, daily quotas of corpses were produced with the same efficiency as the manufacture of appliances. These inhumane policies may have originated in the mind of a single person, but they could only be carried out on a massive scale if a very large number of persons obeyed orders. . . .

General Procedure

A procedure was devised which seems useful as a tool for studying obedience (Milgram, 1961). It consists of ordering a naive subject to administer electric shock to a victim. A simulated shock generator is used, with 30 clearly marked voltage levels that range from 15 to 450 volts. The instrument bears verbal designations that range from Slight Shock to Danger: Severe Shock. The responses of the victim, who is a trained confederate of the experimenter, are standardized. The orders to administer shocks are given to the naive subject in the context of a "learning experiment" ostensibly set up to study the effects of punishment on memory. As the experiment proceeds the naive subject is commanded to administer increasingly more intense shocks to the victim, even to a point of reaching the level marked Danger: Severe Shock. Internal resistances become stronger, and at a certain point the subject refuses to go on with the experiment. Behavior prior to this rupture is considered "obedience," in that the subject complies with the commands of the experimenter. The point of rupture is the act of disobedience. A quantitative value is assigned to the subject's performance based on the maximum intensity shock he is willing to administer before he refuses to participate further. Thus for any particular subject and for any particular experimental condition the degree of obedience may be specified with a numerical value. The crux of the study is to systematically vary the factors believed to alter the degree of obedience to the experimental commands. . . .

METHOD

Subjects

The subjects were 40 males between the ages of 20 and 50, drawn from New Haven and surrounding communities. Subjects were obtained by a newspaper advertisement and direct mail solicitation. Those who responded to the appeal believed they were to participate in a study of memory and learning at Yale University. A wide range of occupations is represented in the sample. Typical subjects were postal clerks, high school teachers, salesmen, engineers, and laborers. Subjects ranged in educational level from one who had not finished elementary school, to those who had doctorate and other professional degrees. They were paid $4.50 for their participation in the experiment. However, subjects were told that payment was simply for coming to the laboratory, and that the money was theirs no matter what happened after they arrived. . . .

Personnel and Locale

The experiment was conducted on the grounds of Yale University in the elegant interaction laboratory. (This detail is relevant to the perceived legitimacy of the experiment. In further variations, the experiment was dissociated from the university, with consequences for performance.) The role of experimenter was played by a 31-year-old high school teacher of biology. His manner was impassive, and his appearance somewhat stern throughout the experiment. He was dressed in a gray technician's coat. The victim was played by a 47-year-old accountant, trained for the role; he was of Irish-American stock, whom most observers found mild-mannered and likeable.

Procedure

One naive subject and one victim (an accomplice) performed in each experiment. A pretext had to be devised that would justify the administration of electric shock by the naive subject. This was effectively accomplished by the cover story. After a general introduction on the presumed relation between punishment and learning, subjects were told:

> But actually, we know *very little* about the effect of punishment on learning, because almost no truly scientific studies have been made of it in human beings.
>
> For instance, we don't know how *much* punishment is best for learning—and we don't know how much difference it makes as to who is giving the punishment, whether an adult learns best from a younger or an older person than himself—or many things of that sort.
>
> So in this study we are bringing together a number of adults of different occupations and ages. And we're asking some of them to be teachers and some of them to be learners.
>
> We want to find out just what effect different people have on each other as teachers and learners, and also what effect *punishment* will have on learning in this situation.
>
> Therefore, I'm going to ask one of you to be the teacher here tonight and the other one to be the learner.
>
> Does either of you have a preference?

Subjects then drew slips of paper from a hat to determine who would be the teacher and who would be the learner in the experiment. The drawing was rigged so that the naive subject was always the teacher and the accomplice always the learner. (Both slips contained the word "Teacher.") Immediately after the drawing, the teacher and learner were taken to an adjacent room and the learner was strapped into an "electric chair" apparatus.

The experimenter explained that the straps were to prevent excessive movement while the learner was being shocked. The effect was to make it impossible of him to escape from the situation. An electrode was attached to the learner's wrist, and electrode paste was applied "to avoid blisters and burns." Subjects were told that the electrode was attached to the shock generator in the adjoining room.

In order to improve credibility the experimenter declared, in response to a question by the learner: "Although the shocks can be extremely painful, they cause no permanent tissue damage."

Learning task.   The lesson administered by the subject was a paired-associate learning task. The subject read a series of word pairs to the learner, and then read the first word of the pair along with four terms. The learner was to indicate which of the four terms had originally been paired with the first word. He communicated his answer by pressing one of four switches in front of him, which in turn lit up one of four numbered quadrants in a answer-box located atop the shock generator.

Shock generator.   The instrument panel consists of 30 lever switches set in a horizontal line. Each switch is clearly labeled with a voltage designation that ranges from 15 to 450 volts. There is a 15-volt increment from one switch to the next going from left to right. In addition, the following verbal designations are clearly indicated for groups of four switches going from left to right: Slight Shock, Moderate Shock, Strong Shock, Intense Shock, Extremely Intense Shock, Danger: Severe Shock. (Two switches after this last designation are simply marked XXX.)

Upon depressing a switch: a pilot light corresponding to each switch is illuminated in bright red; an electric buzzing is heard; an electric blue light, labeled "voltage energizer," flashes; the dial on the voltage meter swings to the right; various relay clicks are sounded.

The upper left-hand corner of the generator is labeled Shock generator, Type ZLB, Dyson Instrument Company, Waltham, Mass. Output 15 Volts–450 Volts.

Details of the instrument were carefully handled to insure an appearance of authenticity. The panel was engraved by precision industrial engravers, and all components were of high quality. No subject in the experiment suspected that the instrument was merely a simulated shock generator.

Sample shock.   Each naive subject is given a sample shock on the shock generator, prior to beginning his run as teacher. This shock is always 45 volts, and is applied by pressing the third switch of the generator. The shock is applied to the wrist of the naive subject, and has its source in a 45-volt battery wired into the generator. This further convinces the subject of the authenticity of the generator.

Shock instructions.   The subject is told to administer a shock to the learner each time he gives a wrong response. Moreover—and this is the key command—the subject is instructed to "move one level higher on the shock generator each time the learner flashes a wrong answer." He is also instructed to announce the voltage level before administering a shock. This serves to continually remind subjects of the increasing intensity of shocks administered to the learner.

Preliminary and regular run.   Pretests revealed that the procedure of reading words and administering shocks requires some practice before it can be handled smoothly. Therefore, immediately preceding the regular run, the teacher is given a preliminary series of 10 words to read to the learner. There are 3 neutral words in the practice series (i.e., words that the learner answers correctly), so that shocks are administered for 7 of the words, with the maximum shock of 105 volts (moderate shock). Almost all subjects master the procedure by the time the preliminary run is over.

Subjects are then presented with a second list, and are told that the procedure is the same as for the first list; the experimenter adds however:

> When you get to the bottom of the list, repeat it over again, and continue giving shocks, until the learner has learned all the pairs correctly.

The experimenter instructs the subject to,

> start from 15 volts and increase the shock level one step each time the learner gives a wrong answer.

Feedback from the victim.   In all conditions the learner gives a predetermined set of responses to the word pair test, based on a schedule of approximately three wrong answers to one correct answer. In the present experimental condition no vocal response or other sign of protest is heard from the learner until Shock Level 300 is reached. When the 300-volt shock is administered, the learner pounds on the wall of the room in which he is bound to the electric chair. The pounding can be heard by the subject. From this point on, the learner's answers no longer appear on the four-way panel.

At this juncture, subjects ordinarily turn to the experimenter for guidance. The experimenter instructs the subject to treat absence of a response as a wrong answer, and to shock the subject according to the usual schedule. He advises the subjects to allow 5–10 seconds before considering no response as a wrong answer, and to increase the shock level one step each time the learner fails to respond correctly. The learner's pounding is repeated after the 315-volt shock is administered; afterwards he is not heard from, nor do his answers reappear on the four-way signal box.

Experimenter feedback.   At various points in the experiment the subject may turn to the experimenter for advice on whether he should continue to administer shocks. Or he may indicate that he does not wish to go on. It was important to standardize the experimenter's responses to these inquiries and reactions.

If the subject indicated his unwillingness to go on, the experimenter responded with a sequence of "prods," using as many as necessary to bring the subject into line.

> Prod 1: Please continue. *or* Please go on.

> Prod 2: The experiment requires that you continue.

Prod 3: It is absolutely essential that you continue.

Prod 4: You have no other choice, you *must* go on.

The prods were always made in sequence: Only if Prod 1 had been unsuccessful, could Prod 2 be used. If the subject still refused to obey the experimenter after Prod 4, the experiment was terminated. The experimenter's tone of voice was at all times firm, but not impolite. The sequence was begun anew on each occasion that the subject balked or showed reluctance to follow orders.

Special prods. If the subject asked if the learner was liable to suffer permanent physical injury, the experimenter said:

Although the shocks may be painful, there is no permanent tissue damage, so please go on. [Followed by Prods 2, 3, and 4 if necessary.]

If the subject said that the learner did not want to go on, the experimenter replied:

Whether the learner likes it or not, you must go on until he has learned all the word pairs correctly. So please go on. [Followed by Prods 2, 3, and 4 if necessary]

Dependent Measures

The primary dependent measure for any subject is the maximum shock he administers before he refuses to go any further. In principle this may vary from 0 (for a subject who refuses to administer even the first shock) to 30 (for a subject who administers the highest shock on the generator). A subject who breaks off the experiment at any point prior to administering the thirtieth shock level is termed a *defiant subject*. One who complies with experimental command fully, and proceeds to administer all shock levels commanded, is termed an *obedient* subject. . . .

Interview and dehoax. Following the experiment, subjects were interviewed; open-ended questions, projective measures, and attitude scales were employed. After the interview, procedures were undertaken to assure that the subject would leave the laboratory in a state of well being. A friendly reconciliation was arranged between the subject and the victim, and an effort was made to reduce any tensions that arose as a result of the experiment.

RESULTS

Preliminary Notions

Before giving an account of the experimental results, it is instructive to consider how persons predict others will perform when commanded to administer powerful shocks to another person. Fourteen Yale seniors, all psychology majors, were provided with a detailed description of the experimental situation. They were asked to reflect carefully on it, and to predict the behavior of 100 hypothetical subjects. More specifically, they were instructed to plot the distribution of obedience of "100 Americans of diverse occupations, and ranging in age from 20 to 50 years," who were placed in the experimental situation.

There was considerable agreement among the respondents on the expected behavior of hypothetical subjects. All respondents predicted that only an insignificant minority would go through to the end of the shock series. (The estimates ranged from 0 to 3%; i.e, the most "pessimistic" member of the class predicted that of 100 persons, 3 would continue through to the most potent shock available on the shock generator—450 volts.) The class mean was 1.2%. The question was also posed informally to colleagues of the author, and the most general feeling was that few if any subjects would go beyond the designation Very Strong Shock.

Result of Experiment I

Subjects accept situation. With few exceptions subjects were convinced of the reality of the experimental situation, that they were administering shocks to another person, and the most potent shocks were extremely painful. In the post-experimental interview subjects were asked: "How painful to the learner were the last few shocks that you administered to him?" Subjects were instructed to indicate their answers on a printed 14-point scale ranging from "Not at all painful" to "Extremely painful." The modal response was 14 (Extremely painful) with the mean at 13.42.

Signs of extreme tension. Many subjects showed signs of nervousness in the experimental situation, and especially upon administering the more powerful shocks. In a large number of cases the degree of tension reached extremes that are rarely seen in sociopsychological laboratory studies. Subjects were observed to sweat, tremble, stutter, bite their lips, groan, and dig their fingernails into their flesh. These were characteristic rather than exceptional responses to the experiment.

One sign of tension was the regular occurrence of nervous laughing fits. Fourteen of the 40 subjects showed definite signs of nervous laughter and smiling. The laughter seemed entirely out of place, even bizarre. Full-blown, uncontrollable seizures were observed for 3 subjects. On one occasion we observed a seizure so violently convulsive that it was necessary to call a halt to the experiment. The subject, a 46-year-old encyclopedia salesman, was seriously embarrassed by his untoward and uncontrollable behavior. In the post-experimental interviews subjects took such pains to point out that they were not sadistic types, and that the laughter did not mean they enjoyed shocking the victim.

Distribution of scores. It had been conjectured that persons would not, in general, agree to administer shocks beyond the level designated Very Strong Shock. The distribution of maximum shocks for this experiment is

TABLE 1

Distribution of Breakoff Points

Verbal designation and voltage indication	Number of subjects for whom this was maximum shock
Slight Shock	
15	0
30	0
45	0
60	0
Moderate Shock	
75	0
90	0
105	0
120	0
Strong Shock	
135	0
150	0
165	0
180	0
Very Strong Shock	
195	0
210	0
225	0
240	0
Intense Shock	
255	0
270	0
285	0
300	5
Extreme Intensity Shock	
315	4
330	2
345	1
360	1
Danger: Severe Shock	
375	1
390	0
405	0
420	0
XXX	
435	0
450	26

shown in Table 1. The obtained distribution of scores deviates radically from the prediction.

Upon command of the experimenter, each of the 40 subjects went beyond the expected breakoff point. No subject stopped prior to administering Shock Level 20. (At this level—300 volts—the victim kicks on the wall and no longer provides answers to the teacher's multiple-choice questions.)

Of the 40 subjects, 5 refused to obey the experimental commands beyond the 300-volt level. Four more subjects administered one further shock, and then refused to go on. Two broke off at the 330-volt level, and 1 each at 345, 360, and 375 volts. Thus a total of 14 subjects defied the experimenter. It is instructive to reprint their remarks at the point of defiance, as transcribed from the tape recordings:

> [0124] I think he's trying to communicate, he's knocking. . . . Well it's not fair to shock the guy . . . these are terrific volts. I don't think this is very humane. . . . Oh, I can't go on with this; no this isn't right. It's a hell of an experiment. The guy is suffering in there. No, I don't want to go on. This is crazy. [Subject refused to administer more shocks.]

> [0123] He's banging in there. I'm gonna chicken out. I'd like to continue, but I can't do that to a man. . . . I'm sorry I can't do that to a man. I'll hurt his heart. You take your check. . . . No really, I couldn't do it.

These subjects were frequently in a highly agitated and even angered state. Sometimes, verbal protest was at a minimum, and the subject simply got up from his chair in front of the shock generator, and indicated that he wished to leave the laboratory.

Of the 40 subjects, 26 obeyed the orders of the experimenter to the end, proceeding to punish the victim until they reached the most potent shock available on the shock generator. At that point, the experimenter called a halt to the sessions. (The maximum shock is labeled 450 volts, and is two steps beyond the designation: Danger: Severe Shock.) Although obedient subjects continued to administer shocks, they often did so under extreme stress. Some expressed reluctance to administer shocks beyond the 300-volt level, and displayed fears similar to those who defied the experimenter; yet they obeyed.

After the maximum shocks had been delivered, and the experimenter called a halt to the proceedings, many obedient subjects heaved sighs of relief, mopped their brows, rubbed their fingers over their eyes, or nervously fumbled cigarettes. Some shook their heads, apparently in regret. Some subjects had remained calm throughout the experiment, and displayed only minimal signs of tension from beginning to end.

DISCUSSION

The experiment yielded two findings that were surprising. The first finding concerns the sheer strength of obedient tendencies manifested in this situation. Subjects have learned from childhood that it is a fundamental breach of moral conduct to hurt another person against his will. Yet, 26 subjects abandon this tenet in following the instructions of an authority who has no special powers to enforce his commands. To disobey would bring no material loss to the subject; no punishment would ensue. It is clear from the remarks and outward behavior of many participants that in punishing the victim they are often acting against their own values. Subjects often expressed deep disapproval of shocking a man in the face of his objections, and others denounced it as stupid and senseless. Yet the majority complied with the experimental commands. This outcome was surprising from two perspectives: first, from the standpoint of predictions made in the questionnaire described earlier. (Here, however, it is possible that the remoteness of the respondents from the actual situation, and the difficulty of conveying to them the concrete details of the experiment, could account for the serious underestimation of obedience.)

But the results were also unexpected to persons who observed the experiment in progress, through one-way mirrors. Observers often uttered expressions of disbelief upon seeing a subject administer more powerful shocks to the victim. These persons had a full acquaintance with the details of the situation, and yet systematically underestimated the amount of obedience that subjects would display.

The second unanticipated effect was the extraordinary tension generated by the procedures. One might suppose that a subject would simply break off or continue as his conscience dictated. Yet, this is very far from what happened. There were striking reactions of tension and emotional strain.

REFERENCE

Milgram, S. Dynamics of obedience. Washington: National Science Foundation, 25 January 1961. (Mimeo)

15.4 JOHN M. DARLEY AND BIBB LATANÉ

When Will People Help in a Crisis?

Social psychologists John M. Darley and Bibb Latané have been interested in discovering the conditions that influence helping behavior, in part because they see a distressingly low rate of helping in emergency situations. One problem they have found is that the larger a crowd of people is, the less likely one of them will help in an emergency. Darley and Latané explain this bystander effect with the concept of diffusion of responsibility, which holds that people feel less responsibility when they are in a large group than when they are in a relatively small group.

Darley (b. 1938) earned his Ph.D. from Harvard University in 1965. He is currently a professor of psychology at Princeton University. Latané (b. 1937) received his Ph.D. from the University of Minnesota in 1963. He taught at Columbia University and Ohio State University before going to Florida Atlantic University. Darley and Latané wrote about their research on helping in their book *The Unresponsive Bystander: Why Doesn't He Help?* (Prentice Hall, 1970).

This selection is from "When Will People Help in a Crisis?" which was published in *Psychology Today* in 1968. In it, the authors examine the conditions necessary for someone to actually provide help in an emergency situation. They also discuss a number of studies and situations in which people's willingness to help was tested, generally with results that support their diffusion of responsibility theory. As you read this selection, notice how Darley and Latané designed their experiments to simulate real-life conditions. How do you think the incidence of helping behavior in our society could be increased?

Key Concept: helping behavior

Kitty Genovese is set upon by a maniac as she returns home from work at 3:00 A.M. Thirty-eight of her neighbors in Kew Gardens come to their windows when she cries out in terror; none come to her assistance even though her stalker takes over half an hour to murder her. No one even so much as calls the police. She dies.

Andrew Mormille is stabbed in the stomach as he rides the A train home to Manhattan. Eleven other riders watch the 17-year-old boy as he bleeds to death; none come to his assistance even though his attackers have left the car. He dies. . . .

Eleanor Bradley trips and breaks her leg while shopping on Fifth Avenue. Dazed and in shock, she calls for help, but the hurrying stream of executives and shoppers simply parts and flows past. After 40 minutes a taxi driver helps her to a doctor.

The shocking thing about these cases is that so many people failed to respond. If only one or two had ignored the victim, we might be able to understand their inaction. But when 38 people, or 11 people, or hundreds of people fail to help, we become disturbed. Actually, this fact that shocks us so much is itself the clue to understanding these cases. Although it seems obvious that the more people who watch a victim in distress, the more likely someone will help, what really happens is exactly the opposite. If each member of a group of bystanders is aware that other people are also present, he will be less likely to notice the emergency, less likely to decide that it is an emergency, and less likely to act even if he thinks there is an emergency.

This is a surprising assertion—what we are saying is that the victim may actually be less likely to get help, the more people who watch his distress and are available to help. We shall discuss in detail the process through which an individual bystander must go in order to intervene, and we shall present the results of some experiments designed to show the effects of the number of onlookers on the likelihood of intervention. . . .

Looking more closely at published descriptions of the behavior of witnesses to these incidents, the people involved begin to look a little less inhuman and a lot more like the rest of us. Although it is unquestionably true that the witnesses in the incidents above did nothing to save the victims, apathy, indifference and unconcern are not entirely accurate descriptions of their reactions. The 38 witnesses of Kitty Genovese's murder did not merely look at the scene once and then ignore it. They continued to stare out of their windows at what was going on. Caught, fascinated, distressed, unwilling to act but unable to turn away, their behavior was neither helpful nor heroic; but it was not indifferent or apathetic.

Actually, it was like crowd behavior in many other emergency situations. Car accidents, drownings, fires and attempted suicides all attract substantial numbers of people who watch the drama in helpless fascination without getting directly involved in the action. Are these people alienated and indifferent? Are the rest of us? Obviously not. Why, then, don't we act?

The bystander to an emergency has to make a series of decisions about what is happening and what he will do about it. The consequences of these decisions will determine his actions. There are three things he must do if he is to intervene: *notice* that something is happening, *interpret* that event as an emergency, and decide that he has *personal responsibility* for intervention. If he fails to notice the event, if he decides that it is not an emergency, or if he concludes that he is not personally responsible for acting, he will leave the victim unhelped. This state of affairs is shown graphically as a "decision tree." Only one path through this decision tree leads to intervention; all others lead to a failure to help. As we shall show, at each fork of the path in the decision trees, the presence of other bystanders may lead a person down the branch of not helping.

NOTICING: THE FIRST STEP

Suppose that an emergency is actually taking place; a middle-aged man has a heart attack. He stops short, clutches his chest, and staggers to the nearest building wall, where he slowly slumps to the sidewalk in a sitting position. What is the likelihood that a passerby will come to his assistance? First, the bystander has to *notice* that something is happening. The external event has to break into his thinking and intrude itself on his conscious mind. He must tear himself away from his private thoughts and pay attention to this unusual event.

But Americans consider it bad manners to look too closely at other people in public. We are taught to respect the privacy of others, and when among strangers, we do this by closing our ears and avoiding staring at others—we are embarrassed if caught doing otherwise. In a crowd, then, each person is less likely to notice the first sign of a potential emergency than when alone.

Experimental evidence corroborates this everyday observation. Darley and Latané asked college students to an interview about their reactions to urban living. As the students waited to see the interviewer, either by themselves or with two other students, they filled out a preliminary questionnaire. Solitary students often glanced idly about the room while filling out their questionnaires; those in groups, to avoid seeming rudely inquisitive, kept their eyes on their own papers.

As part of the study, we staged an emergency: smoke was released into the waiting room through a vent. Two-thirds of the subjects who were alone when the smoke appeared noticed it immediately, but only a quarter of the subjects waiting in groups saw it as quickly. Even after the room had completely filled with smoke one subject from a group of three finally looked up and exclaimed, "God! I must be smoking too much!" Although eventually all the subjects did become aware of the smoke, this study indicates that the more people present, the slower an individual may be to perceive that an emergency does exist and the more likely he is not to see it at all.

Once an event is noticed, an onlooker must decide whether or not it is truly an emergency. Emergencies are not always clearly labeled as such; smoke pouring from a building or into a waiting room may be caused by a fire, or it may merely indicate a leak in a steam pipe. Screams in the street may signal an assault or a family quarrel. A man lying in [a] doorway may be having a coronary or be suffering from diabetic coma—he may simply be sleeping off a drunk. . . .

A person trying to decide whether or not a given situation is an emergency often refers to the reactions of those around him; he looks at them to see how he should react himself. If everyone else is calm and indifferent, he will tend to remain calm and indifferent; if everyone else is reacting strongly, he will become aroused. This tendency is not merely slavish conformity; ordinarily we derive much valuable information about new situations from how others around us behave. It's a rare traveler who, in picking a roadside restaurant, chooses to stop at one with no other cars in the parking lot.

But occasionally the reactions of others provide false information. The studied nonchalance of patients in a dentist's waiting room is a poor indication of the pain awaiting them. In general, it is considered embarrassing to look overly concerned, to seem flustered, to "lose your cool" in public. When we are not alone, most of us try to seem less fearful and anxious than we really are.

In a potentially dangerous situation, then, everyone present will appear more unconcerned than they are in fact. Looking at the *apparent* impassivity and lack of reaction of the others, each person is led to believe that nothing really is wrong. Meanwhile the danger may be mounting, to the point where a single person, uninfluenced by the seeming calm of others, would react.

A crowd can thus force inaction on its members by implying, through its passivity and apparent indifference, that an event is not an emergency. Any individual in such a crowd is uncomfortably aware that he'll look like a fool if he behaves as though it were—and in these circumstances, until someone acts, no one acts.

In the smoke-filled-room study, the smoke trickling from the wall constituted an ambiguous but potentially dangerous situation. How did the presence of other people affect a person's response to the situation? Typically, those who were in the waiting room by themselves noticed the smoke at once, gave a slight startle reaction, hesitated again, and then left the room to find somebody to tell about the smoke. No one showed any signs of panic, but over three-quarters of these people were concerned enough to report the smoke.

Others went through an identical experience but in groups of three strangers. Their behavior was radically different. Typically, once someone noticed the smoke, he would look at the other people, see them doing nothing, shrug his shoulders, and then go back to his questionnaire, casting covert glances first at the smoke and then at the others. From these three-person groups, only three out of 24 people reported the smoke. The inhibiting effect of the group was so strong that the other 21 were willing to sit in a room filled with smoke rather than make themselves conspicuous by reacting with alarm and concern—this despite the fact that after three or four minutes the atmosphere in the waiting room grew most unpleasant. Even though they coughed, rubbed their eyes, tried to wave the smoke away, and opened the window, they apparently were unable to bring themselves to leave.

"A leak in the air conditioning," said one person when we asked him what he thought caused the smoke. "Must be chemistry labs in the building." "Steam pipes." "Truth gas to make us give true answers on the questionnaire," reported the more imaginative. There were many explanations for the smoke, but they all had one thing in common: they did not mention the word fire. In defining the situation as a nonemergency, people explained to themselves why the other observers did not leave the room; they also removed any reason for action themselves. The other members of the group acted as nonresponsive models for each person—and as an audience for any "inappropriate" action he might consider. In such a situation it is all too easy to do nothing.

The results of this study clearly and strongly support the predictions. But are they general? Would the same effect show up with other emergencies, or is it limited to situations like the smoke study involving danger to the self as well as to others—or to situations in which there's no clearly defined "victim"? It may be that our college-age male subjects played "chicken" with one another to see who would lose face by first fleeing the room. It may be that groups were less likely to respond because no particular person was in danger. To see how generalizable these results are, Latané and Judith Rodin set up a second experiment, in which the emergency would cause no danger for the bystander, and in which a specific person was in trouble.

Subjects were paid $2 to participate in a survey of game and puzzle preferences conducted at Columbia by the Consumer Testing Bureau (CTB). An attractive young woman, the market-research representative, met them at the door and took them to the testing room. On the way, they passed the CTB office and through its open door they could see filing cabinets and a desk and bookcases piled high with papers. They entered the adjacent testing room, which contained a table and chairs and a variety of games, where they were given a preliminary background information and game preference question-naire to fill out. The representative told subjects that she would be working next door in her office for about 10 minutes while they completed the question-naires, and left by opening the collapsible curtain which divided the two rooms. She made sure the subjects knew that the curtain was unlocked, easily opened and a means of entry to her office. The representative stayed in her office, shuffling papers, opening drawers, and making enough noise to remind the subjects of her presence. Four minutes after leaving the testing area, she turned on a high fidelity stereophonic tape recorder.

If the subject listened carefully, he heard the representative climb up on a chair to reach for a stack of papers on the bookcase. Even if he were not listening carefully, he heard a loud crash and a scream as the chair collapsed and she fell to the floor. "Oh, my god, my foot. . . . I . . . I . . . can't move it. Oh . . . my ankle," the representative moaned. "I . . . can't get this . . . thing . . . off me." She cried and moaned for about a minute longer, but the cries gradu-ally got more subdued and controlled. Finally she muttered something about getting outside, knocked over the chair as she pulled herself up, and thumped to the door, closing it behind her as she left. This drama was of about two minutes' duration.

Some people were alone in the waiting room when the "accident" oc-curred. Seventy percent of them offered to help the victim before she left the room. Many came through the curtain to offer their assistance, others simply called out to offer their help. Others faced the emergency in pairs. Only 20 percent of this group—eight out of 40—offered to help the victim. The other 32 remained unresponsive to her cries of distress. Again, the presence of other bystanders inhibited action.

And again, the noninterveners seemed to have decided the event was not an emergency. They were unsure what had happened but whatever it was, it was not too serious. "A mild sprain," some said. "I didn't want to embarrass her." In a "real" emergency, they assured us, they would be among the first to help the victim. Perhaps they would be, but in this situation they didn't help, because for them the event was not defined as an emergency.

Again, solitary people exposed to a potential emergency reacted more frequently than those exposed in groups. We found that the action-inhibiting effects of other bystanders work in two different situations, one of which involves risking danger to oneself and the other of which involves helping an injured woman. The result seems sufficiently generally so that we may assume it operates to inhibit helping in real-life emergencies.

DIFFUSED RESPONSIBILITY

Even if a person has noticed an event and defined it as an emergency, the fact that he knows that other bystanders also witnessed it may still make him less likely to intervene. Others may inhibit intervention because they make a person feel that his responsibility is diffused and diluted. Each soldier in a firing squad feels less personally responsible for killing a man than he would if he alone pulled the trigger. Likewise, any person in a crowd of onlookers may feel less responsibility for saving a life than if he alone witnesses the emergency.

If your car breaks down on a busy highway, hundreds of drivers whiz by without anyone's stopping to help; if you are stuck on a nearly deserted country road, whoever passes you first is apt to stop. The personal responsibility that a passerby feels makes the difference. A driver on a lonely road knows that if he doesn't stop to help, the person will not get help; the same individual on the crowded highway feels he personally is no more responsible than any of a hundred other drivers. So even though an event clearly is an emergency, any person in a group who sees an emergency may feel less responsible, simply because any other bystander is equally responsible for helping.

This diffusion of responsibility might have occurred in the famous Kitty Genovese case, in which the observers were walled off from each other in separate apartments. From the silhouettes against windows, all that could be told was that others were also watching. . . .

The evidence is clear, then, that the presence of other bystanders and the various ways these other bystanders affect our decision processes, make a difference in how likely we are to give help in an emergency. The presence of strangers may keep us from noticing an emergency at all; group behavior may lead us to define the situation as one that does not require action; and when other people are there to share the burden of responsibility, we may feel less obligated to do something when action is required. Therefore, it will often be the case that the *more* people who witness his distress, the *less* likely it is that the victim of an emergency will get help.

Thus, the stereotype of the unconcerned, depersonalized *homo urbanis*, blandly watching the misfortunes of others, proves inaccurate. Instead, we find a bystander to an emergency is an anguished individual in genuine doubt, concerned to do the right thing but compelled to make complex decisions under pressure of stress and fear. His reactions are shaped by the actions of others—and all too frequently by their inaction.

And we are that bystander. Caught up by the apparent indifference of others, we may pass by an emergency without helping or even realizing that help is needed. Aware of the influence of those around us, however, we can resist it. We can choose to see distress and step forward to relieve it.

2.2 From "Memory and the Hippocampus: A Synthesis from Findings With Rats, Monkeys, and Humans" by L. R. Squire, 1992, *Psychological Review, 99,* pp. 195, 204–205, 208–210. References omitted.

2.3 From "Serotonin, Motor Activity and Depression-Related Disorders" by B. L. Jacobs, 1994, *American Scientist, 82,* pp. 456, 458–459, 461–463. Copyright © 1994 by Sigma Xi. Reprinted by permission. Bibliography omitted.

2.4 From "Environment and Genes: Determinants of Behavior" by R. Plomin, 1989, *American Psychologist, 44,* pp. 105–108, 110–111. Copyright © 1989 by The American Psychological Association. Reprinted by permission.

3.1 From *The Psychology of the Child* (pp. 3–12) by J. Piaget and B. Inhelder, 1969 (H. Weaver, Trans). New York: Basic Books. (Original work published 1966.) Copyright © 1969 by Basic Books, Inc. Reprinted by permission of Basic Books, a division of HarperCollins Publishers, Inc.

3.2 From "Infant–Mother Attachment" by M. D. S. Ainsworth, 1979, *American Psychologist, 34,* pp. 932–937. Copyright © 1979 by Mary D. Salter Ainsworth. Reprinted by permission.

3.3 From "The Child as a Moral Philosopher" by L. Kohlberg, 1968, *Psychology Today, 214,* pp. 25–30. Copyright © 1968 by Sussex Publishers, Inc. Reprinted by permission of *Psychology Today.*

3.4 From "Children's Understanding of Sexist Language" by J. S. Hyde, 1984, *Developmental Psychology, 20,* pp. 697–701, 703–706. Copyright © 1984 by The American Psychological Association. Reprinted by permission.

3.5 From "Gender and Relationships: A Developmental Account" by E. E. Maccoby, 1990, *American Psychologist, 45,* pp. 513–517, 519–520. Copyright © 1990 by The American Psychological Association. Reprinted by permission.

4.1 From "The 'Visual Cliff' " by E. J. Gibson and R. D. Walk, 1960, *Scientific American, 202,* pp. 67–71. Copyright © 1960 by Scientific American, Inc. All rights reserved. Reprinted by permission.

4.2 From "Perception: An Introduction to the *Gestalt-Theorie*" by K. Koffka, 1922, *Psychological Bulletin, 19,* pp. 531–537, 581–585. Notes omitted.

5.1 From "Weapon Against Pain: Hypnosis Is No Mirage" by E. R. Hilgard, 1974, *Psychology Today,* pp. 121–122, 126, 128. Copyright © 1974 by Sussex Publishers, Inc. Reprinted by permission of *Psychology Today.*

5.2 From *The Interpretation of Dreams* (pp. 33–43) by S. Freud, 1950 (A. A. Brill, Trans.). New York: Random House. (Original work published 1900.) Translation originally copyrighted © 1938; copyright renewed 1965 in *The Basic Writings of Sigmund Freud.* New York: Modern Library. Reprinted by permission. Notes omitted.

6.1 From "Conditioned Emotional Reactions" by J. B. Watson and R. Rayner, 1920, *Journal of Experimental Psychology, 3,* pp. 1–7, 10, 13–14. Notes omitted.

6.2 From *Science and Human Behavior* (pp. 91–93, 98–104) by B. F. Skinner, 1953. New York: Free Press. Copyright © 1953 by Prentice Hall, Inc., Upper Saddle River, NJ. Reprinted by permission.

6.3 From "Relation of Cue to Consequence in Avoidance Learning" by J. Garcia and R. A. Koelling, 1966, *Psychonomic Science, 4,* pp. 123–124. Copyright © 1966 by The Psychonomic Society, Inc. Reprinted by permission.

11.2 From "External Control and Internal Control" by J. B. Rotter, 1971, *Psychology Today, 5,* pp. 37–38, 42, 58–59. Copyright © 1971 by Sussex Publishers, Inc. Reprinted by permission of *Psychology Today.*

11.3 From "Validation of the Five-Factor Model of Personality Across Instruments and Observers" by R. R. McCrae and P. T. Costa, Jr., 1987, *Journal of Personality and Social Psychology, 52,* pp. 81, 85–90.

12.1 From "The Evolution of the Stress Concept" by H. Selye, 1973, *American Scientist, 61,* pp. 692–699. Copyright © 1973 by *American Scientist.* Reprinted by permission.

12.2 From "Little Hassles Can Be Hazardous to Health" by R. S. Lazarus, 1981, *Psychology Today,* pp. 58, 60–62. Copyright © 1981 by Sussex Publishers, Inc. Reprinted by permission of *Psychology Today.*

12.3 From "The Social Readjustment Rating Scale" by T. H. Holmes and R. H. Rahe, 1967, *Journal of Psychosomatic Research,* pp. 213, 215–218. Copyright © 1967 by Elsevier Science Ltd. Reprinted by permission. Notes omitted.

13.1 From "On Being Sane in Insane Places" by D. L. Rosenhan, 1973, *Science, 179,* pp. 250–258. Copyright © 1973 by The American Association for the Advancement of Science. Reprinted by permission. Some notes omitted.

13.2 From *Inhibitions, Symptoms and Anxiety* (pp. 60–67) by S. Freud, 1926 (A. Strachey, Trans.). New York: W. W. Norton. Translation copyright © 1959 by Alix Strachey. Reprinted by permission of W. W. Norton & Company, Inc. and by arrangement with Mark Paterson and Associates, Colchester, England. Notes and references omitted.

13.3 From *Helplessness: On Depression, Development, and Death* (pp. 93–95, 97–105) by M. E. P. Seligman, 1975. New York: W. H. Freeman. Copyright © 1975 by Martin E. P. Seligman; copyright renewed 1992 by Martin E. P. Seligman. Reprinted by permission of W. H. Freeman and Company. Notes omitted.

14.1 From "Intensive Treatment of Psychotic Behaviour by Stimulus Satiation and Food Reinforcement" by T. Ayllon, 1963, *Behaviour Research and Therapy, 1,* pp. 53–61. Copyright © 1963 by Elsevier Science Ltd., Oxford, England. Reprinted by permission. Notes omitted.

14.2 From *On Becoming a Person: A Therapist's View of Psychotherapy* (pp. 31, 33–36) by C. R. Rogers, 1961. Boston: Houghton Mifflin. Copyright © 1961 by Project Innovation. Reprinted by permission.

14.3 From *Cognitive Therapy and the Emotional Disorders* (pp. 213–227, 229–232) by A. T. Beck, 1976. Madison, CT: International Universities Press. Copyright © 1976 by Aaron T. Beck. Reprinted by permission of International Universities Press. References omitted.

15.1 From *A Theory of Cognitive Dissonanace* (pp. 1–5, 18–24, 29–31) by L. Festinger, 1957. Stanford, CA: Stanford University Press. Copyright © 1957 by Leon Festinger. Reprinted by permission.

15.2 From "Belief in a Just World and Physical Attractiveness Stereotyping" by K. L. Dion and K. K. Dion, 1987, *Journal of Personality and Social Psychology, 52,* pp. 775–780. Copyright © 1987 by The American Psychological Association. Reprinted by permission of the authors and The American Psychological Association. Notes omitted.

15.3 From "Behavioral Study of Obedience" by S. Milgram, 1963, *Journal of Abnormal and Social Psychology, 67,* pp. 371–378. Copyright © 1963 by Stanley Milgram. Reprinted by permission of Alexandra Milgram, literary executor.

15.4 From "When Will People Help in a Crisis?" by J. M. Darley and B. Latané, 1968, *Psychology Today, 2,* pp. 54–57, 70–71. Copyright © 1968 by Sussex Publishers, Inc. Reprinted by permission of *Psychology Today.*

Index

abnormal behavior: anxiety disorders and, 290–294; depression and, 295–299; labeling of, 283–289

acceptance, person-centered therapy and, 312, 313

adoption design: in behavioral genetics research, 43–50; in intelligence research, 165–172

aggression, observation learning of, 137–144

agreeableness, as personality factor, 254, 256, 258–259

Ainsworth, Mary D. Salter, on infant–mother attachment, 58–66

alarm reaction, general adaptation syndrome and, 264, 268

ambivalent attachment pattern, between infants and mothers, 59–64

amnesia, 30–31, 33, 153, 154

androgyny, 241–246

animals: dreams of, 115; motivation and, 208–213; teaching language to, 178–184

antagonism, as personality factor, 256, 258–259

anxiety, 257, 284; disorders of, 290–294

anxious attachment pattern, between infants and mothers, 59–64

assimilation, Piaget's theory of, 52–53, 56

association, Gestalt theory and, 100, 101–102

attachment theory, 58–66

attention, Gestalt theory and, 100, 101, 102

autonoetic awareness, 151–155

autonomic nervous system, facial expression and, 217–218

Ayllon, Teodoro, on behavior therapy, 300–309

Bandura, Albert, on observation learning of aggression, 137–144

Beck, Aaron T., 298; on cognitive therapy, 315–323

behavior therapy, 300–309

behavioral genetics, 42–50, 260

behaviorism, 7–10, 99, 119

Bem, Sandra L., 74; on androgyny, 241–246

bias: in psychological research, 11–14; sexist language and, 73–80

birth process, as cause of anxiety, 292–294

boredom susceptibility, as personality characteristic, 221–227

Bower, Gordon H., on the fragmentation of psychology, 15–18

Bowlby, John, 58, 61, 63

brain, split-brain surgery and, 19–28

Brave New World (Huxley), 35–36

business, motivation and, 199–200

Buss, David M., on a cross-cultural theory of mate selection, 201–207

bystander effect, helping behavior and, 352–358

chance learning, 248–249

children: and adoption studies on intelligence, 165–172; anxiety in, 292–293; attachment theory and, 58–66; conditioned emotional responses in, 119–124; depth perception in young, 93–98; dreams of, 112–115; language development of, 173–177; moral development of, 67–72; observation learning of aggression by, 137–144; sensori-motor stage in, 51–57; sexist language and, 73–80

chimpanzees, teaching language to, 178–184

choice, mate selection and, 202–204

classical conditioning, 32, 119, 133

cognitive development, in children, sensori-motor stage of, 51–57

cognitive dissonance, 327–332

cognitive therapy, 298, 315–323

commitment, and triangular theory of love, 228–237

communication theory, recoding and, 149–150

companionate love, 233, 235–236

competition, mate selection and, 202–204

conditioned aversion learning, 133–136

configural memory, 31, 33–34

conscientiousness, as personality factor, 254, 256, 259–260

conscious awareness, memory and, 152–153

consciousness, 3, 8, 10; hypnosis and, 104–108; split-brain surgery and, 19–28

consequence, relationship of, to cue, in avoidance learning, 133–136